F ce Studies in Motion

Martial Rose
Tel: 01962 8

Related titles from Bloomsbury Methuen Drama:

Affective Performance and Cognitive Science, edited by Nicola Shaughnessy
The Methuen Drama Anthology of Testimonial Plays, edited by Alison Forsyth
Modern Asian Theatre and Performance 1900–2000, edited by Kevin
J. Wetmore and Siyuan Liu
Postdramatic Theatre and the Political, edited by Jerome Carroll,
Steven Giles and Karen Jürs-Munby
Theatre in Pieces, edited by Anna Furse
Theatre in the Expanded Field, Alan Read

Performance Studies in Motion

International Perspectives and Practices in the Twenty-First Century

Edited by
Atay Citron, Sharon Aronson-Lehavi
and David Zerbib

B L O O M S B U R Y
LONDON • NEW DELHI • NEW YORK • SYDNEY

Bloomsbury Methuen Drama

An imprint of Bloomsbury Publishing Plc

50 Bedford Square	1385 Broadway
London	New York
WC1B 3DP	NY 10018
UK	USA

www.bloomsbury.com

Bloomsbury is a registered trade mark of Bloomsbury Publishing Plc

First published 2014

© Atay Citron, Sharon Aronson-Lehavi and David Zerbib, 2014

British Library Cataloguing-in-Publication Data
A catalogue record for this book is available from the British Library.

ISBN: HB: 978-1-4081-8316-8
PB: 978-1-4081-8407-3
ePDF: 978-1-4081-8575-9
ePub: 978-1-4081-8413-4

Library of Congress Cataloging-in-Publication Data
A catalog record for this book is available from the Library of Congress.

Typeset by Deanta Global Publishing Services, Chennai, India
Printed and bound in India

Contents

Motion IV	Into the Political Arena

Motion V	At War

Motion VI	Contemporary Rituals: Challenges and Changes

Motion VII	Applied Performance Studies: Therapy,
	Activism and Education

Acknowledgements

Creating and editing this book is the result of a fruitful and inspiring dialogue with many colleagues and friends to whom we are deeply grateful. The idea for *Performance Studies in Motion* originates in the lively presentations and discussions that took place during the 2010 international conference *RS & PS: Richard Schechner and Performance Studies*. In the conference that took place at the University of Haifa, artists and scholars from 12 countries gathered to honour performance studies pioneer Richard Schechner and to discuss current issues in the field. This event led us to embark on this book project, which examines performance studies with a look into the future, and we are therefore indebted first and foremost to all those who participated and presented their research at the conference. We are especially grateful to members of the academic committee: Jeanette Malkin, Carol Martin and Nurit Yaari. We are equally grateful to members of the organizing committee: Sarit Cofman-Simhon, Dror Harari and Olga Levitan, as well as to production assistant Adva Weinstein, and to the Theatre Department and Faculty of the Humanities at the University of Haifa.

The process of editing the book was based on an ongoing and stimulating exchange of ideas, thoughts and feedbacks. We are deeply grateful to Carol Martin for her good advice along the way. We would also like to thank all the contributors for the cooperative, instructive and pleasant dialogue. Thanks to them and their careful attention in taking into account our 'tripolar' cross-readings, this project has led us through an intense process of collective thinking and an enriching pluralist debate.

This book could not be realized without the enthusiastic and professional support of Mark Dudgeon at Bloomsbury Methuen Drama and we are deeply grateful to him. We are also extremely grateful to Emily Hockley and to the entire editorial staff at Methuen.

For enabling us the time and inspiration during this creative process, we are deeply grateful to our families. Atay Citron dedicates this book to Anat and Yael with much love. Sharon Aronson-Lehavi dedicates it with love to Amnon and

Lia. David Zerbib dedicates it to little Eva, who was born during the project, to Milan who often agreed to delay soccer games, and to Valentina for her legendary patience.

Throughout the laborious process, we were all inspired by Richard's vision, and it is with much love and gratitude that we dedicate this volume to him.

List of Illustrations

Introduction

Atay Citron, Sharon Aronson-Lehavi, David Zerbib

Since its inception in the early 1980s at the crossroads of Anthropology and Theatre Studies, the field of performance studies has been in constant motion – advancing, expanding, crossing disciplinary boundaries, spilling over to the praxis of performance, bonding with other fields of knowledge, creating interfaces and escaping rigid disciplinary definitions. This dynamism is reflected in a variety of ways in the 24 essays collected in this volume, which focuses on the present and future of the field. The authors who contributed to this book employ a reflexive approach about their applications of performance studies methodologies to contemporary phenomena, showing in different ways how the field enriches our understanding of these phenomena by creating innovative links between arts, humanities, social sciences and life sciences.

The idea for the book germinated in the 2010 international conference *RS & PS: Richard Schechner and Performance Studies* in which artists and scholars assembled at the University of Haifa to honour Richard Schechner and to discuss current issues in performance studies. Following that conference, it appeared necessary to take the next step and examine the field with a look into the future. As any future is largely conditioned by what is changing at the present, this book offers a concrete and pragmatic view on current research and objects of study, which have the potential of transforming the field of performance studies, based on their methodology, theoretical approach or application.

The eight sections that construct this book and which we describe in this introductory chapter demonstrate this dynamic characteristic of the field in different ways. First, the book starts with sections that discuss fields of research that have been associated with performance studies since its beginning, moving into current directions and issues at stake in the field. Moreover, the essays throughout the book examine topical case studies that touch upon contemporary social and political issues. Each cluster of essays offers a multi-perspective analysis of the domain in question, exemplifying the methodological uniqueness of the field, which is based on and committed to an interdisciplinary approach. What originated in a relationship between performing arts and anthropology is widening into progressive life sciences and cognition laboratories, political research and activism, pedagogy, health care, museology and more.

Other than expanding its links with various disciplines, one of the most visible motions of performance studies is the broadening of its geographic and cultural range. This book reflects this by proposing critical perspectives and case studies from places as diverse as Austria, Belgium, China, France, Germany, Israel, Korea, Palestine, the Philippines, Poland, Rwanda and the United States of America. This multiplicity of cultures and topics brings with it a sense of pluralism that seems to characterize the field from its early days.

Finally, performance studies appears to adapt well to the global and virtual world of the twenty-first century. This, however, does not mean that it embraces the state and evolution of contemporary societies without a stance. Being *in motion* means also being able to step back, or beside, or ahead, in order to build new analytical and critical positions and points of view on our present time, as the critical analyses of the essays that follow demonstrate. It is about taking into account, for instance, the most recent waves of information technologies while keeping in mind the symbolic weight of a human gesture, which has been ritually repeated for centuries. It is also about recognizing the tendency of behavioural adaptation on the one hand, and identifying the potential of aesthetic, symbolic, or political disruption and transformation on the other.

Accordingly, the essays of *Performance Studies in Motion* are arranged in eight sections, which we call 'motions'. This choice indicates that the theoretical, social, artistic, cultural, or scientific objects cannot be fixed and ossified in clear-cut categories and classifications when they are approached through the lens of performance studies. In other words, the motion at stake is the performance of these objects of research as well as the movement that characterizes analytic processes of thinking about them.

Motion I: Performance studies: Perspectives and prospectives

The three essays that open the book exemplify what we mean by the concept of 'motion', as they demonstrate the dynamism of performative objects of research, including the field of performance studies itself. These essays offer a meta-examination of the field, with analyses that simultaneously look backwards on the field's history and forwards into its future. This meta-discourse is a combination of a philosophical account of performance studies (Zerbib), a historiographic model of the changes that have been occurring in the field (Bial) and an inspiring manifesto about the role and importance of those who 'do' performance, written by Richard Schechner.

David Zerbib analyses the interrelations between two theoretical phenomena, which have shaped in the past few decades the so-called 'performative turn': the post-structuralist critique of language's reference to a fixed *truth* on the one hand, and the ways avant-garde performances have demonstrated the embodied relativity of meaning and power on the other. Zerbib's point of departure is a 1966 summit in literary criticism, at Johns Hopkins University, with the participation of Roland Barthes, Jacques Derrida and Jacques Lacan. Richard Schechner was in the audience. In his analysis of the discussions at this summit, Zerbib stresses in retrospect two different ways to approach performance and performativity: the free play of the textual sign, and the presence of the real body. Despite their contradictions, Zerbib articulates philosophically these two paths through the dynamism and force that typify both conceptions of performance.

Henry Bial offers a historiographic yet future-oriented analytic model of the changes and developments that have occurred in the field of performance studies since its inception. Rather than regarding these turns and shifts in evolutionary terms or as stages, Bial suggests we apply the computer operating system (OS) as a methodological framework for thinking about performance studies' perspectives and prospectives. Through this, Bial is able to demonstrate the reworkings of the relations between performance and anthropologically oriented considerations, to a growing interest in identity politics, and from there to contemporary interrelations between performance studies and the internet. These turns, as Bial demonstrates, have not replaced one another, but have rather continued to shape and reshape performance studies as a field in motion, in which traces of the past continually shape the present and the future.

Richard Schechner envisions anew the social role of artists and performers, those 'who play'. He suggestively categorizes those 'players' as a 'new third world', and given the political, social and economic devastating situations in so many places around the world, Schechner looks at performance as a utopian social venue, in which alternatives can be rehearsed, practised, voiced and optimally realized. Performance, according to Schechner, is the social space where difference rather than sameness can emerge. He believes that hope for change is located in the work and play that is done by artists, performers and performance researchers, who team to think creatively about people and societies. In this sense, calling to take (more) seriously those who play, this essay lays the foundation for the kind of artistic activism described and practised by many of the contributors in this book.

Motion II: Beyond experimental theatre

Performance studies has widely impacted the ways the art of theatre is both created and studied. While performance at large often borrows the theatrical metaphor, theatre as a form of art is hardly studied any longer without taking into consideration the 'broad spectrum'. Extra-textual and extra-theatrical components and factors have gained a central status in theatre creative and analytic processes and have increased the need to question the ways theatre produces live interaction rather than 'representation' or 'mimesis'. The three essays in this section discuss characteristics of contemporary theatre, which are central to this kind of performativity. However, these artistic means are no longer based on a literal collapse of the boundaries between performers and spectators as was customary in experimental theatre in past decades, but rather, on the ways life itself infiltrates into creative processes (Kaynar), spectatorial experiences (Miller) or the present and future of the theatre in the age of virtual reality (Martin).

Carol Martin, whose essay opens this motion, has coined the term 'Theatre of the Real', which addresses various versions of contemporary theatre that constitute and interrogate through performance relations with 'the real' and with reality. She analyses the phenomenology of the minimalist setting of the 'table on stage', on which the iconic 'glass of water' (introduced by Spalding Gray) has been replaced by a laptop, and which highlights the blur between fiction and reality in contemporary cultural, technological and political contexts. Martin looks comparatively at two experimental performances, which use the internet to connect to 'the real', and in which the table on the stage functions performatively.

Judith Miller discusses the changes that have occurred in the concept of environmental theatre in recent productions of the Théâtre du Soleil. Although contemporary performances might seem 'traditional' in their positioning of the audience as opposed to the theatre's early environmental experimentalism (in the revolution plays, for example), Miller argues that contemporary spectatorial experience at the Soleil encompasses the memory of the theatre's history, aesthetics, theatricality and vocation, and that this 'performance knowledge' not only enables the use and invention of new artistic methods, but also constitutes interaction through perception, leading to a new form of theatre environmentalism before, during and after the performances.

This motion concludes with Gad Kaynar's essay, which theorizes theatrical creativity from the unique perspective of the dramaturg in German post-dramatic theatre. This theatre, deeply committed to experimentalism, depends, as Kaynar shows, on the extremely subjective and intermediate figure of the dramaturg, which embodies the performance by bringing into the creative process a wide and topical range of cultural associations. Thus, according to Kaynar, the dramaturgical creative process is in fact a hermeneutics that is not anchored either in a play or in a directorial staging concept, but rather, similarly to the legacy of performance, in a strong connection to life itself, which is understood in radically personal and subjective ways. Still, by looking at post-dramatic adaptations of classical drama through the art of the dramaturg, Kaynar demonstrates the social and political meanings embedded in such theatricality, demonstrating the affinities between performance in the Schechnerian sense and the aesthetics of contemporary German theatre.

Motion III: Performance in/of social spaces

In this motion the essays focus on the ways performance activates social and public spaces, calling into attention the dynamic relations between life, memory, identity, locality and social and ethical responsibility. The theatre building, a social space in itself, has long ago ceased to function as *the* location of performance. However, the essays in this section demonstrate not only that performance takes place in an endless variety of spaces, but more importantly how performance studies goes beyond theatrical analyses of such events, fostering new perspectives and relying on interdisciplinary approaches, such as museology (Kirshenblatt-Gimblett), aesthetic political activism (Ben-Shaul) and urban studies (Aronson-Lehavi). All three essays analyse complex webs of social interactions and meanings, as they highlight the coordinators between performativity and the spaces discussed. Performance thus appears able to redefine the identity or render visible an unexpected potentiality of a social space on the one hand, or connect between different layers of time and memory on the other, setting space into motion.

The ethical aspects of performance in social spaces are pertinent when performance takes place in public spaces such as the one discussed by Sharon Aronson-Lehavi. In her essay about an Israeli performance-art venue, 'Performance Art Platform', which is located inside the Tel Aviv Central Bus Station in the rundown part of the city, she analyses the osmotic relations between the socially complex surrounding and artistic creativity. She demonstrates how continuous presence and daily work within this space connect performance to real life, for artists and spectators alike, turning the seemingly passive capacity of 'looking' or 'seeing' into an act that invokes social responsibility. The three pieces analysed in her essay produce a sense of a continuous relational dynamic, which is termed by Aronson-Lehavi as a process of 'relocation'.

Another function that typifies public spaces is their usability as platforms for political power structures to reaffirm authority by means of performance. Daphna Ben Shaul demonstrates the ways in which Israeli performance group 'Public Movement' critically deconstructs choreographic patterns of state ceremonies and other performance routines that take place publicly, challenging their ability to substantiate social normalization and indoctrinate consensus. She shows how the group actually blurs the boundaries between aesthetic performance and political protest, by subversively leading spectators to consider anew the strength of public collective behaviours on the one hand, and to realize the political potential of transformation on the other. Thus performance, like a grotesque smile, oscillates between the aesthetic and the political in ways that critically engage us to redefine our position regarding public spaces and values.

Negotiating the ways historical memory is constructed and transmitted is one of the central goals of the Warsaw Museum of the History of Polish Jews, which opens its doors to the public in 2014, on the former site of the Warsaw Ghetto. Renowned performance studies scholar Barbara Kirshenblatt-Gimblett, programme director of the core exhibition, explains in the interview that closes this section how the cultural-historical exhibition was conceived by applying a performance studies approach, in order to create what could be termed 'an installation of history'. Rather than presenting a collection of original objects, the Museum uses space poetically in order to invoke an experiential commemorative journey of 1,000 years of Jewish presence and life in Poland. Exposing the theoretical assumptions, cultural challenges and practical goals of this project, Kirshenblatt-Gimblett demonstrates the complex and dynamic relations between performance, place and memory as well as the ways our experience of a present space can significantly modify our representation of the past, and impact our vision of the future.

Motion IV: Into the political arena

In the age of information, performance dominates the political arena to the extent that it overshadows ideology and at times even replaces it. Entertainers have become legitimate political leaders almost everywhere, and politicians with no previous experience in the business acquire entertainment skills through frequent participation in TV game, talk and comedy shows. These and other trends have altered the praxis of politics, as well as our perception and understanding of it.

In the essay that opens the fourth motion, Klaas Tindemans describes and analyses performative politics in Belgium during the 2007–11 political stalemate – a period in which that state had no elected government. As Belgian binational society (Flemish and Walloon) came close to collapse, performance filled the political void, replacing other societal organizing powers. Tindemans demonstrates how the relationship between 'real-life' politics and televised political drama series is reciprocal, if not practically a closed circle of endless mirror-like reflections, or simulacra. As TV series borrow plots from the life of contemporary politicians (as they appear in the media), so does the political theatre of 'real life' borrow from its own dramatized reproductions. This reading of the political dramaturgy, designed and performed by the country's two opposing leaders, links the notion of performance to those of national identity and sovereignty, revealing strategies and tactics that are at play not only in Belgium but in global contemporary politics.

The leading parts in today's political performance are not exclusively reserved for politicians, however. The Arab Spring, Occupy Wall Street and grassroots protests in other parts of the world have all been based on the active participation of the masses as well as on their creative imagination. Dariusz Kosiński discusses social drama as performed by hundreds of thousands of Polish citizens in the streets and public Squares of Warsaw in response to the fatal crash of Poland's presidential plane on 10 April 2010. The loss of Poland's political elite in that accident could have caused a political crisis, but it gave birth instead to a year-long series of large-scale public rituals and theatrical street performances in which opposing interpretations of Polish identity and patriotism were embodied and negotiated. Kosiński argues that Polish culture is best understood through the lens of performance, and his analysis of the cycle of rites and demonstrations as a five-act classical drama shows how symbolic public behaviour can eclipse other manifestations of political conflict and effectively question and reaffirm fundamental values and ideologies. The performative acts discussed by Kosiński are significantly more elaborate and sophisticated than ordinary demonstrations. In their opposition, conservatives and liberals were all acutely aware of the paramount role of performance, and exceptionally innovative in composing synthetic rituals as well as their reversal in carnivalesque parodies.

Eva Brenner's essay promotes the idea of social transformance with an urgency characteristic of a manifesto. Brenner contends that in the age of neo-liberal capitalism, performance must be re-politicized in order to empower the disenfranchised and emancipate the avant-garde from the stagnation of deconstructionist aesthetics (as championed, for example, by the critic Hans-Thies Lehmann). When her community-based theatre, the *Fleischerei*, lost its space and financial support due to funding cut backs by Vienna's city authorities, Brenner took her performance work to the streets of the Austrian capital, re-naming her company *Fleischerei mobil*, radicalizing its socio-artistic objectives, targeting alternative funding sources, and adopting new performance strategies and production methods. The essay describes the company's signature project, On Axis – a street procession cum fiesta, which is based mainly on the talents of refugees and migrant workers and is realized with the cooperation of neighbourhood business owners. Moving out of the relative safety of indoor theatre to outdoor public spaces, replacing 'Art' with 'Activism', performance can become, according to Brenner, an effective agent of transformation and an instrument of forging local communities.

Motion V: At war

In spite of imminent danger, and at times precisely because of it, performance finds its way to war zones. On the one hand, fighting itself entails performative behaviour, in animals as well as in humans. On the other hand, fear, suffering, losses and the attempts to recover from them often prompt performance. Whatever the circumstances, performance at war is performance of trauma or the processing of it. This motion opens with performance by soldiers on the front during a break in the fighting (Winograd). It continues with a series of subversive performances by former fighters who are determined never to fight again (Alon), and it closes with war victims and victimizers coping by means of performance with the outcome of genocide (Capraru).

'Theatre of war' is a term denoting a location of fighting, but in Annabelle Winograd's chapter this term gains a new meaning, as theatre is literally present on the warfront. Winograd studies two photographs of soldiers creating their makeshift theatre on the French-German front in 1915. Her performance analysis of still images exemplifies Schechner's argument that performance studies is based on multiple literacies. She analyses shades and light, distances and proximities, gazes and body language, costumes and sets and the details combine to form a thick description of atrocity-as-entertainment. At the same time, Winograd argues, it is ritual performance that by theatricalizing violence purifies it. One cannot but recall the YouTube videos from the infamous Abu Ghraib prison camp in Iraq, where US soldiers performed for the camera the humiliation and torture of Iraqi prisoners. Winograd does not offer moral judgement of such performative behaviour, however. Her essay examines performance as a type of communal self-treatment of men traumatized by their experience and their own actions at war.

The trauma of performing violence led former Israeli soldiers and Palestinian fighters to co-found *Combatants for Peace* – an activist movement that employs non-violent means to oppose the Israeli occupation of Palestinian territories. Chen Alon, a theatre practitioner and scholar, who had served as an officer in the Israeli Defence Force, was among the founders of that movement and the initiator of its thirty-member theatre group. The group practises several of Augusto Boal's 'Theatre of the Oppressed' methods, performing in liminal territories which are neither clearly Israeli nor Palestinian. The audience – or spect-actors, in Boal's terms – are Palestinian villagers as well as Israeli soldiers and policemen. Performances such as dismantling Israeli roadblocks are challenging, tense, almost always on the verge of conflict with the occupying forces, but at the same time playful in the disarming way so typical of Boal's spirit. Through this practice, Alon developed his dialectical understanding of Boal's methods, which he adapted to the unique situation of his polarized group – a group composed of two fractions that differ culturally and politically from one another, yet are united in employing performance as a substitute for fighting.

Closing this motion is Jennifer Capraru's personal account of the role played by Western-style theatre in the healing process that followed the 1994 Rwandan Genocide. A Canadian theatre artist, Capraru is the leader of Isôko Rwanda Theatre since 2008. As a foreigner, she had to be initiated to a variety of complex cultural issues, most challenging among them was probably the juxtaposition of the actors' respective experiences during the genocide with the biographies of the characters they had to play. The building of trust within the company was thus paramount during the workshop and rehearsal process. The performances and the emotionally charged post-show discussions with the audience presented another challenge, which Capraru describes as creating 'a safe space for dialogue' and for processing trauma. Spectators apparently perceived the dramatic plots as an optional scenario of their own lives after the civil war, and in their debates on the dramatic characters' actions, they tended to relate more to ethical issues than to aesthetic ones. The performances thus seem to have become laboratory trials or rehearsal for life.

Motion VI: Contemporary rituals: Challenges and changes

The essays in this section theorize case studies which could be termed 'ritual in motion'. The three essays examine and problematize in different ways traditional/ religious ritualistic forms and their susceptibility to change despite their seemingly fixed nature and due to contextual cultural changes. In all three case studies, it seems that from the perspective of those who practise and perform the rituals, a strong sense of essence remains intact despite changes that occur, such as technological intervention in the production of the ritual (Sarfati), artistic interpretation of the ritual by its practitioners (Cofman-Simhon), or cultural changes that take place (Llana).

Jazmin Badong Llana's essay demonstrates the social and ethical significance of finding new performance methodologies in order to analyse and understand the complexities of a traditional ritual that continues to be performed in the Philippines. Llana applies Alain Badiou's concept of inaesthetics to her analysis of Philippine religious performances – 'dotoc' – carried out mainly by women, and dating back to seventeenth-century Spanish colonialism. In these performances, then and in the post-colonial era, the performers enact a search for the Cross in the 'Holy Land'. Llana argues for a theory that enables her to understand the rituals nowadays as contemporary sites of resistance in which the performers continuously seek identity, as opposed to approaches that mark the participants in these rituals as poor populations who seemingly 'simply' carry on tradition from colonial times.

Liora Sarfati examines the role and impact of the use of technology in contemporary Korean shamanic ritual. Although the ritual she examines is carefully preserved by a new cultural preservation national policy, which sees in it an essential part of a specific Korean identity, Sarfati demonstrates how the seemingly transparent and merely functional part of modern day technology (such as industrially manufactured costumes and sets, documentation of the rituals, or advertising them through the internet) in fact create change in the 'original form' of the ritual. Paradoxically, the official aim of preserving the ritual turns it into valuable asset for the industry that contributes to the commodification of shamanic artefacts. This anthropological analysis opens for Sarfati a rich terrain to examine the concept of 'authenticity' in current ritual practice.

Sarit Cofman-Simhon's essay concludes this motion and offers yet another perspective on the question of ritual in change. Cofman-Simhon examines Israeli Jewish orthodox performers who theatricalize and stage parts of the prayer and other materials that construct their daily religious practice and ritual. Unlike the use of religious and scriptural materials in secular theatre, in this case prayers are performed by orthodox believers who publicly expose and explore their belief. However, by transferring the religious ritual from its original performative and cultural context into the arena of theatre and art, a theoretical question about the changeability of orthodox religious ritual and its consequences emerges. In this essay we move from metaphor to literality: ritual and theatrical performance are no longer reciprocal metaphors, but literally occur on the same stage.

Motion VII: Applied performance studies: Therapy, activism and education

The study of performance has always been linked to practice, as the field has been constituted collaboratively by scholars and practitioners. However, the social applications of performance studies are developing in new directions. The three essays in this section were written by performance scholars who engage in social activism, therapy and education. The first case in point is the professional and academic training of medical clowns who have been integrated into hospital teams in Israel (Citron). The second is the emergence of 'performative psychology', and the establishment of a New York-based international forum of performance activism (Holzman and Friedman). Third is the application of performance studies to educational work in China (Sun and Fei).

From a performance studies perspective, the work of hospital clowns, described by Atay Citron, goes far beyond playful entertainment and diversion. It is associated with rites of reversal, taboo violation and the tradition of ritual clowns, fools and court jesters who defy authority in spite of their ostensible impotence. Citron, who heads the medical clowning academic training programme at the University of Haifa, sees 'audacity and insane courage' as fundamental components of clowning across cultures and generations. It is also the source of the clown doctor's unique ability to empower hospitalized patients and support their transformation into recovery. Taking the risk of overstepping the limits of decorum, these clowns perform an innovative kind of 'provocative therapy' that is also linked to the tradition of the historical avant-garde.

'Can Performance Change the World?' or even 'Save the World'? These were the respective themes of the last two of seven Performing The World Conferences that have taken place in New York since 2001. These gatherings of performance practitioners, grassroots community organizers and scholars from every continent, promote performance activism in its educational, therapeutic, social and political manifestations. The conferences' founding organizers, developmental psychologist Lois Holzman and theatre director Dan Friedman, see the creative and transformative power of performance as a radical alternative to hegemonic socio political structures. Their essay describes the origins of the 'performative turn' in psychology and in social activism, and brings an array of examples, which have been discussed at PTW – the global forum of performance activism. Their ongoing dialogue with the academic field of performance studies is of utmost importance for the advancement of performance activism.

Another unique application of performance studies is 'Social Performance Studies' (SPS), which is described by its initiators, William Huizhu Sun and Faye Chunfang Fei, as performance studies with Chinese characteristics. Their programme responded to the economic and cultural changes in Chinese society during the past two decades. Market economy and the explosion of mass media introduced a public discourse that welcomed and enhanced new kinds of social performativity. In their essay they discuss the concept of *biaoyan* (acting/performing in Chinese) as a tool to improve efficiency at work. A hybrid of Schechnerian concepts, Marxism, Confucian tradition and management discourse, Sun and Fei's performance studies model is distinctly different from Western understandings of the term. This model reflects contemporary Chinese society by negotiating traditional forms of social discipline with new elements of individual freedom.

Motion VIII: Performance studies and life sciences

Whereas in its early stages, performance studies developed mainly through dialogue with the social sciences, today's fertile exchange of information and ideas with life sciences opens new horizons. On the one hand, scientists proactively study biological aspects of phenomena such as creativity, interaction and togetherness in laboratory settings (Noy). On the other hand, performance scholars develop new understandings of performance that are based on findings in life sciences, cognitive theory and their interpretations (Kubikowski). This reciprocal curiosity is not limited to particular studies. It has the potential of opening life sciences to new forms of discourse and creativity (Alon), and of taking performance studies literally into the laboratory.

Opening this motion is an essay by performance theorist Thomasz Kubikowski, who synthesizes the findings of biologist Gerald Edelman with the definitions of anthropologist Richard Bauman to construct a universal approach to performance, in which consciousness is paramount. According to Kubikowski, performance is first and foremost a mental process that involves remembering, comparing and selecting. It occurs through recognition, in the continuous confrontational dynamics of instruction and selection. These occur at the level of the neural system, which is aimed not only at survival but also at learning about the world.

In his laboratory at the Weizmann Institute of Science, neuroscientist and improvisation theatre actor Lior Noy conducts controlled experiments in which several pairs of improvisers perform a simplified model of the well-known mirror game. Applying life sciences methods to an improvisation exercise, Noy studies the fundamental components and the dynamics of unrehearsed synchronized action, or *togetherness*. He records the movement patterns of the participants, measures and analyses them mathematically in order to identify prevailing patterns and to suggest a possible mechanism for what Schechner described as the breaking down of ego boundaries between individuals, what Turner termed *communitas* and what improvising musicians and actors call *being in the zone*. The results of the experiment lead Noy to design further studies that attempt to identify the 'inner critic' that inhabits flow in joint improvisation, and perhaps to the precise location of this inhibitor in the brain.

In 'Performing Science' – the essay that closes this motion and our book – systems biologist Uri Alon calls for a radical change in the culture of science by acknowledging and legitimizing the suppressed subjective, interpersonal and performative aspects of making science. Alon argues that the prevailing myth of science as purely objective and rational deters creativity and frustrates scientists. In order to release scientific imagination and allow for unconventional ideas, Alon argues for the formation of scientists' peer groups, which focus on the emotional and interpersonal performance of science as part of their research. Alon borrows ideas and practices from improvisation theatre, dramatic writing and literary theory. According to Alon, scientific experimentation or performing science is embarking on a journey to the unknown. We hope that *Performance Studies in Motion* takes the reader on a similarly intense journey.

Motion I

Performance Studies:
Perspectives and Prospectives

1

Dionysus in 1966: The Force of Performative Circumstances

David Zerbib

'The theatre was taken in by the Church in the Middle Ages, then some time around the Renaissance it was emancipated, or thrown out from the Church, whence it was taken in by literature; and I think in these last few days it's being thrown out by literature.'[1] It was in these terms that Richard Schechner spoke to Roland Barthes at the famous colloquium, from 18 to 21 October 1966, which for the first time in the United States gave a platform to some of the best-known voices of what later came to be known as 'Poststructuralism'. The accent of this so-called 'French Theory' resounded particularly in the literary studies departments of American universities, notably at Johns Hopkins University where, in that autumn, a crucial moment in transatlantic intellectual history, a rare meeting was held of thinkers linked to structuralism (and for the very first time for the two last named in particular)[2] Roland Barthes, Jacques Lacan and Jacques Derrida.

Yet, this event also needs to be situated within the genealogy of performance studies. In 1966, this original field of research had not been invented. One of its future founders, who would define it as being 'wide open',[3] was the member of the audience who noted, in front of the illustrious French orators at Baltimore, that like the Church literature has – maybe advantageously 'both to literature and to the theatre' – 'thrown out' the theatre. Doubtless there can be no performance study until such a field is opened up, and no doubt the subject of such a study basically can only be the very process or event of opening up this field. What happens when theatricality becomes emancipated from the dramatic text? What effects are measured in the core of the representational apparatus? What transformations take place in language, consciousness, the space and bodies? Performance is constantly bringing us back to such issues, relating to the opening of a field and the setting in motion of an object whose movement indeed is a part of its intrinsic nature.

The Johns Hopkins University meetings shed light on a key dimension of this movement. Up to and including the inaudible question of performance which does not receive an explicit answer in this context, they highlight a fundamental issue for its contemporary theory and practice: the relationship – paradoxical because despite obviously being semantically close it is often contradictory – between embodied performance and textual performativity. What was being looked for and announced on this epic stage of intellectual life, symptomatically through Schechner's fringe speeches between lectures, as the one we quoted at the outset of this essay, was the linkage between at least two falsely converging paths of the *performative turn*: from one side, some philosophical operations leading to the discovery at the core of language, with Derrida, a breach which weakens its link to truth and meaning in favour of a free play of signs; from the other side, a dismissal of the text itself building on the stage of bodies and gestures a literal space of individual and collective transformation.

Against a backdrop of misunderstanding, however, a common dynamic rose up in the watershed years 1966–68 between these paths of the performative turn. Its figure was Dionysus, the god of drunkenness, trance and excess, invoked in a variety of modes and rites, and who at least since Euripides has been in the habit of taking on the features of numerous heroes in this historical tragedy that has consisted in opening up the scene of an end to representation, in literary criticism, philosophy and even the theatre. Dionysus has largely given the measure, in both the rhythmic and evaluative senses of the word, to the performances played out there in the practical and theoretical field. This measure, derived from Dionysian *hubris*, records the immoderation of transformations, and is first of all an indicator of *force*. Now, it is precisely in a certain play between forms and forces that the aforementioned two paths of the performative turn seem able to link together.

Symptom

The reference to the 'symptomatic' presence of the question of the performance in this event devoted to literary criticism and to the sciences of man has a double meaning: in the sense of a meaningful indicator referring to the general balance of an organization, if not of an organism, in which the future of the City of the Humanities in the United States is played out, a stage with its chorus, its heroes announcing the new age, its battles of ideas and its messengers arriving from the Paris left bank. But, the symptomatic question also has the meaning of one brand of philosophy, which sees the theatre as the place for an 'etiology of language', of a disease affecting the ordinary workings of our utterances.

Schechner was not at Harvard when John L. Austin gave his famous lectures in 1955, published in 1962 with the title *How to do things with words*. But Austin answered the question of the theatre. We know indeed that the discoverer of 'performativity', that 'active' property of language whereby words produce deeds instead of merely noting, describing or representing reality, paradoxically excluded from his analysis the declamations of the actor on stage.

'As utterances our performatives are also heir to certain other kinds of ill which infect all utterances . . . I mean, for example, the following: a performative utterance will, for example, be in a peculiar way hollow and void if said by an actor on the stage.' In fact, explains Austin, language in such circumstances is 'used not seriously, but in ways parasitic upon its normal use—ways which fall under the doctrine of the etiolations of language'.[4]

The question of the performance is a distraction even within the performative turn. Thus, there exists a 'performative circumstance' that the theory of performativity considers from the outset as a source of infection, a cause of malfunctions and pragmatic indeterminacy: artistic performance in general and theatrical performance in particular. For, we do understand that art forces us to rethink the criteria of the effectiveness of language above and beyond the conventions of ordinary language. In art, we might say in Austin's terms, the *perlocutory force* of utterances (i.e. the measure of the effects that they produce by the very fact of their performance) lies in their ability to suspend the social and conventional conditions of meaning, making possible their momentary or lasting transformations. That is why, for example, 'the earth is blue like an orange'.[5]

Admittedly, mention of Austin sheds light on another path taken by the performative turn, which was basically only marginally present at Johns Hopkins in 1966.[6] The name of the English philosopher indeed crops up in the introduction by Richard Macksey, one of the organizers of the colloquium, to prepare the audience for the 'language games' that were to bring together the orators and confront them with each other. But the speaker ended up choosing a rather eloquent image to launch the debate that took place between the most formalist structuralism with the first dynamiting of deconstruction, or between the analyses focusing most on the text and the historicist and humanist approach that was heir to Marxism: a lion. 'If a lion could talk, we could not understand him.'[7] Macksey quotes Wittgenstein, who then tells us through this enigmatic formula that a language is only understandable provided the speaker's form of life and worldview is familiar. But this implies an image of the language-game operating as the circus games, in a tension between pure forces and language, with a risk of devouring, exhibiting a symbol of force to illustrate the question of meaning.

Form and force

It is not easy rigorously to address the notion of 'force' in aesthetic theory or critical discourse. There is always the danger of falling into subjectivism, inconsistent metaphorical rhetoric or even occultism. 'Form' is more readily identified and measured, on account of the long philosophical history linking it to the very exercise of *theoria*, the contemplative practice at the origin of all theory. Thus, in Plato we pass *theoretically* from the false form of the perceptible apparition (*eidolon*) to the true Form, that of Ideas (*eidos*). The force is present, however, even in this Socratic method: first in *Eros*, which is in the principle of love of wisdom and incites us to recognize truth, and then it is present in moments when this quest is halted by kinds of parasitic transports. The main interference at issue would be that of the rhetorical effect of Sophistic speech which the Socratic dialogue is fundamentally against. But alongside this main antagonistic force, we also see certain magnetic movements that distract Socrates momentarily from his dialectical elevation. This happens with the poetry of the rhapsodist Io. In the short eponymous dialogue, Socrates recognizes that the rhapsodist has no *tekhne*, in the sense that he does not know the truth hidden behind the verses of Homer that he conveys through the beauty of his song. Nonetheless, this inspired performer who has just won a rhapsody contest when he met Socrates has the power to 'attract' his audience. He creates, acknowledges the philosopher, between the muses and his listeners an unbroken chain of magnetic rings.[8] For a moment, the force of the performance overrides any mimetic and formal value of truth.

There certainly exists in the history of the arts, alongside or through the history of forms, a history of forces that might tie together a series of chains of the type revealed by *Io*. While the art historian Aby Warburg has identified the phenomenon of the survival of forms, that of the survival of forces is necessarily linked to it by co-extensivity or rather by co-intensivity.[9]

Indeed, one can only note how many works, concepts or gestures are able to reactivate effects that have been manifested before, elsewhere. As Antonin Artaud writes: 'Let them burn down the library at Alexandria. There are powers above and beyond papyri. We may be temporarily deprived of the ability to rediscover these powers, but we will never eliminate their energy.'[10] Similarly, the actor 'brutalizes forms, as he destroys them he is united with what lives on behind and after them, producing their continuation.'[11]

Thus, forces are exerted on forms to the point of destroying them but, as in physics, a principle of conservation is observable at the level of the system. Transformations take place but the energy is conserved. The force, in the vector sense, refers back to a constant scalar magnitude. Above and beyond the nature/culture opposition, should we identify a principle of conservation of symbolic energies, comparable to the first law of thermodynamics for instance? An implicit epistemology and a paradigm of a physical conception of space and time function certainly on the artistic forms. This is what Thierry de Duve, for example, was saying about Minimal Art and its characteristic theatricality.[12] According to that art critic, the sculptures of someone like Robert Morris make the performance of space-time itself perceptible and thereby come under the entropic motion as defined by thermodynamics. As heir to the quantum physics revolution, this marks a break with Newtonian physics which measured movements on the basis of a view of space and time as an absolute, fixed frame of reference.

As Robert Crease points out, 'relativity and quantum mechanics have called into question the relation between theory and world in a way that challenges the validity of the image'. Then, science as experimentation has less than ever to fix an image of nature than to frame the 'play of nature'. He specifies: 'The theatrical analogy is thus something to be used rather than proven. In philosophy, as in other disciplines aiming at the recognition of novel worldly structures, disclosure rather than proof is the culminating event.'[13] Between theatre and science, the disclosure which opened the passage from the fixed space-time frame of the theatre to the process-based space and time of the performance cannot be conceptualized without the modern upheavals of physical science. This alone incites us to take an interest in the question of forces beyond the metaphorical attraction of the term.

Classically, we find a seminal dynamic principle in the famous dichotomy introduced by Nietzsche with regard to aesthetics. In *The Birth of Tragedy*, the philosopher describes the struggle, and the complementarity, between the Dionysian and Apollonian dimensions of the works of Aeschylus, Sophocles and Euripides.[14] How are tragic works originally operated on by forces that exceed all measure, and which art tries for a while to stabilize or pacify in the form of the tragic beauty? We are familiar with Nietzsche's critical diagnosis: tragedy has evolved towards a deplorable normalization from the effect of 'Socratic man' who has diverted the dialogue between the Dionysian *hubris* and the Apollonian order, to direct it ever more towards the sterile quest for good and truth. But the forces repressed for a time ended up returning, and have in fact kept coming back. And if necessary they come in through the back door, as Freud said about repressed drives, using the analogy of a lecture from which a disruptive spectator is ejected.[15] Now, in 1966, these forces appeared to be on the speakers' platform, and through the lions' voice, taking their turn to speak.

Performism

Under the title 'Structure, Sign and Play in the discourse of the Human Sciences', over the years, the lecture given at Baltimore by Jacques Derrida has remained the most commented upon of all the papers given at that symposium in 1966. Derrida came to the United States to announce an 'event'. This was nothing less than a body blow to Western metaphysics, coming after repeated attacks from Nietzsche, Freud and Heidegger. But the announcement was a further blow at the very point that seemingly ought to have been restabilizing a modern thought: the structuralism with its setting of new perspectives in the human sciences regarding how man relates to the world. Structuralism wanted to fix the rules of this relationship into a system of signification but, as Derrida explains, the 'philosophical centre' of this system, not to mention its scientific, economic, technical and political centre, was falling apart.

The structuralism of Lévi-Strauss, Derrida shows, deconstructs itself, blowing away the centre from which structure is conceptualized, the metaphysical foundations upon which it is based. How could we fix the structure of signification of a myth for instance, if we take into account the fact that they are tales which are not assignable to any origin, transmitted 'without authors'? Signs (words, writings, languages, etc.) have no fixed origin but they also lack a clear destination: as the origin, the signified misses. The movement of signification, claims Derrida, 'comes to perform a vicarious function, to supplement a lack on the part of the signified'.[16] Seeking to deliver the structural form of the relationship of meaning, structuralism shows – dramatically – 'The overabundance of the signifier, its supplementary character'.[17] Hence becomes the famous performance of the sign for which Derrida becomes the philosophical stage manager: the free play of the sign.

In a claimed Nietzschean attitude, Derrida describes 'the joyous affirmation of the play of the world and of the innocence of becoming, the affirmation of a world of signs without fault, without truth, and without origin which is offered to an active interpretation'.[18] This activation of the sign, its setting in motion in free play, has to be placed within a polarity between form and force, which 3 years earlier the author had made the theme of 'Force and signification'. Criticizing structuralist formalism in the field of literary criticism, Derrida deplores: 'Form fascinates when one no longer has the force to understand force from within itself. That is to create.'[19] Targeting the critical discourse, for instance, that analyses the Cornelian conflict of love and duty in terms of 'rings', 'ascending spiral' or 'helical ascent',[20] the author links structuralism to an operation of geometrization, before which 'one can glance over the field divested of its forces more freely or diagrammatically'.[21] Made up of 'Preformationism, teleologism, reduction of force, value and duration',[22] a pacified landscape is thus drawn to recover like a shroud the very force of writing. Before this 'final peace', this 'peace of the structural *energeia*'[23] which delivers a skeleton of meaning, Derrida tends towards the Dionysian alternative. The latter involves no longer the 'stifling [of] force under form'[24] and, accordingly, revives 'The divergence, the difference between Dionysus and Apollo, between ardor and structure'.[25]

The dynamic in play, however, does not come down to a logic of embodiment. The idea is not to put the literal flesh back on a skeleton of meaning that has been stripped of it by structuralist formalism. While force is 'the other of language without which language would not be what it is',[26] this does not mean that it is a body, material reality or hidden substance, because that would be to bring this otherness back to the binary system of signifier and signified, whereas it is the sign's own power that is being targeted, and not its 'direction' towards an eventual hidden meaning.

Hence, faced with 'preformationism' (or 'preformism' to translate in a lighter word the French '*préformisme*'), which he criticizes, Derrida opposes what might be termed analogically a *performism*. This neologism would clearly set a distinction between the principle of a predetermined form, upon which the process of meaning depends, and a principle of an unpredictable meaning going through this form, destroying it or occurring in excess over it.[27] In other words, *performism* would designate a thought, which involves reviving the forces that run through forms. As in Nietzsche's Dionysism, these forces nonetheless need form: 'For all eternity, [Dionysos] has had a relationship to his exterior, to visible form, to structure, as he does to his death. This is how he appears (to himself).'[28] And Derrida warns against the risk of 'an energetics of pure, shapeless force'.[29]

In art, on the contrary, performance seems to have embodied this 'energetics of pure force', just as it has aspired to attain a pure presence, a gesture that was absolute, unique, unrepeatable, both original and final, reconfiguring the symbolic field on the immediate basis of the real, the body, the event. How, in these conditions which are enunciated in 1966, can a joint between textual performance of the sign and embodied performance be articulated? Would a common *performism* appear on behalf of Dionysus?

In quest for a Saussure of theatre?

At Johns Hopkins in 1966, Richard Schechner was in attendance and questioned Lacan, Barthes and indirectly Derrida as well. At this period, Schechner oriented his theatrical work with his New Orleans Group towards an 'Environmental Theatre'. His 'Six Axioms for Environmental Theatre' came out in 1967 and, in 1966, he asked for the first time a spectator to 'do something (that went beyond the fact of buying a ticket, sitting down, smiling and applauding at the end of the spectacle)'.[30] Would a link be formed between the beginning of the post-structuralist adventure and the ongoing upheavals in the avant-garde theatre scene? 'In regard to the theatre, asked Schechner to Lucien Goldmann,[31] I wonder how you treat the real event of performance, including the audience, the theatre building, and the entire environment of the theatrical event.'[32] What effect does this have on literary criticism 'when the very fact of the theatrical event is introjected into the text?'

Lucien Goldmann had no answer to this 'introjection' of the theatrical parasite. This was not the issue for the conference, and it would appear to have been a lost opportunity for performance theory. But Schechner took his question further with Barthes: 'It seems to me that you describe language and literature as implosive, in other words, turned in on its own laws and explicated by its own laws, while in theatre at least language is explosive – language is a matrix of actions. It doesn't make any sense in the theatre unless language gives rise to action, which is the performance.'[33] What about the relationship between linguistic laws and the 'the spoken word', 'the performance of the text', 'the gestural world'? In the first analysis, Barthes noted how gesture can be related to a common semiological system: 'human gestures constitute a semiotic system' and as such raises the same problem as 'any system of signs'. But Barthes relegated gestures to a grammar as yet too poor: gesture, he explained, is not yet sufficiently 'denaturalised to the profit of a very strong code'.[34] Schechner insisted, hoping for input from the study of the structure of language for the study of the 'language of gesture'. 'If you are to be the Saussure of theatre, that will be wonderful,' replied Barthes to close the debate.

Assuredly, in the years that followed, Richard Schechner evolved, not so much in the direction of a Saussure as of a Derrida of theatre. The thinker of deconstruction had little to contribute to the discussions on theatre at this 1966 conference, but did speak in the exchange that followed Barthes' lecture, not to answer Schechner's question, but to carry on where Barthes had left off and expand on his thoughts on the impossibility of a subject conceived as an original author of a singular speech act: 'I am always already absent from my language, or absent from this supposed experience of the new, of singularity, etc. That would mean that in order for my pronunciation of the word *je* to be an act of language, it must be a signal work, that is, it must be originally repeated.'[35] Schechner's concepts of 'restored behavior', understood as repetitions with no original (unless itself a repetition) or the indeterminacy of a centre of intentionality and identity – when for example he places the actor's identity within the double negative of 'not not me', are epistemologically rooted in the theories of liminality that come from anthropology and tend towards a form of theatrical behaviourism, but their paradoxical formulation and evocative force have more to do with post-structuralist play. Witness also this reply from Lacan to his question, abandoning the battle of the theatre and returning almost artificially to literature, on the subject of 'nothingness' in Sartre: 'the never-here, explains Lacan (it is here when I search there; it is there when I am here) is not nothing'. A 'not not thing' resonates here, attesting to influences above and beyond the lack of answer on the issue of performance.

The meeting between the performance of the post-structuralist sign and the performance of the post-dramatic body on stage is therefore missed only relatively speaking. While Schechner tries to inject the side issue of the embodied performance into the discussion, the meaning of gestures coming for instance from his 'environmental theatre', we understand that it was too early for that, and the issue of the discussions was limited to the terms of Structuralist textual analysis and the question of whether it was destined to fall apart. Nonetheless, Schechner was a symptom. With hindsight, he encourages us to identify on this stage at Johns Hopkins the play of a double performative supplementarity: that of the sign on the signified and that of the body on the linguistic sign. These two dynamics open up the stage for the performance on the basis of a critique of representation, but in different, not necessarily converging places. A mention of Artaud might have bridged the gap.

The real thing

A few months before the Baltimore conference, Derrida published an article, 'The Theatre of Cruelty and the closure of representation', in which he analysed Artaud's project for a kind of theatricality that was to 'traverse and restore "existence" and "flesh" in each of their aspects'.[36] 'How will speech and writing function then?' he asks. 'They will once more become *gestures*.'[37] His answer to Schechner seems to be contained in that essay. According to Artaud, Derrida writes, 'Repetition separates force, presence, and life from themselves. This separation is the economical and calculating gesture of that which defers itself in order to maintain itself, that which reserves expenditure and surrenders to fear.'[38] Hence, we find ourselves in the presence of this other supplementarity, this excess of force, only this time it refers back to the original presence, not repeatable, to the flesh, to life, and not to the specific power of the sign.

Derrida, however, only shows this explosion of presence to demonstrate its re-inscription on the stage of representation. Indeed, presence can only assert itself, Derrida shows, in the form of a tragedy: that of the end of representation. So there is no pure presence, or pure force, life or realities captured immediately in their naked truth. The antinomy with Artaud's theatrical heritage, alongside Richard Schechner's Performance Group for instance, would seem, once more, stronger. 'We want the real thing!' the actor William Finlay shouts for example in *Dionysus in 69*, performed by the Group in New York in 1968. 'Freedom! Delight in the raw flesh! Freedom! . . . I love the smell of riots, the orgasms of death and blood! We will tolerate no more false revolutions, no more rituals and phony bloodbaths! We want the real thing!' The play 'restores' the conflict between the Apollonian and the Dionysian, in a revival of Euripides' *The Bacchae*, wonderfully documented in a film by Brian de Palma.[39]

As the Messenger announces, echoing in some ways the Derridean announcement: 'Yes, it's a death struggle. Dionysus versus Pentheus. The organism versus the law.' Everything appears to corroborate this aesthetic of excess, of a destruction of the theatre frame seeking to revive the transgressive forces of transformation. In one of the versions performed in the Performing

Garage on Wooster Street, the actor playing Dionysus resituated the issue of forces in the contemporary social, linguistic and technological context: 'I want Power Power. Power means power. I mean juice, baby. Electrical power is power. Currency is currency. Power is power. It goes through wires, it's in the tube, in the radio, it comes in little batteries that you can put in your pocket, it makes things move, it is the source of the sense of motion, it makes light, it makes the ticket tick . . . Everyone will be totally in motion and totally informed. Dig it. Power Power! Power Power! Power Power!'

Far, however, from sticking to the pure force, from the literalness of the real body, far from materializing the epiphany of pure presence, and also far from a unilateral merging of the spaces of the actor and audience into a single ritual space-time, the piece is constantly playing on relative, ironic and experimental shifts. As the analysis of the play cannot be set out in detail here, suffice it to note how, in *Dionysus in 69*, the exchange of positions does not happen in only one direction. The actors call each other by their real names, then revert to their tragic mask, while members of the audience strip off to join the Bacchae in the dance, then return to their seats while casting around, under the inquisitive eye of de Palma's camera, for their trousers. Here too, the forces at play are not just vector forces and do not converge ideally in a single direction. The tensions at stake refer back to a global energy in the face of which the theatre issue does not boil down to the illusion of an absolutely and immediately effective political application, that is the final activation of a formerly passive community. The activation of the forces or the setting in motion of positions in theatre is not reducible to a utopia, or to the modern theatrical myth, of the transformation of the spectator into an actor.

A rather simplistic approach of the Dionysian experiments of the sixties tends to reduce them to a literal call for a ritual merging. This is one of the assumptions of the critique of performance theatre made by Jacques Rancière. According to him, this theatre conceives the stage as a 'third term' that is an obstacle to be removed, because of the illusory project of a total activation of the spectator.[40] But the case of *Dionysus in 69* shows a more complex process, a continuous shift between participation and distancing, between identities and positions.[41] The reference to the 'third term' of the theatre stage is constant in this piece. No absolute presence, no direct 'real thing', no 'pure energetics of shapeless force': *Dionysus in 69*, contrary to some appearances, is close to this Dionysus whose epithet would be the god of deconstruction, invoked by Derrida in 1966.

Conduction

In 'The Crash of performative circumstances', published in 1982, Richard Schechner set the conditions for a new situation for performance in the terms of a 'postmodern' and 'post-humanist' theory.[42] Now the historical circumstances of discourses and practices evolve, inciting us to constantly re-elaborate our response to these circumstances. For instance, the inflation of discourses on performativity have tended these days to blur the conceptual differences between performance and performativity. Yet, a look at the seminal encounter of 1966 as a 'primal stage' of performance studies, allows a reappraisal of some of the internal contradictions of the performative turn, in order to rearticulate it on a clearer basis. While there is no merging of the two performance scenes that we have identified (embodied performance and textual performativity), while there is not necessarily a convergence, there is definitely a coincidence.

Now, there is obviously more than one way to understand the relationship between performance in the theatrical sense and post-structuralist theory. Philippe Ausslander, for example, neatly explains how Derridean deconstruction corresponds exactly to the decentring of the actor's identity.[43] Meanwhile, Shoshana Felman, linking Don Juan, Austin and Lacan, has given a masterly demonstration of how the performative 'sui-referentiality' produces an excess on language that we call reality.[44] Reality here appears as the effect of the performative operation, not as its reference, origin, or preconceived aim. This process is also at stake in Judith Butler's view on the embodiment of discursive performativity.[45]

Our attention to the question of forces, coming from the restoration of Dionysism at a given moment in the history of forms and ideas, leads us to envisage another type of link, a dynamic one, which stresses a co-intensivity in the different paths of the so-called performative turn. What is at stake then is a common attention to the *energeia* – to use the Aristotelian notion[46] – which drives the attempt to (re)activate the forces at the expense of forms but with a constant reference to them. This attempt can be called a *performism*. It leads to define performance as the process of actualization which makes sensible or even conscious, efficient or effective what goes *per* form, that is, through the form. The Dionysian force pulses under the Apollonian form (Nietzsche), the force of the sign goes through the form of signification and exceeds it (Derrida), the 'perlocutionary force' operates through the form of the utterance (Austin), an energy may circulate between actors and spectators through the artistic or theatrical framework. This explains why the limits of performance could blur, challenging any project of definition which usually is an attempt to fix an idea on a substantialized form. If performance disappears in the ephemerality of the event, it is not to serve a formalism of absolute presence, but to let the forces operate, to activate a transmission or *conduction* (a transfer of heat in thermodynamics), which is a call for a forthcoming performance and never an ultimate epiphany.

Performance Studies 3.0

Henry Bial

Performance studies is continually reinventing itself. As new scholars enter the field, as new objects and sites of study come under consideration, as new technological, political and social movements alter the contexts in which we think about performance, the methods by which we carry out our analysis inevitably change. This is true of course, of all intellectual disciplines. In many fields, however, scholars choose to emphasize their continuity with the past tradition. The theatre historian, for example, may employ phenomenological theory to explicate digital archives of non-theatrical happenings, and still see herself as heir to the legacy of Terence, Langbaine and Brockett. *This is my father's axe; I've replaced the head, and I've replaced the handle; but still it is my father's axe.*

Performance studies, however, whose origins, at least in part, come from a rejection of more traditional disciplines, has tended to emphasize its own discontinuities and moments of transgression. As Jon McKenzie writes, 'What is performance? What is Performance Studies? "Liminality" is perhaps the most concise and accurate response to both of these questions.'[1] For McKenzie, this emphasis on liminality comes from the central role that rites of passage play as both object of study and organizing metaphor in early performance studies, a valuable idea that I have explored elsewhere.[2] Furthermore, as performance studies initially defined itself in part against literary study, there is significant incentive to focus on the positive value of change, on the unique contribution made each time a new player enters the scene. To put it another way, having been conceived, dedicated and (in a sense) consecrated around the idea of a catastrophic paradigm shift, the field has grown addicted to reinvention. *The Future of the Field, Again.*

It is for precisely this reason that the conventional rite of passage (as theorized by Van Gennep and Turner) is no longer a major site of study for performance studies, nor is the transmittal/transmutation of restored behaviour from one performer/performance to the next. These ideas are not without value, and they are essential to the field's history, but as we consider now both 'Perspectives and Prospectives' of performance studies, we must recognize that academic disciplines take their shape, texture and flavour from the times and places in which they emerge. I suggest, then, that we today imagine performance studies' history of change (and continuity) on the model of the computer OS and its multiple releases: rather than 'first wave' or 'second stage', rather than 'NYU-model' or 'post-Schechnerian', let us speak of PS 1.0, PS 2.0 and so on.

Considering Performance Studies (PS) as an OS allows us to recognize several key principles about the ongoing development of the field. First and most importantly, PS should be understood less as a discrete collection of topics and ideas and more as a virtual environment which can host/facilitate a nearly infinite variety of scholarly and artistic inquiries. Second, just as the period of transition from one OS to the next is highly variable subject to local needs and conditions, at any given moment there are multiple versions of PS 'running' around the world, and even within the same institution. A 'power user' may run multiple versions of PS simultaneously. Thus, a once-critical feature such as Schechner's entertainment-efficacy dyad remains viable, useful and relevant for one user, even while others have 'upgraded'. Third, in order to allow for continuity of use and to prevent the loss of critical data, each OS must maintain some degree of backward compatibility. The new system must be able to read the old documents, and the old system is frequently capable of incorporating some features of the new system. Hence though we mark the major changes, we also recognize intermediate stages (e.g. version 1.5). We further recognize that no OS is ever 'finished', but is constantly being refined as bugs are worked out and new features added: (e.g. version 1.5.1 or even 1.5.0.2). Fourth, some devoted users will not consider the new OS an upgrade at all, and will continue to use a prior version, even if it is increasingly out of sync with everything else. Such users are not (necessarily) victims of inertia or fear of change; often they have specialized needs that the new release no longer serves, and often their 'workarounds' are the source/product of enormous creativity. Fifth, corollary to the previous observation, newer is not always *better*, though newer is almost certainly *newer*. Thus to the degree that novelty itself can be seen as a critical feature, the progress of an OS can be understood as a kind of evolution by natural selection. The system *perceived* as obsolete is gradually abandoned by developers until it actually is obsolete. Sixth, neither the OS nor the refinements and upgrades are understood to be the work of a single genius. The notion of authorship becomes increasingly diffuse and less relevant with each release. Who wrote Windows 7? Who cares?

Different operating systems function similarly because they have similar ends, but they behave according to different interface metaphors: early computing systems, focused on processing, may have been conceived as assembly lines. As the purpose of the computer shifted to data storage, operating systems began to use the interface metaphor of the filing system: directories, folders, etc. The 'desktop' encouraged thinking of the computer as a virtual workspace. Other more recent systems use the interface metaphor of a datebook, a personal assistant, a bag of tricks. Significantly, the interface metaphor that appears to arise in response to users' desires ends up dictating not-quite-performatively the kinds of tasks we use the OS to accomplish: if our system appears to be a filing system, we use it to produce files; if it appears to be a toolbox, we use it to 'fix' things; etc.

In the remainder of this essay, I sketch the history of performance studies as a discipline through three stages that I call (not without irony) 'PS 1.0', 'PS 2.0' and 'PS 3.0'. I note the political and social contexts in which each version of PS arose, and show how that context led to the development of particular interface metaphors. My narrative is centred on the development of the field in the United States, a fact that I shall try, occasionally, not to take for granted, and one that does not, I hope, undermine the probative value of my argument.

PS 1.0 is the by-now-well-rehearsed intersection between theatre and anthropology, as manifested in the fruitful collaboration between Richard Schechner and Victor Turner. Though work from this period continues to be relevant, it is marked by the fascination with ritual and close association with universal humanism that marked the 1960s and 70s counterculture in the United States and Europe. Its interface metaphor is the tribe. PS 2.0 can be understood as shaped by and in response to the postmodern 'identity crisis' of the 1980s and 90s. This version of performance studies is characterized by the highly reflexive deployment of theory and the gradual redefinition of the term 'performative' from a rough synonym for 'theatrical' to a more specialized meaning that emphasizes performance's potential for social efficacy. Its interface metaphor is the solo performance artist. PS 3.0 could be said to have been 'in development' since the late 1990s, accelerating in the 2000s and on up to the present. As the internet and other forms of global communication have provided both the technological and social imperative for a new understanding of performance, the field has attempted to come to terms with the new digital landscape: for example, explorations in cognition, critical re-evaluation of the archive, a revalorization of embodiment. This new interface metaphor is still taking shape, but I suggest that 'open source' will emerge as the central animating paradigm of this next stage of performance studies.

PS 1.0 is, to mix metaphors, a child of the 1960s. Among the most influential of its foundational texts are Erving Goffman's *The Presentation of the Self in Everyday Life* (1959), J. L. Austin's *How To Do Things with Words* (1962) and Victor Turner's *The Ritual Process* (1969). As US and European universities expanded, opening their doors to a wider range of people, including more women and minorities than ever before, conventional academic disciplines increasingly saw their boundaries challenged and stretched. Fields that had previously been organized into neat taxonomies of nation and period found themselves destabilized as those very concepts came under critique. The complicity of the academy in the post-war rise of the military industrial complex was also influential, leading to campus occupations, sit ins and other forms of student protest. As the 1960s and 70s progressed, the academy shifted leftwards, particularly in the humanities and social sciences, with *access* to rhetorics of power as a critical trope.

When Schechner in his 1966 essay 'Approaches to Theory/Criticism', first laid out what would come to be called the broad spectrum approach to performance studies, he did so with the explicit hope that this would expand the field of theatre to groups and peoples previously excluded from formal study. 'If one argues', he wrote, 'that theatre is "later" or "more sophisticated" or "higher" on some evolutionary ladder and therefore must derive from one of the others [performance activities such as ritual, games and music], I reply that this makes sense only if we take fifth-century BCE Greek theatre (and its counterparts in other cultures) as the only legitimate theatre'.[3]

Thanks in no small part to the 1977 meeting between Schechner and Turner, and the two men's subsequent collaboration on a series of influential scholarly/artistic conferences, the origin narrative of PS 1.0 is often framed as a pairing, to use the title of Schechner's landmark 1985 book, *Between Theatre and Anthropology*. What is less often appreciated is that both Schechner and Turner were *seekers* in this formulation. Which is to say, the initial meeting was not between imperial expeditionary forces. Schechner wasn't looking for new territories to colonize with his theatrics. Turner wasn't looking to bring new realms under the anthropological banner. Rather, each man (and let it here be understood that they stand in for a larger group) was, in some sense, a runaway (if not an exile) from his home discipline, and was looking to the other's field as a source of potential inspiration, innovation and change. For Turner, the theatre practitioner's concern with lived experience was a way to revitalize an anthropological discourse that was 'more concerned with *stasis* than with *dynamis*, with texts, institutions, types, protocols, "wiring," custom and so on than with the *how* of performance . . .'[4] Similarly, Schechner, in his 1982 essay 'Points of Contact' (subsequently published as Chapter 1 of *Between Theatre and Anthropology*), emphasized the hope that anthropology's focus 'on human action' would revitalize a field of theatre studies that had become too concerned with literary abstraction.

This mirrors the utopian view of intercultural encounter that marks PS in this phase. When Turner wrote, 'We will know one another better by entering one another's performances and learning their grammars and vocabularies,'[5] it was an expression of the same kind of universal humanism that led other seekers to start communes, take LSD and put daisies in gun barrels. When Schechner sought the roots of theatre in the behaviour of chimpanzees and other 'universals', it was not an imperialist gesture (all people are like me) but an expression of a desire for peaceful coexistence (if we can demonstrate that all people are like one another, we can stop the war).

As other countercultural figures such as Abbie Hoffman did, PS 1.0 valorized tribal cultures, developing a particular fascination with shamanism, trance performance and other apparent triumphs of collectivity. This was echoed in the earliest experiments of Grotowski's Theatre Laboratory, Barba's Odin Teatret and Schechner's Performance Group among others. Many of these artists developed an almost orientalist fetishization of Asia, a turning to the 'mystical east', especially India as a source of inspiration. If this was, in some ways, a valuable counterweight to the Anglocentric establishment that had restricted discussion and debate in the academy for much of the century, it was also very much in tune with geopolitics of the moment, offering a kind of 'one world' utopianism that was especially attractive to the growing pacifist movement.

In sum, we might characterize this initial phase, PS 1.0, as animated by a desire to shift from a dominant understanding of the world as a book – a linear, static catalogue with clear boundaries – to a world as performance. Moreover, because this shift was intended in part to challenge traditional Eurocentric hegemony, the archetype of this performance was not the traditional Western drama, but the coming of age ritual. In other words, the basic unit of understanding – the interface metaphor – for performance studies was the *tribe*, and the field tended to valorize those aspects of theatre that tended towards this *tribal* state. In a parallel development, scholars in the field of speech and oral interpretation also found their way towards performance studies. While the specific institutional histories are different,[6] the idea of doing something that matters, that has efficacy, and that brings people together rather than splitting them apart is crucial. So we might say that the interface metaphor of what Schechner and others have called 'Northwestern's Brand of Performance Studies' is the *community* (which, after all, is a more grass roots US-centred way of describing a tribe, particularly the Tribe That Is Us).

The emphasis on embodiment and mutual interdependence in PS 1.0 positioned it as authentic or sincere, in contrast to a kind of phoniness that was thought to animate the previous generation. The performer was present, real and engaged with his fellow human beings, in a way that, say, the Man in the Gray Flannel Suit was not. And the politics of the period synced nicely with this, so that as politics increasingly involved performance – from sit ins and marches to televised debates to happenings – it was only natural to acknowledge that performance was a force for social change.

What is perhaps striking about this initial PS is that it peaks *avant la lettre* – that is to say, this 'golden age' of the 1960s and 1970s is prior to the institutionalization of PS as a field. Like many operating systems, then, PS 1.0 can be identified and characterized only in retrospect. A product of the 1960s and 1970s, its 'launch' as a platform is more appropriately marked in 1980 by the renaming of NYU's graduate drama department as the Department of Performance Studies and the launch that same year by the Speech Communication Association (later the National Communication Association) of *Literature and Performance* (later *Text and Performance Quarterly*). On the other hand, just as operating systems go through multiple stages, from initial development to beta testing to formal launch to further refinement, institutions being governed by committee and (often) consensus may often be slow to recognize developments that have already taken place. So it is that even at the moment that PS was 'rolled out' to users on a broad scale, the development of the next version was already underway.

It has become fashionable (especially in retrospect) to refer to the 1980s as the 'Me Decade'. This characterization generally connotes negatives such as selfishness, greed and egotism, but for many the decade brought a much-needed reassessment of identity politics, and some important progress vis-à-vis individual freedoms. Identity – particularly marginalized or oppressed identity – was a key component of social movements in the United States and Europe from the 1960s onwards, but the emphasis had tended towards group unity. In so doing, the movements may have eventually become restrictive and calcified. Judith Butler summarizes the problem this way:

> Indeed, one ought to consider the futility of a political program which seeks radically to transform the social situation of women without first determining whether the category of woman is socially constructed in such a way that to be a woman is, by definition, to be in an oppressed situation. In an understandable desire to forge bonds of solidarity, feminist discourse has often relied upon the category of woman as a universal presupposition of cultural experience which, in its universal status, provides a false ontological promise of eventual political solidarity.[7]

For Butler, the emphasis on collective action and shared experience, while laudable, carried its own potential pitfalls: namely, the acceptance of an always already abject position and the 'false ontological promise' that each member of the collective shared the same ideological or material goals and desires. In the language of PS 1.0, we might summarize this critique by saying that the potential value of spontaneous *communitas* is tempered by a recognition that it rarely appears without its counterpart normative *communitas*. Despite the best intentions of the 1960s and 70s counterculture, claims to universality necessarily involve a foreclosure of difference that is experienced as discipline by those who perform their identities outside normative regimes of discourse and power. PS 2.0 responded to this dilemma by reemphasizing the individual. Instead of the shamans and trance-dancers giving themselves over to the larger social whole, the field began to look at the individual and her strategies of resistance to that normative group.

Building on the feminist assertion that the personal is political, scholars examined individuals as both psychic and material subjects. From the realm of comparative literature came critiques informed by Freudian and Lacanian psychoanalysis. If PS 1.0 was, in part, about anthropology and theatre reaching towards one another to explain what each field on its own could not, PS 2.0 saw a similar dynamic. For literary critics, novelists and philosophers concerned with language and subjectivity, the realm of performance offered a metaphorical (and often real) laboratory in which to explore how discourse indeed constituted social relations. Meanwhile, performance scholars saw in critical theory a useful vocabulary with which to explain and systematize much that they had observed experientially. This coalescence reached its apotheosis with, first, Judith Butler's *Gender Trouble* (1990) and subsequently, Peggy Phelan's *Unmarked* (1993). Butler's notion of gender as performance seems at first to be an extension of three lines of thought that come out of the first wave of performance studies: Austin's performative speech act, Goffman's presentation of the self in everyday life and Schechner's restored behaviour. From Austin, Butler takes the idea that an utterance can have social efficacy. From Goffman, she takes that the self involves the enactment of predetermined roles (the illusion of the abiding gendered self) and from Schechner, the notion of restored behaviour (a stylized repetition of acts played out on the body). But whereas Schechner, Goffman et al. were interested in demonstrating how everyone is the same, Butler's strategic deployment of performance theory was about resistance. The pressure to perform one's identity according to universal norms, she argued, was an act of discipline. Such norms constitute a repressive regime. Thus even as performance suggests a possibly transgressive answer to the gender problem, it represents the problem as much as the solution. This is less because Schechner, Goffman, Turner and other foundational figures of PS are white men than because the positive promise of the tribal and collective is gradually ceding centre stage to the discourse of individual self-actualization. So while PS 2.0 is compatible to a degree with PS 1.0, the need of the former to challenge and question the normative assumptions of the latter leads to a distinctly different interface metaphor.

Hence when Peggy Phelan writes of challenging the PS origin narrative and 'the idea that two men gave birth',[8] it is not surprising she looks to performance not as a utopian collectivity, but as a way to speak to the dilemma of the individuated psychic subject. In a Lacanian worldview, the subject is always irrevocably split, yet performance offers, perhaps, the opportunity for moments of jouissance or transcendence. Such moments are fragile and always disappearing; thus it is that Phelan's formulation hinges on performance as that which disappears, or which becomes itself in the moment of its disappearance. 'Performance's being', writes Phelan, 'like the ontology of subjectivity proposed here, becomes itself through disappearance.' Phelan's idiosyncratic (not to say solipsistic) ontology found resonance in the work of solo artists such as Holly Hughes, Marina Abramovic and Tim Miller. If the interface metaphor of PS 1.0 was The Performance Group and its collective ecstasy given social efficacy in *Dionysus in 69*, the interface metaphor of PS 2.0 was Deb Margolin talking, Karen Finley confessing, Ron Athey bleeding.

This is not to say that the emphasis on the individual material body, the individuated psychic subject, completely banished the tribal and collective from the discussion, but rather that this 2.0 release of PS represented a different, more specific claim on the legacy of certain ideas. So that PS became, especially in the United States, a space wherein the queer, the poor, the destitute of all complexions could find a space and a voice, not as faceless 'masses' or nameless acolytes, but as unique individual voices and bodies. This led, perhaps inevitably, back around to the question of the theatre, now figured not as 'high art' but as a marginal space. And here we see the strength of the underlying architecture of PS as OS, for the 'broad spectrum' proved especially broad, especially robust in the areas of performance that were most, well, theatrical, for these lent themselves most to PS 2.0 analysis. Hence, PS 1.5 tends towards PS 2.0 with its emphasis on community-based performance and outsider art. When performance artists such as the NEA Four moved centre, it was in part about staking a claim on a kind of community of radical individualism, pointing to a potential unification of two disparate but compatible systems.

As the culture wars of the 1990s begin to burn themselves out (though brush fires continue to erupt here and there), we see this unification start to emerge in what we might call PS 2.1 or PS 2.2. This refinement of PS 2.0 keeps the emphasis on minoritarian resistance and incorporates the importance of history and genealogy. As Joseph Roach pointed out in *Cities of the Dead* (1996), the disappearance of performance is nearly always incomplete, its memory resurfacing in unexpected and profound ways. Roach's close reading of the intercultural exchanges of memory in a specific historical context provided more than simply a response to the critique that the emphasis on the ontology of disappearance and the transcendence of the immediate had led PS to a presentist bias and a neglect of history. The notion of memory provides a critical bridge between the collective interface of PS 1.0 and the individual interface of PS 2.0. As Roach writes:

> The research strategies I favor emphasize the comparative approach to the theatrical, musical, and ritual traditions of many cultures. To that agenda, however, I would add the qualification of historical contingency: first, the intercultural communication that certain performances enabled at specific times and places and second, the internal cultural self-definition that these and other performances produced by making visible the play of difference and identity within the larger ensemble of relations.[9]

In Roach's reading of the long eighteenth century along the Atlantic Rim, performance facilitates intercultural exchange on a tribal level (as in PS 1.0), while also creating a space to explore 'the play of difference and identity' (as in PS 2.0). Significantly, *Cities of the Dead* also emphasizes the idea that memory is plentiful rather than scarce, that forgetting is not as easy as we previously believed. Because of this, it is essential to trace the genealogy or provenance of ideas, and performance (often through kinesthetic embodiment) can help accomplish this. Diana Taylor's *The Archive and the Repertoire* (2003) extends this principle further, tying together several threads that had come before to crystallize a bedrock principle that had been latent within both versions of PS: that 'performance' can be the method, not simply the object, of 'performance studies'. Or as Taylor put it, 'My particular investment in performance studies derives less from what it *is* than what it allows us to *do*.'[10]

Taylor's strategic reframing of PS can also be seen as a kind of forerunner (a 'beta version') of what would become PS 3.0, an OS with an interface metaphor of an OS. After all, the investment in an OS, like Taylor's investment in PS, is about what kinds of action the platform makes possible. The last 15 years have seen the 'digital revolution' – really a series of interrelated technological changes from the explosive spread of internet access to wireless and mobile connectivity to cloud computing and so on. As with the 1960s' counterculture and the 1980s' identity politics, university campuses were at the leading edge of this social transformation. It is unsurprising, perhaps, that the computer network would come to be our new interface metaphor, surrogating the paradigmatic status of the solo performer in PS 2.0, the tribe in PS 1.0.

We don't yet know what PS 3.0 will allow us to think. Yet such a formulation offers backward compatibility with PS 1.0, for we can see the potential for globalization and digital interconnectivity to create new tribes, and/or to erase the differences between old tribes. Though PS 1.0 verged on a fetishization of the primitive (consider Turner's distinction between the 'liminal' and 'liminoid'), new technology can be and has been assimilated into a PS approach. If we revisit the etymology of the *tekne*, the weaving together, we remember that the theatre, the dance, the ritual, the sermon – these too are technologies, and indeed, the technological or digital performance realm is among the richest areas of current exploration.

Conversely (or complementarily) PS 2.0 users have recognized the potential for digital media to fully realize the individuated psychic subject. The blogosphere, for example, has reduced the barriers of access to media to the point where formerly marginalized subjects can give voice to thoughts and feelings previously suppressed by the gatekeeping mechanisms of a homogenized and homogenizing dominant culture. While such access is still far from universal, and legitimate concerns about surveillance and privacy are still being negotiated, clearly the age of social networking has focused renewed attention on the ways in which 'the personal is political', as well as the ways that individuals can and must perform their identities as ongoing strategic projects in negotiation with sometimes hostile normative discursive regimes. *Relationship status: It's complicated.* Moreover, where PS 2.0 celebrated performative writing, literary work that both tended towards the condition of performance and (not coincidentally) was socially efficacious, the collaborative nature of online dialogue and the accretion of ideas and understanding over time offers a way to think about writing that truly approximates the give and take between performer and spectator that is the *sine qua non* of PS going all the way back to version 1.0 (and perhaps before). Though PS 1.0 privileged the live performance, and PS 2.0's ontology of disappearance seemed to foreclose the value of the mediated record, PS 3.0 redefines liveness as simultaneity rather than presence. Performer and spectator may no longer share physical space, but they share virtual space and actual time. It is still performance, but the network is the medium.

As a generation of scholars and artists for whom the world wide web and its related technologies are *not* 'new media' comes of age, PS 3.0 may also be the first version of performance studies to truly embrace the network paradigm that, though it builds on these foundations, actually has a different kind of architecture, one that is no less utopian but that plays itself out in more contingent, complex ways. In the network interface, transnational flows surrogate intercultural encounters. Memory is a measure of apparently infinite capacity. The ephemeral, the insubstantial shadow is the norm against which even the live body seems hopelessly stodgy and . . . analog. The ontology of performance in such an interface is not disappearance, and not not disappearance.[11]

In a network interface, the 'source code' that enables one operation can be borrowed, replicated or hacked to enable an entirely separate operation in an opportunistic (and broadly accepted) fashion. Thus, work in the recent 'historiographic turn' can be understood as an attempt to repurpose the source code of memory-driven work such as Roach and Taylor. Meanwhile, the growing attention to neurocognitive aspects of performance by Rhonda Blair, Bruce McConachie and others can be seen as an attempt to bring the question of the global network back down to the level of the individual. Interestingly, though, the cognitive turn also seems to bring us back around to PS 1.0's search for universal human characteristics that performance can uncover.[12]

Ultimately, what emerges from this 'perspective and prospective' based survey of performance studies as a series of related operating systems is that PS in all of its forms is essentially a utopian project. In the 'Things to Think About' section at the end of the first chapter of Schechner's *Performance Studies: An Introduction*, for example, readers/students are asked, 'Why do you think "performance studies" can/cannot be helpful in dealing with some of the world's great problems, such as the environment, oppression and exploitation of people, over-population and war?'[13] Though the question technically leaves open the possibility that PS 'cannot be helpful', simply asking the question implies a positive promise for the field. There is a way, of course, in which all academic disciplines are built around a positive promise: that this mode of organizing knowledge will lead to a kind of enlightenment, a better understanding for all mankind, the curing of disease and so on. But I would argue that performance studies is itself more utopian than others, partly because of the circumstances of its genesis at a time when universities were seen as a site for positive social change, and particularly when arts and humanities began to be seen as sites of creative activity and research, rather than simply the 'conservatories' of classic knowledge and wisdom (the sciences had previously been imagined as the site of innovation, but the twentieth century showed that a pure scientific approach could be literally deadly in human terms). And partly because performance activities are themselves a kind of world-making, and such world-making nearly always tends towards the utopian. For if it is in our control to reshape our world, will not most of us choose to do so in a way that is 'better' than what we have now? Yet in a complex and diverse society, utopia is both a contested concept and a moving target, and at the end of the day, the 'performance' in performance studies is not just about what is studied, but how we study. Change, from minor debugging to major reengineering, is as inevitable as it is desirable. As I wrote a decade ago in the introduction to *The Performance Studies Reader*: 'Just as performance is contingent, contested, hard to pin down, so too is its study.'[14] Or as an OS engineer might put it: It's not a bug; it's a feature.

Can We Be the (New) Third World?

Richard Schechner

I sit here this morning (does it really matter which morning?) trying to be optimistic. I want to write how performance studies and the performing arts can save the world, or at least help to save the world. I am typing while rockets and bombs are exploding in Gaza and Israel; Egypt is in turmoil, Syria in the throes of civil war; M23 rebels are closing on Goma in the Congo putting a million people under threat; suicide bombings and assassinations continue in Iraq and Afghanistan; the Somali civil war is ongoing. Sunnis and Shias have warred against each other since the martyrdom of Hussein in 680; in India, Hindus murder Muslims and vice-versa; anti-Semitism is rife in many places; and not long ago Catholics and Protestants were murdering each other in Northern Ireland a few centuries after religious wars decimated Europe. The Shoah is not ancient history.

I am more than halfway through my 79th year. For 71 of those years, the United States has been at war: big wars, small wars, long wars, short wars, good wars, bad wars, just wars, greedy wars, invasions, incursions, missions, actions in Europe, Asia, Latin America, the Middle East, Africa, from World War II and the Korean War to Granada ('Operation Urgent Fury') and Lebanon (twice, 1958 and 1982–84), from Vietnam to Iraq and Afghanistan, from Serbia to Libya and Panama, Cambodia, El Salvador, Colombia, Liberia, Egypt, Zaire, Kosovo, Bosnia, East Timor, Yemen, the Philippines, Congo, Ivory Coast, Haiti, Dominican Republic, Nicaragua, Honduras. . . . And where America has not sent troops it has sent arms, trained soldiers, created alliances and supported proxy armies. Sometimes with grotesque paradoxes such as helping Saddam Hussein invade Iran precipitating a bloody stalemate from 1980 to 1988, a half-million dead, and then barely 3 years later, turning against Saddam with 'Operation Desert Storm', and after that in 2003, 'Operation Iraqi Freedom' where the

United States led the 'Coalition of the Willing' (who's kidding who?). Plus untold covert actions and wars waged by surrogates with American 'advisors'; the 'dirty wars' in Latin America fought in the name of anti-communism; the Cold War with its nuclear build-up still not substantially dismantled. What about the close calls from the Cuban Missile Crisis to the US Seventh Fleet 'patrolling' the strait between mainland China and Taiwan; the continuing 'showdown' against North Korea and Iran over their nuclear arms programmes. The US Congressional Research Service in its 'Instances of Use of United States Armed Forces Abroad' reports that from 1950 to 2006 there were 153 occasions when American forces went on missions outside the borders of the United States. No year was without its particular military excursion, many years had several. Yes, some were for just causes or humanitarian reasons; but most were applications by force of US policy. In addition to active armed intervention is the US 'presence': troops stationed in bases around the world and multiple covert operations. Covert means 'classified', secret, kept from public view and accountability – even in a self-professed 'open' society with its 'free-press'. Who knows how many secret actions there've been and how many continue today? These 'operations' (surgery?) involve 'intelligence' (what a weird name for spying and dirty tricks), terror and torture in camps like Guantanamo and secret 'black sites' around the world. Even the 7 years of peace, my infancy and early childhood, from 1934 to 1941, were gloomed by the 1937 Japanese invasion of China, the Nazi and Soviet invasions of Poland in 1939 and the preparations for the United States's entry into World War II. And what about the wars within American borders – 'war' being used only partly metaphorically? The House Un-American Activities Committee (1938–75) the anti-communist 'witch hunt' led by Senator Joseph McCarthy (1950s), the violent responses to the African American Freedom Movement and gay liberation, the Patriot Act, the War On Drugs.

American society and culture – and through their influence, global societies and cultures – have been deformed by a plague of wars, threats of war (national wars, civil wars, insurrections, 'actions' and 'operations', the war family has plenty of members). Continuous war both creates and requires a political-cultural-social-educational-economic-paranoiac system underpinning weapons research and testing, large standing armies and a spidery stealth apparatus. In the United States, we are bombarded (yes, I am aware of the metaphor) by messages telling us that we can enjoy the benefits of (un)peace – consumer goods, leisure, an open society – while waging (note the metaphor) wars or, rather, crafting on a 'volunteer army' to fight for us. (In quotation marks because economic necessity, and to some degree, racism and sexism determines who volunteers.) The message is disturbingly schizoid: live 'normally' but 'if you see something, say something'. This specific War on Terror slogan-instruction is posted everywhere in New York, and elsewhere I suppose; it is displayed and uttered in a soft voice and reinforced with omnipresent signage and surveillance cameras. Surveillance has been normalized: the panopticon has arrived. Go on vacation, but take off your shoes before passing through the metal detector. The war machine needs both jingoism – America is the best, the greatest, the freest – and paranoia – America is under attack, our 'way of life' threatened, 'they' are crossing our borders actually and figuratively. The military-industrial complex and its concomitant 'disastrous rise of misplaced power' that General and then President Dwight D. Eisenhower warned of in his 1961 farewell address has come to pass. The universities are not exempt but closely knit into the fabric.

The global outcome of all this is that billions of people live on less than $1 per day; billions have no clean water or adequate sanitation. Twenty years ago, people in the top 20 per cent of the world's population were 30 times as rich as those in the bottom 20 per cent. Now they are 70 times as rich. Of the 1,233 drugs developed in the last decade, only 11 were for treating tropical diseases and of these, five cured livestock, not humans. The richest three persons in the world have more wealth than the GDP of the 47 poorest nations; the richest 15 persons have more wealth than the combined GDP of all sub-Saharan Africa, 550 million people. The Occupy Wall Street movement in the United States became famous for pointing out that the top 1 per cent of Americans earned more than 20 per cent of total income.

All the military 'engagements' (married to war?) cost plenty. The expenditure for arms can be averaged out to 330 billion dollars (in 2012 dollars) a year from 1940 to the present. That adds up to about *23.5 trillion* dollars ($23,430,000,000,000). Can you even imagine such a pile of gold? What it would buy if put to constructive uses? Health care, education, public works, arts, housing? Maybe it doesn't make sense to unilaterally disarm. But neither does it make sense to be the world's number one military spender for years, decades, generations, forever. Not since Rome – and remember what happened to Rome, from republic to imperium to decay – has an empire so extended-expended itself. And the cost is not just dollars. The cost is cultural, personal and spiritual.

So what is it about war? Is it all greed and power? No, culture – deep culture, historically reinforced – loves war. Think of it: the foundational Indo-European and Middle Eastern myths are war stories: *The Iliad, Odyssey, Mahabharata,*

Ramayana, Gilgamesh, The Old Testament. Yes, there's a lot happening that is not war; but the core narratives celebrate battle, conquest and heroism: more the glory than the gory of war. These myths admire and even worship the warlike person or deity, male usually but not always because ferocity and valour in battle trumps gender – think Athena and Enyo, Durga and Kali. The Old Testament is warlike, from the Plagues (God's war against Pharaoh) to the tumbling down of Jericho's walls, from the ethnic cleansing of Canaan to David's bloody expeditions, and more. In the realm of literature, the Greek theatre brings against war the claims of women, witness *The Oresteia, Antigone, The Trojan Women* and *Lysistrata*. But heroism is always honoured and war is sometimes celebrated as in *The Persians*. Shakespeare is no pacifist, nor is Milton, Hemingway, or even Joseph Heller. Pop culture from video games to contact sports is driven by violence and saturated with metaphors of war.

When leaders want to focus people on a task, war is a chosen metaphor: not only the jihads and the War On Terror but also the War On Cancer, the War on Drugs, the War On Poverty, the War On Violence, etc. etc. World War I was 'the war to end all wars'. War is what people do, along with sex, death and taxes. Can we change this? Competition for land, hierarchy (power), reputation, honour, mates – overlapping each other – drives human action and, some say, all of nature. Ironically, even the opposite of competition: generosity, sharing and 'love' (in quotation marks because the concept is so malleable), often is a rivalry of who or what can do the most good. Is war natural, is it cultural – or what mix of both?

There is a counter-narrative to this history of violence. In *The Better Angels of Our Nature*, Stephen Pinker deploys impressive statistical and social analysis to show that for centuries violence has declined globally and continues to do so, violence in terms of war, genocide, terror, murder, torture, slavery, capital punishment, domestic mayhem, infanticide and child abuse. He attributes the decline to a set of interwoven causes: the rise of civil societies, democratization, decline in superstition, global trade and affluence and, decisively, the increasing power and influence of women, what Pinker terms 'feminization', where 'female-friendly values' prevail over the 'manly honor' of violent retaliation – on individual, family, tribal and national levels; where contraception allows women to determine if and when to have babies. In summary, Pinker:

> The declines we seek to explain unfolded over vastly different scales of time and damage: the taming of chronic raiding and feuding, the reduction of vicious interpersonal violence such as cutting off noses, the elimination of cruel practices like human sacrifice, torture-executions, and flogging, the abolition of institutions

such as slavery and debt bondage, the falling out of fashion of blood sports and dueling, the eroding of political murder and despotism, the recent decline of wars, pogroms, and genocides, the reduction of violence against women, the decriminalization of homosexuality, the protection of children and animals. . . . All these developments undeniably point in the same direction.[1]

How can Pinker be right, given everything I asserted previously? There are two ways of understanding Pinker's data. As statistics, trends and overall developments clearly show, the proportion of violent acts – individual, societal, national, international – has declined relative to the number of people alive. But the absolute numbers of people who suffer or die has not decreased because there are so many more people alive today than previously – and the world population is going to go up a lot more before it levels off or declines. To put this another way, humans may be regarded as parts of a group – the statistical person, relative to all the others – or as absolute individual 'souls', or 'beings', each endowed with her/his own particular self. From the perspective of unique beings, the number of individuals who suffer or die has increased, even as the proportion of these relative to the whole population has declined. Secondly, violence is not limited to what happens between and among people. Violence is also done to animals and plants, lands and seas: the world as 'Gaia', a unified living thing. This violence against species and habitat, against the planet, is definitely approaching the level of – what words do I need? – specicide and globacide. We are presently living through earth's sixth great extinction, driven by *homosapiens*, us.

It didn't have to be this way. I won't speak about nations other than my own, the United States, but I know that blame also belongs elsewhere. However, the United States has been the leading entity – the 'American Century' and all that – economically, militarily and, after the collapse of the USSR, ideologically. Think for a moment where the world might be if the United States supported the Cuban revolution, opposed the military regimes of Latin America, embraced the democratic socialism of Salvador Allende (instead of being complicit in his murder), helped Patrice Lumumba in the Congo, worked to overthrow apartheid in South Africa and instituted an African Marshall Plan enabling the continent to recover from the horrors of colonialism, refused to take up the cause of defeated French colonialism in Vietnam, worked for the peaceful reunification of Korea and demand a just settlement of the Israel-Palestine conflict. Recognized 60 years ago that dependence on Middle Eastern oil distorted American foreign and domestic policy and therefore launched an all-out moonshot-type effort to develop non-fossil energy sources. Constructed networks of bullet trains and local mass transit, rejected McCarthyism and the hunt for 'un-American activities' which continues under the auspices of the Patriot Act. Some things have been accomplished, but not nearly swiftly enough: an end to racism, sexism and homophobia; comprehensive health-care reform. Other urgent items await action: immigration reform because millions of undocumented persons are an exploited, underpaid underclass; real protection for the environment, the fisheries and the water supply; and meaningful support for education and the arts. In the meanwhile, corporations gain more power increasing the wealth imbalance keeping or transporting millions to poverty (exactly what the Occupy Wall Street movement protests).

'What if?' is a loser's game. However, I am not dreaming when I say that all the possibilities I've just listed were on the table in America, supported by a considerable number of people, and debated in more or less mainstream media (as well as by progressives and radicals). Why were these programmes and reforms not successful? Why were those who actively supported progressive policies wire-tapped, hounded, imprisoned, shot and ground to dust? I am not a conspiracy-theory-type thinker. I don't believe American policy-makers are being controlled by a cabal. I do think that policy-makers didn't fully comprehend the world they were shaping when they made the decisions they made – and continue to make. What they wanted was and is to stay in power in Washington and to expand the new American corporate empire. Even scarier, some American leaders – like the colonialists of former times – believed they were and are doing good. How Brecht would wince and then laugh.

Sometimes clichés and platitudes are useful. So here're some: ignorance is the plague. Xenophobia is the plague. Hatred of others is the plague. Greed is the plague. Disrespect for nature is the plague. Eradicate the plague. Performances are – or at least can be – model utopian societies. Workshops are ways to destroy ignorance; rehearsals are ways to creatively relate to others not by submerging or ignoring differences, but by exploring differences as the group devises a generous common way forward; performances can hold up to public view the outcome of such active research. The broad spectrum of performance studies offers critical lenses to understand societies, groups and individuals who embody and enact their personal and collective identities. Performance studies develops from the axiom that we live in a performatized world where cultures are colliding, influencing and interfacing with each other, and hybridizing at a swift and increasing rate. These collisions are not always politically correct or pleasant. Populations and ideas are on the move, pushed by ideologies, religions, wars, famines, disease, hopes for improvement, government intervention and global trade. The outcome, if there is to be 'an' outcome, of all this circulation is neither clear nor certain. Some argue that change will be radical, stemming from the list I just listed and from almost unimaginable technical progress – robots, nanocomputers, colonizing the moon and mars; others see a new medieval epoch of circulating stasis. I myself shuttle between these alternatives; and all the stops in between.

Performance studies is a particular response to this global circumstance. Performance studies arises from the premise that everything and anything can be studied 'as' performance. The tools of performance studies are drawn from other disciplines and have not yet coalesced into a coherent singularity. Perhaps that's good – it keeps performance studies practitioners alert to what's happening around us. Some of the disciplines that PS borrows from, steals, adapts, and makes use of in our own way include the social and biological sciences, history, gender studies, psychoanalysis, social theory, critical race studies, game theory, economics, popular culture studies, theatre, dance, film and media studies . . . and more: PS is wanton, promiscuous and bold – even as we try to get organized and arrive at consistency and coherence.

There is a problem at the heart of all this. If anything can be studied 'as' performance, if any tool can be used (PS being the ultimate disciplinary bricoleur), then what 'is' performance, what 'is' performance studies? As I theorize it, something 'is' performance when according to the conventions, common usages and/or traditions of a specific culture or social unit at a given historical time, an action or event is called a 'performance'. I know this is a squooshy definition, shape-shifting and unreliable in absolute terms. But it is also useful, throwing the performance theorist back into the concrete social realities she is studying. Over the past 75 years (at least), what performance 'is' has been stretched, twisted and expanded. This expansion was at first driven by the avant-garde and by interactions between non-Western and Western cultures. Later, the expansion was also driven by the internet, with a resulting blurring of boundaries between the actual and the virtual, between so-called 'art' and so-called 'life'.

Performance as distinct from performance studies (except in the dizzying circumstance where performance studies is studied as a performance) – and here I mean performance in its various realms, in social life, in the arts, in politics, in economics, in popular culture and so on – realms overlapping each other, sometimes reinforcing, sometimes subverting each other – performance marks identities, bends and remakes time, adorns and reshapes the body, tells stories and provides people with the means to play with, rehearse and remake the worlds they not merely inhabit but are always already in the habit of reconstructing.

Having written such sweeping generalizations, I must qualify by saying that every genre of performance, even every particular instance of each genre, is concrete and specific, different from every other. Not only in terms of cultural difference, but also in terms of local and even individual variation. No two film showings of the same film are exactly the same as every other. At the same time, that which carries over – which is 'not for the first time' – is the preponderance of every event, even of once-only events. This paradox must be understood and accepted. The tension among permanence, repeatability, ephemerality and originality is what constitutes the process of behaviour and the representations of behaviour at all levels and all instances. Understanding this is powerfully important in a period of accelerating digitization where reproducibility, interchangeability and sameness seem to have the upper hand. But even cloned performances are different from each other when experienced by different audiences or the same audiences at different times. The Heracletian river cannot be bathed in twice.

If we take into account the myriad artworks, personal interactions, rituals, media exchanges, pop culture events and so on that go on everyday all over the world, then both production and reception are incalculably varied even as they appear to become more the same. Ironically, performance and performance studies, as they participate in an increasingly digitized world culture, resist that which they produce. As I noted earlier, what 'is' performance cannot be decided a priori. The same event can 'be' a performance in one instance and not in another. We as theorists, artists and teachers not only must live with this indeterminacy, but devise effective ways to theorize it. The development of performance as a category of theory as well as a fact of behaviour and action, makes it increasingly difficult to sustain the distinction between appearances and facts, surfaces and depths, illusions and substances. More than that: appearances are actualities, appearances drive actions. In modernity, what was 'behind', 'beneath', 'deep' and 'hidden' were (often) the 'most real'. But in postmodernity – and whatever will come after – the relationship between depths and surfaces is fluid and dynamically convective. What was hidden is tossed upwards, what was skim is plunged to the interior.

In 2011, Occupy Wall Street had taken over Zuccotti Park (appropriately located at the corner of Broadway and Liberty). Other 'Occupys' sprang up around the United States and in other countries. Their driving slogan was 'We are the 99%' – meaning that the vast majority do not control the wealth of nations. In Zuccotti Park when I visited, a set of related performances were taking place. The community encamped there were mostly younger people. The mood was performative and academic: seminars, speeches amplified by call-and-response instead of loudspeakers, drumming and dancing, art displays, petitions circulating, food-sharing and many other indications of creativity, goodwill, activism and even irony. The Occupiers knew they were enacting an evanescent utopian moment. Unlike the Weather Underground of the 1960–70s, they did not believe that they could overturn the social order by blowing up the symbols of the powers they detested. They knew that Zuccotti Park was surrounded by police and infiltrated by undercover agents. The Park was quarantined. Then, on 15 November, in the wee hours of the night, the New York police swept the Occupiers from their camp. Over the next few months, other Occupiers were assaulted and evicted from other sites globally.

Nothing physical remains. What lessons can we learn?

In the Occupy movement, I and others hear loud and clear echoes of the great freedom, student and anti-war movements of the 1960s and 1970s; and links – conceptual and strategic – to the Arab Spring, from Tunis through Cairo, on to Yemen, Libya and Syria. Links were forged connecting Occupy also to the protests in Greece, Spain and elsewhere against austerity programmes and to violent labour uprisings in South Africa and China. None of these uprisings and protests is yet 'finished'. Some have turned authoritarian; the one in Syria has devolved into a brutal civil war. In terms of economics, politics, the environment, human rights and health – all the items I began this essay with – the powers are not making changes; or not making them deeply, broadly or swiftly enough. The 99 per cent is angry, dissatisfied and restless. But is it revolutionary? And if so, what form should revolution take? Armed struggle as in the past? Cultural reformation? Something not yet articulated?

In the 1950s, as a way of finding a new path, the 'third world' was imagined. The third world was not communist, it was not capitalist: it was not allied with the Soviet Union or the United States: it was 'non-aligned'. The third world was mostly poor nations, mostly in Africa, Asia, Latin America, and Oceania. On a global scale, the third world was the 99 per cent, the vast majority of people, excluded and exploited by the Great Powers. India's Jawaharlal Nehru was an eloquent spokesperson for the third world. In Bandung, Indonesia, in 1955, Nehru addressed representatives of the third world:

> I speak with the greatest respect of these Great Powers because they are not only great in military might but in development, in culture, in civilization. But I do

submit that greatness sometimes brings quite false values, false standards. . . . I submit that moral force counts and the moral force of Asia and Africa must, in spite of the atomic and hydrogen bombs of Russia, the U.S.A. or another country, count. . . . Therefore, are we, the countries of Asia and Africa, devoid of any positive position except being pro-communist or anti-communist? Has it come to this, that the leaders of thought who have given religions and all kinds of things to the world have to tag on to this kind of group or that and be hangers-on of this party or the other carrying out their wishes and occasionally giving an idea? It is most degrading and humiliating to any self-respecting people or nation.[2]

Today, artists, activists and scholars are a new third world. Nehru's third world had a specific geographical location. Today's new third world is a proportion of people present everywhere with a majority nowhere. What unites the new third world is a community of purpose, a mode of inquiry (the experimental, if you will) and a sense of being other – of not being hangers-on. The new third world is incipient, seeds, not yet fully self-aware. The new third world needs to organize itself as 'non-aligned', neither capitalist, whether of the US or Chinese brand, nor knee-jerk communist/socialist, nor fundamentalist-religious whether Islamic, Christian, Jewish, Buddhist or whatever. The vanguard of this new third world are – and here I hope you won't think me too arrogant – performance theorists and artists who practice collaborative performance research; persons who know that playing deeply is a way of finding and embodying new knowledge, renewing energy and relating on a performative rather than on an ideological basis. What would be a manifesto of this Performance Third World?

1. To perform is to explore, to play, to experiment with new relationships.
2. To perform is to cross borders. These borders are not only geographical, but emotional, ideological, political and personal.
3. To perform is to engage in lifelong active study. To grasp every book as a script – something to be played with, interpreted and reformed/remade.
4. To perform is to become someone else and yourself at the same time. To empathize, react, grow and change.

I am asking 'you' – whoever is reading this – to consider the almost unimaginable because it is so hard for people to take seriously those who are not doing business, making war, or enforcing the will of God; to take seriously those who play, those who create playgrounds and art spaces; to take seriously the personal, social and world-making force of performance. We must reject ideological, economic and religious rigidity in favour of flexibility and fluidity.

All well and good. But can I offer some examples to substantiate my four-point manifesto? There is a lot going on in art, scholarship and social action – especially where these three spheres interact and overlap. Let me offer a very few examples from a very long repertory of possibilities – and in doing so, urge more synergy, more connections among various actions, artists and scholarly pursuits.

Take Eve Ensler's most recent project, 'A Billion Women Rising'. In the aftermath of the rape-murder of a 23-year-old in Delhi in January 2013, women (joined by many men) mobilized to insure that action is taken, not only in India but globally. This action begins as artworks, manifestations, demonstrations and petitions: all strong performatives; and continues as constant pressure for legislation, the enforcement of laws protecting women and guaranteeing them equality on all levels, and a raising of consciousness among women and men. For example, the '1 Billion Rising' action coordinated by Eve Ensler's V-Day movement (boldface on the onebillionrising.org website) asserts:

> Today, on the planet, a billion women – one of every three women on the planet – will be raped or beaten in her lifetime. That's ONE BILLION mothers, daughters, sisters, partners, and friends violated. **V-Day REFUSES to stand by as more than a billion women experience violence.** On February 14, 2013, V-Day's 15th Anniversary, we are inviting one billion women and those who love them to walk out, DANCE, RISE UP, AND DEMAND an end to this violence. One Billion Rising is a promise that we will rise up with women and men worldwide to say, "Enough! The violence ends now."
>
> **HERE'S HOW YOU CAN START A RISING** – Stage a rising in your community, office, college, or school. Organize a flash mob at a landmark building/ site, in the streets or in a nearby mall. Have a dance party, produce a theatrical event, march in your streets, protest, strike, dance and above all RISE!

The '1 Billion Rising' website includes a world map filled with the locales of events. Note that the instigator Ensler is the author of *The Vagina Monologues* and that the February actions are headlined by dances, theatre events and other performatives.

On 1 February, the BBC World Service broadcast *Sita, Draupadi and Kali: Women in Hinduism* (http://www.bbc.co.uk/podcasts/series/heartsoul) exploring the need for a radical re-thinking of Indian religion. Ensler was part of the conversation. A few excerpts:

> **Vandana Shiva:** We've got to reform religion in its ancient exclusions. With all the slokas and mantras saying the woman is secondary, the woman is to serve the

husband and all, and in its new virulent forms that is reinforced plus those forces that are new and are not part of religion in its ancient form but part of a new religion of the market, the religion of greed, the religion of commodification – because these are new forms of religion. And if we don't address the two patriarchies together and deal with them as one process of social reform we will never be able to get safety for women and women's rightful place in society.

Two hundred years of a particular kind of thinking about earth, about nature, about resources has created this false idea, totally false at the scientific level, that the earth is dead matter and therefore you can't violate her – because how can you violate something that's inert. But the earth is living, and the best of science teaches us that. And the same mindset that allows the objectification commodification ownership torture of women is the mindset that allows the commodification ownership torture of the earth.

Romila Thapar: And it's not just religion in this country, but in any country in the world. There is in all religions moments when there are crises, when the religion is being questioned by social custom. Now, the question is: Who is going to be the victor in this confrontation? Social custom, social justice, gender equality, or religious tradition? This is a battle that has to be fought.

Eve Ensler: It is not about asking now, or waiting, it is about rising.

The 'woman question' is as vital today, maybe more so, than when American women assembled in Seneca Falls in 1848 to press for their rights; the injustices as palpable as those Ibsen portrayed. It's not just a matter of equality but of changing the history of violence. Pinker notes the strong correlation – a cause-effect system, I'd say – linking the rise of women, the decline of rape and battering, and an overall fall in violence:

> We are all feminists now. Western culture's default point of view has become increasingly unisex. The universalizing of the generic citizen's vantage point, driven by reason and analogy, was an engine of more progress during the Humanitarian Revolution of the 18th century, and it resumed that impetus during the Rights Revolution of the 20th. It's no coincidence that the expansion of the rights of women followed on the heels of the expansion of the rights of racial minorities. . . . What about the rest of the world? . . . Worldwide, it has been estimated that between a fifth and a half of all women have been victims of domestic violence. . . . I think it's extremely likely that in the coming decades violence against women will decrease throughout the world. . . . Among the grassroots, attitudes all over the world will almost certainly ensure that women will gain greater economic and political representation in the coming years.[3]

Performance supporting women's rights is part of 'social theatre', itself closely related to the project of performance studies. As James Thompson and I wrote in our introduction to *TDR*'s 2004 special issue on social theatre:

> Taken as a whole, social theatre stands alongside of, and sometimes in place of, "aesthetic theatre" (including art theatres, experimental theatres, university theatres, regional theatres, and commercial theatres). We do not deny either the social aspects of aesthetic theatre or the aesthetic aspects of social theatre but rather point out differences of purpose, audiences, venues, and production values. . . . Social theatre may be defined as theatre with specific social agendas: theatre where aesthetics is not the ruling objective; theatre outside the realm of commerce . . . and the cult of the new. . . . Social theatre takes place in diverse locations – from prisons, refugee camps, and hospitals to schools, orphanages, and homes for elderly. . . . Social theatre often occurs in places and situations that are not the usual circumstances of theatre, turning "nonperformers" into performers. . . . Social theatre activists often are artists, but they need not be. The varieties of social theatre . . . can be put into four groups that have a logical and sequential relationship to each other: 1. Theatre for healing; 2. theatre for action; 3. theatre for community; 4. theatre for transforming 5. experience into art. . . . Performance studies as a discipline promises to lead theatre studies out of its parochialism and into a necessary and powerful interdisciplinarity. Performance studies recognizes all areas of social life as topics for the performance theorists. Social theatre carries this banner into practice by going to hospitals, prisons, and war zones and proving that performance itself is a method for understanding what goes on there; for intervening, participating, and collaborating in positive ways with people who live in these sites.[4]

Of course, read 'theatre' in the above to include all of the performing arts. The theoretical underpinning of social theatre – beyond Thompson's writings and those of Guglielmo Schinina[5] – include Paolo Freire's 'pedagogy of the oppressed' and Augusto Boal's expansion of Freire into performance, the 'theatre of the oppressed'.

But of course aesthetic theatre – aesthetic performances of all kinds – is crucial if my proposed Third World of Performance is to become a reality. The number of progressive avant-garde/experimental artists is too great to list even a fraction of them. *TDR* has for decades championed the work of these artists. For example, Rabih Mroué's 'The Pixelated Revolution' about which Carol Martin writes:

> The work demonstrates the ways in which theatre of the real can explore and exploit tensions between fact and fiction, aesthetic innovation and political ideas. Its interpretive intentions are less about literal truth and more about the self-conscious

use of materials to question the conventions of the representation of truth. . . . He notes at the outset that both professional and freelance journalists are absent from the Syrian revolution, making it impossible to know what is going on. . . . Born out of a detailed and forensic analysis of the Syrian protestors uploaded images, like something one might see in a spy film, his performance is a provocative commentary on the aesthetics of post 9/11 warfare and revolution. . . . *The Pixelated Revolution* reveals a strange paradox. Everyday recordings can suddenly become acts of resistance and treated as transgressions that have to be eliminated. Surveillance here is not constant and panoptic. The surveillance of and by both the Syrian Ba'athists and their opposition is a surreptitious pop-up surveillance. There is not one eye scanning the landscape but many eyes, all looking for and trying to capture other eyes. The target of security forces is no longer people with guns with intent to kill, but people with mobile phones with intent to record. The target of people with mobile phones is people with guns, and their intent is to stop the killing by recording it. . . . Mroué participates in an aesthetic and analytical discourse that claims to represent the real and to tell the truth while openly acknowledging the simultaneous use of fiction to do so. He straddles fiction and nonfiction, performance and documentation, entertainment and edification in a performance in which acting, video, photographs, stage design, and text all operate together as equal partners in the creation of meaning.[6]

Mroué's approach is close to that of many others – synthesizing, multimedia, combining fiction and 'real', acting and non-acting, seriousness and parody, scholarship and entertainment: a post-postmodern performative bouillabaisse. I need to stop here, though I could list groups and individuals from Force Entertainment and the Yes Men to Gob Squad and the team, from Nature Theatre of Oklahoma to The Assembly and Builders Association, and many more, who are making concrete the Performance Third World. Added to these are scholars and teachers – for this Performative Third World fuses the academic in the noblest sense (Socrates living/dying for his ideas) with the artistic; the reflective with the active; the critical with the celebratory. Ironically, what's needed now – even in this epoch of hyper-connectivity – is for individuals and groups, movements and tendencies, artists and scholars to coalesce into a single, unstoppable force for positive change.

A PS for PS

PS means performance studies and it means postscript, what is written after. So this, at the last.

In his masterful monograph, *Identity and the Life Cycle* (1959) Erik H. Erikson writes that the crisis of old age – the phase of life I am now entering – is 'integrity/wisdom vs. disgust/despair'. Integrity meaning gaining a view of the whole, what poet Yeats called 'an old man's eagle mind'. So, I am trying to hold things together, to not surrender to 'facts', but struggling to imagine alternatives. I have often said that my brain is pessimistic while my belly is optimistic. That is, what I 'know' reinforces the world I described at the start of this essay. But most of what I 'feel' urges me towards the New Third World. Doing yoga – the very word means to tie together, to yoke as oxen are yoked – keeps my brain and belly in some kind of deep commerce. Every crisis – personal, public, artistic, global – involves choice; choice – a turning this way or that. And, at my age, the turning is a Janus-look peering both forwards and backwards at the same time. More than a half century ago, Erikson wisely and prophetically wrote:

Ideologies seem to provide meaningful combinations of the oldest and the newest in a group's ideals. They thus channel the forceful earnestness, the sincere asceticism, and the eager indignation of youth toward that social frontier where the struggles between conservatism and radicalism is most alive. On that frontier fanatic ideologists do their busy work and psychopathic leaders their dirty work; but there, also, true leaders create significant solidarities. All ideologies ask for, as the prize for the promised possession of a future, uncompromising commitment to some absolute hierarchy of values and some rigid principle of conduct; be that principle total obedience to tradition, if the future is the eternalization of ancestry; total resignation, if the future is to be of another world; total martial discipline, if the future is to be reserved for some brand of armed superman; total inner reform, if the future is perceived as an advanced edition of heaven on earth; or (to mention only one of the ideological ingredients of our time [sic]) complete pragmatic abandon to the processes of production and to human teamwork, if unceasing production seems to be the thread which holds present and future together. . . . When established identities become outworn or unfinished ones threaten to remain incomplete, special crises compel men to wage holy wars, by the cruelest means, against those who seem to question or threaten their unsafe ideological basis. We may well pause to ponder briefly the fact that the technological and economic developments of our day [sic, again!] encroach upon all traditional group identities and solidarities such as may have developed in agrarian, feudal, patrician, or mercantile ideologies. . . . In large parts of the world, this seems to result in a ready fascination with totalistic world views, views predicting millenniums and cataclysms, and advocating self-appointed mortal gods. Technological centralization today [sic, one last time] can give small groups of such fanatic ideologists the concrete power of totalitarian state machines.[7]

Performance studies scholars and performance artists need always to remain actively critical of 'self-appointed mortal gods'. We must imagine, invent and perform alternative ways of becoming.

Motion II

Beyond Experimental Theatre

4

Table on Stage: The Rise of the Messenger

Carol Martin

*It was a wonderful machine. It had the form factor of the original
Macintosh, so if you were seated at it, if you squinted, it looked like a little
anthropomorphic human face staring back at you. And I would type into its
tiny gray-scale screen . . . it was the first computer I used regularly that had
real networking and I would telnet out from it to repositories of information
around the world.*

– Mike Daisey, *The Agony and the Ecstasy of Steve Jobs*

*He even went as far as recording a video of himself while committing suicide;
and this video is now in the hands of the judicial authorities. We were not able
to obtain a copy of it . . . He committed suicide in a public manner, and turned
his suicide into an event relayed by web platforms.*

*   Habib, since all of these events, the Arab revolution, the Arab Spring . . .
started by way of the television image . . . Starting with Bouazizi in Tunis who
decided to immolate himself . . . Is there a connection with Diyaa's actions? Is
there a stand? Against whom?*

– Rabih Mroué and Lina Saneh, *33 rounds per minute and then some*

An iconic rectangle has become a staple of contemporary performance across
cultures. Computers, notes, notebooks and diary entries often rest on a table,
signifying that the table is a surface for intellectual labour, for ideas, for the giving
of testimony, both true and untrue. Alternatively, the table on contemporary stages
has also been empty save for a glass of water. At the table, performers perform
the roles of lecturers, family members, doctors, warmongers, peacemakers, and
above all else, messengers. The messengers who sit at the tables point out the

ways in which we know and do not know what is occurring around us. They transform tables into places, metaphors, surfaces of dreams and ambitions and platforms for social inquiry and justice, as well as boards for dying and death. Messengers summon evidence and archives from appearing and disappearing worlds that are both real and invented; they talk about things that happened, things that might happen and things that never happened. As in Greek tragedy, the messengers report on crucial offstage scenes, but unlike the messengers in Greek tragedy, they are the stars of the show. Their reports are no longer brief summaries but entire narratives from the world of the real outside the theatre. The arbiter is not someone on stage, but the spectators, who perform the role of witnesses in absentia: witnesses to what the messenger reports, but not literally to the scenes reported. Scenes that happened offstage, whether physical, spiritual or social, are told not only to ascertain the course of events already in action, but as the entire event itself. There is no reversal of fortune at the heart of the drama. The reversal has already occurred; the entire performance takes place after the *peripeteia*.

Two works that serve to demonstrate the ways in which tables function as the place from which to narrate scenes occurring in the world beyond the stage: *The Agony and the Ecstasy of Steve Jobs* by American playwright Mike Daisey (2011),[1] and *33 rounds per minute and then some* (2012) by Lebanese writers Rabih Mroué and Lina Saneh.[2] These two works interweave fiction and non-fiction in order to – in the words of Chris Megson and Allyson Forsyth – 'situate[s] historical truth as an embattled site of contestation'.[3] The tables used in these works signify the authoritative domain from which to dramatize, respectively, the working conditions of Foxconn's enormous electronics assembly plant in Shenzhen, China, and the ersatz response, as recorded on Facebook, answering machines, mobile phones and television, to the suicide of Diyaa Yamout, an ill-defined fictional political activist in Beirut, Lebanon. In these works, Daisey, Mroué and Saneh upend notions of personal and political truth by engaging the changes that technology, as both a subject and methodology, has generated.

Both *The Agony and the Ecstasy of Steve Jobs* and *33 rounds per minute and then some* are part of global touring networks. Their sources and destinations are international cosmopolitan cities. Location is defining – not in the sense of a nationalist politics, fixed cultural representation or individual identity, but in the ways it is likened to the ubiquity of the internet. Location is everywhere, anywhere and nowhere. Technology has helped make the way we use tables in performance an authoritative domain, capable of signifying the local and the global simultaneously. The Polish playwright Paweł Demirski explains in *Dramaturgy of the Real on the World Stage* that 'documentary theatre is not only a technique; it's a way of thinking and above all an instrument for acquiring knowledge about the world'.[4] Demirski uses the phrase 'documentary theatre' to identify this way of thinking. I prefer the phrase 'theatre of the real', as it both includes and exceeds documentary theatre. The latter tends to depend upon verbatim quotation of letters, transcripts, court records and so forth, whereas 'theatre of the real' encompasses both theatre about real events *and* the way real events are conceptualized using more diverse means, including fiction clearly identified as such, in the service of non-fiction. We have here a shift in paradigm, perspective, subject, performance and methodology. The signification of the use of tables on stage in the performances I discuss in this essay has shifted from the bucolic or horrific banquets of Shakespeare, the storytelling performances of the past decades and the family scenes and dramas where tables served as a focal point. Discrete locations are no longer separated from a global enterprise. That we exist in a global floating world is the basis of both my case studies.

The unstated assumption of *The Agony and the Ecstasy of Steve Jobs* and *33 rounds per minute and then some* is that the experience that is the object of these works is transnational, due to the presence of personal technology devices, platforms and the internet, even when the experience has the signature of a specific culture or place. Domains of transnational experience are in the process of absorbing a variety of performance traditions, practices and politics. The tables used in these works represent a global 'flat world' that is virtually everywhere and nowhere as well as on the proscenium stage itself. ('Flat world' refers to the technology that enabled countries like China and India to become part of a global supply chain for manufacturing and services.) Taken together, these works, and others like them, demonstrate how contemporary performance straddles oral and postmodern culture, fiction and non-fiction, documentation and entertainment, the local and the global. These performances not only enact the archive, they are a part of the archive. Both works demonstrate what James K. Rilling writes:

> Another of the remarkable aspects of human cognition is our ability to project ourselves into other times and places so that we are not limited to thinking about the immediate here and now. In other words, we can simulate alternative worlds that are separate from the one being directly experienced. We can project ourselves

into the past to remember things that have happened to us, into the future to formulate and rehearse plans, and even into the minds of others to understand their mental states. How do they feel? What do they know?[5]

The tables in these productions situate the stage as a serious social space where audiences learn about tragedies in the real world. Tables signify the authority of the analysis of the live messengers who bring to the representatives of the polis in the theatre audience reports of the nastiness, lying, theft, murder and great financial gain of the masters of the universe as far as we can know them. When the offences are investigated by any board of inquiry, the committees hearing the testimony sit at tables. Courtrooms, legislative committee rooms and performed public reports by television anchors exist in a continuum of events enacted by performers on a spectrum from acting to not acting, from maintaining at least the appearance and sound of equanimity to expressing a wide range of passionate feelings, and from fiction to non-fiction.

In *The Agony and the Ecstasy of Steve Jobs,* Mike Daisey, a large man with a formidable presence, sits at a table as he compares the relationship between Apple product inventors, owners and users (from Steve Jobs to you and me) and the working conditions at Foxconn in Shenzhen, China. Daisey's travelogue begins in Hong Kong and then moves to Shenzhen. There is a war going on right now, Daisey tells his audience. Its foot soldiers are pirates, hackers, jailbreakers, unlockers, the people you go to 'to fiddle with the baseband of your phone, a person who writes tailored viruses'.[6] The war is over who owns all our devices. We may think we own them, Daisey cautions us, but so do the corporations that own the devices that run the networks. The pirates have a small trade in '[giving] people back ownership of the things they think they already own'.[7]

Daisey uses no other objects on stage beyond the table, his notes, and a glass of water: no mobile phone, no laptop, no photos. He leans on the table with the full weight of his body, as if to lean on the audience to make them see what is not literally on the stage: Shenzhen; Apple headquarters; laptops, iPods, iPads, iPhones; workers in China; people in the deep recesses of the Chungking Mansions in Hong Kong; Steve Wozniak, a translator named Cathy and Steve Jobs himself. Early on Daisey describes Jobs, the founder of Apple, as someone 'who believed passionately in the power of technology to transform all our lives, and believed that transformation could be welded to humanist values'.[8]

Throughout his work, Daisey links the destinies of Chinese workers to the voracious Western patterns of consumption of personal technology and our ignorance about the working conditions of those who feed its appetite. In the section of the piece titled *The Gates of Foxconn*, Daisey rails at his audience:

> Shenzhen is a city without history.
>
> The people who live there will tell you that, because thirty-one years ago, Shenzhen was a fishing village. They had little reed huts, little reed walkways between the huts, the men would fish into the late afternoon – I hear it was lovely. Today, Shenzhen is a city of fourteen million people. It is larger than New York City, it is the third largest city in all of China, and it is the place where almost all of your shit comes from.
>
> And the most amazing thing is, almost no one in America knows its name.
>
> Isn't that remarkable?
>
> That's the place where almost all of our shit comes from and no one knows its fucking name?
>
> I mean, we think we do know where our shit comes from – we think our shit comes from China.
>
> Right? In a kind of generalized way? "China."
>
> But it doesn't come from "China" – it comes from Shenzhen. It's a city, it's a place, and I am there, in an elevator, going down to the lobby of my hotel to meet my translator, Cathy.[9]

Daisey's work puts a face to the corporation. In this case, the corporation's products are made in Shenzhen, China, and its boss is Steve Jobs. The workers are no longer obedient Asian automata but real people with dreams and desires and bodies. *The Agony and the Ecstasy of Steve Jobs* is an updated Brechtian learning play in which both Jobs, with his elegant products, and we ourselves, through Job's products, along with the Chinese and Taiwanese governments (Foxconn is a multinational Taiwanese owned manufacturing company), are the fall guys for the exploitation of labour, including the labour of children in China. We can assign an identity to those responsible for the abuses that seem to violate human rights. To drive home his point about the people who make our personal computing devices, Daisey evokes a premodern world of handmade technology. He assures us that our electronics are assembled by hand, by thousands and thousands of tiny Chinese fingers, working in unending motion in vast Kubrikian spaces.[10] The corporate logic of the circulation of this culture is that the workers are as easily expendable as our planned-obsolescence personal technology devices. In both cases, we can throw them away. This world is a product of our making.

Figure 1 Mike Daisey performs *The Agony and Ecstasy of Steve Jobs* seated at a table with his notes and a glass of water. Photo courtesy of Mike Daisey. The Public Theatre 2011.

As a performer, Daisey uses his own hands in a unique gestural system especially designed for each production. In *The Agony and the Ecstasy of Steve Jobs*, Daisey used an iconic roll of the fingers and twist of the wrist while pulling his hand towards his body to sign 'I want it.' He swiped the air to show the movement of images on an iPad. Sometimes he lightly swept his hand from the centre outwards across the surface of his table to part the Red Sea, so to speak, as a means of transition. In so doing, Daisey asserts that the world can be known via live performance, which is a type of handcraft related to but different from the work of the people who assemble our electronics.

Mroué and Saneh take a different approach. *33 rounds per minute and then some* is about the final days of Diyaa Yamout, a young man living in Beirut. There are no actors in this performance installation. On stage we see a table and two chairs in what is assumed to be Yamout's home, where his television, answering machine, mobile phone, computer and Facebook page continue his life even after his apparent suicide. Yamout is absent yet omnipresent in the messages on his answering machine and the recurring ringing of his mobile phone. The Facebook posts on Yamout's wall, which are projected on the upstage wall behind the table, reveal some aspects of the mindset of countries where the circumstances of 2012's 'Arab Spring' still reverberate. Should desperate and/or violent acts continue to be the driving source of change?

The devices in Yamout's room live on even though Yamout himself is dead. Time continues as Azza Darwish, Yamout's friend, keeps leaving messages on Yamout's mobile phone, an image of which flashes on an upstage screen whenever the phone rings. The devices left alone in Yamout's room seem personal even as they continue to work without him. (They are, after all, run by software managed by corporate entities that not only are not present but exist somewhere beyond the imagination.) The ongoing life of the devices is as curious as Yamout's death and is, in many ways, the real subject of the performance installation. The host of an investigative television show broadcast on the television in Yamout's room asks, 'Starting with Bouazizi in Tunis who decided to immolate himself. . . . Is there a connection with Diyaa's actions? Is there a stand? Against whom?' Going forward, should we understand all suicides in the Arab world as acts against the state? No one knows what Yamout's death is really about, leaving the event open to speculation.

Figure 2 *33 rounds per minute and then some* is a performance installation without live actors. The installation includes a table on stage and a television, answering machine, mobile phone, computer and scrolling Facebook page. Photo by Maciej Zakrzewski. The Malta Festival in Poznan, Poland 2012.

Mroué and Saneh's use of mixed media means that performance, video, computers, photographs, stage and sound design and text all operate together. Diyaa Yamout's Facebook page and mobile phone, and the television programme in his room, display confused and contradictory comments. A portion of an exchange on Yamout's Facebook page reads:

Nagham: Only two days ago, he was talking about his new play. He was saying that he uses images in his work, in order to confirm his death. I didn't understand anything.

Daher: He was a deeeeep thinker, and a greeeeat performer.

Azza Darwish: Apparently there is a technical problem in the plane. Waiting to fix it. Screw my luck. [This text message from a friend who is flying to Beirut to see Yamout momentarily flashes on the screen, interrupting the flow of Facebook commentary.]

Joseph: It seems his suicide is due to being part of some atheist sect, that's what I read on some blog out there. His story is weird!!

Samir: Which blog?

Joseph: This one: http://lan/cgi/bic/98.18.1.11[11]

We learn that there have been many discussions about Yamout's suicide. Some say that he was mentally disturbed, addicted to drugs and a devil worshipper. Some of his Facebook friends are praising him as a hero. His friend Walid Hashem says: 'He is no hero and no honor in a pointless death. His suicide is not based on personal philosophy; it is the result of an inner struggle, which he could not come to terms with.'[12]

Georges S: He was listening to hard rock, that's for sure: D

Hamdan: He was influenced by Nietzsche I am sure.

Rita Yamout: You who's saying that he was listening to hard rock, shut your mouth! You have no idea about the reasons that drove him to suicide. Have some respect for the dead!

Jasser: God preserve us from our thoughts. RIP.

Rita Yamout: God preserve us from the thoughts of others! Retarded people!

Jasser: So people are retarded and you are intelligent? What kind of logic is that? Suicide is progress?

Rita Yamout: Stop playing smart with me and twisting my words!

Massoud: Take it easy, guys, for Diyaa's sake.

Hanane: May God forgive him and take him in His love.

Rita Yamout: May DIYAA forgive you! There's really no hope for this country!

Ramzi: I don't understand why he committed suicide. Anyway, who knows in which environment he lived in?

Jim: Some acts in life cannot be spoken but DONE.

Loubnany Assil: The system, the wrong use of power, lies, deceit, all of these can cause one to despair . . . double-dealing, looting . . . some profit, while others gain nothing . . . does God accept this?

Youssef Yehya: Diyaa Yamout's philosophy is more advanced than most people. His thoughts of freedom were way ahead of their time. It was difficult for others to accept them.

Yara: I told him once that he should write to Chomsky and other great intellectuals because only they could fully share his enthusiasm and let his ideas evolve.

Lucid: We should encourage people to see psychologists. His case is nothing but classic depression that can be easily treated!!!![13]

What was the cause of Yamout's suicide? Was it the images he needed to confirm his death in the new play he was writing; being a deep thinker, a member of an atheist sect, or a devil worshipper; his inner struggle, his reading of Nietzsche; hard-rocker depression; the system or his own philosophy? Or is Yamout an unrecognized hero? Is he like Mohamed Bouazizi, the street vendor in Tunis who immolated himself in protest of police harassment, humiliation and confiscation of his wares? Should we link his death to the Arab Spring, the Arab revolution? Was Yamout taking a stand? If so, against whom or what? Can we know?

33 rounds per minute and then some continues Mroué and Saneh's previous semi-documentary artistic inquiries. In their 2005 work, *Looking for the Missing Employee*, for example, half-lies, invented truth, newspaper clips, diary entries, found objects and propaganda are swirled together to tell the story of how and why the civil servant Raafat Suleiman went missing. Mroué and Saneh examine the way documentary evades truth in a flurry of reportage that attempts to piece together a puzzle but never creates a definitive picture. Mroué does not appear on stage in either work. In *Looking for the Missing Employee*, he sits perched behind his spectators with his image projected on a screen until he too disappears from both the screen and the perch. In these works, the real is both invoked and lost in the very act of trying to create it. Information fails as it is revealed. Archives are created and 'disappeared' in the same act of performance. Knowledge escapes us even as information invades us. Truth exists but cannot necessarily be found. What is real are the devices of reportage, not what they purport to report. The medium is the subject. Similarly, in *The Pixelated Revolution* (2012), Mroué discusses how the Syrian revolution can be understood by means of aesthetic analysis of the YouTube clips posted by the Syrian protesters.[14] Video documentation typically used as evidence of a definitive event or past is analysed both for what it depicts and as a source of information, in a manner not unlike the disembodied commentary flashing, flickering and recording in Yamout's apartment after his suicide.

In both *The Agony and the Ecstasy of Steve Jobs* and *33 rounds per minute and then some,* the table is a focused node where virtual realities converge. The multipurpose table – a desk, a pedestal for the laptop, a support for the elbows, an eating place – is where so much of our public and private lives take place. The realities laid out on Daisey's and Mroué and Saneh's tables exist elsewhere. We can be deceived into believing that what Daisey performs and Mroué and Saneh represent is present, when actually what they depict are multiple absences.

Portraying the 'presence of absence' is what theatre has done all along. What has changed is *where* this presence of absence is located. In the development of Western theatre, the Theatre of Dionysus in Athens represented the agora, the public outdoor space where the politically enabled (arguably only adult men) met to thrash out the city's affairs. In the theatre itself, the spectators sat in an open semicircle facing a circle flanked by a *skene*, the façade of a public building, where they witnessed poetic renditions of the fates of their own leaders. In the medieval theatre, the street became the stage. Processions combined drama and pilgrimage, linking the ordinary lives of craft guild members to the sacred life of Jesus. What people experienced was the superimposition of the divine over the human, a window through which to glimpse the eternal and the way it all works out on earth. The Elizabethan playhouse was an outdoor-indoor space, with high walls and a flat playing area suitable for the widest range of places, from bedrooms, banquet halls and throne rooms to streets, taverns, graves and battle-grounds. The rowdy theatregoers were participant-observers within this boisterous, optimistic space, which was well suited to Renaissance exuberance marked with a giddy sense of the ascendancy of knowledge. The modern theatre of Ibsen, Chekhov and their myriad descendants offers great passions in small rooms, the fourth wall removed. The spectators, settled in seats and externally passive (if internally churning), looked at the 'interiors' – both socially and psychologically – of characters supposedly not unlike real people who revealed the social strictures of their most intimate, middle-class lives. The invisible audience looked and listened through this 'as if' space, and was asked to pretend that it was a real space with real people.

Then there is the table on stage in contemporary performance. This table is fundamentally different from the aesthetic conventions of the fourth wall and is actually closer to the ancient Greek theatre than one might at first think: a postmodern agora, if you will. The table is not the representation of another space – as every previous theatrical epoch has offered – but rather is its own thing: a site of discourse, the place where all messages converge. Typically, at the table, the performer sits facing the audience. The audience sees the performer and the performer sees the audience as the performer gives a live report. The space is literally 'real', it is the actual locale from where reports are dramatized and delivered. The discourse is not two-way for the most part; the audience receives what the messenger delivers. Frequently enough, though (and more so these days than earlier), after the formal performance, there is a 'talkback', a continuation of the discursive performance – a reminder that we are all sitting across the table from someone, seen or unseen.

Tables on stage have come to represent a theatre of discourse instead of dramatic text. The performer, of course, has a direct physical presence, as do the spectators. Between the performers and spectators is an imagined presence that is staged in the minds of the spectators: Daisey in China and the labourers he meets there, and Diyaa Yamout and those writing on his wall, calling on his mobile phone, and leaving messages on his answering machine. The post-Holocaust assertion that finally we are only bodies is paradoxically challenged by performance's ability to summon the experience of the real as living in the domains of imagination and conceptualization as well as in the physical world. Complex thought and imagination live on apart from any individual in the performed realities and virtual artefacts of our existence. Communication, in a certain sense, has become continuous, even when very ambiguous, into death. This is part of the virtual conundrum surrounding the fictional Diyaa Yamout. The media as used to reveal Yamout's suicide and responses to it are a real and familiar component of our daily lives, and *33 rounds per minute and then some* relates the media to the real event of the Arab Spring. The responses to Yamout's suicide, however, expose the illusion that the ubiquity of media contains truthful information. As with other works by Mroué and Saneh, *33 rounds per minute and then some* uses the subject of its criticism, the ways in which mass media and personal technology devices provide information, as the means of their performance installation.

Theatre that uses tables in the ways discussed here is modelled, in part, on the cultural ubiquity of global communication nodes, on television newsroom studios, on internet communications. Through all of these, the performers put audiences in seeming communication with distant others as they are told about world events. Whole worlds can pass in rapid succession as the messengers seated at tables on stage report on a vast tract of time and space. The table is a perfect icon of this portable world. Tables wait for the presence of people. They symbolize both solitariness and social life; they are a locus of games, drinks and meals; they are used for interrogation, legal proceedings, political deliberation and decision-making; they serve as altars and as platforms for computers. Tables can be small or large, characterless or elaborate. They can be put anywhere. Tables have become the platforms from which we launch our virtual excursions to get news, contact remote friends, and even access entertainment. They are a modern defence apparatus for excursions and adventures as well as the surface for the ritual partaking of food. Tables are so fundamental to our Western understanding of 'furniture', 'home' and 'office' that a room without tables would seem strange in the Brechtian sense. Sitting behind tables, we are endowed with confidence, and often also with authority over the people sitting across from us, at the table's other side. Tables are metonymic to both order and power. From the table on stage – and in our studies and classrooms – we get in contact with everyone and anyone, with the events of the world.

If we listen to Daisey with his pageantry of one man at a table, it is the corporations that we need to pay attention to:

> The dormitories are cement cubes, ten foot by twelve foot—and in that space, there are thirteen beds. Fourteen beds. I count fifteen beds. They're stacked up like Jenga puzzle pieces all the way up to the ceiling. The space between them is so narrow none of us would actually fit in them—they have to slide into them like coffins. There are cameras in the rooms, there are cameras in the hallways, there are cameras everywhere.
>
> And why wouldn't there be? You know when we dream of a future when the regulations are washed away and the corporations are finally free to sail above us, you don't have to dream about some sci-fi-dystopian-*Blade-Runner-1984*-bullshit. You can go to Shenzhen tomorrow—they're making your shit that way today.
>
> And you need to know that these people are among the best and brightest of their generation. You need to know that when I interview them outside the

factories, they are, each of them, as bright and individual as you are out there in the darkness. You need to know these are exactly the people who fought their way out of their villages, to make a new life for themselves in these cities. These are exactly the people who could have the spirit to think about democracy.

But, fortunately for Beijing, they have a heat sink in the south of the country, they have an economic honey trap that soaks up all those people and keeps them busy, too busy to think about freedom, too busy making all our shit.[15]

Daisey's work is a great example of the ways in which theatre and performance practices not only shed light on contemporary cultural discourses but help form the conversation about our changing epistemologies, whether personal, cultural, historical, social and/or political. If we listen to Mroué and Saneh's performance installation, where human existence is presented only as a digitized reality of sorts, the *aition* is no longer about a mythic origin but about the myth of knowing. How do we come to know, or can we know, anything in the face of myriad contradictory sources of information and our own endless chatter? Mroué and Saneh locate contemporary political events in a mythical, parallel, omniscient but godless world where there is overabundant information but no knowledge.

At least since Spalding Gray's monologues in the 1970s, the recurring use of the table on stage has become an iconic way to signify authorship, truth, presence and authority. It is a reflexive and visible act of translating writing and performing into a critical discourse about personal, social and political life. The performer as social analyst, as public intellectual, as a messenger cut loose from the constraints of conventional drama and scenic representation is the result of a shift in the practice of creating performance and its subject matter, a shift as important as the idea that a broad spectrum of human activity can and should be looked at as performance with the tools of performance theory. Just as the spectrum of what scholars consider performance has changed, so has the spectrum of what and how performers perform.

My thesis is not only that select theatre practices are comprehensible in a variety of cultural settings, but that global culture has its own system of signification. Today's most provocative theatre embraces the cultural and technological changes that are reshaping us globally. Examining the way tables on stage today configure global content and signification has implications for performance theory in that it provides a means to analyse the assemblage, implementation and implications of information. Techniques from oral culture, such as solo storytelling, have combined with postmodern techniques, such as fragmentation of narrative and the disruption of the continuous and integrated presence of the performer. The notion that the archive and the repertoire are distinct domains of separate recorded and performed information has gone by the wayside.

The global shift in patterns of the representation of the real involves a move away from verbatim and documentary sources to methods that openly acknowledge the ways in which theatre about real events straddles fiction and non-fiction, reconstruction and the real. Rather than using the archive as a source of material, provocative theatre-makers construct performance as its own form of archive. Performance as archive, as its own documentation of events rather than as a reference to other forms of documentation, openly portrays events from imaginative vantage points to critique common sources of information. Contemporary performance partakes of the changes in the very idea of the archive brought on by digitization and the internet. The growth of virtual entertainment and personal communication technology has made our ubiquitous cultural experience the result of both live and ambiguous virtual information. Human identity is now understood more in terms of shifting digital realities than in terms of essence: we are what we record. Tables on stage articulate our continuing need for material reality, exchange and encounters, and our search for a physical place to locate ourselves.

Performing History, Performing Memory with the *Théâtre du Soleil*

Judith G. Miller

It would be a stretch to say that Richard Schechner's concept of environmental theatre anchored the celebrated 1970s collective creations of the *Théâtre du Soleil*: that is, the company's critical re-readings of the French Revolution in *1789* and *1793*.[1] Nevertheless, we know that in their design of these plays, Ariane Mouchkine and the Soleil had been influenced by Luca Ronconi's equally famous dramatic treatment of Ariosto's *Orlando Furioso*, in which audience and actors chased each other around the playing space in order to avoid colliding with enormous stage glides. And we also know that before staging in Rome and then throughout Europe in 1969–70 the Christians' complex battles against the Saracens, Ronconi had read Schechner on environmental theatre in a 1968 essay in *The Tulane Drama Review*.[2]

Perhaps to seize the approximate truth in this sketch of influence, it would be better to speak of an internationalized theatre world in which the drive to create a new theatre in the late 1960s and 1970s, both sacred and political, and empowering for theatre practitioners as well as for the audience, crisscrossed Europe, the Atlantic Ocean, the Mediterranean sea, and reached into Asia. In her study of theatre movements of the period, Margaret Croydon calls this a theatre of lunatics, lovers and poets.[3] More prosaically, Christian Biet and Christophe Triau, in their sweep of 'What is Theatre' (*Qu'est-ce que le théâtre?*), echo David Wiles's notion of the spatial as a key organizing concept for how theatre was being rethought by an avant-garde that stretched from New York to Tokyo.[4]

The environmental thinks the spatial in very concrete ways. As Joan MacIntosh remembers from her work with Schechner's Performance Group in the late 1960s and early 1970s, each specific production discovered and created an environment in which performers could find their own relationships with the audience and with each other.[5] Richard Schechner would add that this early environmental work enclosed itself, audience and actors in a form of ritual in which any sense of equating culture with a product to be consumed was rendered impossible.[6] In later theorizing of what theatre should be, Schechner configures differently the environmental. His shift towards 'performance', seen through an anthropological lens, foregrounds meta-theatricality as central to a more general notion of environment.[7] Schechner sees theatre as giving way not only to something relational but also to something self-conscious, a theatre in which physical confrontations and encounters between audience and actors or audience and audience are less crucial than the sense of knowing that what one performs is a performance: a construction of reality that feels real but is also a questioning of how the real becomes 'real'.

This conceptual shift can be read into the work of the *Théâtre du Soleil*, which is not to say that reading Richard Schechner changed the Soleil's engagement with how to do theatre. Indeed, the company, like most French companies born in the 1960s, had used forms of meta-theatricality from its inception in order to decry ideological positions. We might, however, suggest that with his articulation of performance and performance studies in the 1980s, Schechner found a language for theatre practice that incorporates (whether he intended this or not) the questioning of cultural production and knowledge dissemination central to post-structuralist French thinkers of the last half of the twentieth century, including Hélène Cixous, who has been a key member of the Soleil since the mid-1980s. Schechner's vocabulary, then, proves helpful in casting the Soleil's work in performance terms. This essay, accordingly, will attempt to show how the current mental environment of a Soleil production is deeply informed by the memory and history of past environmental productions. To do this, we will move from the Soleil's revisiting of the French revolution to their most recent international success, *Les Naufragés du Fol Espoir*, dubbed here simply 'Mad Hope'.[8]

The *Théâtre du Soleil* opened the doors to a new performance space in the Vincennes woods in 1970. By dint of hours of hard labour, it had gutted and reconfigured one of the hangars of an old armaments factory to house the five platforms, arranged in a rectangle, that comprised the elevated playing space of *1789*. What was startling about the spatial arrangement of *1789* was the role allotted to a doubled audience. One group of spectators stood in the middle of the trestle platforms and had to run, push or shove to take position in front of the trestle where vignettes were performed. The other group sat on bleachers, conferring on the 'active spectators' the role of performers in their own right. Because the Soleil's slant on the French Revolution took the form of actors playing eighteenth-century fair comedians performing the major episodes of the Revolution for a fairground audience, the spectators were effectively positioned as members of an eighteenth-century crowd being addressed by barkers and enjoined to dance, celebrate and later lament the Revolution – shown ultimately as bringing the bourgeoisie to power. Thus, the 'active spectators' not only participated viscerally but also gave the production meaning as a theatre-in-the-theatre experience.

Moreover, the events of May 1968, that other 'failed' revolution – and certainly so in the eyes of most of the theatre-going population who ventured into the Vincennes woods – connected the contemporary to the historical, adding yet another layer of meaning to the refrain heard throughout the second half of the show: 'La Révolution est finie!' (The Revolution is over!) *1789* and *1792* thus performed the reigning mindset of the French Left after the events of May 1968: a dirge for a failed revolution in which all participants, nevertheless, having insisted on the right to revolt, imagine an eventual spilling forth into a more positive energy field, ushering in true collaborative government.[9] The especially strong rapport established between actors and audience, between actors and actors and between the spectators (the three axis of environmental theatre according to Richard Schechner)[10] propelled the production out of any conventional theatrical space into a space where all participants became responsible for moving the theatrical event into a space of political potential.

1789, which played for 3 years before an estimated 350,000 spectators, launched the process of restructuring the Soleil's hangars of the recuperated theatre space for each subsequent production. With each restructuring, a new physical rapport was established with the public, one meant also to capture the questions posed by each production. Thus *1793*, which traced the evolution of a revolutionary neighbourhood committee up to the onset of the Terror, placed the spectators on the floor, so they would surround the outsized banquet tables around which and on top of which actors performed. Less kinaesthetically charged than the mad dashes of *1789*, this position allowed audience members to feel themselves an extension of the 'banquet years' of revolutionary communion and therefore of the debates about who should have the right to represent the people of Paris.

For *L'Age d'or* (The Age of Gold), the Soleil's 1975–76 production, audience members had to climb up and down newly built 'stage' hills to find a viewing space for the constantly moving and highly caricaturized sketches of daily calamities (including the exploitation of immigrant workers) besetting contemporary France.[11] The environment prompted audience members to decide just how close they would allow themselves to be to the exploiters and exploited in French society. For *Mephisto,* Mnouchkine's 1979–80 adaptation of Klaus Mann's novel, two stages representing two artistic attitudes (resistance or collaboration with war mongers), delimited each end of the performance space.[12] Spectators were balloted between possibilities of going along with or subverting Nazism: Positioned in the middle on rotating seats, the spectators had to keep turning, depending on which stage was active. In these productions, the physicalization required of the audience mimicked, in the first instance, the exhausting effort of keeping body and soul together in the daily grind of a war-torn country. On another level, the back and forth movement channelled the pull and tug of situating oneself when faced with making a choice that is immoral but life-saving (collaboration) or moral but almost certainly suicidal (resistance). The environment created by the Soleil invited the audience to think about how one might act or choose not to act during extreme social crises.

In 1980, the nonstop reshaping of the Soleil's performance space came to an end. Guy-Claude François, Mnouchkine's long-time set designer, constructed that year the massive and elegant thrust space, with its front facing bleachers and vomitorium-like entrances and exits, that has hallmarked most of the Soleil's productions since then. For Mnouchkine, this newly recognizable 'stage', appropriate in her mind (as later productions confirmed) for interpreting texts from Shakespeare to Aeschylus to Molière to Hélène Cixous, set up a distance that paradoxically brings the audience and actors into a more ritualized communion. It is part of a larger, carefully gauged ritual of sharing meals, of watching the actors prepare, and of often staying after the production to discuss the performance or the relevant contemporary topics raised by it.

Les Naufragés du Fol Espoir, a production that breaks mental and formal but not physical boundaries, was devised within this ritualized and ceremonial space.[13] Rather than reeling in the audience primarily through its own athleticism and physical engagement as in productions of the 1970s, *Mad Hope* sets up multiple lures for the memory, suturing the audience by large doses of nostalgia, by calling on spectators' own imbrication in the history of the *Théâtre du Soleil,* and through mental gymnastics that move between the many-layered meanings of 'mad hope'. The production thus foregrounds the conscious (and mad) act of doing theatre as a form of participating in a Socialist utopia. It does this within a fictional cabaret called 'Mad Hope', the ostensible locus of the action, while at the same time embodying the making of a film also called 'Mad Hope' (and based on a Jules Verne novel) in the attic of the cabaret – a film in which the fictional steamship carrying its European passengers to a new land is also named 'Mad Hope'.[14] The multiplication of 'mad hopes' reinforces the crazy determination of the fictional characters, fictional actors and real actors to realize their Socialist projects.

All of the 'mad hopes' evoked by this production dwell within one more: The Mad Hope that houses the company and welcomes the public. For the Soleil's actual theatre, space has been transformed physically into a 'dance hall on the banks of the Marne', called 'The Mad Hope'. Thus, the former three-hangared armaments factory sports a new layer of paint and a model hot-air balloon, beckoning spectators on a wondrous ride. Once inside, images of early twentieth-century travel and film posters, blown-up copies of the covers of Verne's books, and a cartographic depiction of Patagonia decorate the walls. This huge map traces the voyage on which the public will soon cast off. On the other side of the entrance hall, in order to get to the performance space, the audience must wend its way through a maze of old lace and trunks, an *ur* attic holding and prefiguring the memory space of the play.

This planned regression into childhood invokes a mental space where colours, tastes, perfumes and pleasure can be easily accessed and reactivated. The film-making within the production reproduces an invitation to the land of 'once upon a time'. Thus, a similar refrain begins each segment of the film-making. The film-maker Jean turns to his sister Gabrielle and commands: 'Gabrielle, crank the machine'. And she answers, 'I'm cranking, Jean'. Such an incantation, reminiscent of the beginnings of storytelling and fairy tales, calls forth the elsewhere of reverie. Many of those spectators who have grown up with the Théâtre du Soleil doubtlessly find their own multiple selves in the reverberations of the doubled plot and manifold frames of the production, hearing again the political debates of the late twentieth- and early twenty-first centuries. We might say, then, that the audience performs itself, that is – 'the audience of the *Théâtre du Soleil*', re-encountering both the rituals and the sociopolitical questions haunting all the work of the company.

The structure of film-in-the-theatre-in–the-collective–memory-of-the-audience/actors highlights the meta-commentary that often marks the Soleil's productions. Since at least 1978 and their film *Molière,* the Soleil actors have frequently played actors examining how an arts organization interacts with political power and the pressing needs of dispossessed peoples.[15] *Mad Hope*, however, gestures to how audiences receive representations of power and how they learn to believe or disbelieve in them. Through the theatre in the theatre (or film-making in the theatre) structure, the Soleil demonstrates that it, too, is aware of its own efforts at crossing boundaries and asking questions.

In this form of self-reflection, *Mad Hope* blends a meditation on leftist politics and art with a rousing adventure story inspired by Verne and reinterpreted by Hélène Cixous. On its most easily readable level and in an attempt at a simplified summary of what happens in the play, *Mad Hope* interpolates nine episodes of 'a silent film' within the story of the making of the film: M. Félix Courage, proprietor of the cabaret called The Mad Hope, has lent three socially conscious artists and their amateur team of international film enthusiasts his attic for their film-making project. It is the eve of World War I and voice-overs of daily newspaper headlines bring the war closer and closer. Scenes of preparing the anti-war, utopian socialist film alternate with filmic episodes.

The film, *The Shipwrecked of Mad Hope*, follows immigrants at the beginning of the 1890s attempting to reach Australia but, instead, shipwrecking on an island that is part of Patagonia. The survivors eventually clash brutally over who should rule their colony. Two long-time inhabitants of the island: a mysterious and compassionate hermit and his young Indian helper emerge intact from the survivors' killing spree. They move forward to construct a lighthouse in order to prevent further shipwrecks from happening. Thus ends the film. Meanwhile, in the world outside the film, in the attic where the film-makers toil, war has been declared and the film-makers disperse for the battlefields of World War I.

This barebones outline of the mirroring plots points to the theatrical wizardry for which the Soleil is so justly famous. The sensory pleasure and incomparable ingenuity of the staging support the Soleil's longstanding theatrical pact – one that sutures the audience to the performance while at the same time reminding spectators that they are witnessing theatre-in-the-making. For example, accompanying the myriad transitions of the theatre-in-the-theatre structure, the melodramatic soundscape also paces the sweep of the choreography, as the 33 actors rush on and off the stage, establishing the decor, moving props and creating the frames for the silent film with its silent, super-titled, dialogue. The sense of the work of theatre never stops; actors playing film-makers and actors playing film actors sweep the stage, man the wind machine, run the spots, or manipulate the seagull puppet – the latter an emblem of hope for the last third of the play. This work of theatre is reinforced by members of the *Théâtre du Soleil*, seen as such rather than as characters, who also manoeuvre backdrops, stage glides, and riggings. All these bodies form part of a continuous moving dance machine. Thus while not losing sight of the fact of theatre-in-the-making, spectators are also carried away by the kinetic and auditory pleasures of the production. This sets up the always dual experience of a Soleil production in which one is inside and outside; part of an emotional, sometimes cathartic ritual, but witness to one's own participation through witnessing theatre being made.

Famous for her stage pictures, in *Mad Hope*, Mnouchkine multiplies awe-inducing moments of stagecraft, such as the fire in the attic studio that has to be doused with buckets of water during the filming. This effect is captured by a camera operator, a producer and more film technicians, who film from side angles or more spectacularly from ceiling pulleys or booms. They are part of the overarching and superbly balanced production frame that prompts the spectators to realize they are looking at pictures, at staged scenes. Seeing both what the camera sees as well as seeing how the camera is manipulated to direct what is seen, spectators learn something about how one 'sees' moving images in general.

Nonetheless, especially in the second half of the production, when huge floor drops and vast backdrops of glaciers transform the performance space into a desert of snow and ice and when the set comprises a close-up of the prow of the ship that takes up nearly the entire stage, the camera, less and less manifest, seems to disappear. The adventures in Patagonia grip the audience outside of any well-defined frame, 'contaminating' it with the ripe emotion of the action. Through this experience of disappearing frames, the magic possible in art's ability to move and subjugate becomes palpable.

Mnouchkine's staging – fluid, mobile, intensifying the senses – echoes what Hélène Cixous called in the late 1970s *l'écriture féminine* or feminine writing.[16] Such a staging realizes Cixous's maternal vision of non-separation and communion: one might understand the company as a paradoxically single and multiple subject, a fragmented whole at the same time coherent in its acceptance of instability, process and disruption. These aspects of the Soleil echo throughout the film-making experience in *Mad Hope* in which the film-makers never arrive at absolute closure. In this, we can locate gestures of the autobiographical. In other terms, the *Théâtre du Soleil* performs a meditation on performing itself.

In the prologue, the searching mind provides the first and encompassing layer of the autobiographical. *Mad Hope* introduces its public immediately into the past in order to illumine both origins and the present. The production begins, then, with actors pulling down the scrim covering the downstage space, a symbolic opening of the mind. The granddaughter of one of the amateur actors from the 1914 film-making has travelled to the attic of the now defunct cabaret, The Mad Hope. She is a graduate student, writing in 2010 a thesis about 'Cinema and Popular Education'. The current owner of the space, another granddaughter of another actor, invites the student to listen to a recording from the front lines of World War I. This pair of young women acts as a connector between temporal zones. On the recorded disk, a male voice, another actor from the film The Mad Hope and the lover of one of the grandmothers, sighs: 'It's not by making war that we'll meet again at Mad Hope.' Thus are the spectators plunged analeptically into not just the past, but into the memory of the past as filtered through the soldier's and the granddaughters' minds. We thus see how memory is constituted through the performance of it.

The quintessential memory space of the attic full of old records and trunks becomes, in a flash, the working studio of the characters Jean La Pallette, his sister Gabrielle and their partner Tomasso. During the next 4 hours, the production will examine just what mad hope really is, the expression 'Mad Hope' serving as a kind of secret moniker for the enterprise of the *Théâtre du Soleil* from its inception. While the present time is not again specifically recalled in the production, the prologue firmly puts in motion the link between the then of the doubled drama (the film-making of 1914/the film-taking place from 1889 to 1895) and the now in which the audience lives.

The film-making scenes, in which the process of making art is foregrounded, give vent to the Soleil's aesthetic inquiries, scattering them between the filmic episodes. Such scenes constitute the second layer of autobiography as they permit the Soleil to review once again its basic interrogations about the role of art in society. Moreover, the film-making allows the company to stage both humorously and succinctly what it has learned about how to do theatre. This second layer consequently becomes a kind of primer to the mission and working methods of Mnouchkine and the *Théâtre du Soleil*.

The dialogue and stage action of Jean and Gabrielle La Pallette, the brother-sister team who have left the world of commercial film-making to enrol in an undertaking of making art that instructs as well as pleases, imparts the Soleil's artistic credo. In their educational film, the La Pallettes consciously choose to tell the exemplary story of how Jean Salvatore, an aristocrat turned 'man of the people', after his encounter with Socialist thought, forges a life that includes lighting the way for future generations. The film they plan also shows how the greed for gold of the Gautrain brothers, the bourgeois passengers on The Mad Hope steamship, ends up condemning almost everyone to a fratricidal, indeed

Shakespearian, pile up of death on the frozen plains of Patagonia. These lessons form the bedrock for both hope and despair in the fictional film-making and in the life story of the *Théâtre du Soleil.*

Just as the story the La Palettes tell reflects the Soleil's commitment to enlightened and allegorical art, the way they tell the story, by positing democracy in action, mimics the Soleil's creative methods. For example, all the actors and members of the film-making crew get to vote on whether to finish the film, given the impending call to world-wide war heard over the radio news. Furthermore, the three conceptualizers of the film have recruited all the local habitués of the cabaret The Mad Hope, including the wait staff, into their artistic project: Art belongs to everyone and everyone can and should participate in the making of it. Yet, everyone must also work to his or her personal best. Hence M. Félix Courage, the cabaret owner – but for the film the spot operator – clearly channels Mnouchkine herself when he chides his overreaching waiter-actors: 'You have to start from what you know.' This advice is basic to every one of the training workshops Mnouchkine conducts.

The third layer of autobiography in *Mad Hope* takes up political choices and ethical conundrums. In studying closely the contents of the film, specific political debates come to light. The company explores either implicitly through allusive example, or explicitly through staged discussions, concerns about the European Union, immigration, colonization, as well as the genocide of native peoples, the end of ideologies, women's rights and capitalist decadence. Almost all of the Soleil's previous productions have exploited dramatically one or several of these issues, including as early as the 1970s – with their queries about political structure and equality – and as late as 2005 – with *Le Dernier Caravansérail's* (The Last Caravanserai's) condemnation of ethnic cleansing.[17]

Inspired by internationalist thinkers, such as Victor Hugo (who is cited) and Jean Jaurès (who is referenced repeatedly), the film lauds the possibility of the fellowship of the world's peoples and thus of a sustainable peace. This hope is realized in the initial camaraderie of the immigrants from many countries singing the *Internationale* and bunking together on the steamship on their way to a new life. The prospect for fellowship is belied, however, by the violent expulsion of some of the immigrants and by their fatal quarrel over leadership which sees former friends flare up into beastly antagonists once in Patagonia.

On the other hand, the film emphasizes the potential for Socialist energies and thought to realize a viable democracy. Once shipwrecked in Patagonia, the survivors envisage several competing formulae for arriving at shared governance. Their positions, and notably the women's forceful advocacy of their right to vote and recognition of their political worth, recapture the heady revolutionary debates seen in the much earlier productions of *1789* and *1793*.

Hindsight, however, embodied by the spectators alive today (spectators enticed to think backwards and forwards in time) helps reconstruct, as does the production through the steady interruptions of news items from 1914, through the portrait of a young, arrogant Churchill, through the portrayal of the British claim to the Falkland Islands off the Patagonian coast, that not only will World War I take place, but so also will World War II and several other wars and genocides thereafter. Governments and nativists still misuse immigrants; Europe flounders; gold rules; and the ideology of progress, including Western superiority, still remains in many quarters an unexamined point of departure for any negotiation on the world's stage. And in contemporary France, the recently 'deposed' President, Nicolas Sarkozy, in gestures reminiscent of Germany in the 1930s, kicked out the gypsy population, made shocking pronouncements about Africa's lack of culture, and restructured public universities to resemble corporate operations. That the *Théâtre du Soleil*, always attuned to the politics of its times, should particularly express its anxiety about the future of egalitarianism is not surprising. Indeed, this broad wink at the contemporary should again be seen as a performance of the political, highlighting the issues that helped defeat Sarkozy in the June 2012 elections.

Mad Hope's three autobiographical layers should best be thought of as resonating chambers, each speaking to, intermingling with and sometimes contradicting the others. Borders are breached; and just as present, past and future times compel our attention through the kinds of questions posed, the inside and the outside worlds of the attic space and downstairs restaurant of the cabaret intersect and create meaning through juxtaposition and infectiousness. The world outside The Mad Hope Cabaret intrudes, for example, on the film actors' ability to maintain their calm: Tomasso, the continuity man in the film-making, an Italian nationalist at heart playing a convict immigrant in the film, attacks against script the actor who is a pacifist, he himself cast in the role of a naïve socialist. Not being meant to do so, Tomasso cannot stop himself from improvising the killing of the socialist in the film. In this way, he evacuates his real frustration with the political situation outside the film and the film-making. This constant interpenetration of layers recognizes how life stories are constructed through putting in relation, as Edouard Glissant would have it, the various mental and material worlds and the many temporal spaces in which we live. The framing of an event helps determine its truth, and multiple frames, as practised in this production, provide multiple angles for approaching 'the truth', while also suggesting that another space always exists for thinking outside the box.[18]

Perhaps what one ultimately comes to see through the work of the Soleil and, to return to him, through Richard Schechner's belief in the value of theatre that is environmentally tuned and consciously performative is that theatre remains one of the last viable political spaces for rehearsing utopia. Such cosmopolitan theatrical communities as the Soleil or as Schechner's, or any of the myriad performance groups operating out of the world's capitals, revel in the 'fol espoir' that dictionaries also translate as 'unreasonable optimism or belief'. In that sense, 'mad hope' not just provides the grounding, backstory, fiction and philosophy of the Soleil's production, but also endows the ethical stance offered to the public as the best possible shared environment. Moreover, it defines the ethical as an awareness of performing memory and history.[19]

Textual Dramaturgy and Dramaturg-as-Text: Traditional versus New Dramaturgy in the Era of German Post-Dramatic Theatre*

Gad Kaynar

This essay sets out to explore some major changes in the notion of dramaturgy and the function of the dramaturg in the German-speaking countries in the era of late post-dramatic theatre. In his article 'Wie politisch ist Postdramatisches Theater?' ['How Political is Postdramatic Theatre?'], Hans-Thies Lehmann defines 'postdramatic theatre' in a nutshell:

> ... A repulsive, controversial attitude of the new theatre to the dramatic tradition, in other words – an abundance of "concrete negations" of the dramatic that began in the historical avant-garde and in the neo avant-garde of the 1950s.[1]

The most conspicuous features of post-dramatic aesthetics and dramaturgy, in the wake of Richard Schechner's formative performance theory and Lehmann's derivative observations in his signature work *Postdramatisches Theater*,[2] comprise inter alia: the transition from a verbally predominant, narrative and sequentially structured poetics, to a performance-oriented aesthetics, distinguished by plot-less, character-less, deconstructed and fragmentary theatrical texts. These texts highlight the performers' corporeal and concrete stage presence, as well as what Patrick Primavesi defines as 'the moment of the performance itself',[3] rather than the traditional coherent and cohesive representation or presentation of a fictional world, plot and characters. For instance, the German director Michael Thalheimer commented on his own dramaturgical interpretation of Friedrich Schiller's *Kabale und Liebe* [*Intrigues and Love*] that undermined and reduced the weight and volume of the classical text and instead accentuated the bodily articulation of the actors annunciating his critique of capitalism as subversion of the natural and the genuine that 'The . . . body speaks its own words . . . since it often says the opposite of what it puts into words'.[4] The post-dramatic idiom is also distinguished by questioning the very nature of theatre and perception. Whereas dramatic theatre is often concerned with the referential import of the play and its stage realization, treating constituents such as plot, character, theatrical language, style, genre and so on as mere vehicles for transporting the message to a passive spectator, post-dramatic theatre focuses on form and process as self-referential, practising a semantics and rhetoric of form proper which conjoins both performers and spectators as active participants. The dramaturgy of *Smarthouse 1 + 2*, an anti-globalization and anti-consumerist project by René Polesch (2003), is based in part on an 'auction', conducted by the performers, of violent and subversive slogans addressed at the young participants who attend Polesch's productions as cult-shows. The well-educated German adolescents come to the stage, 'buy' a slogan, vehemently shout it at their accompanying parents and then meekly return to their seats. The contradictive, self-defeating processual act of 'selling' and 'buying' the anti-commercial slogans and then hurling them at the audience as if they were commercials ironically constitutes both a rebellious gesture and a reification of sophisticated methods through which capitalist society suppresses the revolt by turning it into a marketable commodity.[5] A distinct trait of post-dramatic performance resides accordingly in the encroachment of the liminal borders between fiction and reality, actor and role, *parole* and *langue*, verbal and visual dramaturgy, thereby, through highly theatrical means, trying to refute the exclusive ascription of theatricality to declared performative events in the spirit of Jean-Luc Nancy's dictum: 'There is no society without spectacle, since society itself is a spectacle.'[6] Similarly, post-dramatic performance defies and intermingles 'purist' and solipsist definitions of artistic fields including performance genres, such as 'high' and 'low' drama, burlesque, stand-up, poetry reciting, 'heavy-classical' and pop music and dance. This disposition is even inscribed in the name of the famous German devising group 'andcompany&Co.' whose suffix 'Co.' asserts, as written in the company's manifesto, the decision of the founding members to cooperate, in every new project, on an egalitarian basis, with artists from all fields: musicians, visual artists and writers.[7] Moreover, a specific genre of post-dramatic eclectic and interrelated attributes, such as that of the 'Rimini Protokoll' collective, tries to breach the established dramatic theatre's politics of excluding reality per se from the stage, and to empower 'everyday specialists' to relate to their biographical stories, what Jacques Rancière defines as 're-devising the territory of the communal').[8] Furthermore, similar to Schechner's environmental theatre, post-dramatic theatre replaces conventional and institutionalized venues, associated with bourgeois culinary theatre, with spatial configurations that challenge the diachronic, evolutionary conventions of plot structuring in the dramatic theatre, as well as habitual norms of audience reception (as, for instance, Thalheimer placed the audience around the festive table in his production of Dogma's *The Celebration*, thus incorporating the spectators in the embarrassment of the sexually abused family in the play).[9] It also tends to prefer environments least associated with established performance activities such as the urban sites in which the late radical German theatre-maker, Christoph Schlingensief, staged his scandalous street actions. The rationale underlying the aesthetics, and hence dramaturgy of post-dramatic theatre, is quintessentially summarized in Lehmann's general observation: 'Everything depends on the capability to find theatre where it is usually not perceived.'[10]

The journey that this essay embarks on, leading from traditional dramaturgical approaches to iconoclastic techniques (both of which coexist in practice), is intended to substantiate my main argument that in the post-dramatic era the closed traditional approaches of textual dramaturgy are challenged by the conceptually open-ended and autogenic dramaturgy of the self, or of the *dramaturg-as-text.*

Carl Hegemann – the veteran dramaturg of the *Volksbühne* in East Berlin – provides a simple yet striking demonstration, based on role acting, of the contrast between dramatic and post-dramatic dramaturgical procedures. In his lecture at the International Research Workshop on 'Dramaturgy as Applied Knowledge: From Theory to Practice and Back' (Tel Aviv University 2008), Hegemann, enacting the director, drew a rectangle on the blackboard, representing a show in rehearsal, and asked the audience, casted as dramaturgs, to mention anything of which this form reminded us (a coffin? a shoe-box? a cigarette box?). He then contended that whereas in the dramatic theatre it is the director who would most likely raise these associations in the context of presenting his or her stage 'conception' or 'interpretation', leading to a dialogue with the dramaturg in order to elaborate this conception, the situation in devising processes that pertain to the non-representative post-dramatic aesthetics (alongside other, text-based, modes) is reversed: the dramaturg, as the hermeneutic agent resorting to free, arbitrary associations, interprets for the director – as an integral part of the rehearsal process throughout what he or she considers that the director has done – not *meant*, just *done* as the dramaturg perceives it. This subjective interpretation in turn fuels further developments in the performance script, with the dramaturg thus becoming a kind of 'co-director', as also implied by Cathy Turner and Synne K. Behrndt's contention that: 'the compositional challenge [facing the dramaturg of a devising group] is . . . to define and shape the material from the living process and from the dialogue between the people involved'.[11]

So it can consequently be maintained that whereas in the dramatic theatre the dramaturg conducts a pre-production series of interpretative discussions with the director designers, and actors, in order to help decipher the play and transform it into a performance text (through cuts, editing and adaptation), and serving as the director's critical 'third eye', with limited authority,[12] in the post-dramatic devising production, in which the performance text emerges out of the rehearsal process, the dramaturg becomes an equally privileged partner of the director – if there is any one at all, and their creative functions are blurred. One might therefore say that in this post-dramatic dramaturgical procedure, it is the performance process (i.e. the stage of rehearsals), the *dromenon*, rather than the written text, the *legomenon*, that needs 'translation' in order to be communicative to the implied spectators[13] and involve them in deciphering and gap-filling. We are thus confronted with a reciprocal performance process, which furnishes the dramaturg with the incentives for his/her subjective act. And this act, which evolves from the dramaturg's associative world, leaves its imprint on the fractured, disintegrated performance text. Bettina Milz provides examples from the extreme test case of dance dramaturgy: 'The dramaturg must be the one who takes risks and describes what s/he sees, who stumbles, jumps into deep waters, . . . transforms, gives words to something that still has no words . . .'. To be 'the third eye in contemporary dance means also to move, to risk over-involvement'.[14]

In order to understand the transformation of dramaturgical approaches, one has to outline certain aspects of dominant dramaturgical approaches in the post-dramatic era regarding verbal and synaesthetic translations of play or non-textual performance scripts. 'Translation' in this context means transference from one cultural codification system to another; intercultural translation creating 'hybrid forms';[15] or intracultural translation (either reinterpreting one's own cultural canon or transforming disconnected phenomenological images and concepts into a novel cultural collage, as suggested by Patrice Pavis).[16]

Within these parameters, Central-European dramaturgical translation vacillated at the turn of the millennium between two extremes (with many in-betweens): traditional adherence to a reductive fidelity to the play's inherent interpretative options on the one hand, and devising orientations based on the dramaturg's own environment, biography and socio political ideology on the other. These orientations – which come through by a plethora of audio-visual and imagistic means – fill in the gaps engendered by diminishing (and otherwise changing) the role of the text. The traditional tectonic approaches of *textual dramaturgy* are thus challenged by the non-diegetic, a-tectonic and autogenic dramaturgy of the self, or of the *dramaturg-as-text*. This means that the dramaturg, rather than explicating an extraneous text through his/her perspective, explicates him/herself (i.e. biography, associations, *Weltanschauung*, etc.) through the text, and thereby textualizes him/herself. The dramaturg is thus transformed from a transparent, backstage phantom into an embodied – either personally or metonymically – histrionic presence in a double configuration: as part of an ensemble, and/or as the epitome and incarnation of the entire performance. In this respect, one might maintain that performers and spectators alike are – in the ritual sense as Schechner defines it – 'being possessed by another'.[17]

However, in this 'hesitant, veiled, stammering' context,[18] authorship does not belong solely to the author – if there is any – or to the 'official' dramaturg. The subjective processing of the source material or of the performance's premise may pertain to the hermeneutic agency of the performers, because, on the basis of Augusto Boal's famous dictum – 'I think that everyone can do theatre. Even actors'[19] – if everybody may become a dramaturg, the professional dramaturg loses his/her unique functions. In such cases dramaturgy as a discipline and practice, rather than the persona of the dramaturg, reigns supreme. For example, René Pollesch, starts rehearsals with an unfinished 'meta-text' encouraging actors and spectators to de- and reconstruct it by deciding which sentences 'work' and which not.[20] The German 'Gob Squad Arts Collective' materializes its ideological motto 'we are a collective. Nobody is in charge' by letting spatial circumstances and coincidences act as regulative dramaturgical factors. In the context of their political *Revolution Now!* (2010), members of the group interviewed haphazard passers-by on a Berlin street, trying to influence them to start the revolution by changing their pedestrian habitus. The unforeseen reactions were screened back to the Berliner *Volksbühne*, where the performance took place, and set the course of the subsequent proceedings.

The following classification of approaches to dramaturgy in the post-dramatic era is primarily based on interviews with 25 leading German and Swiss dramaturgs, conducted between 2003 and 2009.[21] The choice of dramaturgy in the German-speaking region (with one exception) rests first and foremost on the recognition that dramaturgy as a practice has emerged, developed and been radicalized in Germany and German-speaking countries for over 250 years. It is therefore reasonable to assume that the well-established and longstanding field of 'traditional' textual dramaturgy in Germany and the German-speaking countries would have experienced the most radical transmutations in the last decades compared to other countries.

A contextualization of the dramaturgical field in the post-dramatic era of the theatrical landscape in German-speaking countries – Germany, Austria and Switzerland after the fall of the Berlin wall is therefore indispensable and provides further reasons for my choice. These are based on the observation that there is a perfect correspondence between the features of post-dramatic aesthetics and the character of contemporary German Theatre. Despite drastic reductions in the theatre's budget as a result of the unification between West and East-Germany (1990) and the economic crisis of 2008, the German Theatre remains the most heavily supported performance institution in the world. The support extends to the average of 85 per cent of a public theatre's annual budget, which – as the renowned Swiss-German director, Jossi Wieler, a former graduate of the Theatre Arts Department at Tel Aviv University maintains – 'increases the readiness to take risks. It encourages heterogeneity, both with regard to dramatic writing and stage realization'.[22]

The most salient characteristic of the current German-speaking theatre is its bent for formal experimentation, relentless challenging and estranging the already defamiliarized definitions and fluid borders of theatre, and continuously seeking various idiosyncratic sociopolitical functions of the theatre. It also subverts, as well as for subverting the dichotomies between artistic modes and institutionalized, repertory, public theatre on the one hand, and the '*Freie Szene*', the independent, alternative or fringe groups that experiment with New Media, process aspects of the cultural and social discourse and rehabilitate formerly excluded elements of pop-culture and 'trash' on the other. These groups are extensively incorporated in the municipal and state theatres and conduce to the development of a 'hybrid' of performative organization forms, genres, methods and techniques, as well as of various forms of cooperation, research of everyday reality and 'intervention' as the theatre scholar Patrick Primavesi describes the situation.[23] The influence of post-dramatic intermediality – especially that of text, dance and video-art – and the diminished stature of the verbal text imprint the stage conceptions of classical plays. For instance, no word is spoken for a long time in Jürgen Gosch's conception of *Macbeth* [2005] while a naked group of male actors, smeared all over with blood – a sensuous *tableau vivant* of 'a band of testosterone-pregnant men'[24] – transforms into whipping, shouting, stamping witches, who are in turn metamorphosed, inter alia, into Duncan and the messenger. The critic of *Theater heute* commented on this approach: 'a new revelation [of a classic] is also a deconstruction of it'.[25] Another post-dramatic feature inscribed in the *Regietheater*'s [Director's Theatre] post-dramatic reading of the classic is the crass non-realistic disengagement of the complementary relations between the text and its theatrical rendering, blatantly articulated, for instance, in Michael Thalheimer's *Emilia Galotti* by G. E. Lessing, in which a fashion-show catwalk stage prescribes the *mis-en-scène* despite eighteenth-century textual demands. Regarding the interrelation of theatre and dance – the influence is mutual: 'Dance conducts a lively dialogue with patterns of post-dramatic performance',[26] as witnessed in the works of Sasha Waltz at the *Schaubühne* Berlin, Nir de Wolf, or in the collaboration of Saar Magal and Jochen Roller dedicated to a mnemonic and phenomenal reconstruction of the Holocaust in a novel, non-manipulative and imagistic manner.[27]

In this cultural environment that encourages the dynamic, permanently revolutionary and explorative thrust which profoundly impregnates even 'dramatic' texts in various ways that constitute an elaborate topic to which I cannot resort here, one witnesses a growing tendency (which germinated in the early heydays of the *Regietheater* in the 1980s between partners such as Claus Peymann and Hermann Beil) of ongoing collaborations between director and dramaturg to the extent that the difference in their functions becomes sometimes obsolete and the one fulfils the functions of the other (outstanding pairs include Jossi Wieler and Tilamn Raabke in the spoken theatre at the Munich *Kammerspiele*, Wieler and Sergio Morabito in Opera productions; Christoph Marthaler and Stefanie Carp at the *Schauspielhaus Zürich*; Falk Richter and Jens Hillje at the *Schaubühne* Berlin; or until recently Frank Castorf and Carl Hegemann at the *Volksbühne*). A similar kind of cooperation exists between post-postdramatic playwrights and director-dramaturgs such as Dea Loher and Andreas Kriegenburg, or Roland Schimmelpfennig and the late Jürgen Gosch. This is alongside cases in which a choreographer, musician or group of performers acts as an autonomous dramaturg to which I shall henceforth refer.

A note on terminology

Before examining the various approaches to dramaturgical translation, it is first necessary to clarify how this term differs from other forms of translation. I contend that Dramaturgical translation does not merely transpose words, cultural notions or dramatic structures from one language into another,[28] but rather *theatre into theatre*. All polysystemic and polyvalent theatrical and extra-theatrical considerations that imbue a potential performance text within a certain reality convention are transferred wholesale through a process of transcodification and modification into a different polysystem operating within a different reality-convention. This is true for any kind of theatre but has a stronger impact in the post-dramatic than in the dramatic theatre, as the verbal layer loses its superior position and draws attention to the all, equally valent, audio-visual constituents of the work. Dramaturgical translation automatically entails the notion of *applied dramaturgy*, which defines the meaning of dramaturgy in this article, and which denotes a dramaturgical interpretative strategy anchored, in contrast to academic interpretation, in purely practical and mostly incidental considerations emanating from the intended stage realization. In other words, dramaturgical repertorial choices in public theatres, production dramaturgy or deliberations underlying devising processes are predominantly 'circumstantial' (viz. accounting for a host of contextual – both inner- and extra-theatrical – conditions), rather than text oriented.[29] This corresponds to Schechner's contention that 'the work of those doing the production is to re-scene the play not as the writer might have envisioned it but as immediate circumstances reveal it'.[30] Bearing in mind the above reflections and concepts, we may now turn to the discussion of current dramaturgical approaches as, inter alia, emerging from the above interviews with German dramaturgs.

Fidelity to the source text

The most salient dramaturgical translation type that promotes fidelity to the source text might be described thus:

'Literary' adherence – regardless of cuts and some editing – to the lexis, syntax, semantics, and general narrative structure of the play.

This approach seems to be highly exceptional in a theatrical environment saturated by post-dramatic experimentation such as seen in German-speaking theatre in the past decade. At the end scene of Michael Thalheimer's above-mentioned 'subversive' directing of Lessing's *Emilia Galotti* at the *Deutsches Theater* in Berlin, Emilia, instead of committing suicide 'by proxy' at her father's hands in order to protect her *Tugend* (viz. her middle-class chastity), lets herself be seduced by the debauched aristocratic society. In my interview with Hermann Beil, dramaturg of the *Berliner Ensemble*, I asked him about Thalheimer's approach. Beil answered:

> I would have never done something like this, because . . . I have too much respect for Lessing. I would never dare to give the play a counter-interpretation. In Thalheimer's virtuoso production, a directing concept is being imposed on the play, and does not emerge from it.[31]

According to Beil and Hans-Joachim Ruckhäberle, the veteran dramaturg of the *Bayerisches Staatssauspiel*,[32] the dramaturg is perceived as a kind of Enlightenment *didascolos*, who seeks to bestow a Humanist message imbued in classical plays, regardless of their theatrical presentation mode. Moreover, what both Beil and Ruckhäberle seem to ignore is that even the most loyal dramaturgical translation of the verbal layer is necessarily thwarted because of the difficulty of transposing the hybrid composition, connotations and emotive charges of the original text, as well as because any play is to a greater or lesser degree de- and re-contextualized in its re-production. This happens not only because it is subordinated to the director's peculiar conception, but because of the changing cultural circumstances. Thus, for instance, Emilia's betrayal of the bourgeois moral values seems in twenty-first-century terms much more plausible than her suicide, and hence in keeping with Lessing's interpretation.

Fidelity to the dramaturg

A good example of the opposite pole to the former approach is the Complicite's *The Elephant Vanishes* (2004). I allow myself a deviation from focusing on the German-speaking theatre both because this is the most appropriate example to prove the point to be made, as well as in order to demonstrate the impact that German dramaturgical post-dramatic practices had on other performative cultures (such as on the plays of the British 'Brutalists', especially Sarah Kane and Mark Ravenhill). In an interview with Synne Behrndt, Steven Canny elaborates upon the process of a triadically focused translation – lingual, phenomenological and medial – of Haruki Murakami's series of short stories into the Complicite's production. Canny delineates the following heuristic approach:

> I was literally . . . underlining things in the book, picking out ideas that I thought would work, then putting them on pieces of paper, putting them on computer files under different tags.

> ... I started to cut apart Murakami's book into very, very short chunks that I knew I could give to an actor, and that they could create a scene from or have a thought about. . . . I would take little chunks of text and give it to the translators and they would re-translate it into Japanese. They would then give that text to the [Japanese] actors who would then present the scene to us. . . . And we would then have a thought about it . . . and then the translators would translate it back into English. I would then shape it into something resembling a text that I'd know Complicite could work from in English.[33]

In this typical devising process, the dramaturg apparently reverses the process of conventional authorship. Inspired by a coherent literary text and by his acquaintance with the performers, he stimulates a hybrid and fragmented chain of actions and then montages it into a coherent play-script. This, however, is not done in order to complete a fully fledged dramatic text (or 'adaptation' in the usual sense), but for the sake of translating the unstructured language of the rehearsals into a structure that moulds the creative energy of the group, as the dramaturg construes it, into an actable performative process. It is thus an original creation in the sense that it reflects the personality and interpretative choices of the dramaturg.

Similar experiences of turning from a subsidiary functionary into a kind of synonym for an open-ended and frameless post-dramatic production have been reported by several dramaturgs whom I interviewed. Stefanie Carp, a leading dramaturg, while working with Christoph Marthaler at the Zürich *Schuspielhaus*, presented herself to me as a 'projector', one who translates the *mise-en-scènic* ideas of her artistic director into her own meta-texts, as she called them.[34] Marvin Carlson refers to the 'often close and long-lasting' ties in the German theatre between directors and dramaturgs, yet notes with regard to the bond between Marthaler, Carp and stage-designer Anna Viebrock: '. . . this trio is still an exceptional one and has developed an aesthetic that clearly owes much to each of the three'.[35] Marthaler himself referred to Carp as much more than a dramaturg: 'She is coauthor.'[36] One of their numerous joint enterprises was *Groundings* (2003), a satirical cabaret-like collage of sketches interspersed with songs (Marthaler often uses popular songs and classical music as lyrics for the most incoherent documentary or dialogical texts) on the bankruptcy of the Swiss national company Swissair, due to failing management, intermingled with critique on the *Zürich Schauspielhaus* board of directors that fired the provocative and aesthetically subversive Marthaler and Carp. In an interview with me, Stefanie Carp claimed that 'since I am acquainted with the impact of Marthaler's directing projects, it is much better that I simply write what he needs'. Having a keen director's intuition, she tailored the text to the specific cast, so that

> each actor could find his character. And then Christoph, as always, started with suggesting songs, choreographic inventions, improvisation, and I knew from experience what he would need, for instance, some crescendo-structured dialogical scenes for board-meetings, or a sketch about a flight-delay that hyperbolically grows from 35 seconds to 10 days, or a self-complimenting text of the company's managers about the Swiss flight history, etc.[37]

Thus, Carp became an equal co-creator, instead of providing ordinary services of a production dramaturg in the dramatic theatre. Irina Szodruch, a young dramaturg at the *Schaubühne* in Berlin – a mainstream theatre that realizes post-dramatic tenets by interrelating and fusing spoken drama, dance theatre, film, video art and theoretical discourses – ascribed this metamorphosis to the fact that 'the repertoire of the public theatres in Germany today includes forms that but a few years ago would have been considered "Fringe,"'[38] all of which are conceptualized, devised and even produced by the omnipotent dramaturg. This asserts itself, apart from the developing function of the dramaturg as festival curator, in the inner-theatrical scene, as elaborated by Bettina Milz:

> It doesn't matter whether you work as a freelance or in the subsidized theatre, as dramaturg in Germany in recent years you were responsible for the classical aspects of dramaturgy, and at the same time you were the constructor of the production, the inventor of the structure, the inventor of projects, a cook, a producer, inventor of marketing strategies, a mediator in catastrophes of various kinds, responsible for budgets, contracts, inventor of novel interaction forms with the audience.[39]

Furthermore, the loss of the authority and authorship of a pre-ordained dramatic text creates a gap of uncertainty and sourcelessness that is filled by the personality of the dramaturg. Dramaturgs' traditional 'objectivity' and remote and liminal involvement as researchers and onlookers at rehearsals becomes subjective, total and holistic. This is because their perforce selective and idiosyncratically biased documentation of the proceedings, which create, according to André Lepecki, 'the memory of the production,'[40] renders them metonymies of the work in which their consciousness is intrinsically grafted. *From interpretive translators of an external text, dramaturgs become translators of themselves as text. Thus, dramaturgical translation becomes self-reflexive and self-referential. It translates itself.*[41]

'Anti'-translation

The second basic approach to dramaturgical translation has had further repercussions that affect even mainstream theatre, although in Germany, the demarcation between 'conventional' repertory theatres and independent groups is deliberately blurred. In January 2010, I saw the Munich *Kammerspiele* Shorsh Camerun's *Konzert zur Revolution* [*Concert for a Revolution*]. An entire philharmonic orchestra in formal concert attire, actors reciting turn-of-the-twentieth-century proletarian and avant-garde poetry, stage hands building a useless and unused two-storey high building while being bullied and urged by their aggressive boss, a huge chorus and video excerpts, converged to devise a concretized *Weltanschauung* of the anarchist auteur dramaturg. He strolled on the stage and in the videos in Tolstoyan peasant clothes distributing Marxist leaflets against consumerism. The spectators were provoked into becoming enraged spect-actors having been exposed to violent verbal, sensory and visceral rhetoric as a protest against a smug and commoditized reality convention. Thus, *the dramaturgy of the performance text becomes 'anti-' or 'counter-translation'*. First, because what pretends to be a rehearsal, the process of creating the performance, is in fact the performance itself. Second, 'counter translation' asserts itself in renouncing the intention of bringing the implied spectators closer to the spectacle's foreign stage language through a familiar cultural terminology. Instead, the aesthetic immunity of the implied spectators is undermined either by problematizing the dramaturgical translation's intelligibility or by blatantly rejecting established interpretations of familiar masterpieces. The spectators are forced to face crude reality instead of a beautified reality convention, as dramaturgs employ criteria such as those expounded by Tilman Raabke: 'We ask ourselves how to translate the play today in the most reality-loyal and contemporary manner possible.'[42] And 'reality loyal' means *eo ipso* not only apparent disloyalty to the source text but deliberate disloyalty to the implied spectators' preconceptions and collective identity as imbued in the prevalent reality convention by professing a heightened yet unacceptable mimetic loyalty to it.

A paradigmatic example is Feridun Zaimoglu's (a Turkish dramaturg living and working in Germany) and Günther Senkel's extremely abbreviated rewriting of Shakespeare's *Othello* into a vulgar German-Turkish Berlin argot. This dramaturgical translation served as the textual version and director's logbook for Luk Perceval's contemporaneous staging of *Othello* at the Munich

Kammerspiele (2003). The production was performed on a bare stage, a space simultaneously physical and mental, reifying Leslie Hill and Helen Paris's postmodern notion of 'placelessness'[43] – a virtual place whose emptiness, nothingness and nowhereness highlighted the existential alienated and identity-less *condition humaine* of the characters. This was sustained by an apparently out-of-context pianist seated mid-stage, who played and shouted in a neo-expressionist style. His very presence and vociferous interventions drowned out the actors' voices and distracted the audience's attention by engendering a dual, synchronous focus, at the same time conducing to an interaction of the performance constituents as autonomous, disintegrated elements, thus constituting an obvious post-dramatic vehicle. The pianist's agonized, ritually connoted chanting articulated the socially suppressed voices of Othello's (and the black Emilia's) African origins.

Zaimoglu engaged here with his own biographic 'otherness' – that of the privileged Turkish outcast in the xenophobic German society. In Perceval's production, Othello, as impersonated by Thomas Thieme, was not a black, noble warrior but a white, elderly, fat, impotent and pathetic anti-hero derisively renamed 'Shoko', who is sexually harassed by an adolescent and horny Desdemona (Julia Jentsch). Thus, on the one hand, the production emphasized Shoko's ostensibly perfect assimilation as a paragon of the 'culturally superior' hegemonic Venetian society, thereby sarcastically alluding to the hypocritical German society. On the other hand, however, this approach also emphasized the characters' awareness that his whiteness is but a histrionic mask for the part that he acts on the void, heterotopic, barren, imagistic stage, of his exploitation as a *Gastarbeiter* (guest worker) or hired army general by the white society; Zaimoglu seems to see no difference. The tragedy of the foreign author dramaturg, as well as of his theatrical agent, lies in the fact that the outsider – especially the privileged and successful one such as Othello or Zaimoglu – is neither capable of being his authentic self nor is he capable of internalizing the 'white' mask that he himself has grafted onto his face, as Desdemona hurls at him in the last scene in Zaimoglu's, not Shakespeare's, words: 'You can be told a thousand times that you are whiter than most white people. . . . Yet you keep on insisting that you are black!'

The most outstanding evidence of the dramaturg's self-textualization and appropriation of the Shakespearean source text lies in the replacement of the bard's lofty poetic style with the lowly gutter German-Turkish slang. The language is unmetered, lewd, flat, apparently 'user-friendly' in its colloquial nature, yet deliberately subversive and revolting, abounding in coarse and colloquial expressions such as *geil, ficken, Arsch, klasse, Fotze*, etc., thus manifesting its 'anti-translational' and hostile character.

Through such means of vandalizing an icon of 'high' European culture, Zaimoglu appropriates and colonizes the symbolic capital of his implied spectators. This production, rather than affirming an updated conception of Shakespeare, subverts the classical notion of the play that is inextricably bound with a phenomenological model of an hierarchical order degrades this order by sullying the language and draining it of any meaning, within an intentionally compressed and 'functional' plot structure, precisely by rendering it as 'explicitly translated' and as unequivocally intelligible as possible.

Such an appropriation of the classical play by the dramaturg-as-text typifies contemporary German dramaturgy. The most salient agent of this dramaturgical conception is the above-mentioned dramaturg and philosopher Carl Hegemann, who together with the other *enfant terrible* of the German theatre, Frank Castorf, led the experimental *Volksbühne* in East Berlin for almost 20 years. In a series of iconoclastic, deconstructed, synaesthetic, conceptually overloaded, and new media sustained post-dramatic (anti-) translations of Russian, German and American masterpieces, they displaced the diachronic-narrative-fictional structure of the original works by creating a common synchronous consciousness space for performers and implied spectators alike.

These strategies and others employed by anti-translation dramaturgies deprive the implied spectators of their 'sacred' anonymity and ensuing immunity. Hegemann sees the existential rationale of the theatre in comparison with the digital technologies, in the live encounter between the bodily presence of actors and performers in their real identities, as the absolute essence of performance and post-dramatic theories.[44] To devise such a reality is the main task of the dramaturg.

A striking implementation of Hegemann's ideas can be found in his and Castorf's hybrid, devised and visual dramaturgy, containing foreign text implantations, converting Tennessee Williams's realistic-psychological *A Streetcar Named Desire* into their own self-referential nostalgic satire, renamed *Endstation Amerika/Endstation America* (2000), about non-adjusting East-European and East-German hard-core communists. The joint reality convention of the performer and the East-German theatre visitor is obvious. Stanley Kovalsky in this production is neither the dramatic character nor its famous Marlon Brando image, but someone much closer to the actor: an elderly, anti-heroic, down-and-out German-Polish type from the streets of cosmopolitan Berlin, presenting himself as an ex-member of *Solidarnosc* who, through the devising mediation of the dramaturg, delivers nostalgic tirades about his friendship with Lech Walensa. When he gets angry, he very slowly and deliberately breaks plates in a ceremonial fashion so that splinters fly into the spectators' faces as if in order to impel the irruption of the real, convert Richard Schechner's notion of 'restored behavior'[45] into a deconstructed, deictic, performatively self-conscious, ironic act and drive Victor Turner's analysis of the ritualized, 'showing' manner of performance *ad absurdum*.[46] The originally Southern belle Blanche Dubois became a German Democratic Republic freak, whose neurotic and fervent nostalgia for her proletarian past asserts itself ironically in goosestep marching to the sound of an imaginary Soviet military band. In both cases, the seams between actor and role, theatre visitor and spectator are torn open, and the theatrical translation turns from an objective mimesis of a detached dramatic metaphor into an ultra-subjective neo-expressionist materialization of the psyche and collective consciousness of the dramaturg/translator as text. In this respect, Hegemann and Castorf's radical dramaturgical approach creates an ultimate synergy between the aesthetic and the social, upon whose interaction the very existence of theatre and performance depends, as described by Richard Schechner:

> Every social drama is imagined in terms of underlying aesthetic principles and specific theatrical-rhetorical techniques. Reciprocally, each culture's aesthetic theatre is performed in terms of the underlying processes of social interaction.[47]

In summary, to wind up the journey conducted in this article through various contemporaneous approaches to dramaturgical translation, it seems appropriate to cite a comment made by Carl Hegemann at one of our meetings: 'Theatre is the model for the fundamental tension between determinism and liberty, between impotence and omnipotence. It keeps us alive because it shows us what will annihilate us.'[48] If we apply this observation to the dramaturg/translator as text, then one might say that in performance and post-dramatic theatre, the dramaturgs are the icon of the stage art. They are the catalysts of the absolute freedom and apocalyptic anarchy that concomitantly underlie the constitution of the performance event. They, especially hyper-subjective, 'anti-translation' dramaturgs, incite, legitimize and embody the artistic and existential chaos of the creative process. They are also, however, the ones that guard this deconstructed process, against ultimate destruction. They constitute the factor that, in a sense, fixates the fixation-resistant, open-ended process, determines its borders and turns it into a performance that safeguards existence because, in Heiner Müller's words: '*Denn das Schöne bedeutet das mögliche Ende der Schrecken*' ('the beautiful signifies the possible end of the horrors').[49]

And yet, to try and grasp the eruption of the post-dramatic German theatre in the 1990s in more concrete terms, one must take into account that it is deeply anchored in the post-traumatic shock caused by the ramifications of the fall of the Berlin Wall, the collapse of the GDR, the loss of Marxist identity and the upsurge of the brutal, alienating capitalist economy and *Weltanschauung*, as well as the consequences of globalization, migration and ensuing xenophobiac trends and the like. These are the symptoms of a society whose centre cannot hold, who once again looks up to the theatre as the *Agora* or *Forum Urbanum* where one cannot rest content with mere 'entertainment', where the public debate becomes an integral part of the repertoire, and where the experimental enterprise is not only a provocative, subversive gesture, but an attempt to transform the theatre again into a politically meaningful institution.[50] In this climate, the function of the dramaturg becomes intellectually detached, and at the same time political, pragmatic and reality-oriented, or as dramaturg Stefanie Carp self-reflexively puts it echoing Piscator and Brecht: 'It becomes daily more and more important to deal dramaturgically in the political sense, in the framework of a political ethic. I mean, theatre is after all a public meeting place, and there you encounter, or have to encounter, statements, public statements.'[51]

However, how do the political expectations from theatre and dramaturgy benefit from the unique faculties of post-dramatic aesthetics? This has to do with the relentlessly inquisitive nature of the post-dramatic, with its laboratorial, sceptical character that questions the most basic and preliminary ingredients of the medium, that thematizes the very encounter between performers and audience, conducing to a situation in which, according to Primavesi, 'rather than fixating on the practice and ideology of politics, the *politics of practice* itself comes into play'.[52] This means, again in Heiner Müller's words in the wake of an idea by Godard, that to make theatre political is not a question of contents, 'but of how you deal with the contents, namely, a question of form'.[53] And in our context, it is not a question of the dramaturg versus form, text or import, but of the dramaturg as form, text and import.

Motion III

Performance in/of Social Spaces

Re: Location

Sharon Aronson-Lehavi

The question as to where a theatre performance is located seems to have a simple answer: in the theatre, on the stage, on site. We are accustomed to accepting a frame designed by the creators of a performance, which demarcates our understanding of its location, and we recognize the signifiers that tell us which spatial elements are supposed to be included in our experience and which are not. Theoretically and phenomenologically, however, this is a much more complex question.[1] Before theatre studies became a discipline, the performance was located in the *text*, and theatre was studied as 'drama' and as a subcategory of literature. With the rise of 'theatre studies' during the twentieth century, the performance was 'relocated' from 'page to stage' but semiotic approaches still regarded the stage as a signifier of a 'fictional world' and therefore – theoretically at least – the performance continued to be located in the text and continued to be conceptualized as 'text'. However, both the written text and the stage as the locus of performance were seriously challenged by performance studies. Emphasizing the real and performative characteristics of theatre not only once again shifted the location of performance from the fictional realm to the real happening and from image to body, but also, at the same time, destabilized an option for determining the location of a theatrical experience at all.

Accordingly, the phenomenological question I pose here is: what is the location of a performance? On the stage? In the performers' bodies? In the bodies of the spectators? In the space that opens up between performers and spectators? In the larger geographical, political and contextual space that surrounds the performance? In all of the above? And if so, where and how do we draw the boundaries in order to avoid generalizations that overshadow analysis of artistic creativity and intentionality? Or, perhaps, as I would like to suggest, rather than determining a fixed location on the one hand, or arguing for 'dislocation' of performance, it should be understood as an ongoing process of *relocation*; an aesthetic and social experience that is in constant state of motion between creators, performers, spectators and environment. I am interested in the interrelations and interdependence of the various locations that construct the experience for both creators and spectators.

The case study that evoked these questions and which I shall discuss in the following pages is that of Performance Art Platform, an Israeli venue dedicated to performance art, under the artistic direction of Tamar Raban. Performance Art Platform has been located since 2004 within the Tel Aviv Central Bus Station in the rundown southern part of the city, having been relocated to this space following a fire that destroyed the group's former premises. This relocation not only opened a new era in the ensemble's history and creativity, but also compelled spectators to contend with the unavoidable impact of the bus station area on their experience, even when the performances did not interact with this social frame, at least intentionally as in site-specific work. Accordingly, I use the term 'relocation' in this essay in three ways, which all demonstrate the unsettledness of performance as both practice and object of research: (1) 'relocation': as a defining event in the specific history of Performance Art Platform, which did not occur as a matter of choice. As I shall explain, although working within the bus station went well with Raban's understanding of performance as socially engaged, her art is aesthetically sophisticated and could be categorized as 'high culture', and she did not attempt to create performance 'for' this area; (2) 're: location': the social, aesthetic and experiential meanings of the actual location of Performance Art Platform inside the bus station, and its impact on both artistic creativity and spectators' experience; and (3) 'relocation' as a theoretical concept for performance analysis, emphasizing the dynamic and relational aspects of a performance's location and environment. Although my analysis examines a very special case, this methodology can be a useful tool for analysing artistic experiences in relational dimensions, *whether or not* they are site-specific events or intentionally created in what Nicolas Bourriaud formulates as 'relational art', which is 'an art taking as its theoretical horizon the realm of human interactions and its social context rather than the assertion on an independent and private symbolic space'.[2] In addition, I examine not only the spectators' experience of a performance but also the location's osmotic impact on artists and the ways it permeates into creativity. While this theoretical approach might be relevant for many forms of art, it gains specific importance in the case of performance, because of the liveness of the medium, its susceptibility to change and its sensitivity to human encounters and interactions.

I find support for this relational methodology in what environment-behaviour and place studies scholar David Seamon terms 'environmental embodiment', which, drawing on Maurice Merleau-Ponty's phenomenology of perception, is 'the various lived ways, sensorily and motility-wise, that the body in its pre-reflective perceptual presence engages and synchronizes with the world at hand, especially its architectural and environmental aspects'.[3] 'In short,' Seamon, following Merleau-Ponty, explains that 'perceptual experience always involves a continuously shifting figure and ground housed in a broader constellation of significances and actions'. Similarly, Henri Lefebvre theorizes that 'the form of social space is encounter, assembly, simultaneity. But what assembles, or what is assembled? The answer is: everything that there is *in space*. . . . Everything: living beings, things, objects, works, signs, and symbols'.[4] Accordingly, the first step of my analysis is to examine and to elucidate the 'broader constellation' and the complexity of the environment in the case of Performance Art Platform and its bus-station habitat. Spatial osmosis, relational affect and environmental embodiment are the basis for analysing aesthetic choices and ethical implications that are the outcome of creating socially engaged performance within such an area, even when the performances are high culture and not site specific.[5]

Relocations: The history of Performance Art Platform

Performance Art Platform, a platform for the advancement of interdisciplinary art in Israel, founded by the Shelter 209 Foundation in memory of Dan Zakhem, was established at first as 'Ensemble 209' in 1988 by performance artists Tamar Raban, Anat Schen and Dan Zakhem (d. 1994). Their first venue was inside the north Tel Aviv bomb shelter no. 209 that was made available by the municipality, and which became the name of the ensemble. In 2001 they moved to a space inside a huge industrial building (Beit Mercazim, in Hebrew 'House of Centers'), in the south of Tel Aviv, which the municipality turned into an artists' space, and there they worked side by side with other studios and dance ensemble spaces; this second venue was named 'Performance Art Platform' ('Bamat Meizag').[6] When a fire destroyed the entire site in 2003, they had to be relocated once more. In 2004, Raban and her ensemble moved to a space inside the New Bus Station in the rundown south of Tel Aviv where they have been creating performance art during the past decade. At this location, Performance Art Platform is home to Ensemble 209, and both are artistically led by Raban. The ensemble creates experimental and innovative performance art pieces, three of which I shall discuss below. In addition, the Platform offers performance art workshops, hosts artists from Israel and abroad, and runs an annual international performance art festival.[7] In all three locations, the bomb shelter, Beit Mercazim and the bus station, there is a clear link connecting an artistic credo dedicated to fringe and experimental art to geographical fringe locations. There is also a link connecting the transformation of industrial spaces into artistic ones (as has happened in so many places in Europe and the United States), the parallel tendency to artistic experimentalism and the support offered by the Tel Aviv Municipality and the Ministry of Culture who have been willing to fund art in such spaces, in the hope that artists will contribute to upgrading the social fabric of the area by virtue of being there and by attracting culturally aware audiences. This was certainly what motivated the municipality to offer Raban and other artists a space inside the (new) bus station. I emphasize this point because moving into this space after the fire was not a matter of artistic choice as in site-specific cases, and also because many of the other artists who at first moved to the new bus station had left after only a short while.[8]

The bus station area, unlike the group's two former spaces, is itself performative, and as such has had an impact on both creativity and reception in complex ways that go beyond the usual relationship between a surrounding area and a building that frames artistic creativity. It is performative because the bus station is an utterly heterogeneous social space, which thousands of people cross daily, and more importantly, it is located in a neighbourhood peopled mostly by underprivileged migrant workers from poor countries, who are by and large 'transparent' to the Israeli society. Although it is an extremely lively heterotopia, the bus station is, as I shall detail below, a rundown and architecturally troubling facility which is home to a distinct subculture. Despite, or perhaps because of those characteristics, such a space becomes not only inspirational but also performative, turning Performance Art Platform into a unique kind of a 'theatre within a theatre'. If *theatre* (in the original Greek, *teatron*) is 'a seeing place', being located within the bus station – where life touches life – necessitates the act of seeing, by artists and spectators alike.

Re: Location: The Tel Aviv New Central Bus Station

There is a strong dissonance between the highly aestheticized performances created at Performance Art Platform and its surroundings. A long grey corridor full of vacant shops and graffiti leads to the performance space. This corridor through which spectators pass on their way to the performance space, having encountered first the bustling area of the bus station, testifies to the grand failure of what originally was planned as the largest and most impressive 'Grand Central' of the Middle East and the biggest building in Israel, built on an 11-acre lot and which opened to the public in 1993. It was supposed to be the 'gateway to Israel' as envisioned by architect Ram Carmi (1931–2013), a modern version of the biblical 'shaar ha ir' (city gate). In his *White City, Black City* Sharon Rotbard quotes a 1992 interview Carmi gave to Roni Hadar in *Tel Aviv*, a local weekly: 'The inspiration for building the central bus station came to me from the biblical concept of the city gate. That's where the wise men, judges, and old men sat . . . it is supposed to be the gate to the country'.[9] The project that was originally envisioned by entrepreneur Arye Piltz already in the 1960s, and which took decades to realize, was according to Carmi intended to be a gleamingly white architectural edifice full of upscale shops and cultural centres. The idea was that by replacing its neighbour, the poor and dirty 'Old Bus Station', the new one would turn the whole area, the neglected south of Tel Aviv, into an attractive and vibrant district. This, however, was not to be the case. The New Bus Station is a gigantic six-floor grey concrete mega-structure plus an underground level, surrounded by four big streets, and it overshadows all human proportions. Its complicated architecture, which includes innumerable corridors and levels, is utterly disorienting. Following its failure as a merchandizing and cultural centre, hundreds of spaces are vacant, and many others are home to a huge variety of small businesses, including shops, kiosks, tattoo parlours and enterprises that serve the migrant workers and their communities. In addition, the migrant worker communities use spaces in the station for Christmas markets, karaoke competitions and other forms of popular performances and entertainment, especially over weekends. The surrounding area is otherwise notorious for its impoverished population and high crime rates, including drugs and prostitution. Rather than facilitating gentrification, the new bus station reconstituted this area as the backyard of Tel Aviv. Notwithstanding this development, and even though this is how this area is perceived by the majority of Tel-Avivians, the bus station has at the same time evolved a unique atmosphere, which is quite different from any typical Israeli locale especially because of its striking heterogeneity, its chaotic arrangement and its lack of aesthetic appeal.

It is difficult to conceive how surprisingly close this place is to an extremely fashionable neighbourhood of the city, called 'the heart of Tel Aviv', an upscale

Figure 3 The Tel Aviv New Central Bus Station. Photo by the author.

area which was declared by UNESCO in 2003 to be an architectural world heritage site, and yet how distant and unvisited by local people the new bus station is. Entering the new bus station is a disorienting experience, since one instantly becomes aware of the poor and neglected condition of the area hand in hand with the multicultural mixture of identities that one sees, the polyglot languages that one hears and the energetic dynamism of all who frequent the bus station.

It is this mixture of impressions and experiences that inspires and infiltrates consciously and subconsciously into the work of performance artists such as Raban. Raban understands performance as socially engaged by its very nature, as an art form that is sensitive to human conditions and that opens up to situations in their complexity rather than shutting them out. Indeed, the first work that Raban's ensemble created in this space, *The Second Law of Thermodynamics* (2005), which she co-directed with Guy Gutman, took the bus station area as the point of reference and the source of inspiration for the work. Even though the performance took place within the intimate space of Performance Art

Platform, it is easy to see the relationship between the two spaces. It is in later performances, such as *Old Wives' Tales: Rise Woman and Make Us a Cake*, also co-created with Gutman (2006), *Ding Dong* (2010), a reworking of the first act of Lorca's *House of Bernarda Alba*, and other pieces, that the direct reference to the bus station is harder to trace, and yet, as I will now discuss, these performances reflect and embody the environment in profound ways.

Discipline and difference: *The Second Law of Thermodynamics* (2005)

This performance was actually a set of lessons, taught to an audience of about 40 spectators who were placed in a highly aestheticized sunken class surrounded by seven teachers/performers. The title of the piece, *The Second Law of Thermodynamics*, which is also the title of one of the lessons, refers to the physics law according to which entropy, the general disorder of a system, always increases. By examining social and educational systems in this performance in social terms, Raban's idea had to do with the ways these systems try to impose order, discipline and sameness where in fact difference, otherness and alterity disable any attempt to do so, as these factors always rise to the surface.

At the beginning of the performance, each member of the audience received a notebook which also served as the performance programme, and in which one could find the various lessons, the ID cards of the performers and a quiz that one had to fill in at the end of the performance. Significantly, the notebook was designed just like the easily recognizable notebooks all Israelis used in school for many years, and on which a familiar slogan was printed: 'We all say "thank you," "please," and "excuse me"; one nation – a beautiful nation'.[10] This slogan that was used in a naïve and optimistic manner in Israel's early days – a time when Israeli society regarded itself as a 'melting pot' for its many immigrants and newcomers from around the world – is treated here with subversive irony, especially in the context of the social environment of the performance.

One of the first lessons in the performance is based on personal recollections which each performer shares with the audience, and which have to do with his/her experiences in buses or transit stations. The performers who come from different backgrounds and homelands (Israeli – both Jewish and Arab, Russian, Ethiopian and Turkish), often recall events at those stations as traumatic and sometimes humiliating; these are almost always incidents in which, although they take place in a completely anonymous and transitory milieu, paradoxically, the performers are sharply encountered with their own identity, with their sense of alienation, with their need to explain who they are, and with their being marked as 'others'. For example, Yana Fridman, who was born in Kazakhstan and arrived in Israel in 1994, tells the following story:

> I was rushing to the Ministry of Absorption. I was riding on Bus 31. On King George St., a little before the stop, I rang the bell. It was broken and the driver drove past the stop. I panicked. I was afraid of being late. I was eight months pregnant with Tamar. I knew I wouldn't be able to run all the way back with my big belly. I screamed for the driver to stop, "I want to give birth" [Hebrew: *laledet*]. The driver stopped immediately, in the middle of the street. I found myself surrounded by women who asked me questions I didn't understand. I didn't know what labor pains were, I didn't understand what "breaking water" they were talking about. I just wanted to get off the bus [Hebrew: *laredet*]. Today Tamar is seven years old and my Hebrew is a bit better. Yana.[11]

Although this event is a result of a mere linguistic mistake, a trifle, such experiences are formative in one's perception of oneself vis-à-vis society and it is precisely the impersonal framework that enhances a sense of otherness.

Other lessons in the performance include sharing and teaching childhood songs in various languages, language lessons, 'hygiene and cleanliness' instructions, gymnastics and more. Since the performance focuses on education systems and childhood memories, especially those originally experienced as children, and now relived from an adult perspective of the performers, a troubling and unsettling feeling of nostalgia and naiveté is mixed with a growing recognition of the critical perspective the performance adds to these memories. Thus, the performance constantly navigates between reconstruction and memory on the one hand and deconstruction and a realization of the impossibility to organize everything into a coherent system on the other. It also necessitates spectators to realize their own constructions of identity through the "lessons" as well as to become aware of the passers-by they encounter on the way in and out of the theatre.

In the programme, Raban specifically mentions the bus station as a source of inspiration for this performance:

> While Performance Art Platform was being built in an abandoned space on the ground floor of the Central Bus Station, we were given a few rooms for temporary use. These were empty classrooms belonging to a college on the sixth floor that had closed down. While wandering around the station, I discovered that amongst all

the different kinds of shops and kiosks, there are 40 Russian language bookshops (and one Hebrew bookshop) and a similar number of hair salons, specializing in a variety of communities – Ethiopian salons, Russian salons, and Philippine salons.... Between all these are the empty shops that have been rearranged for morning use as classrooms. In these classrooms, mainly new immigrants with "unnecessary" professions and social patterns prepare, according to the need of the moment, for their new positions – "vocational retraining" as it is called in the professional jargon.[12]

Significantly, the performance not only mirrors the sense of social alienation Raban experienced in the bus station, but also takes it further by defamiliarizing local notions of education and identity; and through the stories of her performers she voices those of dwellers of the bus station area. This is an example not of a 'site specific' performance that intentionally locates itself in a certain site but rather of the specificity of a site that permeates into the process of creation, and leads to an osmotic and relational dynamic I term 'relocation'.

Community and creativity: *Old Wives' Tales: Rise Woman and Make Us a Cake* (2006)

Whereas in the first performance the relationship between the bus station and the ensemble's creativity is clearly evident, in their following performance in this venue, *Old Wives' Tales: Rise Woman and Make us a Cake* (2006), this relationship is seemingly less clear. As can be seen in the image, members of the audience watch through a glass window a group of bakers at work in the back of a patisserie. The two people sitting and watching in the first row are Raban and Gutman, the co-directors who also perform in the piece (See Fig. 4 on page 114).

Old Wives' Tales is a textual and visual collage, made up of children's tales by the Grimm Brothers, stories by Italo Calvino, W. B. Yeats and other writers, personal recollections, and songs about women, femininity, childhood, cakes, ovens, feeding and eating. It takes place in the kitchen (the backspace) of a fictional but real patisserie. In the patisserie that was designed and built (by Oren Sagiv) especially for the performance and located inside the ensemble's performance space, a professional chocolatier, a group of performers who learned bakery especially for the performance, a young child and two mentally challenged performers prepare and bake pastries throughout the performance. The baking takes place before an audience of about forty spectators who watch, desire and eventually eat the desserts.[13] The patisserie's kitchen is located behind

Figure 4 *Old Wives' Tales: Rise Woman and Make Us a Cake*. Created by Tamar Raban and Guy Gutman. Ensemble 209, Performance Art Platform, Tel Aviv, 2006. Front Row: Guy Gutman and Tamar Raban (with their backs to the audience); Behind the glass screen, l-r: Yael Even-Zohar, Yossi Doister, Talya Lewin, Daniel Brook, Yana Fridman, Effi Ben-David. Photo by Fartush.

a glass window through which the spectators can watch the kitchen at work, while Raban and Gutman perform in front of the glass window, in the same space where the audience is seated. Employing the act of preparing the desserts, *Old Wives' Tales* constitutes a performance about reconnecting to childhood memories (good and bad) and at the same time about the communal creativity of performance itself.

The performance space, especially the highly aestheticized section of the patisserie kitchen behind the glass, seems escapist; an almost cinematic or even illusionist image of an Italian or French bakery, definitely not reminiscent of a typical Israeli locale. The set, the activity and creativity, the music and the European aroma all over, emphasized by the hallway at the rear with the red carpet, vanilla walls and the staircase that as in a realistic illusionist set leads to the 'front space' of the patisserie, quite easily enable spectators to sink into this fantasy of beauty and chocolate, and forget where they just came from, and where they actually are. And yet, the continuous trembling of the buses that pass underneath every now and then prevents such an option.

When the performance begins, the kitchen area is darkened. For about ten minutes, the spectators who listen to Raban and Gutman reading a tale by Yeats about witches preparing cakes see themselves reflected in the glass window, a materialized version of the 'fourth wall'. Suddenly a small light goes on in the rear, and the staircase area is revealed, evoking a strong sense of disorientation.

Still under the impression of the bus station, one isn't sure for a moment whether the two figures that quickly pass in and out of that space are bus passengers passing by or part of the performance. Then, they enter and start assembling the kitchen, but this very moment heightens the uncertainty and relational spatiality of the locations that are experienced in this space within a space. The glass window is a 'fourth wall' that paradoxically emphasizes the act of seeing, of looking at someone or something who seems untouchable, who is there and not there at the same time, who is both real and fictive. This is an experience which is similar to that of looking through an imaginary transparent wall at the inhabitants of the bus station area, and is also reminiscent of Foucault's articulation of heterotopias in terms of a mirror:

> I believe that between utopias and these quite other sites, these heterotopias, there might be a sort of mixed, joint experience, which would be the mirror. The mirror is, after all, a utopia, since it is a placeless place. In the mirror, I see myself there where I am not, in an unreal, virtual space that opens up behind the surface; I am over there, there where I am not, a sort of shadow that gives my own visibility to myself, that enables me to see myself there where I am absent: such is the utopia of the mirror. But it is also a heterotopia in so far as the mirror does exist in reality, where it exerts a sort of counteraction on the position that I occupy. From the standpoint of the mirror I discover my absence from the place where I am since I see myself over there. Starting from this gaze that is, as it were, directed toward me, from the ground of this virtual space that is on the other side of the glass, I come back toward myself; I begin again to direct my eyes toward myself and to reconstitute myself there where I am. The mirror functions as a heterotopia in this respect: it makes this place that I occupy at the moment when I look at myself in the glass at once absolutely real, connected with all the space that surrounds it, and absolutely unreal, since in order to be perceived it has to pass through this virtual point which is over there.[14]

During the performance, the glass window is used in different ways that enable the connection between the spectators and the performers to become real. In many ways, the kitchen inside represents Raban's childhood memories, highlighted by the presence of a child performer; and Raban's own presence in front of the window is her means of bringing us into her world. When she wants us to sensually feel and touch that 'inside', a chocolate bowl that has just been prepared is served to her from inside, and in a Eucharistic act she feeds each member of the audience a biscuit which she takes out of her apron/body and dips in the chocolate. This act connects the spectators with the bakers, a community that performs throughout mini rituals of its own, some recognizable to everybody and some understood only by the performers/bakers, similar to the rituals that are carried out outside the performance space by the various communities of the bus station. At another moment, Raban and one of the actresses almost touch each other with their fingers but are kept apart by the glass window, touching and not touching at once. One of the strongest moments is when Raban enters the kitchen through a small hatch on the side. Finally, the glass window, this intermediate space, enables the group of performers to gaze at the audience as well. This is especially felt at moments when the mentally challenged actors who are free of the social/theatrical convention of ignoring the spectators examine the audience by leaning on the glass window and peeping back at the peeping audience. This window then challenges performers and spectators to peep, gaze, look and *see*. The glass window, it could be said, becomes the location of the performance, and its reflections extend beyond the immediate space of the performance to that of the wider social environment.

Relocation: *Foreign Work (Avoda Zara)*: *Siteseeing Performance* (2012)

Analyses of the type offered above are applicable to almost all of the performances created at Performance Art Platform, whether or not they literally refer to the bus station, as they all emphasize (in different ways) the immediacy of the event and its location. However, unlike the two works discussed above, one of the ensemble's most recent works, *Foreign Work*, which premiered in 2012, is a performance that straightforwardly relates to the bus station. This performance was created almost a decade after the arrival of Performance Art Platform at the bus station, and is a site-specific performance in a very full sense. It consists of a guided tour through the gigantic space of the station led by Raban and other members of the ensemble who put on mini-performances at different locations during the tour. One could possibly regard this performance to be a result of the group's gradual familiarity and sense of belonging to the larger area of the bus station, acquired from years of daily presence within this space, although it might well constitute a response to the reaction of Raban's spectators and visitors to the dissonance between the bus station area and the fringe cultural experiences offered by Performance Art Platform.

The tour lasts over two and a half hours of quick walking and it includes short visits to different spots in the station. These visits are coordinated in advance by Raban and include meetings with different people who actually work and dwell in the bus station, including a security guard, a portrait artist, a Russian bookstore seller, a Druze baker, a Yiddish cultural centre manager and others. In each place, the person introduces him/herself to the group and interacts with the group. In a manner different from the performances created inside Performance Art Platform, these people truly *perform themselves*, as they are not actors or artists. By introducing Raban's cohabitants to the spectators on the tour, she makes the enormous and alienating building more familiar and turns it into a human space, a space that, regardless of better or worse architectural and municipal decisions, is nonetheless home to real people.

The tour itself starts at Performance Art Platform, and after climbing up to the seventh floor the group gradually descends all the way down to the underground level, analogous to the seven levels of Dante's *Inferno*, as indeed Raban mentions. Towards the end of the performance, Raban takes the group to a surreal world at the underground level, a complex of five cinema halls that were in use for *five months only*. In one of them, a film is screened in which all the people who were met along the way tell their personal stories. Once again, theatre, cinema and magic are able to reveal and touch life in the most direct way while introducing the spectators to the complexities of this space.

It is clear that the Central Bus Station, with its complex social, political, urban and aesthetic contrasting realities, has inspired and influenced the work of Raban and her ensemble. Although this creativity does not necessarily 'change' or 'improve' the environment, I argue that it is nonetheless socially and politically effective and meaningful. Working daily and persistently in this area, finding and creating beauty and humanity in this space and bringing audiences to experience real life inside and outside the performance space, makes people who do not usually come to the station temporary residents of this place. This is an artistic act of turning a place into a *teatron*, a seeing place and a performative act of relocation.

Critically Civic: *Public Movement*'s Performative Activism

Daphna Ben-Shaul

Public Movement, a group established in 2006 by Israeli artists Dana Yahalomi and Omer Krieger, defines itself as a performative research body that investigates and stages actions or public choreographies in public spaces.[1] Performed in Israel, Europe and the United States, their actions offer a radical configuration of social and ritualistic patterns embedded in power structures, such as national and military ceremonies, as well as in civic behaviour such as demonstrations.

Topical and innovative, and equally equivocal and intriguing, PM's events are part of a fertile performance history of public activism. Its work is not directly derived from a specific model, but rather continues to explore the possibilities of what Claire Bishop ascribes to the vast social turn of the 90s – mainly as 'producer of situations' in public spaces and initiating 'projects' (instead of products or shows) in which the addressees function as participants (and not only viewers) and the action takes place with collaborators and agents.[2] Being, as Bishop observes, 'a *return* to the social',[3] it is possible to note numerous affinities to influential performative precedents. For example, some of PM's actions are based on re-enacting, while deconstructing, critical events – reminiscent of situations already created around the 1917 Russian Revolution, and especially the re-enactment *The Storming of the Winter Palace* (1920), directed by Nikolai Evreinov.[4] Keeping in mind Guy Debord's and the Situationist operations, PM's actions interfere with reality.[5] Without a clearly defined art frame, some of the members marched in uniforms and 'security-guarded' bank branches in the midst of the 2011 summer protest in Tel Aviv. On 28 September 2012, they launched in Graz, Austria, the elaborated event *Re-Branding European Muslims*, led by Yahalomi, aimed to re-imagine and counter-image Islamic cultural identity. It was defined and performed as a competitive campaign in which European Muslims are the 'brand' presented by experts (such as in publicity or mass media) and by actual and re-enacted public figures.[6]

Defining its founders as 'leaders', PM links to its own structure of work a deep interest in social structures and counter-structures, which include hierarchical relations.[7] In 2011, Krieger left the group while Yahalomi remained its sole leader. She initiates, conducts research and organizes major PM's projects, while group members can initiate actions or take part as co-creators. The initial idea is developed until it finally takes shape as a score. This process takes place per project, without regular meetings or studio work. The projects are cumulative multifaceted investigations of contemporary and future performative models. Within the larger context of performance studies, the group's actions, being reconstructions and deconstructions of public patterns, may be seen as performances of performances. They are creative variations of restored behaviours, tightly connected to changing circumstances and research about places, such as the Ghetto in Warsaw, University Campuses, or areas of governmental institutions.

The meta-discourse of this paper, which is connected to the group's Israeli ground, presents two related performative strategies: first, the political aestheticization of ceremonial codes and their crucial connection to crisis, characterizing PM's early actions – mainly *Also Thus!* (2007), simulating a military ceremony, which includes a collision between a car and performers; and *Emergency* (2008), a re-enactment of rescue routines in a state of emergency connected in PM's performance to terror attacks and political violence.[8] The second strategy is that of site-specific civic acts, some of which are invisible interventions. In this context, I will focus on participatory actions.[9] These two strategies are deeply related to each other and sometimes intermingled. They are both based on an overlap between the aesthetic and the political, as well as on a tight correlation between artistic and cultural public performance.

These close and fluid relations in PM's work sharply evoke principal questions. What is the extra-value of such an attitude in days of utterly performative protests and revolutions world wide? What social efficacy can be ascribed to aesthetic-political practices which intensively act, react and enact without an explicit articulation of a political position? The actions frequently create tensions between activism on the one hand and identification with social systems on the other, as well as between a group's manifestation of force and authority and between oppositional disruptive stances. In what sense can such a dual and even perplexing perspective be considered critical? I could generally argue that PM explores ways to implement a critical overview which includes different perspectives, reversible roles and sides, or interwoven time layers in its actions. Moreover, although these are most concretely performed under specific circumstances, they are – to varying degrees – abstractions of ceremonial patterns and activism. As the generic name 'Public Movement' indicates, the actions can be considered as paradigmatic behavioural options. PM's aesthetic-political position can thus be regarded as visionary – aiming at non-monolithic critical introspection and creatively practicing the fundamental opportunity and passion for civic involvement and change.

Ceremonial crisis: *Also Thus!*

Also Thus! was premiered at the 2007 Acco (Acre) Festival of Alternative Theatre, to a frontally seated audience, in the schoolyard of the local Al Amal Arab elementary school at the seaside.[10] It was followed by many performances in Israel and Europe, performed by about ten performers in white uniforms (neutral yet reminiscent of those of the Israeli navy), as in many of the group's actions.[11]

The choreography of *Also Thus!* is based on a series of very familiar, although creatively arranged, Israeli military and nationalist exercises. In Acre, the group used the school yard against the backdrop of the Crusader fort. The performers raise the PM flag – actually the blue, black and white Estonian flag (contingently selected and unfamiliar, yet bearing a visual affinity to the blue-and-white Israeli flag); they march ceremonially in single file, saluting, their faces turned towards the audience. Then they join hands and dance Hora-like circle folk dances. Their gestures create a sophisticated simulacrum – an explicit resemblance which is at the same time a non-particular ceremony.

These acts evolve into acute crisis, a *gestus* of rupture and disruption: A black Jaguar sporting a flashing light, an objet trouvé associated with the formal power of authority, slowly circles the performers and menacingly accelerates. The car re-appears as two female performers are sitting on its hood and suddenly roll down to the ground. The car re-emerges and drives across the yard's width while a performer walks its length. The unavoidable geometry of an accident is thus outlined in space, first as a potential occurrence and moments later realized in a powerful head-on collision between performer and car.

Figure 5 *Also Thus!*, Dialogue of Four Cultures Festival, Lodz, Poland, 2008. Courtesy of Public Movement.

The performer is hurled to the ground, his or her limbs spread apart, and is then lifted horizontally and carried off by others, resembling an evacuation from a site of crisis. The collision, strikingly incongruous with the rest of the ceremonial patterns, is repeated five times (its first occurrence also including an apparently lifeless performer falling out of a car door thrown open), and thus turns into a cyclical movement phrase.[12]

This detailed description can give concrete shape to the aestheticization of ceremonial codes in PM's practice. This strategy was pushed to an extreme and revealed its complexity when *Also Thus!* was performed in Berlin in 2009 at the Olympic stadium arena built by the Nazis in 1936 and was renovated. The military drills merged with a collective memory of Nazi aesthetics. The car used in the accident was a Mercedes. In this context, the notion of a Jewish-Israeli return to Germany in a position of strength was manifested both as a recuperative counter-event and as an appropriation of disturbingly analogous power. Following Bishop's attitude, a tension is created between the ethical (connected to the social efficacy of the action) and the aesthetical (manifested within artistic framework and criteria).[13] One may wonder whether the politicization of ceremonial aesthetics does not in fact turn into the aestheticization of the political which is characteristic of nationalist or even fascist movements.[14] Nevertheless, acting out the aesthetics of military power related to fascist connotation, in Berlin or elsewhere, does not literally strengthen the fascist model, but has sharp critical value.

In Israel, in the framework of alternative events or fringe theatre that attract mostly liberal, left-wing-oriented audiences, the equation of identity and power is strongly connected to the everyday performance of sovereign unity which has never ceased to be relevant. In the first decades of the State of Israel, after 1948, when my parents were dancing and practicing solidarity in folk-dance circles while losing friends who died in wars, a visionary ideology of unity was deliberately promoted. Actually, such governmental ideology was promoted even before the creation of the State, in order to construct a national and cultural common ground in a country whose sovereignty has never in fact been bound within the lines stipulated in the United Nations partition plan. Its armistice borders known as the 'Green Line', breached in 1967, remain challenged and indefinite to this day. European Holocaust survivors and immigrants from various Arab countries constituted a major part of the growing need for communal and cultural values and a collective Israeli ethos. The rhetoric of unity still prevails in today's Israeli eclectic and developed society, embedded in the school system where it forms the basis for the 'institutionalization of total Israelization'.[15]

In its ceremonial performances, PM turns this total experience into a choreographed syntax of images and movements. An aesthetic of unity is immediately apparent in the white uniforms of PM's performers, as well as in their unison or circular choreography. Nevertheless, the generalization of military ceremony functions as a layout for an ongoing specific crisis – such as the long periods of intense terror and lack of any solution of the Israeli-Palestinian conflict, as well as the periodic and ongoing wars. 2006, the year PM was established, saw the Second Lebanon War. In *Also Thus!* the ceremonial presentation of militarist orientation echoes the repetitive annual calendar that integrates religious holidays with Memorial Day and Independence Day. This cycle, which can be understood as a national libidinal inertia, has been apparently celebrated and commemorated forever, since the 'first' mythical time, *in illo tempore*.[16]

While these patterns explicitly indicate the group's Israeli breeding ground, they are also a de-familiarized abstraction and an expression of the group's critical overview, and therefore relevant to an international spectatorship. It is not simply a simulative transposition of a cultural performance, but rather a hyperbolic stylized extraction of a social behaviour. The military gestures have strong generic quality; the uniforms are simply white without any identifiable markings; the group's tricolour flag is a pseudo-national symbol. As insinuated by the presence of the flag, the ceremonial performance is in fact a demonstration of public life by being an alternative territory, a realm of creative critical practice. Thus, a duality or a sense of 'glocality' is created – a territorial overlap between sovereign local space and action space, which also has characteristics of a non-local artistic 'Everynation'.[17]

The sense of a recurring accident is indeed central in Israeli public space, and at the same time is relevant to every social structure. It can be understood as the counter-point of the reassuring ceremonial stability and a manifestation of power, as if the car representing formal authority has gone astray. The sequence of ostensible accidents entails a practised virtuosity. Its carefully choreographed slow and repetitive performance intensifies a sense of radical danger and horror, while at the same time generating aesthetic fascination. It is a controlled bio-political *gestus* – a singular bodily act which is, in Foucault's terms, an embodiment of institutional, systemic regulation and thus a manifestation of social plurality.[18] The act not only disrupts the unifying, festive formality of the previous acts, but also imposes an arbitrary order of hitting (killing, assassination) – a cycle in which the performers/soldiers actively participate, anonymously hitting and 'miraculously' recovering, joining the file once again.

The substantial symbolic value of this act can be viewed through Paul Virilio's discourse on cultural structures and urbanism, in which 'accident' and 'accidentology' are most relevant key notions. Apparently a chance occurrence, the 'accident' – not literally a car accident – is in fact a predictable disruption. Deriving from technological and socio-economic developments, this conceptualization is associated with speed and acceleration. Its understanding involves the exposure of technological weaknesses and of the predictable dis-synchronization of control systems which might, potentially, lead to disaster.[19] The accident in *Also Thus!* is a live, concrete performance and not a technological image reducible to pixels. It is nevertheless a shocking but cumulative predictable motif, associatively related to the mass-media's addictive repetition of segments of horror. Arriving in the wake of several forceful acts, such as whirling round in circles and repetitive violent wrestling (involving two performers at a time) to the sound of Rammstein's Industrial Heavy Metal music, the accident is propelled by the force of ceremonial routines. It is the externalization of a potential acceleration of ritualistic codes finally reaching an inevitable point of collapse.

One of the links made in *Also Thus!* between distinctly physical states and verbal motifs is the final ceremonial pattern.[20] The performers stand close together and recite an oath, repeating after Krieger, who stands behind a podium: 'I am within the boundaries of a State / I stand firm / I feel a great presence /

I am a member of a group / I feel the presence of my friends who stand by me / My place is here, my cause is just / I may be wrong / I am not wrong / I am right / I am here / I am alone / I am held captive / I swear / At this time / Now! / Now! / Now!'[21] The hollow repetitive consent of indoctrination is combined with expressions of selfhood and loneliness, sobriety and doubt: 'perhaps I am wrong,' 'I am alone,' 'I am held captive.' Following an announcement proclaiming that 'the ceremony has come to an end', the performers lie together, after which they energetically stand up, run off the site and then storm back, inviting the audience to join them in a circle dance to the music of a popular mainstream Israeli song. This is a troubling inclusive event, leading to joyful solidarity while displaying the inertia which seems to begin anew, over and over again, since time immemorial, 'also thus'.

Critically regulated: *Emergency*

In 2008, PM created *Emergency* (in Hebrew *Pigu'a* – Terrorist Attack), as a project of the Acco Dance Center and intended for the Acco Festival. I attended this action twice in a festival that actually did not take place. On 9 October 2008, the eve of Yom Kippur (Day of Atonement), an Arab driver from Acre's Old City entered a predominantly Jewish street in Acre. As part of this off-routine holiday, the common tradition in Israel is to avoid driving, expressing comprehensive respect to this fasting day. The car was stoned in anger. The predictable escalation of the 'accident' soon bore violent confrontations, many wounded, dozens of damaged stores, cars and buildings, massive police intervention and several arrests. The Mayor of Acre, overruling the protest of a group of theatre artists, cancelled the Acco Festival which was supposed to take place a few days later.[22] *Emergency* was thus performed only for an audience of invited guests, mainly artists.

The programme description of the intended performance, which was planned months before the riots, could have been formulated in direct response to them:

> A festive power manifestation combining an emergency preparedness drill, a mass casualty incident and various disaster scenarios. The event takes place with the involvement of expert-performers from official rescue forces together with local volunteers.

As if one step ahead of the collision choreography, the political aestheticization of rescue routines expresses a direct acknowledgement of the disturbing similarity between functional regulated patterns of crisis and national militant gestures etched in collective memory.

Rocks and concrete-block fragments were lined up in an empty field near the Festival Gardens, with the group's flag on one side and a screen on the other. The audience sat on mats in front of the line of rocks. The uniforms worn by the seven performers, joined by volunteers, included protective vests and dark trousers. As they entered the space, they performed various gestures associated with rescue and defence forces. They created carefully arranged shapes combining found objects manipulated to Techno-Rock music: an X was outlined with yellow tape that is regularly used to demarcate emergency zones; they performed CPR such as transporting orange-coloured stretchers and a first-aid bag. The differentiation between rescue forces and victims became blurred when some of them also lay down in the gaps and cracks amidst the stones and blocks, and were evacuated by others, dragged through the dust on stretchers, one by one. Death played an integral part in this routine by repeatedly inserting bodies into white body bags of the Zaka rescue organization, whose emblem includes a blue Star of David.[23] Another line was crossed when performers who acted as rescuers rose from the ground, retreated to the rocks and began to hurl stones. Without any coherent dramaturgical justification, the *a posteriori* time of rescue intermingled with the violent confrontation as rescuers became attackers.

The state of emergency simulated the collaboration typical of crisis situations by involving readymade factors, thus reinforcing a sense of temporary utopian solidarity. By the end of the performance, an actual first-aid ambulance arrived and real paramedics performed medical acts such as checking people's pulse and attaching 'deceased' tags to bodies. Eventually, a fire-truck arrived and its water hose was directed at the other side of the field, with no clear aim in sight, playing its role – including logo and colour codes – in the ceremonial crisis.

As a concrete reaction to both intrusive TV representations of horror and to the widespread sociocultural and philosophical discourse on terror representation, especially following 9/11, the action was further underscored by broadcasting the live action on CCTV. It was selectively photographed (by Krieger) with a camera attached to a flashlight. The camera lingered on faces and on the bodies' distinctive marks as an act of identification, while spectators' eyes kept shifting from the image projected on screen to the live action itself. This multidimensional perspective thus unified the live crisis and its documented iconization, virtualization, or what Richard Schechner explains as 'specularity'.[24] As Boris Groys points out, distinction should be made between the empirical function of an emergency image and the symbolic value of images that, as part of media economy, turn into a political sublime: strong, awe-inspiring, intolerable yet fascinating.[25] The media factor in PM's *Emergency* intensified the actions that were modelled to render an implicit political sublime. This was clearly exemplified in the Pieta poses through which the encounter between the wounded and rescuers was interspersed and isolated on screen, as well as in various carefully choreographed and reframed one-on-one interactions, such as mouth-to-mouth resuscitation.

Through the performance, emergency acts are viewed not as an inevitable crisis *per se*, but rather as aesthetically arranged political constructs which demand regulated ruling systems and a chain of representations. It is patently clear, however, that apparently solid codes stabilize dynamic positions; they do not shield one from death or fragility, either, and can always reach their 'accidental' point of collapse.

Civic visions: Participatory actions

Live acts of involvement in public spaces are a central part of PM's work and most of them entail public participation. Referring to a constellation that challenges the opposition of viewing and acting, manifested in re-appropriation of the place by the participant, Jacques Rancière draws an analogy between the counter-positions of passive and active citizens and those of passive and active emancipated spectators.[26] Like most of the participatory actions dealt by Bishop (2012), in PM's actions as well the two parts of the analogy – viewing versus acting/ passive versus active – merge in the figure of the participating citizen; but it is a complex figure, based on dualities and tensions between citizenship which is also a subjection to systems, as well as between being active and being manipulated.

PM's profound interest in national memory was manifested in several actions in Poland, a highly charged location, especially but not only for Jewish Israelis.[27] Following extensive research, PM organized the massive *Spring in Warsaw* (2009), which they described as 'A walk through the Ghetto led by Public Movement'.[28] It was a participatory re-enactment of what seemed to be an official educational Israeli ritual. The event took place 3 days before the 'March of Life' from Auschwitz to Birkenau concentration camps, an annual Holocaust Memorial Day event in which hundreds of mostly Israeli adults and high-school students take part. For *Spring in Warsaw*, PM – with the cooperation of local performers – guided a group of about 1,500 mostly Polish citizens, thus shifting the national perspective of the narrative.

Figure 6 *Spring in Warsaw,* Warsaw Ghetto, Mordechai Anielewicz memorial, 2009. Photographer: Tomasz Pasternak. Courtesy of Public Movement.

During this journey which lasted about 2 hours, participants followed PM's members who carried the group's flag and performed military drills and acts of evacuation. They stooped down on the road, together with the participants, following Islamic-like prayer prostration movements. One of the sites on the march was the Mordechai Anielewicz memorial – a bunker turned monument commemorating the leader of the Warsaw Ghetto uprising. At the monument PM members stood and sang a Polish protest song from the time of the Solidarity Movement.

Detouring from the official route of the March, they stopped in front of the home of Esperanto's Polish-Jewish creator, Doctor L. L. Zamenhof, and sang a song in Esperanto. In yet another stop, they knelt in front of a bronze relief monument commemorating the German Chancellor Willy Brandt's kneeling in front of the Memorial to the Heroes of the Warsaw Ghetto. The route ended with a wreath-placing ceremony at the Memorial of the Heroes of Warsaw Ghetto itself – a monument erected by Natan Rapoport, a Warsaw-born Jewish Holocaust survivor. The ceremony included a speech which began with the exclamation: 'Oh, Humanity!' and continued with the well-known opening lines of T. S. Eliot's *The Waste Land*: 'April is the cruellest month'. 'Cruel' April is also the time of chain of rituals validating Jewish-Israeli national identity: a week after Passover Israel marks the Holocaust memorial day, which is followed only a week later by Memorial day, and which leads directly to Independence day, thus constructing the shift from disaster to resurrection. 'Let us remember', the speech continues, 'the Jewish fighters of the ghetto, fighting in Warsaw not for Judaism but for life; fighting not for a state but for human dignity, for survival. . . . Poles, Jews, Christians, Muslims, Europeans, Africans, Asians, Americans, Australians, Israelis and Palestinians: Our stories are different, but all our lives are sacred.' By this experiential occasion – and this time with unequivocal articulation of an ethical stance – PM expanded the spectrum of collective memory, removing it from any exclusive nationalist ownership.

The participatory actions which practice protest skills can take the form of a creative rally or disruption. For example, PM's traffic-blocking circular dances, performed on several occasions, including the Tel Aviv mass protest of summer 2011. It was followed by a version of the Arab Dabka Dance, organized by group member Saar Székely, which gave a new perspective to the duality of disruption (and a potential accident) and solidarity. In one of the latest actions, *Civil Fast* (*Ta'anit*, religious fast in Hebrew), led by the members Hagar Ophir and Saar Székely and took place at the streets and at a city square in Jerusalem on December 2012, the religious custom to fast turned into a declared establishing ceremonial routine which will celebrate and mourn the political options of self-sacrifice, such as hunger strikes and self-immolation. The 24-hour action included marches in uniforms in front of main institutions, choreographies of treatment and purification, a collective participatory feast – after which PM's members started to fast – and a press conference.

Civic actions can also take the form of a dimension especially added to a given protest event. For example, *May 1st Riots* performed by PM on 1 May 2010 at the Kottbusser Tor area in Berlin's Kreuzberg neighbourhood, where since the riots on 1 May 1987, a protest action has been acted out by left-wing activists and the police. Without interfering in the event, PM supplied participants with an interpretative discourse and an experiential dimension – headphones playing a soundtrack with a choice of five channels, including 'Live Sociology' offering commentary about the live event (by sociologists Robert Schmidt and Thomas Scheffer), 'Music for Riots' and edited recorded conversation with Joseph Vogl from Humboldt University who addresses the performative aspect of the revolutionary act.

A university campus, another location historically charged with protest and political activism, was the venue for another PM's action practicing civic involvement. It was performed in two different versions – *University Exercise* (2010) at Heidelberg University, and *Exercise in Citizenship* (2010), at Tel Aviv University. More than a mere public place, the campus was thus displayed as a public sphere. In Jürgen Habermas's terms, it is *Öffentlichkeit* ('Publicness');[29] an arena for freedom of speech, but at the same time a part of the overall sovereign power – a microcosmic hierarchical power structure.[30] This ambivalence was apparent in Heidelberg, where the action included collaboration with the police and fire department, embodying official force and participating in an evacuation re-enactment of protestors, together with dozens of students.[31] In the Israeli version, the action included a previous establishment of a 'student body' which then took active part along with all the participants in a demonstration-like walk on the campus grounds without a defined purpose, and in campus choreographies (such as 'making out' on the grass). Among other acts, the audience attended a lecture (by Igal Dotan) in a university hall, combining insights about the functions of the university and live rock music. The action ended at the library square, where military drills were performed and speeches were delivered on a podium by actual representatives of various extreme stances of Israeli public life. The practice of taking a stand was then physically exercised by performing *Positions*, a participatory choreography of demonstrations, and then the whole action concluded with a party.

I will resume with a closer look on *Positions* – which was performed autonomously or as part of other performances numerous times since 2009, in Israel, Europe and the United States.[32] It consists of two performers standing on two sides of a public space, while other group members mark the performance space with red-white caution tape. The two announce: 'You are asked to choose a side, to take a stand!' and audience members are required to position themselves on one side as two diametrically opposed stances are proclaimed – that is, men/women, smokers/non-smokers, capitalism/socialism, or, in particular local contexts, pertinent stances such as 'Ariel (a city in the Occupied Territories) is part of Israel'/'Ariel is part of Palestine', or 'The Poles saved Jews'/'The Poles supported the Nazis'. For every proclamation, the action space is divided in two, but for a while an intermediate zone is left between the caution tapes, briefly trapping those who waver between the two positions.

This playful action is a paradigmatic act – a binary matrix of activism experienced through the body and its position which still contains different perspectives wherever it is performed. Like the other participatory civic actions, expressing a position seems to be in opposition to the group's performances of governmental power structures. The strict binary movement of *Positions* is more complex for it evokes the problematic issue of ideological choice. Are we actually making a free choice or have we been chosen to take a side? Do we oscillate between positions, or rather between an idiosyncratic choices and socially structured acts? *Positions* is an extreme example of the meta-political extra value of PM's attitude. Its bodily and concrete spatial experiences offer dialectic overviews of social positions and visions of optional activism; it is not a direct reflective criticism or a 'rehearsal' of specific activism.

Positions does not directly express the notion of accident which has been realized in the ceremonial performances and is explicitly visible in most participatory civic acts. However, the potential crisis is ingrained in the performative score of actual resistance acts, which commence by taking a stand. It is equally embedded in governmental or military structures, as well as in economic systems. Such piercing real or potential moments, which should not be reduced to pessimism, are acute points of contact between the aesthetic realm of performance art and the performative reality of public life. This close relation, apparent in PM's creative research as a whole, is what enables participation in the choreography of change.

9

Rising from the Rubble: Creating the Museum of the History of Polish Jews

An Interview with Barbara Kirshenblatt-Gimblett

The core exhibition of the Warsaw Museum of the History of Polish Jews is scheduled to open in the second half of 2014. Its programme director, Barbara Kirshenblatt-Gimblett, was interviewed on Skype on 17 February 2013, responding to questions about the development of the project, her curatorial concepts, and their relation to the field of performance studies.

DZ: Please tell us about the history of the project and the process of creating the Museum.

BKG: When the United States Holocaust Memorial Museum opened in Washington, Grażyna Pawlak, then executive director of the Association of the Jewish Historical Institute of Poland, and her associates were inspired to think about creating an exhibition in Warsaw about the history of Polish Jews. After all, Poland has its Auschwitz-Birkenau, Treblinka, Sobibór, Majdanek, Belżec and Chelmno – but nowhere in Poland or the world is there a museum dedicated to the 1,000-year history of Polish Jews. Poland was not only the place where millions of Jews died. It was also where millions of Jews lived for a millennium – and without a break, until the Holocaust.

She was supported by Yeshayahu Weinberg, the visionary who conceptualized the permanent exhibition of the Holocaust museum in Washington. He was also the person who conceived Beit Hatfutsot in the mid-seventies.[1] He said, 'If there is a Holocaust museum in Washington, there should be a museum of the history of Polish Jews in Warsaw.' He worked closely with Jerzy Halbersztadt, who became project director of the planned museum in 1998 – and founding director of the Museum when it was officially established in 2005. It was Jerzy who developed the full concept for the Museum, including the architectural competition for the

Museum building, Outline of the Historical Program and Masterplan for the Core Exhibition at its heart. Alas, Weinberg passed away in 2000. I often feel that I have him looking over my shoulder and hoping he would be happy with what we have created.

Weinberg was a pioneer in the development of the storytelling museum. Beit Hatfutsot (The Museum of the Jewish People in Tel Aviv) was extraordinary when it opened in 1978, and I was privileged to have served as a consultant on the project when it was being developed. It was to have no original objects. Instead, it would tell the story of the Jewish diaspora through every conceivable medium. Without original objects, was it a museum? I put this question to Weinberg. His answer: a museum tells a story in three-dimensional space. He didn't want to start from original objects. He didn't want to be limited by a collection. He wanted to start from a story, and he wanted to use, as would a theatre director, every method and means to tell the story. First and foremost, he would tell that story in space, and he would make the space itself tell the story. In essence, the Museum was a theatre.

Like other Jewish museums in Europe, the Museum of the History of Polish Jews tells the story of Jews who lived in that place. But how that story is told and the building in which it is told set the Museum of the History of Polish Jews apart. Unlike the Jewish Museum in Berlin and the one in Copenhagen – in both cases designed by Daniel Libeskind – the architecture of the Museum of the History of Polish Jews does not carry a Holocaust message and does not encase a millennium of Jewish history in a Holocaust shell. Quite the contrary: our building is a box of light. Its surface of glass fins is luminous, transparent and reflective. Inscribed on the glass is the word Polin in Hebrew and Roman letters.

The Museum of the History of Polish Jews is also a site-specific museum. It stands on the rubble of the former Warsaw ghetto, facing the Monument to the Warsaw Ghetto Heroes, in Muranów. This was the pre-war Jewish neighbourhood and home to perhaps *the* largest community in Europe before World War II: more than 350,000 Jews, about 10 per cent of Warsaw's population. At the Ghetto monument, you mourn: you honour those who died by remembering how they died. In the Museum, you honour them by remembering how they lived. The Museum completes the memorial complex.

As for the exhibition itself, our approach is scenographic in the full sense of the word. We have tried to create a seamless scenographic environment that transforms as you move through it. You don't feel like you're in a gallery full of exhibits. You walk the plot. The path itself tells the story. The path might be more

Figure 7 Designed by the Finnish Studio Lahdelma & Mahlamäki Architects, the Museum of the History of Polish Jews faces the Monument to the Warsaw Ghetto Heroes, designed by Nathan Rapoport. Photo by Barbara Kirshenblatt-Gimblett.

linear and the story more chronothematic. Or, the path might be more flexible. An open plan and thematic approach are better suited to the long durée of the early modern period.

Several of our designers are opera and theatre designers – Steve Simons and Arnaud Dechelle. *Kraków Under the Occupation*, the permanent exhibition in the former Schindler factory, was also designed by theatre scenographers, and it has a very Krakow, very Tadeusz Kantor, feel about it. So there's something happening here in Poland, where a great Polish tradition of theatre scenography is starting to make itself felt in exhibition design.

DZ: Would you say it is more related to the kind of experience we could have in installation art?

BKG: Exactly. Installation art and environmental performance are inspirations for sure. We aim for an immersive experience, first and foremost immersion in the story, and we see immersive space as a way to achieve that experience. The visual arts and theatre – art as performance and performance art – meet.

AC: It seems to me that there is strange nostalgia for Jewish culture in Poland, a revival of the Jewish presence, but with very few Jews who actually live in that place. Some people attribute this to the understanding that a Jewish revival is potentially a profitable enterprise. Can you offer your own explanation for this, and do you feel that the Museum of the History of Polish Jews is part of that?

BKG: I consider the Museum of the History of Polish Jews to be part of the very history that it presents. It is an expression of both Jewish renewal and Jewish presence in Polish consciousness. The number of Jews in Poland today is small, but there is a renewal of Jewish life here on a small scale – being small in scale should not diminish its significance. To be here today – and in my case to actually live here, though I have been visiting Poland since 1981 – is to know that there is also a sincere commitment to this museum on the part of those who are making and supporting it: the Association of the Jewish Historical Institute of Poland, the City of Warsaw, and the Ministry of Culture and National Heritage, as well as the international donors, staff and hundreds of volunteers. Cultural economics rules all over the world. Of course, museums need money in order to function, and they also contribute economically to the region. But, they are first and foremost driven by their mission and this one is no exception. If anything, the mission of this museum is monumental, as is the cost of creating, running and maintaining the building, its exhibitions and its programmes.

I have absolutely no doubt that the Museum's mission is supreme: to tell the story of Polish Jews and to transmit the legacy of the civilization they created to future generations in Poland and the world. The way in which we do this will be the key to our success in Poland, for Jews living across the globe, and for everyone else. Our Polish visitors will see a history they will recognize as their own – but from a new perspective. To engage the Polish audience in the history of Polish Jews *as integral to the history of Poland* is to recover Poland's historic diversity. Our Jewish visitors will discover a 1,000-year history of Polish Jews that has been overshadowed by the cataclysmic events of the Holocaust. This is a story of the best of times and the very worst of times. We will create a trusted zone, a safe place for dangerous ideas, a space of conversation, dialogue and debate.

When I speak before Jewish audiences in North America, the first question is often, 'Why in Poland?' My response: 'Would you ask that about any other Jewish museum? The Jewish Museum in London, Paris, Vienna, Berlin, Moscow? Why would you not make a museum that tells the story in the very place where the story happened?' Their response, as you yourself remarked: 'Because there are no Jews there'. From a strictly practical perspective, would it not make more sense to take the Museum to Jews elsewhere, rather than bring them to Warsaw? That may be practical, but the impact will be exponentially greater if Jews come to Poland – to the very place where this story took place, a place utterly saturated with the tragedy of the Holocaust, but also with 1,000 years of history.

The Museum will be a bridge across time, continents and above all people – and it has a special role to play in reconnecting Jews around the world with the places where their families once lived and with those who live here today.

Indeed, if we know anything about tourism, we know that the point is to go *there*. Encountering 'there' 'here' is not the same thing as encountering 'there' 'there', so to speak. Otherwise, why travel? Our first asset is therefore the power of the place. We must harness the emotional power of the site, the very place of the Warsaw ghetto uprising, but also the space where a large Jewish community thrived. You have to come here to experience the story in a way not possible anywhere else.

This museum would have been inconceivable before the fall of communism – and *not* because capitalism followed communism. To open up to the history of Polish Jews here in Poland is to be fully European – indeed, this is a powerful way to recover the historic diversity of Poland, a diversity that was lost with the genocide, redrawing of boundaries and relocation of populations. Poland, the place where the largest Jewish community in the world once lived, was once a centre of the Jewish world. If anything, you have to wonder how such an important story could have gone untold. There was not only a genocide, but after the Holocaust, there was also silence – indeed, material traces in many places were simply erased. *That's* what you have to explain – seven decades of relative silence. Emigration radically reduced the already small number of Jews in Poland. The vast majority who remained were assimilated – and more and more so. Countless others hid the fact they were Jews, and many who were children during the Holocaust simply did not know that they had Jewish birth parents or grandparents. Polish suffering during the Holocaust was terrible, and most Poles who helped Jews hid that fact for fear their neighbours would ostracize them.

In Europe today – Germany, Austria, France, Italy, Poland and Ukraine among others – people avoid saying 'Jew'. Yes, the word is in the dictionary and it should be a normal word, but it is not. Say anything – 'of Jewish origin', 'Jewish roots', 'Jewish background', 'of the Mosaic faith', 'our older brothers', Hebrew, Israelite, *ebraismo*, anything – but not *Juif, Jude, giudeo*, and certainly not *Żyd* or its variants in other Slavic languages. In Ukrainian, *zhyd* is tantamount to saying Yid or kike and is considered an anti-Semitic slur. What will it take to be able to say Jew, in any language, and not cringe? I would like to think that the Museum of the History of Polish Jews would help to normalize the situation. Indeed, in one of our branding workshops, someone came up with a brilliant idea – brilliant in my eyes though not in everyone else's – to change the name from Muzeum Historii Żydów Polskich to Mużeum Polin – adding a dot that reminds one of the word that makes everyone anxious: Żyd. Imagine the logo, Ż, and the conversation it would prompt.

There is no denying that the number of Jews in Poland today is small, no matter how you calculate – they say almost 8,000 who are prepared to identify themselves as Jews and anywhere from 20,000 to 60,000 that cannot be counted but that by some measure – Jewish origin of some kind – can be estimated.

I think of this museum as part of the post-war, post-Holocaust, post-communist story. It is part of the story of Jewish renewal and above all, of Jewish presence in Polish consciousness. This museum and all that it represents speak to what it means to be part of the new Europe and the world. Poland today has a relatively vibrant economy and is building a post-communist society based on democratic values and civic engagement.

That is why I feel sad when I encounter cynicism about the motives for creating this museum. No doubt there are some whose motives are cynical – How could it be otherwise? – but the project cannot be reduced to money, kitsch and bad faith.

What does Jewish presence in Polish consciousness mean? For many years, courageous individuals who saved Jews, the Polish Righteous, hid their acts of heroism for fear of what their neighbours would think. Since the fall of communism, interest in Jewish history and culture has expanded exponentially. This interest should be taken very seriously. There is no reason to question its sincerity. We can debate the various forms this interest takes, but of one thing I am sure: the Museum of the History of Polish Jews will provide an incomparable resource for raising the standards.

DZ: As a performance studies scholar, one could have expected of you to focus on the performative aspect, the 'Event' with a capital 'E', which took place in Poland. This event, which is considered as a disruption of history, has a specific name – Shoah. But instead, you turned your attention to a 'non-event': a millennium of Jewish presence in Poland. A museum exhibition curated by a performance studies scholar and focusing on a non-event may seem paradoxical.

BKG: That's very interesting. The staging of process requires good dramaturgy. Process is not without drama, and a millennium is not one longue durée. Nor is a millennium made up of periods of stasis interrupted by crises and turning points, as if they are the only 'events' in history. But first, take a step back. What constitutes an event? Stanley Eveling, the Scottish philosopher, is said to have said that 'A thing is a slow event'. The period of 1,000 years of continuous

Jewish presence in this territory is made up of events of many different orders of magnitude. In fact, we make every effort to resist the gravitational pull of the Holocaust – to resist the teleology of the Holocaust, as the biggest event, as the logical and inevitable outcome of a history of anti-Semitism. We do not set the Holocaust within the history of anti-Semitism, which is what Holocaust museums generally do, but rather within the history of Polish Jews, a distinction that makes a difference.

The first event in our millennium narrative is arrival: our visitors will descend a grand staircase and enter an artistic installation inspired by a forest. This is intended as a priming experience. In this space of historical imagination, in this time before time, they will hear legends that Jews told themselves about how they came to Poland and why they stayed. The Polin legend, as retold by Agnon, conveys the sense that it was divinely ordained that Jews should come here and stay here until the Messiah arrives. That is our starting point – a multimedia poetic installation.

The moment visitors leave the Forest and enter the medieval gallery they cross the threshold between legend and history and begin their journey through seven historical galleries. The medieval period extends from the tenth century until 1506, at which point this territory was becoming the centre of the Ashkenazi Jewish world – Jews were living in about 100 locations, with Jewish communities in about half of them. The second and third galleries are set in the period of the Polish-Lithuanian Commonwealth. It was here that the Jewish population expanded exponentially and distinctive forms of Jewish life specific to this territory emerged. With the partitioning of the Commonwealth, Jews found themselves in the Russian, Prussian and Austrian empires, a period that we characterize as encounters with modernity. World War I, the empires collapse, and the Second Republic forms. Despite economic hardship and anti-Semitism, this short period – just two decades – has been characterized by some historians as a second golden age. In the gallery that follows, the focus is on the Holocaust within the territory of occupied Poland – what happened here, what was known and how it was understood. The story does not stop here but continues into the post-war years and comes forward to the present and into the future.

I am sometimes asked, 'Which is the most important period?' This I take as a rhetorical question because the person usually knows. For some it is the Holocaust. For others it is the post-war years, the period of most recent memory through which they themselves lived, or the inter-war years. Some insist that the entire exhibition, or most of it, should focus only on the modern period. My answer is always the same: the most important period is 1,000 years. I believe visitors will be surprised and intrigued by the galleries they assume will be of least interest: the medieval gallery, where 'there is nothing to show', and the post-war years gallery, where 'there is nothing to say', because for many people, the Holocaust simply closed the book.

A period of 1,000 years is not simply a state of being without a shape. Nor is the story we tell a master narrative. In a sense, this story has been lost because of a single defining and definitive event, the Shoah – this is pretty much the only thing most people know about the history of Polish Jews. The Germans created the ghettos and built all the death camps here. The most traumatic sites of the genocide are all here. For visitors to Poland with any interest in Jews, their itinerary, more often than not, is organized around Holocaust sites. There are exceptions: some visitors go back to their home town, pursue their interest in genealogy or attend reunions, but overwhelmingly, their visit to Poland is defined by Auschwitz-Birkenau. No question, it is essential to remember the Holocaust, and there is no more powerful way than to go to the very epicentre of the genocide. But, lest the world know more about how Jews died than how they lived, we have an obligation to tell the story of their lives and to transmit the civilization they created to future generations in Poland and the world.

One could say that 1,000 years is an event in its own right, a very long one. And, there certainly are events in the story. Some of them are small, and some are big. Among the most dramatic is the Khmelnytsky Uprising – we do not treat it as the 'first holocaust', even though it is etched in Jewish memory as one of the great catastrophes, but we do present it in all of its brutality. That said, we don't treat it as a turning point, as some historians have done. The Commonwealth rebounded after a century of war, and Jewish communities renewed themselves. Jewish life after this event was not radically different than before, though long and deep historical processes were at work and new spiritual trends, such as Hasidism, emerged. The partitioning of the Commonwealth was of course an 'event', actually a series of events that constitute a tumultuous process. Even the Holocaust, the most singular event of all, had duration, was made up of many events and was most definitely a process – indeed, we place an emphasis on life in the shadow of death and then in the face of death and present the many little events that were the reality of Jews in occupied Poland. That is not how this period is usually narrated. We do not begin the Holocaust gallery with the rise of Hitler and follow the Germans from there.

Our lead scholars for this gallery are Barbara Engelking and Jacek Leociak. They published *The Warsaw Ghetto: A Guide to the Perished City*, a landmark contribution to our understanding of the Holocaust. Barbara is trained in social psychology, and Jacek in literature, which explains in part why they are especially sensitive to inner life – to the emotional and psychological experience of those whose story we tell, as well as to the experience of the visitor.

This gallery, insofar as possible, is based on documents that were written on the spot, in the moment. They have an immediacy that you cannot deliver in any other way. This presentation of the Holocaust is unusual in not including post-war testimony. There are no video recordings of survivors, and I can't think of a Holocaust museum that doesn't use such material in the exhibition itself. Visitors will have access to post-war Holocaust testimony in our Resource Centre. While our approach limits the material we can use, it is coherent and very powerful. And, it is consistent with the mode of narration that we use throughout the entire exhibition. We try to keep our visitors inside the period, to bracket what he or she knows happened later, to see the world as those in the period saw it – no fast-forward, no foreshadowing, no back-shadowing. Stay in the moment. We try to achieve this by using documents from the period and quotations from first-person accounts of the time.

Here is how we do it. Two narrators accompany our visitors through the first part of this gallery. Adam Czerniaków, head of the Warsaw ghetto Judenrat, kept a diary in Polish. Emanuel Ringelblum, head of the Oyneg Shabes archive, an underground effort to document everything that happened in the Warsaw ghetto, kept a diary in Yiddish. We quote from each diary at each stage in the story – in the original language, with translation into Polish and English. We juxtapose these two points of view, these two heroes – it is as if they're walking with the visitor through the story.

We also use space and light to create a psychological place that is hard to describe. You will feel the story even before you've seen or heard anything. This is a double-height gallery with a mezzanine. Taking inspiration from the bridge that joined two parts of the Warsaw ghetto, the team came up with the brilliant idea of having visitors walk up a set of stairs and stand on a bridge, from which they could look down to what looks like normal life on the Aryan side outside the ghetto. Later, when visitors enter that space from below, they will look up and see others on the bridge – and they will discover the reality of occupied Poland under German terror.

I would compare the experience to that of *The Purple Rose of Cairo*, only in the opposite direction. Instead of walking out of the movie and into life, we walk out of life and into the movie. This requires a combination of rigorous discipline in terms of the script – it is largely in the first person, the moment, the place, and we try not to break frame. We carefully use the scenography to position the visitor in narrative space. There is the view from above, then from below. That is definitely theatre. What else could it be?

AC: Do you want the visitor engulfed in the period as in realistic theatre, or do you apply a Brechtian approach that will be fragmentary: you will witness, think, analyse, walk on to a different period?

BKG: I would like to think more Brechtian. We never try to recreate realistic settings and events. That said, we do want to create something more or less seamless and to avoid the feeling that you are in a gallery with displays, one after the other. Museum exhibits don't generally form a seamless whole. By their very nature, there are breaks – spaces between discrete elements and displays, especially in exhibitions based on objects.

Our scenographic approach aims to be seamless without being a recreation. We do not recreate a World War II 'bunker experience' or make a theme park simulation of anything. We never replicate a period room with every detail. We have no costumed actors, and our visitors don't dress up in costumes. So the feeling of being in the moment and in the place is achieved in other ways. Our approach is more evocative than realistic. It's more suggestive than a complete replica of something.

When we present local violence in Poland right after the war, you don't see any violence when you come towards this area. What you see is a high wall that is rather ominous – it is covered with a massive black and white photograph of the exterior of the building where the Kielce pogrom broke out, but there is no address on it, no name. There is just something ominous about that wall. On it there are names of about eight of the many places where violence against Jews broke out. Those names are not printed on the wall, but rather cut out almost surgically so that you have to look inside the letters to discover what happened – in all of its brutality. The effect, while subtle, is very powerful. The ominousness of the scenography tells you that this is not going to be a good story.

There is a jarring dissonance between this ominous wall and the hopefulness of a group of vibrant young Jews, their bags packed, ready to set out for Palestine, as seen on a large photograph nearby. This is how our lead scholars for this gallery, Helena Datner and Stanisław Krajewski, decided to start the narration of the Kielce pogrom in 1946 – not with the violence but with the moment *before* it begins. Turn the corner and on the reverse side of the display, you will find the bare facts: no images, no photographs, no scenography, simply the facts. This text appears on the back of a suggestion of doors, to indicate that you are outside. The facts take you from point A to point Z. Nobody contests the bare facts of what precisely happened. Rather, the question is what happened next?

What happened next is also not scenographic at all. Essentially, the centrepiece of the aftermath is a section of the trial testimony. In essence, the judge asks: why did you kill the woman? The accused answers: because everybody was killing. The judge asks: then why did you kill the baby? The accused answers: Who would take care of the baby? You simply read a section of the trial record. Who needs commentary? Who needs scenography? A quotation from the stenographic typescript of trial proceedings suffices. There follow four interpretations from the period – the Church, the Polish underground, the Communists and the 'moral voice'. The structure is bare facts, funeral, trial and interpretations from the period.

SAL: I wanted to ask you about the youth tours of the death camps. How do you think the Museum could integrate such overwhelming experiences?

BKG: One of our goals is to change the itinerary and not just in terms of where these groups go, but also psychologically and emotionally. The best way is to convince those who organize these groups to start with the Museum. Much is to be gained from a perspective of 1,000 years, not least a better understanding of the spectrum of relations between Jews and their neighbours. These marches have been going on for many years, and we have been told that the organizers are genuinely interested in doing something new and in enriching them with a broader perspective. Some young participants – or prospective ones – are pushing back. They are feeling oversaturated with the Holocaust message, and that is a real danger. The Museum of the History of Polish Jews offers these groups a new resource for innovating and refreshing the way they design these experiences.

SAL: I found it interesting how you spoke not only of Jewish visitors, but everybody who comes there, including Polish visitors who want to learn about their own history through the Museum. Is the visit perceived as an individual experience, or, do you see the experience of the Museum as communal in any way?

BKG: First, the museum experience is first and foremost a social experience. People rarely come alone. Indeed, museums are increasingly aware of the important role they can play as a 'third place' – neither work nor home nor formal setting for formal events, but rather an informal social space. Communities form within and around the Museum, not least when our public participates actively in the creation of the Museum itself. This is what happened when more than 300 people helped to create our magnificent wooden synagogue ceiling and roof, inspired by the one that once stood in Gwoździec, near Lviv.

Second, I see the Museum of the History of Polish Jews as an international museum – a history museum in the nation's capital on a world stage. That international profile is something that I hope I can bring to the project as somebody from outside of Poland but inside Polish Jewry – my parents were born and raised here, and I became a Polish citizen on the strength of my father's pre-war Polish citizenship. The great opportunity both in Poland and for Jews around the world is the international character of the institution. Everyone agrees that the Museum will be important for our Polish visitors, who are expected to make up about 65 per cent of the audience. The Museum staff understands well the importance of the Polish visitors. This is an audience they can identify with and with whom they have direct and continuous contact.

From a Polish perspective, the issues are anti-Semitism and the Holocaust – and for a segment of our Polish stakeholders, assimilation and Jewish contributions to Polish society and culture. It follows that tolerance education is a priority, though not the only one. From my perspective, the exhibition provides an opportunity to reconnect Jews to their own history and to the history of Polish Jews more generally, whether or not their families descend from this territory. This is an important part of Jewish history, the history of probably 70 per cent of the almost 14 million Jews alive today.

I do not mean to suggest that we have two completely separate audiences, with two separate sets of expectations and needs. Indeed, the greatest opportunity of all may well come from cross-audience encounters. Without such crossover, each audience will be in an echo-chamber; they will talk only to each other.

There is of course an international audience as well. I can imagine that for audiences coming from other places that experienced genocide or who know what it is like to belong to a minority, they too will find themselves in the story. They will of course talk to one another, but if they also talk with others, we will have achieved something more.

I do worry that this sincere concern with anti-Semitism and Holocaust, the effort to overcome stereotypes about Polish anti-Semitism and at the same to time to promote tolerance, will make us into a Holocaust museum by another name. The starting point of Holocaust museums is precisely the lessons of intolerance. I'd like to think that we can offer a different model, a model of constructive engagement.

DZ: How, in your opinion, can performance studies transform the curating work in a historical museum?

BKG: Here is what I learned from performance studies that helps me make a better exhibition and museum: first, a critical edge. Performance studies works against the grain. It had to separate itself from theatre history and drama as an exclusive field of interest, and I think of performance studies as oppositional from birth. It suits my thinking also because it is inclusive of many media, artistic forms and theoretical perspectives. Performance studies is not preoccupied with only the best and most famous. This is Schechner's broad spectrum, and I think his broad spectrum is everywhere in evidence in the work that we're doing in this exhibition.

I had to fight against the idea that this exhibition should showcase distinguished individuals and their achievements as a first principle. I had to argue that history is not only about elites and the great things they did. It's about everyone. It is social and cultural history. It is about historical process.

Like performance studies – and unlike many history museums, which work only with historians – our team is truly multidisciplinary and our approach interdisciplinary. Our scholars represent not only history, but also anthropology, sociology, art history, social psychology, literature, philosophy, religious studies, philology and last but not least performance studies. As a result, we can approach history with a broader range of perspectives and materials than if we took a strictly and more conventional historical approach.

I have always valued the way in which performance itself can be a generator of theory. It is not a matter of having performance in one hand and theory in the other and applying the theory to the performance. Artistic practice is theoretically informed and it generates theory. Artistic practice is illuminated by theory, but these are not separate enterprises, and one doesn't precede or follow the other. What excited me about working on this project was the idea that I would think new thoughts about museums, not by watching what others did but from doing it, from the practice. I hoped that I might generate new theoretical insights or a new theoretical approach from the practice, and that's performance studies.

So too is the idea of the agency of display. Above all, this exhibition is performative. It is part of the story it tells, and it does what it is about. It is the impact it can have, the changes it can bring about, that are ultimately what make it so important. The sense of mission – of making performances that matter – that is performance studies at its best.

Motion IV

Into the Political Arena

10

The Impossible Disappearance of Belgium: Notes on Politics, Dramaturgy and Performance

Klaas Tindemans

Introduction

Belgium, as a nation, is an atypical construction. Belgium never matched the homogenizing tendency of nation states, in the direction this process has taken after the congress of Vienna in 1815.[1] Rather, Belgium could be considered as a 'leftover' of the late medieval Burgundy, which was a non-continuous zone of 'federated' counties between the Kingdom of France and the Holy Roman Empire of Germany, a patchwork of territories systematically 'eaten', since the late fifteenth century, by its larger neighbours.[2] Pre-Belgian territory served as the battleground for West-European wars of religion, succession and hegemony. With its independence in 1830, the new country derived its own identity from the sentiment of the 'underdog', the eternal victim of imperialist ambition. Due to this almost 'colonial' history, internal divisions within the small territory remained invisible, especially the fact that the frontier between Germanic and Romanesque languages cuts the territory in two regions. Benedict Anderson demonstrated the importance of language as one of the foundations of the 'imagined community'.[3] So the difficulty, since its independence, to forge a national (political) culture in Belgium which is not dominated by one of these (Dutch or French speaking) cultural groups was never a surprise. The solution to this problem was, in 1970, the creation of a complex constitutional structure of a federalist nature.[4] Belgium is divided into three regions – Flanders and Wallonia, each of them linguistically homogenous, and Brussels, with a bilingual regime – and three communities – the Flemish and the French-speaking communities, both with specific administrative competences in bilingual Brussels, and the (small) German-speaking community. This process of 'defederalisation' is rather exceptional: most federal states, such as Germany or Switzerland, are historically created as a union of formerly independent unities. But in Belgium the opposite continues to happen. This process has resulted, some 40 years after its first implementations, in a profound separation of political cultures. There are no Belgian political parties anymore, no Belgian mass media, no Belgian universities, there is almost no shared public opinion. The political competences of regions and communities have only augmented since 1970, and a 'Copernican revolution' has gradually taken place: the language-based entities are now the centres of political power, not the federal government. Sovereignty has been displaced along specific cultural lines, resulting in a new artificial construction, since none of these regions is linguistically or culturally homogenous anymore, if they ever were in the first place. One important aspect of this separation between political cultures – resulting from institutional separation – is the disappearance of a unified Belgian political class: Flemish- and French-speaking politicians don't share a common political past anymore, even the relations between ideological 'sister parties' – Social Democrats, Christian Democrats, Liberals, Ecologists – have become merely informal. Electoral accountability, even in federal elections, is reduced to the regional electorate, nobody represents Belgium anymore.[5] The elections of 2007 and their aftermath of nearly endless governmental negotiations were the culmination point of this process. In Flanders, the conservative alliance of Christian Democrats and Flemish Nationalists won convincingly. They had the right to start negotiations, but these finished in a first stalemate: a sequel of provisional governments, finally resulting in new elections in 2010. In the process between 2007 and 2010, the conservative alliance had split up, and the Flemish nationalists became the biggest parliamentary party, principally at the expense of their Christian Democrat ex-partners. The negotiations, with Flemish Nationalist leader Bart De Wever in the pilot seat, ended with a second stalemate: his party left the tables.

This paper will try to analyse this process of democratic self-destruction of Belgium as a nation in performative and theatrical terms, by identifying some of the mechanisms of 'restored behavior' in the political culture of this divided country, by reading this public performance as a dramaturgical structure. Two examples of Belgian theatrical drama should clear the path for this analysis.

Political fiction

Political fiction – the legendary *The West Wing* TV-series about an idealized Democrat president of the United States, or the recent Danish series *Borgen* – often reproduces the performative character of politics. Techniques such as the 'walk and talk' in *The West Wing* translate the combination of the pressure to perform, on the one hand, and the uninterrupted flow of information, on the other: how do politicians reconcile, in a theatrical gesture, the inadequacy of the information and the urgency of the decision? These series also use the classical dramaturgical device to expose the intertwinement of privacy and publicity in order to aggrandize the real (political) drama: the melodrama of the Prime Minister's divorce in *Borgen*. But this fiction would not have been written the way it was without the inherent and peculiar performativity of this political landscape itself. In this essay, I will concentrate on recent political developments, as they belong to the 'real' script of this microcosm of globalization Belgium sometimes seems to be: Belgium as a laboratory of peaceful conflict, once visited by officials from Jerusalem to study the possibilities of a capital for two nations. This analysis will focus on three aspects of Belgian political reality. First, I will show the influence of mass culture in its 'electrified' and televised form on the Flemish and Belgian nations as political entities. The isolated, provincial character of the development of the Flemish nation – as a concept and/or societal fact – and the conservative nature of this emancipation movement shed a particular light on this assimilation of mediatized politics. Second, I will deal with the relationship between the public appearance of contemporary politicians, in the actual crisis, and the intrusion of elements from their private lives – elements which have always a performative relevance. Finally, more structural conclusions are drawn from these accounts on the performative nature of daily Belgian politics. In this context, I will use the notions of 'performative' and 'performativity' to describe the specific relationships between political discourse – as a 'logocentric' expression of (ideological) means and goals – and its embodiments and enactments, whether consciously scripted or not. Applying the insights of Joseph Roach, I could define political performances as the rarely successful but socially necessary attempts to bridge the gaps and fill the vacancies between collective memory, societal norms – that is, legality, with the legitimate state as its source – and the 'theatre' of the public space. Political performance 'surrogates' the black holes of sovereignty.[6]

Political facts

Between June 2010 and November 2011, Belgium had only a government of 'current affairs'. This government didn't have full executive powers, because it had no parliamentary majority after the general elections of 13 June 2010. So this government couldn't be held accountable by the newly elected Parliament. However, the elections had shown clear results in both constituencies of the country: the Flemish nationalists – N-VA, a conservative party – won in Flanders, while the Social Democrats – PS, the last 'Old Labour' party of Europe, as their enemies say – won among the French-speaking voters. But, as I explained above, Belgium functions as a 'double democracy': the French-speaking and the Flemish (Dutch-speaking) parts of the country have completely different political landscapes and, to a certain extent, separate civil societies. Only in the larger Brussels region do politicians of both languages compete against each other. But even there, the voter has to choose between two 'language regimes' before s/he can vote for a party or candidate. The most popular metaphor for the nature of Belgian government negotiations is that they are permanent diplomatic conferences.[7] The clear results of the elections of 2010 drove the leaders of the victorious parties to start this conference. In fact, this conference had already started with the federal elections of 2007, only to be interrupted by the bailout of Belgium's largest bank, Fortis, in September 2008. In 2007 the Flemish conservative parties – nationalists and Christian Democrats – joined forces in an electoral alliance. After their victory, they demanded a radical reform of the state in a 'confederal' sense, before pledging any loyalty to a fully empowered federal government.

During these negotiations, the Flemish conservative alliance broke up, but the genie was out of the bottle: this was no longer a negotiation between political parties, but between political communities claiming – and performing – their homogeneity. Until November 2011, we had four provisional governments and a resigning government, in short: a diplomatic stalemate. With the electoral victories of Flemish Nationalists – now by far the biggest fraction in the federal Parliament – and the (French-speaking) Social Democrats – traditionally the powerbroker in Wallonia – the leaders of these parties were doomed to take the initiative for the talks. They concluded, quite swiftly, a 'gentlemen's agreement', whereby Bart De Wever, the sharp-minded and eloquent leader of the N-VA, obtained a confederal reform of the Belgian state, implying a large transfer of competences to the regions, and Elio Di Rupo, the smart and charming leader of the *Parti Socialiste*, got the guarantee that the financing system, advantageous for his poorer region, would continue without too many alterations. After 2 months of conferencing with seven parties – Social Democrats, Christian Democrats and Ecologists from both languages, plus the Flemish Nationalists – De Wever found the agreed transfer of competences too insignificant and raised the financing question once again, thus blowing up the gentlemen's agreement. As it happened, the next year was spent driving the Flemish nationalists away from the conference table and replacing them by the two liberal parties. An agreement to reform the state was reached in September 2011, and a government – with the Liberals and without the Ecologists – was formed in November 2011. Social Democrat Elio Di Rupo became the new Prime Minister.

One should be careful, however, to interpret facts from a very recent political past as meaningful for structural features of a political, let alone a societal, system: this would be as arrogant as the newspaper columnists who couldn't stop to describe the present events as 'historical'. But since this political crisis in Belgium can be considered as the deadlock – albeit a provisional one, as every political impasse is – of the coexistence of two political 'scenes', it legitimates this particular scrutiny. The virtual disappearance of Belgium as a political unity requires more attention than just a story from a dated newspaper.

Political theatricality

Political theatricality, in Christian Western Europe at least, probably started with the decision by the medieval clerical hierarchy to use performative devices – ranging from sculptures in church porches to enacted hagiographies and mystery plays – to convert the large population to dogmatic Christianity, a strategy which intended to mobilize the masses in their struggle with the emperors of the Holy Roman Empire.[8] From an ecclesiastical point of view, this strategy was extremely counterproductive and quickly denounced. Medieval theatre both laid the foundations for the Reformation by allowing reflections about the contingency of established world views through theatrical impersonation,[9] and it stimulated the early modern concept of sovereignty – in the unconscious transformation of theological ideas into political theory. So we witnessed, during the seventeenth century, extremely theatricalized displays of absolute sovereignty, with, particularly in France, a shift from masque, where the *Roi Soleil* 'exhibits' himself as the literally incorporated centre of attention, to a display of his effigy as a mechanism, the *Roi Machine*.[10] Even more remarkable is the performance of physical, even sexual energy in the early years of Restoration England. A lifestyle of radical libertinism, with the Earl of Rochester as its clearest example, reflects, quite paradoxically, both the short-lived euphoria after the defeat of puritanism in 1660 and the constitutional abyss wherein the restored Stuart regime was about to fall.[11] Modern political theatricality changed profoundly with the revolutions of the eighteenth century. Where you could say that the American Revolution uses theatre in the first place as a rhetorical metaphor for establishing the idea of 'exceptionalism',[12] the French Revolution puts the nature of theatrical representation itself at stake. There are obvious parallels between the creation of the 'fourth wall' by Diderot and his idea of 'mimetic' representation by actors – instead of direct 'imitation', as classicism saw it – and the debates about the mandate the population gives to its representatives in the *Assemblée Nationale*, a discussion fed by the early revolutionary activist Emmanuel-Joseph Sieyès. The latter advocated the fullness of representative mandates without direct intervention from the electorate – a political 'fourth wall', one could say, with the parliament itself as a stage and the general public watching in darkness and silence.[13]

Even Robespierre's *tragédie sanglante* could not prevent this 'bourgeois' idea of representation from dominating the next centuries, despite being challenged by revolutions and other phenomena of direct political participation. After the 'representational turn' of Diderot and Sieyès, the twentieth century witnessed, due to the electrification of the public space and the consecutive emergence of mass culture, another paradigmatic turn in the performance of the political, this time to be qualified, paraphrasing Walter Benjamin, the 'reproductive turn'.[14] The politician – first by his or her voice, then by his or her image – can be reproduced endlessly; his or her discourse should no longer be represented by artistic devices such as the theatre or the visual arts. The twentieth-century politician doesn't need cultural representation anymore, but reproduces himself as a work of art of the highest resolution. Ronald Reagan provides the perfect example. He was raised in the context of the Chautauqua movement, which spread its conservative Christian message by promoting rhetorical and theatrical skills among its devotees, and was subsequently influenced by the genius of President Franklin Roosevelt as a mass communicator on the radio – his voice was all over the nation. He translated these devices and impressions into a radio presence and a moderately successful movie career. His breakthrough as a celebrity and a successful personal brand came when he hosted the so-called 'consumer republic' for the *General Electric Television Theater*, a prelude to his political ascendency under the ultra-liberal banner of 'no taxation but plenty of representation'. The success of his political brand was due to the split he realized between his unmatched and unchallenged 'electric' histrionics and the historically low popularity of his political decisions. The most symbolic image of this relationship is the opening sequence of the 1984 Republican Convention, where he is called to appear, by his wife Nancy, on a gigantic video screen, overlooking the public of the convention and, indirectly, the whole nation watching the live coverage of the event.[15]

Belgian theatricality

The most obvious difference between the Reagan Revolution – an unprecedented and definitive transformation of both communicational and economic politics – and Belgian politics is of course its geopolitical scale. Nobody in the international community cares much about unity or discord in Belgium, especially since the linguistic conflict never resulted in any casualties. The conflict isn't even comparable with Cyprus or Northern Ireland, given the absence of powerful allies behind the quarrelling parties or communities. This qualitative distinction is not without consequences, also from a performative point of view, since it limits the repertoire of its actors. Belgian politicians are doomed to provincialism, but even on this small scale there is a split between communicative appeal and ideological premises. Political opinion polls and research show that a large majority of the voters of the Flemish nationalists do not agree with the claim for total Flemish independence, although this party has never made a secret of its ultimate goal.[16] The key, however, to their 'counter-ideological' success lies in the discursive and performative qualities of Bart De Wever, the party president. In a way certainly comparable to Reagan's effort, he manages to unite an image of conservative solidity with contemporary appeal for electronic media and a strategic vagueness about his final ends. To this he adds a firm Flemish nationalist pedigree. Flemish nationalism is rooted in nineteenth-century romantic nationalism. The separation from the Netherlands at the end of the sixteenth century resulted, two and a half centuries later, in a small country where the ruling elite, like almost everywhere else in continental Europe, spoke French. The early Flemish awakening, not long after independence in 1830, was basically a cultural movement of Catholic schoolmasters in provincial towns, with modest claims about the use of standardized Dutch in administrative and judicial affairs. But since their strongholds were rural and conservative, they were only exceptionally linked with the workers' movements of the same era. The experience of World War I, where French-speaking general staff led an army of young men speaking only their local Flemish and Walloon dialects, accelerated this emancipation process. From that moment on, their struggle became openly political and their cultural image changed considerably. During the 1920s, a number of symbolic Flemish leaders – such as the poet Paul Van Ostayen – embraced expressionist Modernism, but this modernity was quickly silenced with the advent of Fascism. When, in 1933, the VNV – Vlaams Nationaal Verbond, or Flemish national association – was created, the short lived idea of pluralism and cultural openness was sacrificed for a truly Fascist party organization and ideology, including anti-Semitism.[17] Collaboration with the Nazi occupation during World War II was no surprise,[18] although the SS preferred its own political allies in Flanders. The Flemish movement of the inter-war years, perhaps due to its cultural roots, was always conscious of its theatrical force and built its early electoral success upon a large network of local cultural associations, mostly with a Catholic signature and, to some extent, comparable to the Chautauqua movement in America. Cultural skills such as eloquence were important, both as an affirmation of Flemish identity and as political tools. The theatricality of their mass meetings was impressive, often staged by the best Flemish theatre directors.[19] Even after the catastrophic collaboration with Nazism, these cultural assets continued to mobilize, after a short period in the political desert, an important part of the electorate for Flemish nationalist parties, finally resulting in the success of Bart De Wever's N-VA. He finally managed to liberate Flemish nationalism from the neofascism of the Vlaams Belang, the ideological successor of the collaborationist VNV and the Flemish version of European extreme right populism. Crucial to the popularity of De Wever – a historian specializing in the politicization of the Flemish movement – was his media appearance. He is Belgium's most gifted debater – a classic skill of a political performer – but he also reached the finals of an immensely popular TV quiz show appreciated both by the cultural elite and by the larger population. Only a few months later, he cashed in on this success in his first independent election victory, in the 2009 elections for the Flemish regional parliament. De Wever polemicizes constantly, using worn-out clichés about dynamic Flemish entrepreneurs and lazy Walloon trade unionists. But his popularity is also due to two other factors: a shrewd use of the traditional provincial network of cultural associations – no longer Catholic, but still pretty conservative or 'petty bourgeois' – and, quite importantly, his alliance with the employers' lobby, where he recruits his most professional political staff. De Wever succeeds in forcing his strategy upon the media, dictates the political agenda of the Flemish regional government, and subtly forces cultural policies, even in the arts[20] to subscribe to his ideas of national identity – a conservative, essentialist identity. He turns an invitation as a guest lecturer in political science, at Ghent University, into a major media event, openly pleading for the construction of national identity as a precondition for democracy itself.[21] So his 'performative habitus', his strategy to overcome the contradiction between long-end goals and the daily requirements of political negotiation is a combination of traditional romanticism and sharp wit, in perfect harmony with contemporary media formats.[22] His French-speaking socialist opponent, now the Belgian Prime Minister, Elio Di Rupo, uses a leftist variation of this strategy: an equally successful merger of 'Old Labour' rhetoric and networking and ideological pragmatism of the 'Third Way' type.

From a performative point of view, the places a politician chooses to deliver his different messages are significant. Political scientists Maarten Hajer and Justus Uitermark analysed the aftermath of the murder in 2004, by a Muslim fundamentalist, of Dutch film-maker and anti-Islam activist Theo Van Gogh. Job Cohen, mayor of Amsterdam, perfectly controlled the internal political discourse, but failed to translate this discourse of moderation in the media, especially in TV talk shows. However, his alderman Ahmed Aboutaleb – now the mayor of Rotterdam – held a very mediatized speech in one of Amsterdam's biggest mosques, scourging his own Muslim community for not being attentive to the radicalization of youngsters' right under their eyes. Aboutaleb's staging was perfect and his discourse, by being provocative, has helped defuse the situation.[23] In the same sense, De Wever has won over, in the media, in the parochial venues in Flemish villages and on symbolic locations of the Flemish movement, both protest voters who voted for 15 years for the neo-fascist Vlaams Belang and moderate conservatives who would never have imagined another vote than a Christian Democratic one. His commonsensical neo-liberal discourse has won over the 'dark blue' right wing liberals.[24] At the same time, he is very present in the French-speaking media and speaks before Walloon businessmen but firmly refuses to talk with the leading French newspaper in Brussels, *Le Soir*,[25] which once associated his name with concentration camps. For the contemporary Flemish movement, this is insult added to injury, since De Wever's most potent claim is that he saved nationalism from neofascism and extreme right populism.

Conclusions about Belgian political performativity

In my introduction, I suggested that the performative character of politics – as a more general regime – is linked to the 'contamination' of rational political discourse by personal, biographical incidents. This is of course a dramaturgical technique known since Friedrich Schiller's *Don Carlos* or even since the St Crispin's Day speech in Shakespeare's *Henry V*. But with the advent of the 'dramatised society',[26] this intertwinement has become a structural element of 'performative' politics itself. Here too, the Belgian example is telling. During the negotiations leading to the present government, which started in June 2010, the process was twice interrupted for medical reasons: the first time in August 2010, at the exact moment when Bart De Wever decided to terminate his gentlemen's agreement with Elio Di Rupo about the financing of the regions. When Di Rupo raged furiously against this 'betrayal', De Wever turned white and eventually fell unconscious at the negotiation table. Ironically, it was one of his most fervent political enemies, French-speaking Christian Democrat Joëlle Milquet, who brought him to the ER. The rest of the party drank champagne and prepared for the much awaited breakthrough that never happened.[27] This was no deliberate gesture of course, but the coincidence of these two 'performances' at least delayed a major blow-up of the situation. More consciously, the grave illness and eventual passing of the mother of the last mediator between Di Rupo and De Wever, Flemish socialist Johan Vande Lanotte, caused several pauses and time-outs during a crucial episode in the negotiations.

The unexpected empathy between Vande Lanotte and De Wever – major ideological rivals and both shrewd tacticians – was even mediatized: De Wever briefed the press about the condition of Vande Lanotte's mother and its consequences for the political agenda. He pacified his discourse and shifted his image from stubborn hardliner to compassionate human being. But in the end, this script – if it existed – failed to deliver any political results.[28] In both cases, De Wever mastered the dramaturgical setting, as if he had scripted a docudrama. If this crisis is seen as a 'social drama', in Victor Turner's sense, these accidents are used as secular ritual adjustments to the 'breach', the second phase of social drama: redressive mechanisms to reduce the fall-out of the actual and ongoing societal disaster.[29]

In the context of the general performative regime of contemporary politics, Belgium suffers under specific and important burdens. In the first place, the gap between the legal-political notion of the state and the sociological concept of the nation is extremely deep, in the consciousness of both the population and the political elites in Belgium, and even more outspoken in Flanders. Even when you consider that this gap is constitutive for democracy itself, as Hans Kelsen does,[30] the strategy of Flemish nationalism is directed towards a continuous performance of the widening of the abyss. By conceiving national identity as a precondition for a functioning democracy, by blaming the supporters of Belgian unity for exactly reversing the logic in their rejection of identity altogether, Bart De Wever in fact denies political contingency as such. He denies the contingent character of both the legal-political and social realities that political performance feeds on. Political scientist Marc Hooghe remarks that nationalism, as an ideology, requires every citizen to be a nationalist, or at least to affirm his or her national identity. Social Democrats, Christian Democrats or Ecologists however, will never reproach their adversaries for not joining their ideology.[31] The second aspect is even more fundamental. Political parties, as discursive formations, could be defined as political 'aggregates'[32] an antidote against forced consensual policy-making. Parties assemble a myriad of sometimes even contradictory political claims, and they try to rearrange their priorities according to the political objectives they consider as the most imminent. For a nationalist party, this priority is clear: it is the autonomy of the nation, Flanders in this case, and it is independence in the long term. Given the general political discourse, the performative habitus accompanying it and the above structure of Belgian politics as a diplomatic conference, the necessary shifts in priorities can never take place. For almost 30 years, the 'communitarian divide' has dominated every political debate, serving as the final touchstone for political right or wrong. It makes any 'agonistic' type of policy-making impossible by affirming and even imposing the necessity of national consensus.[33] There is no alternative for Belgium, one could say, but this affirmation sweeps, in daily political practice, any other ideological difference under the carpet.

The final phase of the Good Friday agreements of 1998, which put an end to the Troubles in Northern Ireland, is an interesting example of forced consensus. Sinn Fein, the Irish nationalist party, used the same tactics the Flemish nationalists did during the governmental crisis in Belgium, as they participated in the negotiations that would eventually lead to these Good Friday agreements. They raised the stakes when an agreement approached, a maddening experience for the result-driven British government of Tony Blair. Finally they called in President Clinton, once, twice or more, who forced everyone, Sinn Fein to begin with, to become reasonable.[34] Unfortunately, we Belgians cannot call in anyone. Even the European president is a Belgian, which in his case means: a Fleming. So the performative efforts of all Belgian political gatekeepers – both the defenders of a federal status-quo and the proponents of more regional autonomy, or independence – lead to the effective impossibility of real political deviance. The relative autonomy of the rare or even hypothetical politician who wants to talk about global warming, social inequality, cultural differentiation or the like is indeed very relative.

And finally: can the aporetic situation of Belgian politics shed light on the 'performative turn' in politics in general? The crisis shows how both the dramaturgical and performative characteristics of public policy come (sur) determine a key issue of politics as such: the question of sovereignty.[35] The separation of political cultures in Belgium are said to have led to distinguishable, different features in political style among Dutch- and French-speaking politicians and their electorates. But it is exactly the discourse of distinction (or separation) that shapes the performative habitus of the Belgian politician. It is, among other discursive attitudes, constitutive for her or his 'political self'. The reproductive, the mediatized aspect of this political *persona* is only one element in the wider theatrical and performative character of political dramaturgy. In this sense, the aporia between 2007 and 2011 reveals indeed a link between performativity and sovereignty: the habitus of separation is based upon narratives of identity which are meant to fill in or to hide the black holes of a politicized society. When Flemish Nationalist leader De Wever makes a joke about the employers' lobby being his real master, this is not as innocent as it looks. He is performing an image of a nation whose sovereignty is based upon the structure of its economy. In other words, a performative analysis could uncover fundamental notions of societal structure, whether they are already politicized or not. This is of course just the prologue of a performative theory of sovereignty, but Belgium remains a well-equipped laboratory.

National Street Theatre: Large-scale Performances in Poland after the Crash of the Presidential Plane

Dariusz Kosiński

Saturday morning on 10 April 2010 heralded a quiet and sunny spring day. At the break of dawn, when most of the nation was not yet fully awake, the unsettling but as yet unconfirmed news spread that the government aeroplane Tu-154M carrying President Lech Kaczyński had encountered problems landing in Smolensk, in western Russia. The President, together with an official delegation of several dozen representatives from the major offices of state, senior military officers and former prisoners-of-war had boarded a plane to Katyn to take part in an official event marking the 70th anniversary of the mass execution of thousands of Polish military officers by the Soviet NKVD (People's Commissariat for Internal Affairs).

The news that the government transport had crashed due to thick fog around the former military airbase of Smolensk North Airport, killing everyone aboard, at first seemed utterly improbable and unbelievable. But this was soon confirmed, and the crash became a starting point for a political crisis as well as for a series of large-scale performances, which lasted for a full year after the disaster. The performances were diverse, including public rituals and ceremonies along with street protests and mock carnivals that spectacularly re-actualized and negotiated values and symbols that had been central to enactments of Polish patriotic identity since the nineteenth century. This extraordinarily sustained and animated set of responses reinforced the view, which I have advanced elsewhere, that Polish culture is best understood through the lens of performance.[1] But these performances also served as tools for reinterpreting the traumatic catastrophe and re-establishing the political, ideological and symbolic order of

Polish society. From this point of view, they provide an important example of the role performances play in contemporary political and social life. They function not only as ideological or hegemonic vehicles, but also as ways of enacting community and establishing a shared understanding of past and current events. Although some of the Polish 'post-Smolensk' performances were organized by traditional political institutions, the dispersed flow of the whole drama suggests it would be inaccurate to consider the crowds simply as 'masses' manipulated by the politicians. They should be considered rather as co-performers or 'spect-actors', ready to join in and even take over the action.

Below I attempt to recount some crucial aspects of the aftermath of the crash, including several of its most important performances. Taken together, I suggest that these performances formed a kind of cycle: a five-act drama, with extraordinary mass events serving as its dramatic climaxes.

Act I: The performance of mourning

Cynical as it may sound, given the horrors of the plane crash, one could say that the entire cycle began according to Hitchcock's formula, with an 'earthquake followed by rising tension'. Rather than a slow exposition and gradual exploration of the field of conflict, the post-Smolensk 'drama' started from the most significant event: the crash, which set reality into action. To some degree, this structure can be seen as a variant of analytical drama, in which the action is shaped by the unravelling of 'pre-scenic' events, as in plays such as *Oedipus the King* and narratives from the 'whodunit' genre. However, there is a key difference: the circumstances of the crash continued to be hotly contested and were not subject to closure. Besides the officially documented explanations – fog, pilot error, inaccurate information from the airport staff and poor technological equipment at the Smolensk airbase – many sensationalist conspiracy theories have been aired. But in the cycle I will describe here, the meaning of the event and the way it should be memorialized have been socially negotiated and ultimately resolved for some parts of the community, by means of performance.

The cycle of performances started almost immediately following the first news about the crash. In reaction to this sudden and terrible event, people came out into the streets, lit candles and brought flowers to places connected with the victims of the disaster. Prayer meetings and impromptu services were held in public squares and churches, often followed by discussions that provided an instantaneous and spontaneous reaction to the events. The need to go outside and get involved often resulted from individual shock, and the participants in those mass spectacles would probably regard such spontaneous expressions of grief as authentic. However, these forms of action also drew on pre-existing vocabularies, since most of them belonged to the 'repertoire' of Catholic funeral celebrations, based on the pattern of salvation through sacrifice and suffering. The fact that the crash took place only a week after Easter strengthened this Christian interpretation, and served as the base for immediate heroization of the victims, especially President Kaczyński.[2]

The impact of the mourning rites was so great that for a short while they overshadowed the rising political conflicts and tensions, which receded into the background. The definitive proof of this force could be seen in the unwavering defence of the decision, taken 2 days after the crash, to bury the presidential couple in a crypt beneath Wawel Cathedral, set among the tombs of Polish kings. Small protesting groups were ignored in the name of respect for the dead and for a funeral ritual at this time-honoured burial site.

However, the differences and divisions in the ways of understanding the traumatic event became more pronounced at the two official funeral ceremonies themselves: the public commemoration of the dead organized by the government in Warsaw and the burial of the presidential couple in Kraków. Both ceremonies respectfully followed the Catholic tradition, and both treated the dead as victims and heroes who died while fulfilling the national mission of serving the memory of the Katyn massacre, commemoration of which had been officially disallowed for many decades under the communist regime in Poland. Yet there were some obvious differences between the two. The first ceremony was intended as a tribute to all the deceased in the crash, perceived as representatives of the entire pluralistic nation. This intention was clearly embodied in the altar built for the occasion, at Piłsudski Square (formerly known as Victory Square) in Warsaw, which includes photographs of the victims. All pictures were of the same size and ordered alphabetically, with no priority given to particular individuals. This intention was also clearly expressed in Prime Minister Donald Tusk's speech. Although this ceremony was by no means secular (it took place at the giant stone cross commemorating the famous papal mass from 1979, and its central element was a Catholic funeral service), it had a much more official and less overtly religious character than the burial at Wawel Cathedral. The latter was a ritual act of exaltation and glorification of Maria and Lech Kaczyński, which situated them as protective spirits of the entire community. During that ceremony Janusz Śniadek, chairman of the Solidarity Trade Union, which supports the right-wing opposition, swore an oath of allegiance on behalf of 'the people', thus establishing the cult of the heroic virtues of the presidential couple. These differences between the pluralistic and metonymic representation of the entire society on one hand, and the idealized national hero who was considered to have sacrificed his life on the other, were played upon and deepened in the later phases of the drama.

Act II: The game of the election campaign

The process of reconciliation and closure, initiated by the performance of mourning, was at least partly continued in the subsequent act: the June 2010 presidential election. In the aftermath of burying the dead, the living – in many cases still grief-stricken – had to return to more humdrum activities, and to the mundaneness of everyday life. Established political process and activist campaigning began to take over from the vitality of large-scale community performances.

Nonetheless, the presidential election fulfils a very particular function within the entire structure of the post-Smolensk drama. The relationship between its first and second acts immediately recalls the paradigmatic Western play, William Shakespeare's *Hamlet*. In both the post-Smolensk drama and Shakespeare's play, the action takes an unexpected course and the protagonist suddenly changes strategy. Hamlet does not avenge his father. And when Jarosław Kaczyński – the President's twin and apparent successor – announced that he would stand for election in his brother's stead, he did not pursue the anticipated line of attacking the Russian government and the Polish Prime Minister Tusk (of the opposing Civic Platform Party) as being responsible for the crash. Although such accusations had been put forward vigorously by many Kaczyński supporters, Jarosław Kaczyński himself adopted a moderate stance and initially avoided appealing to the tumult of emotions stirred up during the immediate aftermath of the disaster.

When this politician, notorious for his aggressive statements and radical opinions, abruptly switched to a more conciliatory approach, he caught his political adversaries off-guard. Consequently, they started to voice similar suspicions to those the Court had harboured about Hamlet. Jarosław Kaczyński was said to be mentally unstable, or at least putting on an act for the presidential election.[3] For their part, the campaign staff of Kaczyński's Law and Justice Party sought to convince the electorate that the less severe image of their candidate was a direct consequence of the traumatic events in April, which had profoundly changed him. They even organized mock performances to show that it had never been their intention to pick fights with their opponents. Among these was a 'happening' called *Give Peace a Chance* – a word-play on the Polish acronym for the Law and Justice Party, PiS[4] – during which Kaczyński supporters sang protest songs while wearing stock 'hippie' costumes, wigs and flowers. But innovative as it may seem, this strategy failed to convince a majority of the electorate. For many Poles, the man who had undergone such traumatic experiences would be stepping onto the stage of the presidential campaign (commonly regarded as a space of inauthenticity and pretence) only in order to execute his brother's last will, to clarify the mystery of the crash and to punish those he considered responsible. These widely suspected underlying motivations were heavily downplayed during the campaign, and as a result, Jarosław Kaczyński's words and deeds were regarded as a bad theatrical trick to conceal them.[5] Sham actors have rarely been appreciated in Poland, even if their play was just part of a cunning strategy of delayed revenge. Consequently, Jarosław Kaczyński lost the election to Bronisław Komorowski.

Act III: The drama of the cross

After a momentary calming of the atmosphere and a return to a 'subfebrile' state, the third act of the post-Smolensk drama brought a return to the main course of the action. And it is significant that this return was prompted not by the main political actors and parties, but mainly by former spectators, who now entered the stage; or more precisely, the square in front of the Presidential Palace, at Krakowskie Przedmieście in Warsaw. Its centre was occupied by a wooden cross, erected in the first days after the crash by a group of scouts. It stood there until 22 May, when it collapsed during a spring storm and was taken inside the Palace by functionaries from the Government Protection Bureau. The decision to withdraw the cross provoked an impassioned reaction among the people who had been gathering each day in the square to carry out their own rituals of mourning and commemoration, and who now opposed governmental attempts to clear their 'street stage'. They created the Social Committee of the Defenders of the Cross, and organized various protests. As a result, on 27 May, the cross was restored to the front of the Palace. However, it returned with new meaning, as the emblem of a community who combined memorialization of the crash with an ongoing struggle against the politicians they accused of being responsible for the tragedy.

This meaning was reinforced soon after the election, when the incoming President Bronisław Komorowski stated in an interview for *Gazeta Wyborcza* on 10 July that the cross should be relocated to a place more suited to its religious significance. This statement seemed provocative for many, and it resulted in a new wave of protests from conservative politicians who vocally supported those still gathering at the site. But there remained a chance for reconciliation. On 20 July, the Chancellery of the President, the Archdiocese of Warsaw, the Student Chaplaincy and the scouts who had first erected the cross signed a document agreeing to its transfer elsewhere. It was agreed that on 3 August a ceremony would be held, during which the cross would be moved to St Anne's Church.

The events on that day led to a spectacular triumph of performance power, proving that underestimating the latter holds the potential for political downfall. The relocation of the cross, planned in concord by the state and church officials, was expected to put the conflict to rest. The symbolic power of the Church, for which the cross is the essential symbol, and the power of the State, exercised (by definition) through the apparatus of necessary coercion, were expected to reduce the likelihood of conflicts in and around the square. However, the unexpected happened. The church and the state, on seeking to intervene in this space – which had by that time become the central stage of Polish public life – performed weakly, displaying few of their characteristic traits. This could be explained partially by the fact that the state, aware of the sensitive situation, did not wish its intervention to be perceived as a kind of power play, nor to provoke the crowds to counterattack and riot. But the ineffectiveness of the Church officials seems inexplicable. Young priests with hardly any assistance were sent to moderate between groups in a public square teeming with tension. This testifies to either utter naivety on the part of the Church administration or a lack of desire for real reconciliation. Given that priests and their superiors are specialists in ritual and have vast experience in organizing public ceremonies, the non-deployment of their customary 'symbolic weapon' for major public events – that is, a show of strength by a monumental procession of priests, headed by a cardinal – should be regarded at least as a symptom of their unwillingness truly to engage in the conflict, or perhaps even as signalling the start of a provocative political game.

Irrespective of motivation, due to the lack of a firm stance on the part of the state officials, the Defenders gathered around the cross and made the relocation impossible. After some further quarrels and jostling for position, the surrounding space was eventually abandoned by both the State and the Church officials. The stage at Krakowskie Przedmieście was proclaimed 'independent' and became a space for an ongoing series of performances, now directed at once against the State and Church authorities. The defenders continued to perform narratives of the dead president as hero and martyr, while simultaneously attacking the ruling powers for betraying the 'true nation'.

Soon the square became the theatre for a 'war of performances' between the Defenders and their opponents. Through the ensuing weeks, both sides staged provocative and scandalous performances, including ceremonies and rituals based on the official 'actors' that were far from politically correct. The Defenders appealed strongly to nationalistic and messianic resentments, positioning themselves as chosen ones ready to sacrifice everything for their faith in Poland and God (the order is not accidental). Their enactments were serious in tone, full of prayers, liturgical gestures and quasi-religious actions. But very soon counter-performances appeared. On 9 August, a mock street protest called *Cross* took place, coordinated via Facebook. According to the organizers, the event was an 'artistic-political happening', comprised of a series of actions that parodied or blasphemously played on the rituals of the Defenders. During the most radical of these mock-rituals, a cross made of empty cans of 'Lech Beer' (with clear reference to the name of the deceased President) was carried aloft with great ceremony. A group of young men tossed around a yellow duck-toy,[6] while rhythmically shouting 'One more' (a typical shout of football fans, demanding one more goal from the terraces). The solemnity of the Church service and the studied engagement of the Defenders contrasted sharply with the carnivalesque play of their counterparts, typified by a reversal of meanings and hierarchies. During this Polish summer carnival, the most painful and serious aspects of the events of the preceding months – death, suffering, sacrifice, martyrdom, memory and respect – were ridiculed and dethroned in a series of improvised and playful performances, the effectiveness of which resulted from their subversion of accepted norms and taboos.

As a response to this mockery, on 10 August, the 'mensiversary' of the crash, the supporters of Law and Justice organized a demonstration to express 'sacerdotal' values, such as the memory of the victims, their honour, the care of the nation and allegiance to the Catholic faith. Both types of performances continued side by side for several days, only partially kept apart by the police. Demonstrations and counter-demonstrations continued for the entire month, and the conflict was fuelled by both sides as they contested the national stage.

As a result of the 'drama of the cross', two diametrically opposed concepts of Polish community gained increased visibility and prominence. One envisioned the nation as united around a central point, the common faith. The other was based on belief in a dispersed community that could provide a framework for diverse, individual initiatives and various ways of dramatizing identity. The group associated with the former employed traditional symbolism as well as national and Catholic myths, especially the Romantic idea of a small group of reckless knights defending the last bastion of freedom and truth, ready to die and convinced that their blood will nurture a new, better Poland. The second group radically rejected the idea of sacrificial death, together with its most significant symbol, the Christian cross. Though later both sides would leave the stage, giving way to a more traditional form of political theatre (see below), this summer 'theatre of conflict' seems to be the climax of the whole drama – the radical act of exposing two irreconcilable images of society that divide contemporary Poland and disrupt any broad agreement about a shared identity through a recurring conflict between 'tradition' and 'modernity'.

Act IV: The struggle for memory

When fall came, the unruly, summer street protests started to lose their momentum and again gave way to more ceremonial acts, dominated by traditional dramatic patterns and actors. Such was the character of a series of consecutive mensiversaries of the crash, organized by Law and Justice on the tenth day of each month, and increasingly more structured and well thought out. The climax of each of those events was a 'Memory March' with torches, culminating with a speech by Jarosław Kaczyński. Due to the ceremonious repetitiveness of those events, the fourth act took on a more serene and stable tone.

Its main theme was memory, which was to emerge as a complex and further contested topic. It became increasingly evident that this memory is not a 'natural' cognitive capacity, but a collective and individual practice that enacts multifarious shifts and reinterpretations. As Jarosław Kaczyński put it, the memory of the Smolensk crash was 'active memory', because it emerged in the form of actions and performances (which had come to dominate what I earlier called Act III). They emphasized the role of Lech Kaczyński as the most significant community figure, the protagonist of memory and the personification of the core meanings and values worth preserving for future generations. Simultaneously this emphasis entailed a necessary, public forgetting of those victims of the crash who did not fit within the framework of the symbolic and political meanings deemed worthy of remembrance. Such people as the left-wing politician and representative of post-communist factions Jerzy Szmajdziński, or the feminist activist Izabela Jaruga-Nowacka, fell into oblivion. Those victims, pushed to the background by the figure of the 'President killed in action', receded into apparent insignificance on the public stage of memory established at Krakowskie Przedmieście, and their deaths resonated publicly only at those sites which commemorated them individually. Thus, the fourth act exposed the ambivalent power of performances described by Joseph Roach in the introduction to his seminal book *The Cities of the Dead*. Roach argues there that 'performance offers the substitute for something else that preexists it' and that it 'stands in for an elusive entity that it is not but that it must vainly aspire both to embody and to replace'.[7] The performances of 'active memory' replaced the metonymic representation of the actual society, instead embodying the 'nation' as personified by Lech Kaczyński and substituted almost perfectly by his double – his living twin brother, Jarosław.

Act V: The anniversary

This performative substitution found its *grande finale* during the commemoration of the first anniversary of the crash. Of course, there were official state events for this occasion, but they were understated and held at Powązki cemetery – far from the central stage at Krakowskie Przedmieście. The square in the front

Figure 8 Commemorating the first anniversary of the crash of the presidential plane, Warsaw, 10 April 2011. Photo by Kamila Sarzynska, courtesy of Dariusz Kosiński.

of the Presidential Palace was again occupied by supporters of the Kaczyński brothers who started their performances early in the morning with ritual actions such as lighting candles and shared prayers. In the afternoon, after the official celebrations had concluded, the post-Smolensk community of remembrance was institutionally and performatively established by these groups as the 'true' nation. The first phase of this enactment took place in an enclosed space of the Congress Hall, where the Lech Kaczyński Social Movement was proclaimed, confirming the former president as the major object of post-Smolensk memory. In the second phase, the gathering moved to Krakowskie Przedmieście, where a rally was staged. Jarosław Kaczyński was the protagonist of both events, giving speeches in the Congress Hall and in front of the Presidential Palace. In the second speech in particular, the leader of Law and Justice drew together and reinterpreted various narratives and threads from the year after the crash, in order to formulate a prophecy about the future of the community and articulate a new imperative to fulfil the national mission. This speech was especially distinctive since, on the anniversary of the former president's death, Lech Kaczyński's twin brother effectively stood in as his effigy, or as a kind of manifestation. In response to his inspired speech, a new Hero was called forth to cries of 'Jarosław! Jarosław!', and a community was re-asserted around him as the crowd continued to chant 'This is Poland!'.

This event ended a year-long dramatic process in which a metonymic representation of Polish community was replaced by a vocal and demonstrative minority, who usurped the exclusive right to prominent social representation. From this point of view, the post-Smolensk dramatic process can be regarded in some way as genuine and effective 'national theatre', in which the place of an incomplete, contested representation is taken by an assertive, activist community. But the consequence of performing this national drama by Jarosław Kaczyński and his followers is a paradox. By repeatedly enacting their community on the basis of a perceived originary fidelity to the tragic event, to memory, to the dead and to their 'mission', Jarosław Kaczyński and his supporters weaved together essence out of contingency. The faith that they profess and practice is the claim of a substantive and real nation, regarded as an entity that is given and cannot be questioned – a 'fact' that is natural or supernatural (which is ultimately one and the same thing). At the same time, this pre-existing nation emerges from affective experiences and a decision rooted in Polish right wing ideology. As the journalist Bronisław Wildstein comments, 'There is no community based solely on rational premises. It must be experienced. . . . At such moments it is possible to establish whether or not one is a member of a given community. This is the moment of choice.'[8]

Therefore, the community is posited as originary, but simultaneously must be created and re-established. This (ostensible) paradox describes the underlying principles of the national theatre at Krakowskie Przedmieście. The nation exists and provides foundations for an identity, but only for those who make the 'right' decision, recognize their place within the framework of the nation and remain faithful to this essential experience.

An obvious question emerges here: how can one know that a certain experience or a certain choice is one that constitutes the nation at a given historical moment? And should we not consider the choice of silence or even mockery just as 'traditionally Polish' as the choice of martyrological heroism? However, if one accepts the givenness of the nation, such questions lose their validity. Asked whether it is possible to feel alienated from a 'national-Catholic' form of Polish community, Wildstein responds that, in effect, an alienated individual simply does not belong to the community, and that any revolt against such an entity runs up 'against the real formula of Polish community, in the name of one that is unreal and therefore non-existent'.[9] Wildstein is right. There is no other form of Polish community that manifests itself so coherently and thus exists as drama/representation. Accordingly, there is no other Polish community that is able to produce the performative 'reality effect'.

Paradoxically, these views resonate with the dynamic concept of nation put forward by contemporary anthropologists and historians.[10] They argue that nation is not a 'naturally' conditioned community but a construct; it is not a community founded on blood ties and the earth, but a result of long-term cultural processes and socialization mechanisms, already in place from the beginnings of an individual life. If nation is not a natural entity, then nobody belongs to it 'simply' because of being born or living in a certain place, or speaking a certain language. In order to become and remain part of a nation – or indeed any other community, including a family, for that matter – one has actively to contribute to its creation, to collaborate in building and rebuilding the symbolic complex that guarantees the uniqueness of national identity. This view opens up a space for alternative identity projects; however, whether these are to be included in the stock of 'national tradition' is dependent on their effectiveness and general acceptance, and not solely their presentation.

In this process, a key role is played by the performative operations that take place among a community of actors and spectators. They enable the unique 'spark' responsible for mutual understanding and unity between the participants, and which constitutes the core of a vital experience recognized as 'the discovery of truth' or even a 'revelation'. This 'truth' – the truth of experience and revelation – is created performatively and reinforced by processes of shared faith and bonding, which can endure even if a group of spectators or co-participants disperses right after the performance. It was to this truth and the forces that it produces that Jarosław Kaczyński referred, whether intentionally or not. It is a community of 'true Poles' who did not rationally create their Poland, but experienced it.

This process was governed by such forces as dramatization and staging, and it unfolded within a heightened, extra-daily context; that is to say, it had a dramatic and theatrical character. These features link national tradition with contemporary politics, neither of which acknowledges the rights of the absent, the silent and the passive. By the same token, the patriotic and nationalist mechanisms of inventing tradition seem to be allied with the paradigmatic order 'perform, or else . . ', which has been proposed by Jon McKenzie as the main power governing contemporary life. At the dawn of the new millennium, McKenzie wrote that 'performance will be to the twentieth and twenty-first centuries what discipline was to the eighteenth and nineteenth, that is, an onto-historical formation of power and knowledge'.[11] In the light of McKenzie's insightful analysis, the Polish post-Smolensk drama seems to be at the crossroads of the two paradigms: by means of performance, it led to the (re)construction of a mission, to be accomplished with all the discipline and obedience of crusaders faithful to a heroic leader. The transformative power of performance, so highly valued by performance art and performance studies, is used here not as a tool of revolution, but as a weapon of conservative restoration. The opposition between traditional theatre and experimental and liminal performances seems to be no longer valid. The same can be said about the theatrical metaphor in general, with its tendency to set apart actors and spectators. In these respects, it seems no longer to be effective as a tool to describe and analyse contemporary political and social life. Of course, some of its elements may be redeployed, as I have attempted myself in this essay. But the crucial thing is to address this traditionally Western notion of theatre and performance as something illusionary or superficial, and thus not 'real'. We are surrounded and ruled by performances. Sometimes we are also damaged by them. So it is misleading and even dangerous to believe that if something is dramatically constructed and performed, it is not effective. It is quite clear why pioneers of performance studies such as Erving Goffman,

Victor Turner and Richard Schechner used theatre and drama as optics for researching social life, but now, several decades later we have to look for such analogies in the much wider field of the performing arts. First of all, we should cast aside the concept that large-scale performances are merely 'expressions'. We should rather regard them as prepared experiences of an unstable nature, always in danger of being reshaped and taken over by the participating spect-actors.

'Social Transformance': In Defence of Political Performance/Art

Eva Brenner

What is 'transformance'?

The notion of 'social transformance' departs from recent socio-theatrical practices developed by the experimental theatre company, Projekt Theatre Studio/ FLEISCHEREI in Vienna, Austria, by taking steps beyond dominant paradigms of 'performance' and 'transformance'. Thus it reconstructs the goals, purposes, theories and practices of political theatre for our age. Social transformance calls for an activist performance/art created for and in local communities by engaged artists and amateurs in dialogue with civil society, human rights groups, political activists, neighbours and non-theatre-going audiences.

Over the past decade (2004–13), a small ensemble of 10–15 artists experimented at a local storefront space, the FLEISCHEREI ('Butchery') in Vienna's bohemian seventh district with new work-formats in order to serve as models for a transformational political kind of performance, cooperating with migrants, refugees, unemployed, senior citizens and other minorities. We call the group 'intercultural' because since its inception it consisted of artists from different cultures, countries and backgrounds – among others, Austria, Germany, Switzerland, Belgium, Italy, France, Greece, Slovakia, Poland, Hungary, Mexico, Singapore, Brazil, Israel, United States and various countries of Africa. This sociocultural laboratory aims at advancing strategies for a 'Theatre of Empowerment', and rests on a critique of postmodern/post-dramatic performance. It outlines the concept of 'social transformance' as fusion of artistic 'performance' works and socially activist 'transformation'.[1]

We must redirect the future organization of all areas of life towards human beings. Human beings must be in the centre of our concern and not like it is practiced today, the forces of economics in a totally isolated way.

– Joseph Beuys, Every Man an Artist [Jeder Mensch ein Künstler], (translation by the author[2]).

In the 1970s, Richard Schechner established the term 'transformance' as part of his performance studies theories to denote social and aesthetic transformational processes, particularly in his essays 'From Ritual to Theatre and Back' (1974) and 'Towards A Poetics of Performance' (1975).[3] Referring to anthropologist Victor Turner, who locates 'the essential drama in conflict and conflict resolution',[4] Schechner situates the dramatic effect in the act of 'transformation' – in how people use theatre as ways to experiment with change. Accordingly, transformation in theatre occurs 'in three different places, and at three different levels: (1) in the drama, that is, in the story, (2) in the performers whose special task is to undergo a temporary rearrangement of their body/mind, what I call "transportation," (3) in the audiences where changes might either be temporary (entertainment) or permanent (ritual)'.[5]

In his essays, Schechner outlines differences between ritual, theatre and performance using his research into tribal settings while analysing the goal of Western avant-garde theatre as acts of approaching community. Referencing Claude Lévi-Strauss, he asserts that 'at its deepest level, this is what theatre is "about," the ability to frame and control, to transform the raw into the cooked, to deal with the most problematic (violent, dangerous, sexual, taboo) human interactions'.[6]

In addition to Schechner's understanding of transformance as characterizing 'transformational' acts of performances – communal (tribal) or aesthetic (theatre) – my use of the term refers to 'social' aspects and locates performance within a political framework based on concrete alternatives, fusing social and aesthetic concerns, and giving voice to processes of change. This concept underscores performance as communal activity in public space, uniting actors (professional and amateur) with partners in local communities (migrants, women, youth, unemployed, political activists and small entrepreneurs). This emphasis of 'social transformance' targets transformational processes capable of co/creating new sociopolitical contexts of emancipation and empowerment.[7] The difference between this and Schechner's approach is a legitimate, but at the same time fundamental acceptance of his observation that performances of various types have transformative power. The 'communal' – tribal or urban – that

Schechner refers to is what I am focusing on, stressing its political function and character of performance.

While Schechner's work remains highly influential, a shift of focus with an eye on societal changes since the 1970s seems necessary. Today we are faced with a crisis of civilization caused by neo-liberal capitalism. This necessitates new responses and new kinds of transformations. At a time when avant-garde performance largely adheres to 'postmodern/dramatic' genres which privilege aesthetic instead of social concerns, people experience startling states of economic crisis, social downgrading and cultural lack of innovation. In Western European societies, today many people experience increasing social stagnation, political pessimism and artistic lack of experimentation. Accordingly, predominant feelings of artists expose a sense at confusion, angst and a loss of hope – sentiments which are also expressed in many postmodern/post-dramatic works.[8]

On the other hand, new inspirations are rising with uprisings in the Arab world and movements across Southern Europe where unemployment is encountered with violent protests ('Indignado' and 'Occupy' movements). It remains to be seen how these movements will help form a new version of political performance.[9]

FLEISCHEREI – A mission

In 2004, the new performance space FLEISCHEREI opened its doors, following a geographic move out of a white-cube avant-garde theatre into the streets in response to funding cutbacks on the heels of a newly instituted 'Theatre Reform' (2003) by Vienna's Social-Democratic City Government. The name 'butchery' refers to the old store-front space's history as a former butcher-store and is also an ironical commentary on neo-liberal reform processes threatening to 'butcher' small cultural initiatives.[10]

The mission of the new intercultural and interdisciplinary ensemble was to develop innovative socio-theatrical working formats based on alternative funding sources and modes of production, by building bridges with the community and attracting new collaborators, audiences and supporters with the goal of re-politicizing and emancipating experimental theatre in our age. Faced with issues such as increasing poverty, violence against women, society's treatment of foreigners or the elderly, and a gradual dismantling of the social welfare state, new challenges are put forth to artists. They are called to participate in social activism, reappraise conditions for art-making and strive to integrate marginalized communities such as migrants, refugees or senior citizens in their work.[11] This programme is based on the belief that consequences of enforced capitalist globalization produce not only precarious working conditions and rising poverty, but more severe migration- and refugee laws, rising xenophobia and a destruction of our environment.[12]

The focus of socio-theatrical projects lies in new concepts of empowerment theory and practice. This can be achieved by taking theatre into the streets, creating new alliances between local, cultural and community groups, and finally counteracting the results of diminishing public funds, the loss of public space and the destruction of micro-social urban infrastructures. This concept of a 'Theatre of Empowerment' privileges process-oriented works, builds on the heritage of the political avant-garde of the twentieth century (from Breton to Artaud, from Grotowski to Boal, from Brecht to Müller) and supports research and development of grass-roots cultural movements based on local autonomy and subsistence.[13]

As noted, Brazilian theatre revolutionary Augusto Boal stated in his book, *Theatre of the Oppressed* – there exist two theatre perspectives. Theatre is for the people when it sees the world from the perspective of, that means understood in constant transformation, with all contradictions and movements of these contradictions, if it shows roads towards the emancipation of man. This perspective makes clear that the people who have been enslaved through work, habits and traditions, can change their situation. It is paramount to push forward those changes.'[14]

The 'Theatre Reform' and the project On Axis as constructive response

The unconventional community-based experimental theatre FLEISCHEREI, established in 2004 in the wake of Vienna's abovementioned 'Theatre Reform', works since 2011 as an itinerant company under the title FLEISCHEREI *mobil*. Having lost its space due to reform-cutbacks, the company continues its course, stresses socio-theatrical formats and tours city-wide and abroad.

The reform's motto 'Less is More!' as laid out in a strategic study paper[15] promised alternative (so-called 'free') theatres of Vienna, by granting larger funds to a chosen few while cutting funds from the rest. This was not easy to legitimize and execute in a social-democratic environment of grass-roots activity, which had blossomed in Vienna since the 1970s. All of a sudden the support for community-based institutions, neighbourhood theatres and experimental groups of little commercial interest was discredited under the sign of efficiency, innovation, festival-compatibility – a stance which marked a radical change from over 20 years of grass-roots oriented social-democratic cultural politics. Although some groups, including the FLEISCHEREI, protested against the reform, a large majority consented, hoping that in the newly instituted competitive game of appointed funding committees, evaluation processes and elite jury decisions they would remain 'winners'.[16]

However, 10 years after its initiation, the reform has revealed itself as a neo-liberal 'de-form', producing 'less' instead of 'more', that is, less funding and fewer projects and cultural spaces. Negative repercussions include a significant depletion of cultural venues, a commercialization and centralization of culture as a whole, a rise of mainstream at the expense of fringe production. Under the spell of the neo-conservative concept of 'creative industries', public funding was redistributed while private sponsorship for the arts promoted. The process resulted in the loss of alternative spaces, in smaller productions, a decline in risk-taking programming, a reduction of general media coverage for the fringe – which has harmed both artists and local audiences. Viennese alternative culture, which used to be the pride of western European social-democracies in support of non-commercial art, has given way to a 'neo-feudalistic' kind of culture of highbrow artefacts for the rich. Espousing a post-dramatic amalgam of new corporate art, remaining 'free theatres' now operate in established institutions, present 'retro-chic' nostalgic projects lacking reference to concerns of ordinary people, favour formalistic experiments and cater to young manager classes and tourists.[17]

The Vienna 'Theatre Reform' produced a successive decline of alternative theatres through a redistribution of resources from 'below to above' (i.e. from smaller to large theatre institutions) – hurting above all small, intercultural and women-led companies – and ended up in an increasingly controlled, economically driven relocation of venues into large 'production-house-clusters' in the city centre. By streamlining the city's alternative theatre scene, the reform produced unemployment among artists and a commercialization and concentration of selected companies with international ties. Groups rooted in the community disbanded, local spaces closed and artists went unemployed.

Figure 9 © Derya Schuberth, Projekt Theater Studio/FLEISCHEREI, 'On Axis: Village Place 2010: everyone is coming here', Performance in public space for the festival Soho-in-Ottakring, May 2010, Vienna, Austria. From left to right: Anne Wiederhold, Francis Okpata, Maren Rahmann.

Socio-theatrical experiments

Simultaneously with the ensuing reform-process, the FLEISCHEREI reduced infrastructural costs and began to operate without entrance fees, turning towards amateurs and community groups, expanding into public space, gaining new funders and audiences, and opening up its space to migrants, refugees, civil and human rights groups, local media and small businesses.[18]

In reaction to the pitfalls of the reform-process, the new artistic team questioned the classical approaches, methods, techniques and efficacy of experimental performance in a period of neo-liberal political, social and cultural decline. Under the title of 'socio-theatrical' experiments, the FLEISCHEREI struggled to create new ways to transcend the prevalent formalistic character of contemporary avant-garde performance, situating itself at the crossroads of intercultural performance, community activism and anti-globalization movements.[19]

From 2004 onwards, a succession of socio-theatrical installations and community performance projects were tested out: from cooking shows with migrants to refugee benefit parties, large street processions and fiestas, talk-shows on radio and local television, performances in local restaurants and marathon productions lasting several days and nights. In 2008 these projects culminated in the creation of an intercultural street-theatre procession project titled On Axis. This has become the group's signature-project, held since annually, and ending with a multicultural and multidisciplinary community fiesta. Artists, neighbours, friends, local entrepreneurs, as well as tourists and casual passers-by celebrate community in this event. They join forces with local businesses, social activists, schools, women's, human rights and refugee-organizations, including Verein Ute Bock, Asyl in Not, Radio Orange and Okto.tv, to demonstrate solidarity against neo-liberal reforms of social austerity and cultural downsizing.[20] These people 'celebrate' as a mixed community of middle-class people, neighbours, business people, artists, but also underprivileged such as migrants and refugees. In terms of the once-a-year art event On Axis, it is an ad-hoc community whereby the project brings together people from different backgrounds, so that they continue to live and act together as a community when the project is over. In that sense the project, now going into its fifth anniversary has created remarkable sustainability – each year new businesses have been added to the list, neighbours offer their help with the next project, and migrants have lost fear of freely moving in and out a quite upscale bohemian neighbourhood.

On Axis is a 'work-in progress', which has been expanding over the last 5 years throughout the urban area of Vienna.[21] The project's precursor was a 3-month migration workshop, Asylcafé, with a final public showing at the FLEISCHEREI with artists, refugees and sociologists co-financed by *KulturKontakt Austria*.[22] Asylcafé combined the teaching of social communication skills, storytelling, singing, dancing and theatre improvisations to a group of 15 refugees of different cultural backgrounds, such as, Afghanistan, Bosnia, Chechnya, Iraq, Kurdistan, Nigeria, Angola, Gambia, Senegal and Republic of Congo. Meeting once a week, the sessions combined singing, dancing, body work, theatre games and improvisations leading to the creation of a performance based on live stories.[23]

Four editions of the eco-cultural event On Axis took place in several of Vienna's districts, each time focusing on a different theme, such as migration, integration, promoting shared community culture, and peaceful coexistence. In 2010, the project received the innovation prize of IG Kultur Vienna (a local grass-roots cultural group) in the category of 'International exchange', following which it has been invited to diverse communities for lectures and presentations and widely covered by the media.[24] This successful socio-theatrical format changed the theatre's theory and practice, pushing it away from classical avant-grade approaches to new sociopolitical concepts, participatory modes of encounter and interaction, and the use of theatre and performance for impacting social change.[25] We call the project 'eco-cultural platform' whereby the 'eco'-part refers to our local district's over 40 per cent Green-Party supporters, and signals a low-energy, low-technology, sustainable undertaking.

Structurally, On Axis consists of two elements: (1) On Axis, the street theatre procession through the district, and (2) the intercultural street fiesta called 'Dorfplatz' (City Plaza) at the end of the event, which celebrates diversity with music, an art auction, communal dancing at the central plaza, a concluding music concert and a party. The procession is constructed of a montage of about 15 scenes, which are created in autonomous workshops led by five independent curators who each direct small groups of intercultural artists. During a few months of preparation, they develop individual scenes at site-specific locations such as shops, shop-windows, cafés, restaurants, the central plaza, back-yards, and at local cultural organizations. Scenes include scenic reading, theatre, cabaret, dance, music and art installations, which mount to a theatrical loop of about 12 stations that form a full mise-en-scène. About 25–45 artists and migrants participate in the processions themselves, while hundreds of spectators, neighbours and passers-by witness the 'grand finale'.[26]

Whereas initial editions embraced wider topics of migration, On Axis 2012 focused specifically on African migrants' stories, songs and dances, which dealt with their experiences after leaving home. Activities included a children's workshop, lectures by migration experts on new refugee legislation which took place at a fictitious 'Mobile Office of Refugee Consultation' and which engaged spectators in discussion. These led to the theatrical procession around the plaza, where spectators joined in singing, dancing and conducting interviews with shop owners, culminating at the 'fiesta of diversity' with up to 300 and more participants.[27]

More specifically, On Axis 2012 included original poetry by Gambian artist, David Jarju, about impressions of an African refugee in Vienna, a freedom-speech by Nigerian actor, Francis Okpata, cabaret scenes by South-African actress, Jenny Simanowitz, accompanied by African-American singer Margaret Carter, street jamming by African rappers Nigerian ethnic group Ofu Obu, Kurdish songs by singer/poet, and Sakina, songs with texts by Jura Soyfer – the 'Austrian Brecht' – composed by Austrian-German duo, Maren Rahmann (Accordion) and Rudi Görnet (Bass), music by Senegalese artist Amadou at a local hairdresser's shop, a Heiner Müller-monologue on slavery by Jewish actress,

Dagmar Schwarz, installations and processions of a 'community dragon' built by visual artists, Markus Kuscher, and Spanish social artist, Marta Goméz.[28]

The format of On Axis has expanded in impact and size and today presents a journey through a local community with participants entering a collective experience; it also exemplifies a collective reflection process on issues of migration and integration through discussions, dance and celebration. A theatrical project turns into a neighbourhood project of communal sharing, perhaps not unlike historical carnival processions and fiestas – traditions which continue to exist in some rural Austrian areas, all but disappeared from the cultural life of our cities. The project gives testimony to multicultural diversity and demonstrates ways to overcome social divisions. Shared acts of performance create moments of encounter, solidarity and recognition of 'the other' through singing, dancing and playing together. It offers a performative context in which the notion of 'community' acquires a new meaning as one close observer remarked who has extensively written about the project. Here are comments by progressive Viennese journalist, author, cultural producer and editor of Europe's largest homeless magazine, Augustin, Robert Sommer, on the 2010 edition of On Axis:

> ... The concept of this astonishing street procession means ... improvisation. ... First of all because of the refreshing unaccountability of amateurs, secondly due to the steady flow and disruption of non-theatrical city life ... the concept is, in my view, ingenious! – Firstly it is a demo following the motto "reclaim the streets." Secondly it is a city tour. ... Thirdly, the real city and its nooks and crannies are ... fairytale like settings for theatre. Fourthly, ... real space acquires a certain aura which otherwise it would not have: a trivial courtyard ... becomes idyllic or enigmatic. ... Fifthly, the integration of shops and businesses, of galleries, and cafés with the lives of owners and clients is an extremely exciting socio-cultural model. Sixthly, the project brings people together. Seventhly, it functions as homage to chaos and indeterminacy. ... And last but not least: It is great theatre! A wandering theatre of bafflement.[29]

While On Axis developed into the group's signature-project in the public arena, the new theatre FLEISCHEREI had established itself within seven short years as new cultural hotspot and vibrant meeting place for political performances, discussion and sociocultural experimentation bringing together artists, intellectuals, audiences and neighbours from all walks of life – people who usually never meet in our society. This quality shapes the work until today. Under the banner of creating a non-elitist 'Theatre of Empowerment', which differentiates itself and takes distance from postmodern/post-dramatic avant-garde projects, performance-, musical- and visual artists from diverse cultural backgrounds (including Eastern/European, African and Asian countries as well as artists from the United States and Latin America) come together in what some might call a new form of popular theatre.[30]

As noted experimental theatre director and visionary, Peter Brook, wrote about the meaning of popular theatre: 'It is always the popular theatre which saves the day . . . the theatre which is not theatre, theatre on carriages, on wagons, scaffolds, with spectators standing, drinking, seated around table, participating, screaming in between; . . . theatre in back rooms, attics, stables, performances of one night, the torn sheet drawn across the space, the movable Spanish wall hiding quick changes – this one theatrical genre covers it all.'[31]

Post-democracy, post-dramatics – and its discontents

'Post-dramatic theatre' was introduced into the critical debate by renowned West-German theatre scholar, Hans-Thies Lehmann, in his standard work 'Post-dramatic Theatre' (1999).[32] There he offered a broad overview of 30 years of radical avant-garde theatre development in Europe and the United States (1970s–late 1990s) subsuming it under the label 'post-dramatic', which is proclaimed a new theatrical paradigm. Over the past decade, the term has been widely disseminated if not overused as it has come to denote each and every performance that no longer adheres to the classical unity of space, time and action.

Lehmann defines this new genre as theatre beyond drama – encompassing experimental, avant-garde, subversive, radical, risk-taking and postmodern strategies – or 'theatre after theatre' which seeks to overrule social norms, conventional notions of character, theatrical space, time and storyline. While experimenting with non-linear structures, it erects aesthetic 'practices of exemption' to produce states of heightened perceptivity in the audience. Traditional Brechtian fables (narratives) are abandoned and psychological characters, dramatic teleologies and Aristotelian unities are suspended.

Theoretically, post-dramatic theatre reflects the postmodern performative turn of the 1990s and is indebted to the strategies of deconstruction, destabilized meanings and ambiguous constructions of identity ('simulacrae') leading up to pessimistic societal visions often emanating from Francis Fukuyama's notion of an 'end to history' (1992).[33]

In contrast to traditional theatre since Greek drama, which operated under the order of text, the 'post-dramatic' genre uses such diverse inspirations as visual imagery, music, dance, poetry, news reels or oral histories as source material, as Lehmann outlines in quoting the later works of East-German playwright, Heiner Müller: 'Müller calls his post-dramatic text "Description of a Picture," a "landscape beyond death" or an "Explosion of a Memory" in a dead dramatic structure.' This describes post-dramatic theatre: the members or branches of the dramatic organism are, even as dead material, still present and form the space of a memory breaking open in a double sense. Also the prefix 'post' hints at a culture which has stepped out of its previous horizon of modernity, yet [still] in relation to it – a relation of negation, liberation or playful exploration of what's possible beyond this horizon.[34]

Lehmann asserts that since 1990, theatre has lost its social impact or efficacy. While giving credit to the importance of historical avant-garde traditions (1920s and 1960s), 'post-dramatic' theatre has left revolutionary potentials behind. It shares with postmodern art characteristics of neo-expressivity, hyperrealism, ambiguity, process-orientation, subversion of codes and anti-mimetic qualities.[35] As post-dramatics privileges an 'aesthetic behaviour of transgression', the stakes no longer lie 'in themes, but in ways of perception'.[36]

In his newer work, *Writing the Political*,[37] Lehmann advances the 'post-dramatic' and substantiates the concept of an 'aesthetics of interruption', reflecting on post-dramatics as bringing the radical analysis of a 'society of spectacle' by Guy Debord full circle.[38] In Lehmann's eyes, traditional political theatre is restricted to deceitful media images which cater to audiences while the 'postmodern' genre locates the Political where it is not perceived, giving representation to disclosed issues which transcend the realm of visible political 'realities'.[39] He declares any theatre of explicit political intention as non-effective and leading into a void. Quoting Derrida, he substantiates a postmodern 'aesthetics of interruption' whereby theatrical discourse breaks 'reality apart' and disturbs spectators' false naiveté.[40] Theatre as something 'fundamentally other' has impact, according to Lehmann, only as far as it is not re-translated into logic, syntax and political vocabulary:[41] 'The truly social in art is the form.'[42]

Over the past years, younger scholars have sought to supersede Lehmann's theses promoting a more aggressively a-political stance of a post-dramatic and 'post-spectacular' paradigm. By quoting the French philosophers Derrida, Baudrillard and Rancière, Jan Deck declares most political theatre as 'not advanced', and the engaged intellectual as having lost his/her field of discourse in an age of neo-liberal capitalism.[43] Post-dramatic approaches 'offer the chance to locate the political in theatre in the void of political theatre: In the very situation of making theatre, in its production, staging and reception.'[44]

> Making theatre politically moves beyond the poles of engaged art and "l'art pour l'art" insofar as artistic processes in art become the political act themselves. . . . The "political" resides in the artistic approach to the material.[45]

Although much can be technically learnt from postmodern und post-dramatic aesthetics – that is, rhizomatic narrative structures as well as anti-hierarchical, multidisciplinary and intercultural aesthetic values – I take issue with its philosophical, social and political repercussions. While the label 'post-dramatic' reaches back to the 1990s, it continues to resonate today as having pessimistic, often cynical perspectives on life. The post-dramatic has abandoned the 'principle of hope'[46] and articulates a kind of 'aesthetics of surrender' which, as formulated by the team of FLEISCHEREI and myself neatly fits phenomena of neoliberalism: (1) hostility towards and/or loss of working-class history, political and avant-garde; (2) lack of theoretical foundation; (3) neglect of (socio-) economic theory; (4) abstract constructions accessible to mostly elitist audiences; (5) expropriations of 'first' and 'second' avant-garde formal innovations (interdisciplinarity, change of awareness, reorganization of actor-audience relationship, environmentalism) while denouncing radical politics; and (6) discharge of social efficacy, that is, socially transformational qualities of theatre.

In my view, this paradigm refutes visions of emancipation, empowerment and social change, leading to the conclusion that an avant-garde turned 'mainstream' cannot effect positive sociocultural transformation, as it is existing outside of societal rules, agreements and conventions.[47]

Recent publications of Lehmann's disciples tend to reiterate the master's findings and continue to advocate ambiguous ideas of a radical 'theatre of interruption' which undermines 'prescribed modes of behaviour'.[48]

As opposed to post-dramatic paradigms, which are ambivalent towards phenomena of 'real' life, 'social transformance' aligns itself with concrete social issues and movements, heralding a new era of political theatre. This happens at a time when protest movements against worldwide crises as a result of neoliberalism – producing austerity, new poverty, a dismantling of the social welfare state, even a threat to democracy – are on the rise worldwide.

Motion V

At War

Beyond the Boundary of the Agora: The Hilltop Performance at the Western Front, 1915

Annabelle Winograd

Figure 10 The presenter, combatant performance: North of the coast of Talou, Meuse, France, October 1915. Photog. Lieut. Barbier, © BDIC, Paris.

Socrates had a friend called Simon. He was a sandal-maker. According to legend, he let Socrates use his house for discussions when the conduct of such discussions was not allowed in the Agora. Simon's house was just outside the *horos* of the agora. That boundary was defined by fascinating stone markers about three feet high, one of which declares *Horoseimi tes agoras,* "I am the boundary of the Agora."[1]

I begin *in medias rés*. A photograph. A rudimentary performance space on a hilltop patch of earth. Blankets stretched between five poles suffice to raise a warfront scenography; a 'poor' theatre. Establishing shot: October 1915, near the old mill at Côtelette, north of the coast of Talou in the Meuse, France, WWI. A squad of artillery soldiers sprawls on the ground; some look away, not yet fixed on the show. I'm drawn at first to the tight circle of spectators, the absence of costumes. All the participants, in some form of their regulation daily-life army clothes, seem to be in a more egalitarian relationship to one another than they might be in the regimental space down the hill. Then I note the photograph's sunlight and shadows, its shades of light and dark and grey. But above all I'm struck by its sense of intimacy. 'This is ours,' the photo says, 'we are doing this.' This intimacy, this drawing in, this elected-enclosure creates a self-organized pocket, a small world shaped so that its participants might pursue their practice, quite autonomous of the immediate surround – the war. One of the men addresses his comrades. I call him 'the presenter'.

I would not have stayed with this image long had I not found, elsewhere in the same archive, that is, by chance, a second.[2] In the decades the photographs had sat cramped in the long wooden file drawers of the Photothèque of the BDIC, the Paris archive of all photographs, both amateur and professional, of France's wars

Figure 11 The soldier-victim, combatant performance, Meuse, France, October 1915. Photog. Lieut. Barbier, ©BDIC, Paris.

since the beginning of photography, no one had set the second alongside the first to create a series: the visual narrative of at least part of a performance.

The shift to the second image is transformative. Time has passed; sun and shadow have shifted; the wind has come up, and the audience thinned. The photographer, one Lieutenant Barbier, has moved in close, and following his camera's eye, we face the soldier-victim: eyes blindfolded, pants pulled down around his ankles. At his side stands a soldier with a stick. I call him 'the powerful one'. And then suddenly, the image grabs me with its hook, the unanticipated emergent action from the audience: three soldiers have turned to acknowledge Barbier, probably one of their own. Their grins, complicit, implicate him and themselves, folding him into the group, the movement of social life suddenly and spontaneously forming a powerful curve, a bonding, suggesting that what they are watching, what he is photographing, should not be watched, not be photographed, not be done.

Torment, suffering inflicted upon the other, a canonical subject in art, is often represented in painting as a spectacle, something that one observes (or chooses to ignore), and our own viewing of the second photograph is one of those occasions that a mediatized life provides for us to, as Susan Sontag has told us, '[regard] – through the medium of photography – the pain of others'.[3] Through thousands of photographs taken at the front, I've searched for the acting-out of the violence of the war and of the complexity of combatant sexuality – not photographs of atrocities, but of the performance of an act of atrocity, the performance of an act of violence or of sexual taboo. Here, I think I have found it.

In his *Violence and the Sacred*, René Girard argues that actual violence always threatens the social life of a group. 'The function of ritual,' he writes, 'is to "purify" violence, that is to "trick" violence into spending itself on victims whose death will provoke no reprisals'[4]; and Performance Studies theorist Richard Schechner responds to Girard: 'All this sounds very much like theatre . . . dramatic narratives and theatrical actions are so often . . . explicitly violent'.[5]

In the hilltop photographs, the violent encounter *is* the afternoon's activity; no soldier downtime theatrical, but performance retaining its power and danger to wound, to terrorize, even to kill. The important thing here is what you do, not what you think, believe or say. Is the palpable tension in the second photograph of a simulated ('trick'), or actual sadism? Has the photographer in this warfront photo-shoot, caught an act of surrogation in progress, a spectacle in which one person is sacrificed on behalf of, or instead of, others; in which ritual or ritual-like practice becomes popular entertainment? Or are we in the presence of a real flaying of Marsyas? Will the humiliation and shaming end in sodomy? Is this 'action' – and I choose precisely this extremely political term to set what we see as antecedent to the later performance activities of the Vienna Actionists who, in their carnal and bloody actions of the 1960s, blurred the line between art and daily-life – is it a forbidden action, as Schechner, invoking anthropologist Victor Turner, describes the ritual process in some of its incarnations: 'unauthorized, anti-structural, subjunctive, subversive'[6]? Is it, as in Russian Roulette – a common and outlawed life and death game played in contemporary armies – a repeated high-stakes practice, in which warfront madness is so rampant that no one pays much mind to the danger of a spun barrel on a loaded revolver, and the spectators, all intimate participants, laugh in anticipation of the shot that will bring in its wake a death or a reprieve? I cannot know the answers to these questions but suffice it to say that on the hill, a meaningful number of both performers and participant-observers are getting what they need, what the group needs to function as a group: signals of solidarity, displays of power, of sexual prowess/sexual coercion, the marking of boundaries, identifying an 'other', perhaps blood. Certainly by 1915, into the second year of the war, soldiers were functioning in extreme-trouble: all their accepted texts, accepted feelings, accepted ways of using their bodies had, like worn cloth, been rent apart; their readiness for the life of the liminal/liminoid, the betwixt and between was, by then, all. Soldier was marked person: bearing the wounds of the break-up of everything he recognized.

All violence is performative for the simple reason that it must have an audience, even if that audience is only the victim. The hilltop 'action', the performance, the series of photographs, is a pornography. *Yo lo vi* as Goya wrote beneath one of his *Disasters of War* images. 'I saw this', and beneath another, *No se puede mirar*, 'One can't look', and finally, *Estto es lo verdadero*, 'This is the truth.'

The hilltop photographs, while set within my category of representations of performance-at-the front, sit at the far end of its spectrum, different and distant from the kinds of combatant performance based on soldier 'trench-scripts', those sketches written by soldiers to be performed by soldiers before an audience of soldiers. These overexcited, disorderly, ranting, funny, filthy texts were, in performance, sung, danced and improvised with a pronounced 'low' Bakhtinian carnivalesque sexuality, physicalized on stage and particularly displayed by the x-dressed soldier-woman. The *poilu*-voice ('*poilu*', the hairy one, is the name affectionately given the unshaven French foot soldier) in the combatant trench-scripts is the last of the unheard soldier voices of the Great War and offers a kind of testimony that Samuel Hynes in his *The Soldier's Tale*[7] calls the 'pre-tale' of soldier life, the immediacy of speaking before the story had achieved literary coherence as in novels and memoirs. The audience of soldiers for these performances at the front in 1914–18 comprised the largest *coterie* group of spectators since fifth-century BC Athens, and the performance spaces at the front were, in the terms of sociologist Erving Goffman, a 'backstage' area, an *ob-sceneum* where ordinarily proscribed impulses might be indulged: a dangerous space as the theatre has always been. Here is secret knowledge.

Still, in the hilltop 'action', there is something most deeply secret, more deeply 'other' than the widely shared culture of soldier theatricals I have described briefly above. The hilltop 'action' seized in the two photographs presents an encounter best defined by Performance Studies theory's apposite terms 'is performance' and 'as performance'. 'Is performance' refers to the theatre – an aesthetic genre which we can define simply as 'I know it when I see it'. And I know when I see it, that the hilltop performance at Côtelette is not theatre; it is an 'as performance' event – a way of being in the world, unstable, unpredictable, unscripted even when scripted; it is how we perform in our daily lives: sport as-performance, ritual as-performance, identity as-performance, war as-performance.

Misreading the hilltop performance as benign rather than confronting its liminal praxis is the kind of pitfall that Performance Studies researcher Ian Maxwell (using his own examples) cautions his colleagues against, alerting them to beware the siren call of Victor Turner's focus on the liberating efficacy in ritual-derived forms of cultural performance – what Turner calls its 'fructal chaos': ways of making the social structure work without causing too much friction. Maxwell warns of both 'the allure that such an intensity of experience holds for participants, and no less the allure of that state as a theoretical construct',[8] one, Maxwell argues, foundational to the project of Performance Studies. Turner's faith in a fundamental human goodness, Maxwell writes, has proven irresistible to Performance Studies:

> By elevating and sanctifying the rapture of intense shared physiological, psychological and phenomenological experiences as moments of liberation, of a beneficent fundamental humanity, we run the risk of mis-recognizing the flip side of the picture . . . something altogether darker and dangerous at the heart *of communitas. . . .*"[9]

What happens at the hilltop leads us to the issue of the impossibility of knowing the other, the praxis of an 'other' – soldier-as-other – and demands for its moment, our 'ignoral'[10] of anything we thought of as soldier performance at the front. 'When we study other cultures', Dutch ethnographer Johannes Fabian writes, 'our theory of their praxis is our praxis . . . and the foremost problem of ethnographic writing is the meeting – I prefer confrontation – of kinds of praxis, ours and theirs,[11] and Clifford Geertz dictates: 'we have met the Not-us and they are not-Us.'[12]

The hilltop performance cracks open combatant cultures at the front, challenging me to pursue, what Don Handleman, in his essay 'Why Ritual in its Own Right? How So?'[13] describes as a 'thought experiment': first, to separate, to an extent, arbitrarily, the phenomenon of a ritual (and I say, of a performance), from its wider sociocultural order, its environment, so as to analyse it 'in and of itself' – exhausting what can be learnt of ritual from ritual (of a performance from its performance). This analysis, Handleman writes, is not an end in itself, for the second step will be to re-embed the ritual (the performance) in the social order with the added knowledge of what has been learnt about it. The intention here, 'is to explain ritual more as … form, and less so as social order … a premise of a-representativity of ritual phenomenon, a position neither pro- nor anti-representation.'[14]

The hilltop performance in-its-own-right is intimate, self-enclosed. It has been initiated and is being performed and observed by what Elias Canetti has called 'the pack' (as in wolves) – the smallest unit of a fighting force always seeking to enlarge itself, to become 'more', to eventually become 'the crowd' of Canetti's towering treatise, *Crowds and Power*.[15] In his book, Canetti posits the bleak ethical void, the fundamental amorality, at the heart of the crowd (of which 'the pack' is its primal-category). The pack is not beneficent, it functions out of hunger, it bares its fangs, it pulls aside the curtain on the potential for the dark and dangerous at the heart of *communitas*. Pack-performance is filled with an intensity of experience; it is doing something to its participants; they will come out elsewhere, otherwise. 'Ritual performers may wish they were in the theater', Schechner writes in his essay 'Living a Double Consciousness', where 'when the play is over, they can step out of their roles and show that everything that happened onstage was make believe. But no such luck. … Ritual's actions are not make-believe, they are make-belief. … The outcome is binding'.[16]

The barren space of the performance at Côtelette has separated itself and its participants from the sociocultural order that is – for the time it has taken the sun to move – elsewhere, apart, and what happens on the hill is autonomous of its surround. But surely, what has gone round there will come-round with a difference. The outcome is binding. The soldiers, many times betrayed, were not to be betrayed by their own performances. That this performance's twisting back and torquing into the social order of the warfront, that its re-embedding itself into that world and that order has been, and remains, problematic, is attested to not only by the displacement of the two photographs in the Paris archive, by their having been secreted away in plain sight, but by the fact that years of research have not turned up anything remotely resembling them in the multiple collections of either texts or images of the Great Wars' three major powers: France, England and Germany.

British war historian John Keegan tells us,

> Soldiers are not as other men—that is the lesson that I have learned from a life cast among warriors. The lesson has taught me to view with extreme suspicion all theories and representations of war that equate it with any other activity in human affairs. War . . . must be fought by men whose values and skills are not those of politicians or diplomats. They are those of a world apart, a very ancient world, which exists in parallel with the everyday world but does not belong to it. . . . It follows it at a distance. The distance can never be closed for the culture of the warrior can never be that of civilization itself.[17]

Numerous claims insist that ritual does something, often transformative, whether temporarily or permanently to cosmos and participants. To do controlled transformation, a ritual form must 'know' it is doing this, it must recognize change as both property and product of its operation.

The hilltop performance 'knows', it 'recognizes' what it is doing. It is a marker place of soldier culture[s], unique in exactly the ways it is different from what theatre researchers think of as theatre at the front, and from what war historians have allowed themselves to look at in soldier culture[s]. Reading soldier trench-scripts and photographs not as literature or illustration but as performance, and performance itself as a critical wedge to open soldier identity at the front, enables the raising of a lost soldier voice, a different history.

What is dramatically different in the hilltop 'action' is that it is the 'doing' that is critical, and the form that the doing has taken, and not the act of reflecting or reflecting-upon combatant culture[s], as in the soldier trench-texts and performances. At the hilltop, the social order, for a time apart, lives down the hill. The hilltop performance can only be enacted beyond the boundary of the Agora.

Dismantling Road Blocks: Non-Violent Resistance of the Palestinian-Israeli Group 'Combatants for Peace'

Chen Alon

Combatants for Peace is an activist movement founded in 2005 by former fighters, Israeli and Palestinian, determined to abandon the vicious circle of violence. Committed to non-violence, the movement's aim is to put an end to Israeli occupation of Palestinian territories, to stop the Jewish settlement project in the West Bank and to establish a Palestinian state alongside the State of Israel, with East Jerusalem as its capital.[1] This chapter discusses the activities of one of the movement's five regional groups – the theatre group 'Tul Karem-Tel Aviv' – that comprises 15 Palestinians and 15 Israelis and practices a unique form of the Theatre of the Oppressed method.

In recent years, the Theatre of the Oppressed method created by Brazilian director and philosopher Augusto Boal has become one of the most popular and useful types of theatre worldwide. Since its inception during Brazil's military dictatorship of the 1960s, the Theatre of the Oppressed has been part of the field of social and community-based theatre. Its aim was to function among specific homogeneous communities, at the centre of which were the members and groups of society, namely non-actors;[2] the Theatre of the Oppressed has expanded since the 1980s – when Boal's writings were first published in English; today, hundreds of groups practise the Theatre of the Oppressed in many places worldwide. In Israel and Palestine, the practice and research of the Theatre of the Oppressed are still in their infancy. Only a minority of theatre creators and social activists in the region is familiar with the possibilities offered by the Theatre of the Oppressed, its variety of methods and techniques.

Some of the initial rituals of the Combatants for Peace movement, such as the exchange of personal stories and testimonies, were performative. As co-founder of this movement, I found myself the only member familiar with the practices of Theatre of the Oppressed, and most significantly with the function of Joker – not only a theatre director but also facilitator, teacher, political leader, ethnographer and researcher. As such, I believed that the movement could benefit from establishing its own activist theatre group. It was difficult, however, to persuade the Palestinian members that theatre-making can in any way relate to political activism. For them, making theatre with Israelis was perceived as compliance with normalization which they rejected, as engagement in cultural activities in times of struggle, even as collaboration with the oppressor. It took 2 years of cooperative theatre-making and building of mutual trust to establish an awareness of the impact of theatre as a political instrument and even as a non-violent weapon.

One should keep in mind that the present depiction is written with an awareness of the paradoxical telling of one story that is in fact two – Palestinian and Israeli. Furthermore, the violent past experiences of the members of Combatants for Peace and their respective societies dictate the different dynamic readings, interpretations and narratives of the concept 'violence' and of its opposite, 'non-violence'. Different interpretations of violence are part of this polarized process: to this day, Palestinians find it difficult to see the act of throwing stones at Israeli tanks as violence. For them, it is an act of defiance symbolizing the asymmetry of heavily armed oppressor and unarmed, oppressed civilian. To Israelis, it is similarly difficult to perceive the soldier manning the checkpoint as violent. For them, he acts in self-defence. Consequently, there are also two different approaches to the concept of non-violence.

Boal speaks of the cathartic, transformative moment that is unique to the *Theatre of the Oppressed*[3] – a moment in which the 'I' turns into 'we'. Not dissimilar to Victor Turner's concept of *communitas*, this moment normally occurs in a homogeneous community. Our group, however, is polarized. It consists of Palestinians and Israelis who share a vision but have differing affiliations, memories and experiences. We therefore seek three phases of communitas: one for each subgroup, and a third one for the entire, polarized group.

A central and unique feature of non-violent struggle is the fact that the strategy and the tools of the struggle and its aims are identical and not separate. It is important to note that the concept of 'non-violence' is not characterized solely by the absence of violence, but precisely by the fact that it is nearly always one side, the non-violent one, that absorbs the violence of the other, violent side.[4] The reflection and the experience of Combatants for Peace have taught us that non-violence is first and foremost a performance, because its deepest goal is not to defeat or to win power, but to *show*. In our case this means showing the enemy, the world, a transformative image of power relations, and at the same time showing that this image exists as reality, made of the same social, historical and human matter. Dr Martin Luther King Jr repeatedly argued that the aim of non-violent struggle is not to defeat the adversary, and assuredly not to bring about its downfall and humiliation, but to establish a new and equal justice, stressing equal rights and creating dialogue and a culture of equal rights. The means to achieve this aim must be as pure as the aims of the struggle itself.[5]

The interdisciplinary research field of art and non-violent struggle is surprisingly sparse. Apparently the reason for this is that the field itself, integrating art and activism, also termed by practitioners as 'artivism', has only recently begun to flourish, research of the field developing along with it.[6] One of the pioneers in non-violence research, for example, Gene Sharp, makes only brief mention of the use of the arts, including theatre, in the field of non-violent struggle. There are evident performative elements in Sharp's scheme, in the form of political satire in humorous skits, plays and singing.[7]

From its inception, our activist theatre group has operated under the tension of an inevitable polarity: the need (mostly represented by Palestinians) to present activism and resistance against the occupation, versus the need (mostly represented by Israelis) to construct dialogue and establish trust within the group. This tension has been explained by social psychologists specializing in inter-group relations. The oppressed side is more interested in action in respect to power relations and oppression and their political foundations – collectivization of the discussion. The privileged side generally attempts to direct the discussion to a personal, individual, emotional – 'non-political' – level.[8]

Through direct action: The Shuffa performance

Bearing this principle in mind, and being aware of the urgent need of our Palestinian partners, subjected to close scrutiny and pressure by their surroundings (again, a performative concept), preference was initially given to activism on the ground.

A decision was reached to postpone to a later stage proper theatrical activity, characterized by dialogue and reconciliation. The reasoning was that any direct action would include performative elements that would allow us to reflect on the process as in direct theatre.[9] The group defined its vision as the aspiration to reach a point where the group's common non-violent struggle would be essentially realized by means of theatre and performance.

In the early phase of theatrical work, it already became clear to the group that the most urgent issue was that of the heaped cinderblocks used to obstruct entrance to the village Shuffa. The group decided on a direct action of dismantling the roadblock, which held the most destructive significance for the Palestinians villagers, as it had turned the road – previously linking the village of Shuffa and the city of Tul Karem – into one accessible exclusively to Israeli settlers and soldiers. This was not the first direct action taken against barriers in the territories, but it was uniquely designed in performative terms. So was the agreement that the shared design of the act following the event would be carried out in a group with theatrical means. This constituted a link in the protracted circular process to which we were obligated – of action and reflection.[10] Among other things, this process enabled examination of the connection between direct actions and different forms of activist theatre that we strove to develop as a shared, polarized, Israeli-Palestinian culture of non-violence.

Planning the action thus included conscious performative elements: first, the choice of stage and action – the space in which it would take place and the specific action it would follow, namely the action as 'a display', presenting the Tul Karem-Tel Aviv group to its 'new audience', most importantly the Palestinian inhabitants of Shuffa; second, the group determined who would be 'the actors on stage' – those who would dismantle the roadblock, Israelis and Palestinians together; and facing them, who would serve as spectators at the performative events: an audience of Palestinians and Israelis who would watch the action but not take active part in it. Moreover, we knew that besides the invited audience, an audience not officially invited was certainly expected – soldiers and settlers. Some members of the group, Israelis only, were assigned as a buffer between the soldiers and the action itself. Their role was to speak a previously written text about the non-violent principles of the group and the fact that its Israeli members were former soldiers. This, done calmly and persuasively, was an attempt to mitigate any violence by the military forces present. Eventually the action, surprising us, took place exactly as planned, right up to dismantling the roadblock, without any resistance by the soldiers and settlers. This was primarily due to the controversial (among the Palestinians) act of unceasing calming talk with the soldiers, and our affirmation that the event involved a non-violent group and non-violent action.

This issue – of either holding dialogue with the army or ignoring it in direct action – remains controversial. We suggested to the Palestinians to set aside the basic political assumption held by the group, according to which we are all in the same boat – oppressed by the army and not negotiating with it. We were sure that this assumption, in this situation, effectively served those in power. However, the reasons for a dialogue with the army were not solely pragmatic. It seems that both ethically and politically there is no reason for the oppressed to communicate with the oppressor while the boot of the latter remains on the neck of the former. A more complex observation of the situation as a theatrical scene shows that through the dialogue, the soldiers and officers become participants in the action against their will. It even demands them to make moral decisions, allowing for their transformation. Despite the fact that in their helmets and bullet-proof vests they look impervious to transformation, sealed, impenetrable, we insist on seeing the transformational potential within them, their humanity. Through engaging the oppressors in the space of action with a dialogue that subverts the foundations of Boal's homogeneous model – denying any dialogue with the oppressor – we turn them from spectators into spect-actors.[11]

Usually, of course, we fail. In this case too, the success of the action was cut short in the second phase. After dismantling the roadblock, we stopped at the next obstacle with the intention of marching together back to Shuffa along the road that was forbidden to Palestinians. However, as soon as we began to march, the soldiers fired stun grenades immediately followed by rubber-coated bullets at us. Ten participants were injured – half of them Palestinians and half Israelis.

Figure 12 With IDF soldiers becoming spect-actors, 'Tul Karem-Tel Aviv Theatre Group' is performing near the village of Izbat-Tabib in 2013. Photo by Combatants for Peace.

Site-specific invisible theatre and the vision of a utopian space

Boal's first book briefly recounts the Invisible Theatre technique,[12] and his second book, *Games for Actors and Non-Actors*, surveys its technical development in depth.[13] Essentially it consists of the covert mounting of a piece of provocative theatre in a public place, so as to cause discussion and debate among unknowing 'spect-actors'.[14] Boal emphasizes that Invisible Theatre is first and foremost theatre: it is perceived as a play, including actors who play characters and a prearranged text. The chosen subjects for invisible theatre are of utmost importance to the actors and spect-actors. Invisible Theatre is only staged in public spaces that are not defined as theatre spaces, and only to an audience that does not know that it is an audience.[15] 'Invisible theatre is not realism, it is reality.'[16]

In conventional theatre, the consent of the audience and theatre-makers is that the architecture can add and remove meaning in accordance with the needs of the play. The same space can be a fifteenth-century open field or an American kitchen in the 1950s.

In activist theatre, the space is a dimension in itself,[17] and in the polarized model, it is sometimes even the decisive element.

Site-specific theatre is usually dependent on the given space defined by the architecture.[18] In the case of a performative resistance group, site-specific theatre actually depends on the political context, as place is not merely architectural space but also charged with the political significances of the system of power relations that functions on and in it. With an intimate performative process, it often becomes a utopian space, enabling one to experience and imagine a place in which external power relations are cancelled and no longer exist.[19] However, in such cases, neutralizing the power relations from actual reality and leading to their apparent disappearance effectively reaffirms their presence.

The concrete embodiment of polarization in space facilitates mobility and transformation of the individual, the single-nation group and the polarized plenary group. The possibility of imagining and then embodying crossing borders between polarized spaces within the framework of theatrical exercises – in which one can cross the imaginary 'line' and appear next to or inside the opposite group – is charged with performative utopian potential.[20]

Boal contends that the non-violent performative act constitutes trespassing.[21] The fact that non-actors create a theatrical space for themselves challenges the accepted perceptions of 'who is allowed where'. This is a fundamental principle of the main technique of the Theatre of the Oppressed, Forum Theatre. Its ethics and aesthetics require and transgress an additional border, as it enables the oppressed (the spectators) to go on stage and replace those who have already trespassed (the protagonist/s).

The choice of a liminal space, between two areas – between two roadblocks that separate Area A and Area B,[22] when it is unclear whether we are in Area B or C and the authority is not defined – has led to many conflicts with the army and to several grotesque situations. One of the main elements in oppressed space is the issue of observed and observer – the oppressed are already in strange/alien spaces, controlled through monitoring and surveillance.[23] Similar to hegemonic space, at the roadblock we find ourselves in a space under observation, a fact replete with theatrical implications.[24] The space is undefined, but nonetheless it is a space we have defined as ours. We have gradually developed a type of connection with the area as a performative space. We have chosen to act in the space in which we are being observed by soldiers and military cameras, by settlers and by Shuffa farmers.

Due to the proximity of the military surveillance camera, soldiers constantly approached our gathering. The regular presence and intervention of the soldiers at encounters had different effects on the polarized group. On a fairly regular basis, the following scene ensued: we sat in a circle at the foot of the olive tree, between the two roadblocks. An officer and soldiers arrived, and immediately perceived that Israelis and Palestinians were sitting together. They asked 'Who are you?' We replied, 'Human beings, and who are you?' The officer said, 'I am in charge here, you are forbidden to be here'. We: 'Who is "you" and what is "forbidden"?' and then confusion took over: the officer said 'You are in Area C' and we said 'No, this is Area B'. For 3 years, we had never met a soldier, officer or policeman who could officially define the 50-metre space between the two roadblocks. This fact surprised us, but also helped, enabling us to turn the situation into Invisible Theatre.

Who is in charge? Unidentified power in a blocked area

We did not know ahead of time that the blocked area would serve us as a work space for an extended period of time, but realizing this we began to consolidate different strategies of Invisible Theatre. On the one hand, we inhabited an imaginary space, utopian, from which we sought to achieve a dialogue, equality and justice; on the other hand, reality itself penetrated into the same space. We chose a strategy that would not allow external interference to cancel the encounter for which we had gathered. Travelling to the Occupied Palestinian Territories, where different laws and borders restrict our presence either individually or as a group, is part of the principle of the non-violent struggle.[25] Our defined aims were to eliminate disruptions, create a protest and confront our internal needs as a polarized group, experiencing external interference in different ways. In other words, one of our aims was to show understanding of and sensitivity to the emotional and political needs of both sides of the polarized group. We asked ourselves how we might protest together by means of theatrical activity against the incursion and trespassing of the army into the intimate lives of the group, while also preserving one of the central principles of Theatre of the Oppressed – making invisible oppression visible.[26]

Our initial tactic against military interference was to sit in a circle and, when we noticed soldiers on patrol, two previously selected Israelis from the group would go and speak to them. The result was positive, as the group's representatives embarrassed and confused the soldiers, and consequently we were never asked to leave the place. Nonetheless, our talking to the soldiers led to feelings of resentment among the Palestinians, despite their appreciation and understanding of the motive – to avoid conflict between them and the army.

Figure 13 Making oppression visible. 'Tul Karem-Tel Aviv Theatre Group' performing near the village of Shuffa in 2009. Photo by Einat Gutman.

They contended that avoiding conflict did not serve the group's aims, but established an element of normalization. They were also concerned about how things might look to Palestinians in the 'audience' of this Invisible Theatre.

In response to the feelings and needs of the Palestinians, and wishing to examine additional modes of action, we initiated responses based on theatrical games and playing. In one encounter, aware that in a matter of minutes the soldiers would show up and disrupt the meeting, I suggested playing 'King of Movements', a game that would warm us up and prepare us – as in Theatre of the Oppressed – for the encounter with the oppressors in reality. Invisible Theatre allowed us to determine the conditions of the situation and create a different reality, imaginary and subversive.[27]

In the 'King of Movements' game, a volunteer leaves the circle and the group decides who will initiate the movements and the sound. When the volunteer returns, the group is to imitate the leader's movements without exposing him/her. The volunteer stands in the centre and tries to detect the focus of changes in movement. When s/he discovers who is 'king', the 'king' goes out and a new leader is chosen, and so on. When the soldiers arrived as expected and asked 'Who is responsible for the group?', we suggested that they join the game and work it out for themselves through the rules of who is the 'king'. They were taken aback and stood aside. Even though the action we practised was only a protest against oppression rather than direct confrontation, it created a new link in the encounter/conflict with the soldiers.

We often chose to ignore the soldiers as a tactic. On one such occasion, as we sat in a circle, the soldiers shouted from the road, 'Who is in charge?', and we did not reply but continued to play our childish games. 'Hello, I'm talking to you,' shouted the patrol commander. We did not reply. The soldiers joined their officer and asked 'Who is in charge of the group?' We remained silent and continued to ignore them. The soldiers noticed the Israelis in the group, and realizing they were not authorized to deal with Israelis in that situation, they summoned a civilian police patrol car. The policeman who arrived immediately entered the circle and aggressively asked in Hebrew and Arabic, 'Who is responsible for this group?' Again, we did not answer. The policeman stood confounded, wondering what to do. Suddenly shots were heard – first the sound of a single shot and then a volley. The atmosphere became charged as everyone tried to discern the source of fire. Only after a few seconds, as the embarrassed policeman took his mobile phone out of his uniform pocket and the sound of shots as its ringtone became evident, was that 'source of fire' revealed. In the ensuing silence, he answered the call, his voice greatly lowered and, while he was leaving the circle, the group burst into laughter, giving new meaning to the concept of comic relief, resonating Boal's definition of catharsis in Theatre of the Oppressed. The written situation that included gathering in the space and deliberately ignored those representing the powers that be also included the policeman as a spect-actor, interacting in the Invisible Theatre – writing, directing and playing his own role.

Utopia displaced: An experience outside Palestine or Israel

The performative principle operating in the space of the action can be compared to a certain extent to some avant-garde artistic processes, such as Happenings. Boal relates to the concept of a Happening when he defines Invisible Theatre, while emphasizing that it differs from Happening and guerrilla theatre.[28] Francis Babbage contends that Boal needed to distance himself from the new and experimental theatre phenomena of the 1960s to which he was exposed in the United States. Babbage explains that the reason for this distancing was his strong nationalist sentiment in the time of struggle against dictatorship. Those years led him to stress the authentic Brazilian culture of the Theatre of the Oppressed.[29] Susan Lacy – a performance artist who, in the early 1970s, engaged in social issues by means of place-dependent community performances with local residents – connects Theatre of the Oppressed and performance art. Lacy asserts that they are connected not only in their temporal proximity, but also in their aesthetic and thematic similarity. Lacy compares Kaprow's demand to add to art the possibility of concealing from the audience the fact of its being a spectator or present at a work of art, with the principles that Boal outlines for Theatre of the Oppressed in general, and Invisible Theatre in particular.[30] To support this claim, she cites a relatively early statement by Boal: 'If you make any change within the theatre – a theatre that has a proscenium, a stage, an arena, or a combined version of stages – this is but reformism, you are not really changing anything. We believe that you can go any place and make theatre.'[31]

Elsewhere, Boal clarifies that he also considers Happening and guerrilla theatre to largely preserve the old theatrical patterns.[32] Lacy contends that these types of performance allow artists to embody different characters (personae) concomitantly – the experiencing, the reporting, the analysing and the activist.[33]

Lacy bases this on her contention that 'man is political', in the sense of an unbroken line of artistic experiencing that embodies the journey from the personal to the public.[34] In connection with this theory, linking between Theatre of the Oppressed and theories of performance art, one should comprehend the events of the polarized group in spaces that are obviously not theatre performances venues.

Two principles combine to define these events as polarized invisible Happenings: space and time that are neither Israel nor Palestine, undefined areas – occur beyond the space and time of the conflict, beyond its signs and representations.

In the year 2009, the group was invited to Ireland and England. This visit to a space that was neutral for the two groups allowed performative and theatrical events that were not possible in the conflict zone. The Irish and British hosts functioned as part of the event, but their presence was that of observers. (Customarily at a Happening there are several degrees of participation). The local audience experienced the event neither as life nor as a work of art, but as an intermediate experience in between.[35] The sense was one of space and time detached from reality for a while, and the event created and presented conciliation, tranquillity and harmony, an experience detached from reality and concomitantly constituting the concrete reality of the polarized group.

Finding new territories to exchange identities:
The example of a football game

Schechner, following Geertz and his reading of different human behaviours as symbolic acts,[36] claims that a tight link exists between performance, ritual (religious or other) and sports. The difficulty in separating the shared components in these fields raises the question what differentiates them, and leads the observer to discern the functions they serve, the place in which they occur and the social circumstances of their existence.[37] Moreover, the expected behavioural codes of both their active participants, the actors and the spectators at the event, differ and therefore provide different experiences to everything concerning the event.[38]

Towards the end of the group's intensive journey in Ireland, aiming mainly to deepen the internal theatrical process, the group decided to take a break and go to the beach at Donegal in western Ireland. It was a short distance from the work space. The spontaneous arrangement for all the group members included a football game that divided the members into teams, set up goalposts and meticulously followed the score. Despite the fun and leisure framework, a sports game ostensibly devoid of importance, the question arose how to divide the group. One of the participants suggested Palestinians against Israelis, another suggested mixed teams ('We're Israelis and Palestinians here, but also men and women, and that's a more significant factor where football is concerned'), and then a suggestion was made and unanimously accepted – to integrate: we would play in mixed teams – Palestinian-Israeli and men-women – but each group would be defined in advance as a national group. In other words, there was an unconscious desire in the group not to disconnect completely from the reality of the conflict, to continue to imagine ourselves within our national framework. The mixed team, through the football game, displayed nationalism by imaginary means, representations and symbols: for all those present – spectators and players – it was agreed (as in theatre) that the game being played was between Israel and Palestine. The entire process was accompanied by quips and laughter, jeers and jokes, as well as cheers of encouragement and booing inspired by and related to reality. The irony and the laughter continued even after the game, when 'Israel' beat 'Palestine' to a 7:3 score, mainly due to the fact that none of the Israelis scored even one goal, which were all scored by Palestinian players. The latter taunted the Israelis (as part of the imaginary reality that establishes mutual relations with the reality of the dispute): 'You're not players, you were just statistics, we could have played without you'; while the Israelis replied: 'What does it matter? Whatever you do, in the end Israel wins . . .' It seemed as though the Irish and British watching us didn't really understand us. It was once again cathartic to laugh, let go, roll around until we could hardly stop, Palestinians and Israelis, caught up in the way in which reality, game and performance had all intertwined.

Theatre as Metaphor: Isôko Rwanda's Trilogy of Time

Jennifer Herszman Capraru

You can be performing it as theatre yet at the same time it's reality . . . I know that I am performing, and I have to pass on the message at all cost. Yes, because the message is to tell the people—then people will do everything they can to fight against genocide all over the world."[1]

Isôko Theatre Rwanda is engaged in a three-part performance project begun in 2008 and called the *Trilogy of Time*. The first part concerned the past of Rwanda (*The Monument*, 2008), the second interrogated the country's present (*Littoral*, 2010) and the final part will speculate on the future, in an interdisciplinary performance piece to be created by Rwandan artists and presented in 2014, the 20th anniversary of the genocide. In this paper, I will refer to personal experience as the founder of Isôko Theatre, and analyse how Isôko's work enlists metaphor in performance to help create safe spaces for dialogue. To accomplish this, I will discuss the two plays the company has already mounted, both in terms of text analysis and in order to argue that their real meaning can only be situated in their live performance. Additionally, I will discuss how performances evolved in the Rwandan context. In order to take the reader into the experience of the work, it is cogent to enlist personal recollection – and from there raise theoretical questions.

Isôko Theatre was founded with the aim of creating contemporary intercultural theatre with a focus on human rights, and also as a contribution to social harmony and cultural growth in Rwanda. The company was awarded local NGO status (No. 52/2009) and is partnered with Theatre Asylum, Canada. The group was founded on 4 July 2008 in Kigali, as 4 July marks the end of the 100 days of the 1994 genocide.

What might 'safe spaces' mean in performance in post-conflict Rwanda? In the work of Isôko, they consist of performance-driven non-judgemental spaces, built through trust developed over time, and further bonded by communal labour. In this way, safe spaces were first created among our group in rehearsals. Later, we endeavoured to communicate them to audiences during and following performances by creating performance that uses metaphor to suggest, but not directly surrogate for, Rwandan realities. Discussion framed by performance is the methodology Isoko enlists to deploy performance as ritual, ritual as an element of catharsis, catharsis – and the lacuna created when it is not forthcoming – as healing, and healing as hope.

The two productions of Isôko Rwanda, *The Monument* (written in 1995) by Colleen Wagner and *Littoral* (written in 1999) by Wajdi Mouawad, are by Canadian authors, and are set in unnamed post-conflict landscapes. Performance, in the case of such non-localized Canadian texts, serves as a bridge across cultures and human experiences by exploring mimesis in the social arena. 'A play is play', as Peter Brook has said. Plays should reflect us back to ourselves. In these texts, 'us' signifies the human race. The writers are not Rwandan, but through the use of theatrical metaphor, their writing articulates universal truths. It is the open-endedness of these works, described in detail later in this paper, that makes them adaptable to a new cultural context. Both narratives are universal in their geography – neither name-specific locales – but are written as poetic transpositions. They are apolitical in that they do not take sides, but present characters, in the genre of Brechtian social constructs. Characters are represented without moral judgement, thus letting the audience decide whom to side with. The works speak of anger but do not seek to create anger, and achieve this by keeping a critical distance from specific realities. Both plays offer a dramaturgy that dances with catharsis, in that they lead to it, then pivot away without the satisfaction of an expected resolution. In doing so, rather than providing relief, the texts open a questioning space for dialogue by revealing rather than telling. They invite the audience to complete the labour of the live with our troupe in an atmosphere in which they are encouraged to ask questions, or to answer them. The artists of Isôko – whom, apart from myself and past collaborators from Canada, France, Benin and Lebanon – are all Rwandan, want to tell their country's story by using socially engaged performance to contribute to building a world where genocide is no longer possible.

In my position as a foreigner, having first come to Rwanda in 2006 to work on the crew of the Canadian feature film *Shake Hands with the Devil*, it has been crucial to observe and learn from my Rwandan colleagues. To never forget that the Rwandan people are working through immense emotional pain and will continue to do so for generations. Artists and audiences welcomed our theatre company. Both texts were approved by Rwanda's Ministry of Youth, Culture and Sports, whose officials attended performances. Isôko is now touring internationally, to the World Stage in Toronto in 2011 and the Dialog Festival in Poland in 2013.

Isôko's productions in Rwanda evoke the past by letting conflicts in Bosnia or Lebanon, though unnamed in the plays, surrogate for Rwanda to some degree, and enlist metaphors to send signals: for example, an actor embodying a soldier or a prisoner, via material signs such as properties (a rifle) and costumes (a prison uniform). In Rwanda, contemporary performance is undergoing a renaissance, and theatrical metaphor has the power to speak to an audience via the collective memory of a people engaged in witnessing a story that is about them, yet simultaneously, not about them. Though the two plays in Isôko's repertoire stand in for Rwanda, neither was adapted to be set there. This is not theatrical metaphor in a non-local universal classical sense, such as in the Greeks or Shakespeare, but metaphor 're-localized' in a local ground of meaning which connects immanent sites: Bosnia and Lebanon suggest Rwanda. By avoiding the grafting on of another locale to be read on stage as Rwanda, lacuna are created, providing spaces for the audience to imagine their own experience, and perhaps provoke critical thinking.

Rwanda is engaged in a paradoxical journey through time, in which a people does not want to forget 1994, yet at the same time must move on and renew its country. This drive forwards, out of the past, through the present, into the future, combined with the renaissance of contemporary art, is deeply engaging, as it affirms the value of performance in rebuilding civil society. It is a country that can be contradictory in that it is undergoing an unprecedented process of reconciliation, yet at times appears to be a land trapped in memorial. Adding hope transforms recollection from the passive into the active. Honouring yet moving beyond tradition is a venture into the unknown land of the imagined – and this is the territory of theatre.

Out of the past: *The Monument*

Isôko Theatre Rwanda's first production was *The Monument* in 2008, an award-winning drama which has been translated into six languages. The context is a barren post-conflict landscape that suggests Bosnia. The narrative begins when a widow (Mejra) rescues a young genocidaire (Stetko) at his moment of execution, on the condition that he will do as she wills for the remainder of his life. As her captive, he is forced to re-trace his thoughts, re-live his deeds, until he finds again the site of genocide. In the climactic scene, Mejra forces Stetko to unbury and name each of his 23 victims, among them her missing daughter Ana. After this final and shared ordeal, she releases him, and he asks for forgiveness. In the final tableau, Mejra freezes with one foot in the past and one in the future. This metaphoric space is one of potential forgiveness, and is the space that Rwanda is moving through today as the government continues its project of 'promoting national unity and reconciliation'.[2]

Thus, the play ends with a question for the public: is it possible to forgive after genocide? And if so, how? The question is asked by creating a 'safe space' – one which does not embody literal history onstage as it is too recent and would fail to create the necessary distance to critique or understand, neither does it deliver a universal metaphorical truth that would not touch local audiences. The question, and perhaps the answer, lie in the search for the right scale, the elusive temperature of distance between and from other historical spaces. *The Monument*'s eternal story of war, retribution and the need for co-existence has fit contexts from Germany to Romania to China. Isôko was the first to premiere it on the African continent. For Rwandans, engaged in an immense project of rebuilding, restoring and cohabitating, watching their actors speaking in their language, Kinyarwanda, while embodying the struggle towards forgiveness, and the ambivalence inherent in this act, is memory as memorial, and a living metaphor in service of accepting the other. Finally, this space of meaning appears as a liminal one, in transition between there (Lebanon, Bosnia) and here (Rwanda).

The context

Rwanda is a beautiful country, composed of hills and lakes, and was referred to by the neo-colonial regime of past president Grégoire Kayibanda as the Switzerland of Africa – a name contested by the Rwandan Patriotic Front's more self-sufficient government. It is home to the rare silverback mountain gorillas, a string of volcanoes, leapfrogging technology and genocide. In 1994, a million people were killed in Rwanda during a murderous campaign of horrifying efficiency.

During the 100 days that began on 7 April, priests killed parishioners, students killed professors and parents killed children. All Hutu were to be implicated, and of the Tutsi, none were to be left to bear witness. The shadow of 1994 is long. It stretches over the land in liminal and subliminal space. Due to this history, the government's focus is on strengthening national unity and rebuilding social infrastructure. In a grass roots movement, artists and audiences are engaged in a project of rebuilding cultural infrastructure. What contemporary culture – or modern theatre or drama – that existed pre-1994 is largely lost. But new voices are making themselves heard.

Richard Schechner writes in *The Future of Ritual* that 'the best way to understand, enliven, investigate, get in touch with, outwit, contend with, defend oneself against, love . . . others, other cultures . . . is to perform and to study performances and performative behaviours in all their various genres. . . . And what is performance: behaviour heightened, if ever so slightly, and publicly displayed, twice-behaved behaviour?'[3] Why perform genocide twice through theatrical surrogation? Why perform it once, even, or the aftermath of it? Because what happened in Rwanda concerns us all and as such should be made visible. As the Ivoiran writer Veronique Tadjo argues, it is 'not only a unique affair of a people lost in the black heart of Africa . . . but to forget Rwanda is to walk blind . . . into obscurity, arms outstretched, into a certain collision with the future'.[4]

Artists placing the aftermath of trauma on stage come face-to-face with a lacunic dilemma: there is the moral obligation to bear witness to crimes against humanity using artistic mediums, yet artists may be rendered mute in the face of an event of unimaginable magnitude, such as genocide. This event, beyond imagining, is somehow to be imagined. Moreover, it is to have performative language imposed upon it. If bringing trauma into representation while balancing the ethical dimensions of the task is so problematic, why do it at all? The most fundamental argument, as Blanchot states, is that shining a light on disaster may enlighten us about why such tragedies have occurred throughout history.[5] Yet this leads to another dilemma: *who* may attempt it? Only those who have experienced the trauma? But what if they lack the necessary skills to bring the work into being? Can they be trained, and if yes, should they be? Conversely, if the artists are trained but have varied knowledge of the trauma they represent, that is another road into the same conundrum. And what of the slippery politics of voice: who is speaking, who may speak, who is not speaking, and why? Your trauma is not mine, just as your performance is not mine. However, one of the currencies theatre trades in is metaphor. Archetypal figures on stage performing a narrative can serve to access universal tropes across time and cultures. And universal experiences collapse boundaries through the communal witnessing of human stories.

Performance is memory, it is a memory-act. It may not be possible to look at something head on. To see it, one must glance to the side, and wait for it to shift into focus. In performance, we enlist metaphor to achieve this glance, to carry the narrative above the experience of life. In the case of Isôko Theatre, the issue is to anchor metaphor in the local, and carry the narrative of genocide above the experience of daily co-existence by suggesting but not simplifying universal contexts.

While a rich tapestry of ancient performance traditions dating back to the fifteenth century continues in Rwanda, the country has a small but growing contemporary theatre culture. Much theatre in Rwanda falls under the rubric of 'theatre for development' – community and NGO work designed to spread awareness about social issues such as HIV. There is a focus on theatre as a tool for reconciliation, less so on the viability of theatre as a cultural resource. Modern languages scholar Chantal Kalisa notes that theatre in Rwanda is deployed primarily as a vehicle for bringing social issues to the public's attention. But, she cautions, representations of trauma remain problematic:

> It is my observation that theatre is present in Rwanda and is perhaps the most visible form of artistic expression. The subject matter often relates to the question of reconciliation as well as other economic, health, and social issues in post-1994 Rwanda. The idea of enacting genocide raises ethical questions such as how do you "create a spectacle" based on disastrous events?[6]

Though two theatres existed in the defunct French Cultural Centre in Kigali until 2006, there was in 2007 only one purpose-built theatre in all of Rwanda, at the National University in Butare. In late 2008, Ishyo Arts Centre opened its doors. It was founded by Carole Karemera, an artist from the diaspora raised in Belgium and one of the three Rwandan women dedicated to creating sustainable theatre that also includes Odile Gakire Katese from the Democratic Republic of Congo, and Hope Azeda from Uganda. Ishyo Arts was closed in May 2013 as the building was sold, but for 5 years formed the centre of Kigali's artistic hub.

After completing field-testing workshops and readings with audience feedback of *The Monument* and *Littoral* (at Gisozi Genocide Memorial and the National University of Rwanda in 2007), I was convinced by local audiences that these plays would be acceptable to a Rwandan public. I moved forward with *The Monument* and decided that the language on stage should not be that of the colonizing forces, but the local language of Kinyarwanda. The trained actresses from the diaspora whom I had worked with in French and English readings told me they did not speak Kinyarwanda confidently enough to perform in it.

Eventually I was introduced by Katese to an artist at the University Arts Centre named Jaqueline Umubyeyi, leader of the all-woman drumming troupe *Ngoma Nshya* (New Drums). Umubyeyi is a teacher who has acted in a few public service announcement films – but never in a play, let alone a two-hander about the aftermath of genocide. She is a confident public speaker who speaks excellent French. In rehearsals, French would be the lingua franca, and the text was translated into Kinyarwanda. She was also a survivor who had lost most of her family in 1994, and was struggling to raise her two children and support her traumatized brother. I was seriously concerned about how working on the play would affect her emotionally, but she assured me that she would be able to handle it.

Meanwhile the search for an actor to play the part of Stetko was ongoing. I auditioned anyone who had performed in high school, as a traditional dancer, singer, or hip-hop artist. During my search, I ran into Jean Paul Uwayezu, a student in management who had been a natural talent in a youth group I led collective creation with. In auditions, I did not discuss ethnicity, since colonial forces had made a disaster out of imposed differences. Casting was based on talent. It was only later that I learnt that Jean Paul was a survivor. His family objected to him taking the role because for one thing, for his costume he would have to wear the hated pink prison uniform of the Rwandan genocidaire, just like real prisoners. This was a troubling and interesting moment. Theatre and reality blurred, as the material elements in the daily life of Rwandans were 'twice performed' on stage.

Material and performance realities

Materially, creating theatre in Rwanda presented constant challenges. But trust was more crucial to locate than infrastructural solutions. Trust between Rwandans has been a matter of renegotiation since 1994. Paul Kagame's government has discouraged tribe-based terminology in order to unify all ethnic groups as Rwandan. We prepared our work within this official context, and also remained hyper-vigilant about re-traumatization. Solange Umuhire who, with

Ruth Nirere, played one of the two characters I added in my mise-en-scène, said of their roles as the disappeared girls Ana and Ini:[7]

> To be a part of this play and make sure it doesn't happen again, at least we have hope, that it happened, but we don't want another generation to face it. . . . It's very heavy, it's very intense . . . sometimes among the cast it's hard to pull ourselves together, and I really thank God that so far we haven't flipped.[8]

Biographical questions to actors about their characters – why am I here? Where do I come from? Where am I going? – wave flags for performers in post-conflict Rwanda, where colonially imposed notions of ethnic division fuelled attacks from 1959 onwards. In rehearsal it remained unsaid but implicit for both the cast and I that questions of ethnic identity would only arise around the fictional lives of their characters. We navigated together. The word – together – was essential to our work in Rwanda in a more crucial way than in theatre I have directed in less heightened circumstances. The project became larger than a theatre production. To be able to work as an ensemble meant we had to learn intimately how to co-exist. We built solidarity through a long and demanding creative process, balanced with commitment to our Rwandan audiences, who

Figure 14 Jaquline Umubeyeyi as Mejra and Solange Umuhire as Ana, 2008. Photo by Nick Zajicek.

would ultimately include survivors, perpetrators and everyone in between. As artists from different cultural backgrounds, we built trust through the daily labour of rehearsal.

As Isôko rehearsed, trust among us transformed into action on stage. Jean Paul, who lost many members of his family in Cyangugu Province, played the hated militiaman Stetko, who was ordered to rape and murder. That story is not Jean Paul's. Yet, in terms of the given circumstances of the character, Jean Paul had traits in common with this young man who talks of family, his girlfriend, having a beer and taking a leak more than he does of his crimes. In this way, actors and characters crossed ethnic lines to meet the rigorous demands of live ensemble performance.

> MEJRA
> The truth has a way of emerging.
> Nothing can stop it
> once it's started.
> I may be gagged
> my husband tortured
> my house burned down
> my land stolen
> my children savaged
> but the wind will speak my name
> the waters will tell the fish
> the fish will tell the hunter
> "I am".
> I am.[9]

Rwandan audiences

As we stood before the audience at talkbacks, informing spectators that the play had been written in a universal sense, for Bosnia, for East Timor, we often heard – mostly in rural areas – 'that's not possible. We thought it had only happened here'. This gave us the impression that it helped Rwandans to learn that yes, it had happened in other cultural contexts. Many times.

My reflections on the Rwandan reception of *The Monument* reveal the risks and benefits of using metaphor as a theatrical strategy. Audiences hungering for justice reacted personally to a story informed by the Balkans, but also struggled to reconcile that story with their need to move forward. Some saw it as re-enactment of a genocide event, while others read its divergence from strict Rwandan reality as a flaw. This clash between expectation and outcome came to life after each performance. However, the point of attack in the play, of a survivor securing the release of a prisoner, was born out of the playwright's imagination.

> At our version of Gaçaça [traditional courts], the post-show talk, we the artists stood trial. Discussions lasted hours after the performance, and often had to be cut short. At times a few people would leave, or sit sobbing quietly. A few times, survivors would stand after the show and give testimony. But the first questions we invariably received at talkback sessions were not emotional and were from men. Women were mostly shy to speak. For the men, legal questions came first, fast and furious, emotional responses later, as they questioned the verisimilitude of the play. "How did this woman manage to do this?"; "Did she bribe the judge?"; "Who is she in fact?"; "Are you advocating this become law in Rwanda?"; "What if everyone took a prisoner home?"; "What then?"[10]

The labour of the live is a large element of the production's outcome or result. By embodying the journey we took to realize our work on stage, the Isôko team enacted the work of building trust in post-conflict zones as essential, difficult and without a discrete end. This 'outcome', however, can be hard for Western audiences to accept. At Toronto's World Stage, the four actors and director came face-to-face with audiences in discussion every night. We replaced the pleasure of closure as the curtain fell with a call to witness. Rather than a positive ending that performed reconciliation, the play ends with a question: 'Can you forgive me?' asks the boy soldier. 'How?' answers the widow. Catharsis is not on the menu.

My staging brings the final monument from which the play takes its title, that of 23 girls' bodies, to the audience, rather than as specified in the stage directions: 'The corpses have been seated. Stacked in a circle, looking out.'[11] I never conceived of the 'bodies' as life-sized representations of women. They were remnants dug from the red earth, informed by the murky glass cases I had seen in Auschwitz. These personal fragments (a comb, a notebook, a crucifix, a pair of broken glasses, a baby's blanket) are carried by the twin ghosts of Ana and Ini to be laid to rest at the audience's feet. Only the circle of 23 candles, one for each missing girl, is nearer. The remains of victims dissolve into the forest, just as the production dissolves into memory and forms a counter-monument rather than one of stone: a monument that will disappear into remembrance. This leaves the audience with the work of memory, as the ontology of performance resides in its ultimate disappearance.

Performance studies scholar Peggy Phelan reminds us that the live, or liveness, exists only in the present moment and in a shared space. It cannot be saved, documented or represented. Once it is, it is something other than performance.[12] Live performance is the most palpably human of art forms, with roots linking us back to ritual and the sacred. In Rwanda, one could feel the audience owning that, by how they leaned into the circle, took breath with the actors, drank in each word. Most stayed in their seats after the curtain call, waiting. If we had not planned talkbacks, they would have occurred spontaneously. Unknowingly, these first Rwandan audiences contributed to the work by increasing our awareness of our responsibility in asking them to journey with us for 90 minutes back to the 100 days.

While the play offers a glimpse of hope in a final moment of possible forgiveness, it does not answer the question of how forgiveness is achieved. In our production, this invitation to closure never marked the end of the performance. The talkbacks formed the second half of the evening, and exposed a crucial challenge to audiences and artists alike. The function of performance is to lead us to the source (isôko in Kinyarwanda means source) of theatre, deeply planted in communal cleansing, witnessing and justice.

> This thing called reconciliation. . . . If I am understanding it correctly . . . if it means this perpetrator, this man who killed my son, if it means he becomes human again, this man, so that I, so that all of us get our humanity back . . . then I agree, I support it all.
>   —Cynthia Ngwenyu, facing the state-sanctioned murderer of her son at the Truth and Reconciliation Commission, RSA.[13]

Into the present: *Littoral*

Lebanese-Canadian playwright Wajdi Mouawad's works are steeped in the political and social context of his homeland. Lebanon's themes of exile, war and the journey into identity provide the landscape of his texts. *Littoral's* (*Tideline* in English) intertwined stories of collective trauma, ethnic conflict and laying loved ones to rest intersect sharply with contemporary Rwandan realities. Unlike *The Monument*, *Littoral* (performed in French), though violent, contains scenes that are absurd, erotic and ludic. Its diversity of characters mirrors the population of Rwanda, who are composed not only of the three ethnic groups of Hutu, Tutsi and Twa, but also of a diaspora returning from every corner of the globe, returning refugees who were absent for decades and returning genocidaires from DR Congo whom the government is re-integrating. This social experiment is happening in the most densely populated country in Africa (300 people per square kilometre) – in a country that in 2009 changed its official second language from French to English and is the only former French colony to have joined the Commonwealth. Isôko's second production brought to the stage a fictional world and a theatrical mythology that would acutely pinpoint the realities of a fragmented nation striving towards unity, in an attempt at social acupuncture.

The Canadian poet and classics professor Anne Carson points out that,

> "there is a theory that watching unbearable stories is good for you . . . but do you want to go down into the pits of yourself all alone? Not much. What if an actor could do it for you? Isn't that why they are called actors? They act it out for you. You sacrifice them to the action. And this sacrifice is a mode of deepest intimacy of you with your own life" (Carson xi).[14]

This returns us to the origins of drama as myth. *Littoral* begins in the mythical, when, as Oedipus did, supposed orphan Wilfrid discovers he does have a father, but one who returns only after death, demanding that his son bury his body in his ancestral land. Due to ethnic differences (in this case Muslim and Christian, which refers to Mouawad's own mixed parentage), Wilfrid's mother's family refuses to allow the father to be buried next to his wife. Accompanied by the walking, talking, rotting body of his father, the son voyages across the sea and begins a journey into the territory of the self – just as Rwanda's returning diaspora are in the process of doing as they reclaim their identity. Touching upon the trope of lost biography, the play excavates the mind of a young man born in exile whose life is terrorized by memory in many forms; testimony, dreams, letters, spirits and by the metaphysical pull of 'home'. The central dramatic action, Wilfrid's indecision in how to bury and honour his father (referencing Hamlet), generates subtext intimately familiar in a country where many citizens have never found the remains of family who have been missing since 1994.

Le Chevalier, Wilfrid's guardian, a character written as a knight of King Arthur's court, accompanies him. In the Rwandan context, this pivotal figure was portrayed as the warrior Muteraçumu, Thrower of Spears – pure spirit and mythical Rwandan protector of the *mwami* (king). The Rwandan actors selected this legend to remind modern audiences of dignity and right action. The first act of the play takes place Ici (Here), and the second Là-Bas (There). Here and There in Mouawad's text stood for Montreal and Beirut. In our production, workshopped in 2007 and 2009 and performed in Kigali and on tour in Rwanda in 2010, the plan was to stay true to the author's world, which hints at Lebanon but is not set there. The geography and characters populating *Littoral* are symbolic, which made cultural transposition possible. Audiences readily understood archetypes such as survivor, militiaman and orphan. There is universality in the specificity of war, and though the written text gave few clues to locale, our performance text grounded parts of the play in Rwanda with signifiers such as certain costumes, properties and music. The balance again is to find the universality in the specificity of a local performance. This functions when the universal meaning is paradoxically delocalized and re-localized in a new context. Thus, the liminal 'safe space' provides the key between 'there' – the universal, and "here" – the local. A narrowing of the context to represent only Rwanda, when this was never the playwright's intention, would forfeit its meta-level. It is through metaphor that *Littoral* achieves its epic power.

Wilfrid: I opened letter after letter to find, to understand. My whole life was spilling out of those envelopes, my memory, my imagination, everything, was slipping away and dissolving. I suddenly had the overwhelming feeling that I wasn't me anymore, that there was another Wilfrid and that *that* Wilfrid was someone I could almost see and touch. All those letters my father wrote me, what were they if not proof that I never really existed, since they weren't addressed to me but to someone other than me, another who looks like me, who's the same age, whose name is also Wilfrid, and who, by the most amazing coincidence, lives in my body? I spent the night poring over those letters. Many talked of the land, my parents' homeland, of childhood. Always the sea, often the sea. With my mother. Sometimes death, often love. A lot of love.[15]

The play is divided into six sections: There, Yesterday, Here, The Other, Road and Tideline. Premiering the play in Africa – which was over *there* to a Canadian audience – meant that in Africa, *there* became Canada while *here* was Rwanda. The son encounters familiar archetypes from oracles to soldiers who help or hinder his task of burying his father's body in a country where one additional corpse is one too many. This need for closure echoes a ritual that takes place each April during *içyunamo*, or mourning, when all bodies found throughout the year are buried. The national mourning period lasts for 1 week, during which there are memorial services, candlelight vigils, televised documentaries and radio broadcasts about the genocide, and public billboards about commemoration. Businesses are closed and classical, if any, music is played. On 7 April, apart from groups of survivors bearing candles, the darkened streets of Kigali are eerily empty.

In his search for a holy burial, Wilfrid will be aided by the figure he meets last, Joséphine, just as returning diaspora seeking the remains of their loved ones are helped by local Rwandans. Joséphine is also an orphan. First, she is heard but not seen, whispering the names of the dead as she struggles to inscribe them into her memory, a ritual that echoes the mourning period, when groups of survivors share testimony and recite the names of the dead. Upon meeting the other travellers, Joséphine's first act is to demand a pencil to write down the names. Draped upon her are pre-war telephone books. Through these repositories and by her recital of the missing, she is memory incarnate. She represents the survivor, determined not to walk into oblivion and lose the past, but to instead carry the names – to *Carry The Word*, as Holocaust survivor and author Charlotte Delbo titled one of her plays. As our actress Natacha Muziremakenga was 7 months pregnant, she carried the past on her back and the future in her belly, both her real and metaphoric identities embodying Rwanda's push towards the future.

Walter Benjamin, borrowing from Freud and relating experience to art, speaks of two kinds of memory – voluntary and involuntary. Benjamin states that consciousness is essentially a filter that registers events by categorizing them. This is voluntary memory, in which one recalls events. When consciousness is unable to process an event, one may not have a full memory of it, and what is left are traces. Involuntary memory can be brought about by a shock and, unlike voluntary memory, it is closer to lived experience.[16] Actors develop a memory-mechanism through the study of techniques such as Stanislavsky's sense memory. It is in order to register an experiential mode of memory that art must go beyond meaning, narrative and language. It must awaken the traces left by experience that live in our subconscious. This is the domain of involuntary memory. It lives in the realm of the imagination and the domain of theatre, where reality is re/created, re/membered and possibly made whole. As French literature and genocide scholar Jean-Pierre Karegeye puts it, 'art, in the context of genocide, relates to bearing witness, while at the same time to social engagement.'[17]

To connect to the diversity of Rwandan audiences, I chose for the mise-en-scène of *Littoral* a metaphysical compass between the binaries of dream and reality. The production utilized an expressionistic style, gluing then un-gluing the narrative from reality in order to place spectators in a subjective world through the use of a mise-en-scène which enlisted imagery built of repetition, doubling, mirroring, in order to create an element of the uncanny. *Littoral* is an unpredictable world where the dead speak and the living listen. Its ontology balances on the *littoral*, or edge, between dream and reality, living and dead, past and present, there and here, self and other – binaries that are deeply relevant in Rwanda. However, the foundational narrative upon which the text rests is that of exile. Successive waves of refugees fled Rwanda in 1959, 1972, 1990 and 1994. Like Wilfrid, returning exiles are suspended in an ambiguous state of otherness. They are neither here nor there, but balanced on the edge, between memories preserved for years in the diaspora and the current realities of their inherited nation, one in which they may be perceived as strangers. This feeling of estrangement, brought to life through a theatrical language of metaphor, is the space Isôko created in performance each night in front of its diverse yet somehow unified audience.

Through performance, questions on how to sustain a more humane world can be raised, whether by intercultural plays standing in for Rwanda, verbatim post-apartheid performance, or improvising with spect-actors as in Boal's theatre. This paper offers reflections on working in the field in Rwanda since 2007 with a consistent ensemble of artists, in a country recovering from profound wounds, yet one that is undergoing a cultural renaissance, which, I believe, will prove instrumental in healing those wounds. No easy answers are given, as performance should not seek to explain, but to reveal. Art is the art of asking questions. In Isôko's performances, it is a liminal space that is at stake and made flesh by the experience of being both 'there' and 'here'. That is the threshold to the heart of our work. The ultimate meaning, like a god, may lie elsewhere.

"Imana yirirwa ahandi igataha mu Rwanda."

(Rwandan proverb: God spends the day elsewhere but sleeps in Rwanda.)

Motion VI

Contemporary Rituals: Challenges and Changes

At the Site of the Void: Inaesthetics of Performance in the Bicol Dotoc

Jazmin Badong Llana

The women huddle close to each other under umbrellas as strong winds and rain lash against the fragile temporary shelter. It is 3 May 2008 and I am in Canaman, Camarines Sur, in Bicol, Philippines, for the last day of the annual performances in adoration of the Holy Cross. The women are singing the dotoc, visibly cringing when thunder and lightning strike, but continuing to sing even when the accompaniment of the electronic organ stops as power fails and fierce gusts of rain wet the instrument. Elsewhere in other parts of the Bicol region, other performances are being held or prepared. I would be witnessing some of these other performances, in Legazpi and Nabua, on that month of May 2008, for the second time, and going back to the dotoc practice in the town of Baao for the third or fourth time as a researcher and for the nth time as a native of the town.

How might performance studies be used as a kind of thinking about performance in the post-colonial context of the Philippines? The performance practices of formerly colonized countries pose a challenge for research and knowledge production, problematizing generally accepted principles of theatre and performance studies. Understanding the variegated aesthetic, cultural and political forms intertwined in post-colonial performance practices is a complex, reflexive process for the local researchers, who are now no longer only informants but theorists of their own context, facing the challenge of examining and articulating the historicity and contemporary significance of these cultural practices of performance. For these local scholars, including myself, the process of knowing is both enabled and burdened by colonial education – the post-colonial predicament famously discussed by Spivak,[1] Bhabha[2] and Said.[3] These figures have become highly influential in theorizing the post-colonial condition, claiming a discursive space for the subaltern and the oppressed in ways that diverged from Fanonian radicalism by emphasizing ambivalence, contingency and hybridity. The framework of post-colonial deconstruction has been, however, strongly contested by Marxist critics, especially on the grounds of denying the subaltern a specific voice and creative political agency. Concomitantly, in the field of performance studies, performance ethnography from Turner[4] to Conquergood[5] has redefined ways of speaking about the practices of conquered, silenced or peripheralized populations, and many new participants working in the 'field' have been 'contesting performance',[6] insisting on 'the situatedness of local sites of research'.[7] This paper follows that trajectory of contestation, in order to address the key questions of political agency and innovative creative practice in the post-colonial context, by exploring possibilities opened up by Badiou's theory of event and related concept of 'inaesthetics'.[8]

In the Philippines, the poor persist with sustaining performances dating back to the colonial period.[9] These are religious, devotional, practices and, specifically for this paper, the *dotoc* and *komedya*. Why would this be the case when the performers exist on the margins, victims of poverty and social ills, unable to escape their victimhood? In Fenella Cannell's research, they refer to themselves as *'kaming mga mayong-mayo'* or, in Cannell's translation, 'we who have nothing at all'.[10] Are they Spivak's subalterns without voices, able to speak only through representatives? The performers' commitment to, and enjoyment of, the mainly presentative styles of their performances strengthen the suspicion that something else is going on here. Filipino scholar Vicente Rafael[11] has explained fidelity to the practice of this cultural form as a work of translation, while Reynaldo Ileto[12] has examined the connection of the Lenten ritual chanting of Christ's passion with popular movements and revolution. Badiou has remarked that 'the age of revolutions' is over, for the West at least,[13] but what space is there for hope and freedom in the present age of continued pauperization of the already poor? What modes of action are possible or are in fact being taken? What forms of practice enable seeing of this situation? Can contemporary performances which enable the poor to appear and count for something be thought as acts of resistance *sui generis*? If the acts and their contexts are regarded through the framework of traditional aesthetics, admired from a safe distance, and appreciated only as the weak rumblings of the powerless crying out for divine justice, then their meaning and significance remain occluded, and the marginalized people themselves are rendered excluded from the political situation they might otherwise be seen as seeking to represent.

The Bicol dotoc

My investigation of performance has focused on the practices of religious devotion in Bicol, Philippines, specifically on the *dotoc*, (no English equivalent except perhaps 'pilgrimage'),[14] a homage to the Holy Cross performed for 9 days each year, usually in April and May. Texts in the vernacular Bicol language[15] that date back to the Spanish colonial period are sung by female performers who play the role of pilgrims journeying to the Holy Land to visit the Holy Cross and communities re-enact the search for the Holy Cross by Helena and Constantine in 325 CE. Through field work in 1998–99 and again in 2007 and 2008, I found four distinct practices of the dotoc: the cobacho dotoc (dotoc performed using a shelter called 'cobacho'), the Canaman dotoc (dotoc performed in Canaman town), the dotoc as *komedya* (dotoc that is komedya in form – that is, following the conventions of komedya, a play more known in theatre history as the medieval *moros y cristianos* or similar to the *capa y espada* plays of Spain), and the *lagaylay* (a song and dance praise also performed in Canaman town). For the purposes of this essay, let me cite only three important points about these performances: the rich variety of the ways that the performances are conducted, the performance mainly by females and the communal effort in financing and producing the performances, and the clear articulation of a sacred vow as the reason for the continuing practices.

The dramatic action in all four practices follows a basic pattern: a group of pilgrims sets out to look for the Holy Cross, finds it and, on finding it, adores and praises it and submits petitions for peace, justice, prosperity, good health and deliverance from evil. The ways that this basic action unfolds in the performances are however varied and stamped with a distinct local style.

The cobacho dotoc text tells of a group of pilgrims meeting another group of travellers who dissuade them from continuing the journey, because the latter had heard that the Cross has been stolen. The first group says the Cross has been returned and tells the story of how the Emperor Heraclio waged war against the Persian king Cosrohas and recovered the Holy Cross that Cosrohas had stolen from Jerusalem.[16] This dotoc is called *corocobacho* or *cobacho dotoc*, because of the use of a *cobacho*, a shed or small shelter by the roadside where the pilgrims meet and the Heraclius story is told.

In the village of Tinago, Bigaa, in Legazpi City, this same text is performed, but all other performance elements are different and it is performed with the *komedya* depicting the search for the Holy Cross by Helena and Constantine.

Figure 15 Pages 2–3 of an extant copy of the 1895 corocobacho dotoc text which is part of the Bicol Special Collections, University of the Philippines Main Library.

The komedya is a distinct performance style adapted from the Spanish *moros y cristianos* and characterized by stylized speeches, marches for entrances and exits, choreographed fighting and the use of distinctive costumes of the main and minor characters.[17] In the town of Nabua, the community of Santa Elena, Baras also performs the dotoc as komedya, but in a longer form that includes fighting between Constantine's troops and Moors, which ends with the surrender of the non-Christians to Constantine. In Canaman, the action is set at the end of Helena's pilgrimage, when the cross had been found, and Helena's entourage perform the *lagaylay*, a song and dance praise for the cross. The dotoc at this site, performed before the lagaylay, uses a variety of texts all of which can be traced back to the Spanish period.

In all of the sites, the texts are of colonial origin, but the ways that these are performed show contemporary (re)interpretations of the narratives and embedded sets of symbols. The communities freely improvise with the music, the decorations and the costumes, only keeping intact some key features such as the endless marches, the stylized verse recitation and the practice of having the director[18] dictate every line of the komedya to the actors. And it is through such improvisations that the devotions become celebrations, *fiestas*, made even more special with a lot of eating and drinking where even strangers can partake of the food and drink after watching the performances.

Performed outside of the church and managed by the laity,[19] 'the dotoc is *pagsa-Dios*, which means it is "for God," an act of faith or religious longing.

This is the reason given by the dotoc participants for why they do what they do. . . . [But the] vernacular faith expressions do not neatly cohere. Seeking coherence of the articulated intention and vow of faith with its exterior expressions, one can see the latter as empty form, shallow ritual, just words mouthed or said and people dressed up in fancy costumes. In some instances there is even no attempt at having any kind of "show" even if the performers are dressed in shiny satin dresses. One could find oneself asking what the point of it all is, as I have done.'[20]

Inaesthetics in the dotoc

The performances raise the disturbing question about whether or not the texts and how they are performed have a direct connection to the faith experience of the participants. The text obviously tells only half of the dotoc story and there is a whole set of meanings that cannot be accessed only from seeing the performance. Performers I spoke with said only that the dotoc shows their faith in the '*Amang Dios*' (God, or Father God). The connection of such expressed faith to the ways of its expression was not a point they interrogated or critically analysed, and my co-performative methodology did not allow probing that could possibly (however unintended) hint of doubt about their 'sincerity' – the correspondence of word or deed with 'interior states'. Webb Keane's ethnography of Christian belief among the Sumbanese Protestants in Indonesia points out how 'sincere speech' and interiority are strongly valued, but the way that these are evaluated comes in the form of a public performance. 'The doctrinal stress on interiority works in tension with the highly formalistic procedure that enacts not belief per se but rather the discourse of belief.' What stands out is 'its schematic nature, its theatricality, its lack of psychology'.[21] What stands out is the public performance that becomes the mark of the faith professed. But the opacity of performance is such that the researcher is left to figure out how the performance appears and what it may mean in the light of one's experience of it. Intention is very difficult, if not impossible, to account for. With the komedya and dotoc, one is faced with a challenge and a demand to think of agency and memory not in terms of an interior state but of a performance, a behaviour, a public declaration. According to Badiou, 'Genuine subjectivation has as its material evidence the *public declaration* of the event . . .'.[22] Agency will have to be understood from the consistency of the expression, even if such consistency or persistence actually comes in the form of inconsistency, incoherence, dissonance, a seeming disconnection between behaviour/performance and interior state.

And, yet, having said this and recognizing that faith drives and sustains the performances, one still seeks that the intention, sincerity, is physicalized in the performance, perhaps in the face and body of the performers or in the artistic elements, the expected exterior embodiments. Alas, this seeking for unity of thought and action, the logical agreement of intention and performance, is useless and unnecessary in the case of the dotoc.

The performances are a ritual display of faith by both the performers and their audiences. There is no aim to represent the text through the dramatization, even in the komedya where roles are taken and played by 'actors', but where the director is part of the show, because she is dictating the lines to them in full view and hearing of the audience. The lines have in fact been memorized by many of the spectators whose participation in the singing or recitation can be heard occasionally, if one listens hard enough. Many in the audience used to be active performers themselves or, if not so, have memorized the lines out of familiarity, from repeatedly hearing them every year. Spectators mouth the words of the dotoc and at times suddenly burst out in song, or tap the rhythm on their thighs, on their arms or on the bamboo fence of a nearby house. In the Bigaa komedya, as the performance extends from the afternoon to the early evening, the audience crowd around and into the performance space. Watchers and watched mingle and 'backstage crew' strive to clear spaces for the unfolding drama, not always quietly. The spectators follow the performers or go several paces ahead to the next stop in the 'pilgrimage'. Children cross the road this way and that, or look down onto the poor 'old man' dropped into a pit, punished by Helena for refusing to say what he knew of the whereabouts of the Cross that she seeks. The defiance of this old man was repeatedly cited by the community folk, both of Bigaa and Nabua, as the high point of the action – curiously, not the finding of the cross that is the point of the 'pilgrimage' in this komedya.

One may say a wholly different aesthetics is at play here. Certainly there has been a strong concern among the performers and practitioners of the dotoc (and the komedya and lagaylay) in all four sites that aesthetic standards be followed and preserved. But this is certainly not the aesthetics that Feodor Jagor had in mind when he spoke scathingly about the komedya he saw in Daraga, Albay, in the 1800s:

> The actors stalked on, chattering their parts, which not one of them understood,
> and moving their arms up and down; and when they reached the edge of the

stage, they tacked and went back again like ships sailing against the wind. Their countenances were entirely devoid of expression, and they spoke like automatons. If I had understood the words, the contrast between their meaning and the machine-like movement of the actors would probably have been droll enough; but, as it was, the noise, the heat, and the smoke were so great that we soon left the place. . . . Both the theatrical performance and the whole festival bore the impress of laziness, indifference, and mindless mimicry.[23]

Filipino scholar Resil Mojares remarks that Jagor judged what he saw using criteria totally alien to the experience, and propounds that the komedya's 'flaw is its aesthetic', with the 'purposeful act of exoticizing the foreign, of rendering it as Other (L. exoticus, "outside")'.[24]

Also writing on the komedya during the colonial period, Vicente Rafael says the komedya 'rehearsed' the appearance of the foreign, preparing the natives for its onslaught and thus enabling them to deal with it, to give it an orderly presence in the vernacular and thus to domesticate it. The komedya thus contains 'the colonial uncanny'[25] and '[threatens] to disarticulate laws from above and mobilize desires from below'.[26] He cites the Spanish Juan Alvarez Guerra who like Jagor had only snide remarks about the actors' 'flat tones . . . drained . . . of affect' and wrote about the dangers posed by the 'comedia'[27] – 'the comedia is not only bad art, it is also a corrupting influence on native youth [making] them think that they can be other than who they are . . .'[28]

For Guerra, then, 'the vernacular plays were aesthetic abominations that reflected the innate inferiority of native thinking'; they '[lacked] historical veracity and narrative coherence', were 'truly absurd' and 'thus appeared to be literary monstrosities'.[29] But worse than this, the elite native nationalists (called *ilustrados*, literally the enlightened ones) thought the same way of the komedya. It was 'a source of shame' and 'had to be disowned, or at least reformed'.[30]

A key learning here, however, is Rafael's view that, in 'domesticating the foreign', the vernacular and its speakers were also forever altered, 'rendered estranged' . . . 'uncanny', 'appearing to possess what in fact possesses them'.[31] Looking at the costuming practice in the dotoc and komedya of the twenty-first century that remains much like what Guerra saw, one might ask if the 'colonial uncanny' persists and if this might explain the particular aesthetic that seems to also persist in the dotoc enactment.

Even as I say this, I have to unsettle this thinking and start all over again. The dotoc is multiple, peculiar and new at its local site, and the images jar and clash as one struggles to make sense of its logics. After going on about how the devotion is made special by the rich improvisations in music, decorations, costumes, I could not explain why in the Baao and Canaman dotoc practices, the contemporary performers are not all concerned about dressing up and would perform just as they are, in everyday dress. Why do Helena's soldiers in the Bigaa komedya wear dark glasses which are totally at odds with their 'medieval' costumes? Why is Constantine in the Nabua dotoc played by a boy and the non-Christian soldiers played by females? Why is a transvestite allowed to join and yet the dotoc is described by practitioners as being performed by females? These details confuse the observer and the field work did not produce any coherent explanations, largely because the performers themselves were not sure of the answers but did not mind the fact. But perhaps indeed this is because the mayong-mayo in Bicol rarely speak their minds. It is as if, again, this supports Cannell's observation that the Bicolanos avoid explaining who they are, would not even say 'who they are' or 'draw on a notion of what they do to construct a declaration of who they are',[32] which explains why they are 'a vexing puzzle for social and political theory'.[33]

But something persists: not a memory, says Badiou, but active thought, and what remains to be done is to tell it as I have encountered it. 'To tell it like it is, and to draw the consequences of this "telling" situation, is . . . a decision "by logic" that "[bears] a possibility for action"'.[34] Badiou's concept of inaesthetics allows the thinking of post-colonial performance as agentic action and the writing and talking that articulate it.

The dotoc in its varied forms is pilgrimage, a 'journey to the sacred',[35] but there is no actual journey to the Holy Land. Instead, it is a performance of pilgrimage that transforms the act into the real. As I have said elsewhere,[36] the dotoc is a 'utopian performative' in the sense that Jill Dolan describes the term,[37] with the utopic 'agenda' embodied by the act of performance itself',[38] which might be equated to Dolan's notion of the 'never finished gestures towards a potentially better future'.[39] But the 'restoration of behaviour' as Schechner might put it,[40] with the emphasis placed on restoration as process, the repetition and persistence of the practice, might at least be partly explained by the pleasure of realizing the desired end which is also repeatedly felt, because the performed pilgrimage always ends with the finding of the cross; the pilgrims triumph; they reach their destination.

The experience of seeking and finding in the dotoc is poignant and significant because the performers are, in the main, the *mayong-mayo* – the 'people who have nothing at all' who are constantly on the losing end, whose vulnerability is beyond material poverty but includes 'having to endure humiliation, disapproval and rejection, of constantly having one's dignity challenged, and of being shamed'.[41] Peter Hallward's description is instructive: they 'have nothing which entitles them to belong to the situation', [but] '[h]aving nothing, they occupy the place from which the void as such might be exposed, via an event'.[42]

The dotoc is an act of seeking that reveals the mayong-mayo at the site of the void.[43] They may be inexistent in the state of things, without presence, without voice as Spivak would have it, capable only of 'bad art', but they transform this situation with their performance.

A truth surges out from the garishness of the dotoc appearance, piercing through the discrepant performance. 'A truth and a subject of truth do not derive from what there is, but from what happens, in the strong sense of the term "happens"'.[44] '*What there is*' in the dotoc are the costumes, movement, stylized delivery, which might be thought as marks of the particularities of religion as colonial imposition. These are empty of any emotional, even mental, investment, *subtracted* from thought until what remains only is the presence, the coming-to-presence, of the performers and their act of performance. That is the point of it all. '*What happens*' is the post-evental affirmation of the event of Christian conversion, which may not necessarily conform to common knowledge or what the institutional church expects. The truth that is seized by the dotoc practitioners and to which they have been faithful comes about through the process of subtraction and the act of performance becomes a process of subjectivation that bores holes in the common knowledge of devotion, faith, religiosity, and even of what performance, of how drama and theatre, are or should be. The dotoc subjects are revealed and lay claim to a space that is theirs and with the performance of pilgrimage declares their fidelity. The dotoc walking whether real or imagined becomes the creative embodiment of this fidelity, performed in all its corporeal possibilities, even in the face of a poignant lack of material means – fidelity of performance which becomes fidelity of hope, for hope is 'the simple imperative of continuation, a principle of tenacity, of obstinacy'.[45]

Thinking of performance as an event of thought, says Adrian Kear, '[re-acquaints] us with the "void" of the situation'.[46] And shouldn't this be the case? Should we not, indeed, seize the thought, cultivate a fidelity to an event that changes the quality or intensity of appearing – 'whereby what once appeared as nothing comes to appear as everything – the process whereby, paradigmatically, the wretched of the earth might come to inherit it'?[47] This is the beauty of Performance Studies and also its potential for surfacing ways of thinking that used to be inexistent, akin to the effect of making the invisible visible in and through performance.

Acknowledgement

The author is grateful to Adrian Kear and Richard Gough (Aberystwyth University) for much of the theoretical work, to the Ford Foundation International Fellowships Program for the research funding, to the Commission on Higher Education of the Philippines and Aquinas University of Legazpi for the conference support, to the editors Ati Citron, Sharon Aronson-Lehavi and David Zerbib and the University of Haifa, and to Richard Schechner for the inspiration that has animated all of us.

New Technologies in Korean Shamanism: Cultural Innovation and Preservation of Tradition

Liora Sarfati

In contemporary South Korea, the performance of shamanic rituals (*kut*) is an appreciated cultural trait and a valuable commodity that produces economic gain.[1] Kut rituals have been documented for hundreds of years, and are performed both privately for clients (*sonnim*) who wish to appease their ancestors or other spirits, and publically as symbols of national heritage. The cost of private rituals begins at 2,000 US dollars/day.[2] Since the 1980s, the South Korean government and several municipalities have begun to sponsor apt performers of this tradition by monthly stipends. This is a new form of turning kut into a high-yield asset. The fast integration of new media into the shamanic world marks the vitality of this vernacular religion and its ability to adapt to changing cultural and technological contexts. It also demonstrates that continuity in tradition does not mean maintaining the same practices that existed in prehistory, rather constant adjustment to social conditions. New media has opened innovative arenas for discourse and communication among practitioners, and between them and the rest of the world.

In the past 100 years, Korea has undergone fast modernization coupled with occupation by the Japanese (1910–45) and a harsh civil war (1950–53), which ended in division of people and land into North and South Korea. One of the outcomes of this unstable period is a robust national effort to preserve traditional performances in order to construct a unique cultural identity. In the early 1900s, imperial powers, mainly the Japanese, often stated that Korea lacked a culture of its own, and therefore does not deserve political autonomy. South Korea has been struggling against such claims already before its independence and throughout its fast transformation from an agrarian society in the 1950s to a post-industrial one.

Korean shamanism (*musok*) has survived this political turbulence and is still widely practised. During kut, Korean shamans (*manshin*) induce themselves into altered states of consciousness through dancing and drumming. Spirits of natural elements and ancestors descend into their bodies and are available for consultation by other ritual attendants for the purposes of healing, fortune-telling and blessings. In village settings and in Seoul during the 1970s, altars were mounted at houses of clients or manshin, and audiences included mainly villagers and their acquaintances.[3]

Twenty-first-century post-industrial Seoul offers a variety of technologies that enhance public visibility and easy access to musok practices. Manshin and clients travel a few hours by car to distant mountain shrines that used to require long foot-pilgrimages. These shrines provide larger and more impressive offering altars than the ones depicted in photographs from the late nineteenth century, because now, with relatively small investment of time, a manshin can purchase artefacts at stores rather than labour to prepare them. Electric light and sound amplification enhance the ritual's effect. Practitioners advertise their services on websites, and people can watch filmed rituals at home before they choose a manshin. These technological innovations suggest that the framework of musok has changed significantly in terms of choosing a personal manshin, ritual locations, ritual preparation and altar presentation. At the same time, public and scholarly discourses in Korea echo the idea that a ritual is more valuable when it follows the 'original form' (*wonrae ŭi mosŭp*). In the discourse of Korea's cultural preservation policy, *original form* means that rituals 'remained truest to the celebration's original form, capturing the very essence of this ancient festival'.[4] In the Korean Cultural Heritage Administration (CHA)'s website, Kim Chan explains that 'The Cultural Heritage Administration strives to conserve our precious cultural heritage in its *original condition* to bequeath to future generations, while promoting it as a *catalyst for national development*'.[5] Since the 1980s, this effort to produce a homogenized genuine independent local culture brought musok to the fore.

Musok is viewed as the only indigenous religion of Korea, because Buddhism, Confucianism and Daoism were imported from China. Despite Confucian and Christian objections to religious aspects of musok, the beautiful rituals have attracted policy-makers who offered official recognition of kut as artistic manifestation of the 'Korean spirit'. This essay explores the context of Korean shamanism in the early twenty-first century describing how rituals and their role in society have changed following technological innovations. My anthropological research also revealed that musok is more prevalent in Korea than most Koreans are willing to admit. The official stance of the South Korean government has been that 'Today, only token traces of this ancient indigenous religion can be found – and then rarely – in rural areas'.[6] Such statements ignore more than 200,000 active registered practitioners.[7]

The official recognition of musok's value as a national heritage is a novelty because throughout Korea's history, the educated elites have regarded manshin with disdain because of their contacts with dangerous spirits and their strange behaviour.[8] However, in the 1980s, the government began to acknowledge manshin as Holders of Intangible Cultural Assets (*ingan munhwaje*).[9] Nominated manshin are expected to perform and teach specific rituals in a prescribed manner.[10] The nomination committee ignores technological innovations in contemporary musok. It determines the correspondence of a kut to ancient 'original forms' using only verbal and musical criteria. Analysing the evaluation criteria that the Korean government uses in order to nominate rituals demonstrates that the main characteristic sought is affinity with historic performances, judged by comparison of the performed songs to documented ritual texts from 50 to 100 years ago.[11] I suggest that the Korean CHA observes technological innovation in kut with caution because if technology incorporation is considered an alteration of the 'original form', then it would be difficult to find performances that deserve preservation. Modern technology has become such an integral part of contemporary musok that it would be hard to imagine a kut without it. Had the nomination committee insisted on restricting the use of technological devices in kut for the sake of 'authenticity', there would have been few manshin able to practise it. However, acknowledging that technology plays a part in the ritual would require constant updating of the preserved kut protocol. Finally, CHA itself uses multiple venues of mass media in all of its efforts to disseminate Korean heritage. Therefore, it would be unimaginable for CHA to demand that manshin would not document their own rituals. Such pragmatic arguments resulted in CHA's overlooking technological aspects throughout the designation process.

During my fieldwork, I worked closely with Dr Yang Jonsgsung, whose research focused on the designation process of Korean performers.[12] He has been a member of the Korean Committee for Cultural Assets since 1998, thanks to his academic and artistic acquaintance with musok that extends over three decades. A unique feature of his knowledge is that in his early twenties, he was an apprentice of a famous manshin. Two decades later, in 2007, he was the folklore researcher in charge of planning the kut ritual that was performed as the opening event of the first Korea Traditional Performing Arts Festival.

New technologies in the Shamanic artefact market

On a rainy evening in September 2007, Manshin Sŏ Kyŏng-uk performed at the World Cup Stadium Park. Near a lovely pond, altars for a staged kut were constructed and decorated. The ritual served as the opening performance of the first Korea Traditional Performing Arts Festival, which has been repeated yearly, enabling wide public exposure to various traditional performances including kut. The rainy weather complicated mounting altars and background screens. Manshin Sŏ often performs in open air events and has therefore created unique, synthetic, factory-made ritual props that can endure stormy weather. Instead of displaying delicate gods' paintings on paper, as manshin have apparently been doing for generations, she took photographs of some fine examples of this art at her home shrine, and used those images to create polyester banners. The banners can be rolled into plastic water-proof tubes. In harnessing technology to improve her paraphernalia, the manshin deviates from norms of producing musok goods by hand from natural materials. Many manshin in Seoul maintain their habit of hanging paper paintings even in wet weather, thinking that these artefacts signify the traditional value of the ritual. The academic discourse on ritual preservation that is practised by scholars who choose rituals for nomination as assets has thus increased the value of being true to 'original form'. However, the vagueness of this term allows for different interpretations of its meaning and application. Interestingly, practitioners put much effort in material aspects that are hardly commented upon by scholars, who in turn avoid designing evaluation criteria for this aspect of the ritual.

Most manshin buy ritual artefacts from specialized stores that keep a constant inventory of drums, costumes, paper flowers, paintings and statues of gods. The Korean government did not nominate any musok craft artist as a Cultural Asset.[13] Such designation would have entailed a new evaluation process and budget. With no official supervision, musok artists and art dealers are free to alternate the material aspects of kut to suit clients' tastes and price ranges. Some shop owners have become so knowledgeable in ritual production that manshin ask for their advice when planning a kut. A common practice in the busy lifestyle of famous manshin is to send a driver to pick up ritual props trusting that the shop owner's choice fits the needs of both the manshin and the gods. Old manshin have told me how in the past, the need for a new ritual prop was initiated by dreams in which gods and spirits asked them to prepare specific items. Nowadays, while associating with friends and shop owners, manshin are often tempted to buy various items on display. Shop owners intentionally exhibit beautiful kut costumes and decorations in order to entice manshin to purchase them.[14] This alters the ritual both in the extent of personal involvement of manshin in the creation of ritual props, and in aspects of communication with the supernatural. Another outcome of commodification is that manshin have fewer opportunities for socializing within the performance team.

Manshin often gather with their assistants in the days before rituals in order to prepare together a pile of paper decorations. In such sessions of work that I observed, a sense of feminine communities was created. In urban settings, there are few other occasions for the whole team to get together outside rituals. Ready-made props result in loss of important opportunities for transmission of tradition and for group solidarity construction.

The commercialization of ritual props has influenced also the cosmology of musok because manshin show interest in costumes that attract clients' appreciation rather than centring their choice on the identity of the worshipped supernatural entity. A beautiful costume presented in a store downtown might result in the incorporation of a less appreciated spirit into a kut, as happens with the nymph spirit (*Sŏnnyŏ*). That outfit was rarely purchased by newly initiated manshin in the past, but its bright pink sateen together with a decorated crown and sparkly hairpin have made it so popular that it is sold just as much as outfits for more powerful gods.[15]

Ordering musok costumes from famous wedding-dress designers or from specialized artists results in a homogenization of gods' attires, which was not the case before commercialized musok artefacts took root. Manshin Kim Nam-sun states that she keeps her tradition of designing costumes individually, and indeed I have not seen similar ones in other practitioners' collections.[16] Designs appear while she dreams, and accordingly, she explains to the dressmaker how to draw them. Using the services of well-known costume designers rather than taking part in practices of commercial mass production asserts the manshin's status as a successful professional. Popular new designs are later copied and mass manufactured. Mrs Lee, a musok goods shop owner in downtown Seoul, showed me several academic books that she consults while preparing kut outfits. I have seen her offer several design options to manshin clients while presenting drawings of historic attires and musok regalia from those books as proofs to her abundant knowledge and cultural expertise. The use of academic research in material religious context blurs the boundaries between the intended academic audience and artefact producers. Academic knowledge is, in this manner, disseminated through the print industry and applied to the religious realms of musok, reducing the need of direct inspiration from gods and spirits to earn the necessary knowledge about appropriate costume preparation. Filmed rituals also avail manshin with images of various costumes that other manshin use. The commodification of musok artefacts reduced the need of personal apprenticeship for manshin and musok artefact producers, and increased reliance on knowledge mediation by factory-produced images and texts.

During the first Korea Traditional Performing Arts Festival in 2007, Dr Yang introduced the ritual as an ancient practice, ignoring completely the production process of the artefacts. As a senior curator of the National Folk Museum and an avid collector of musok art, Dr Yang knew that many artefacts were mass manufactured or prepared with new synthetic materials, but he did not mind this, as long as the ceremonial words matched officially legitimized ancient texts. The contradiction between the ritual's reliance on technological innovations and its declaration as ancient was also not perceived by the manshin and her audience, who were concerned mainly with the ritual's efficacy.

New media changes musok knowledge dissemination

New media has become a lively arena for musok practitioners to communicate, advertise services and learn of upcoming staged rituals. Films and other digital documentations also serve as a means for learning about musok. Interestingly, while many Korean scholars are photographed and quoted on practitioners' websites, discourse of new media usage in musok is absent from most academic publications by Korean scholars. The effort and time that is dedicated to filming and promoting the broadcasting of kut rituals on television and internet venues marks a shift of practice from word-of-mouth self-promotion and knowledge acquisition to media-mediated activities.

Professional manshin organizations established internet portals such as www. kyungsin.co.kr in the 1990s, when internet usage in South Korea expanded.[17]

Figure 16 Manshin Kim Mi-ja performing in front of cameramen at a yearly ritual on Bonghwa Mountain. Photo by Liora Sarfati.

The portal www.neomudang.com offers an interactive map where one can click on a region of Korea and find a list of manshin who practise there along with their specialties. Service providers such as musok goods stores and shrines for rent use such portals for advertising. The result of online flows of knowledge has been increased numbers of manshin who practise a hybridized style of musok, overlooking the strict regional classification that Korean scholars regard as very important.

A common product of online musok is manshin's personal website – *hompeiji* – in which visitors can learn basic facts about their line of religious practice, read their biography and communicate with them. Manshin Sŏ Kyŏng-uk hired a professional IT specialist in the mid-1990s to construct her website www.mudang.co.kr. She updates her website regularly with photos and information of upcoming performances. She also replies to readers' queries, and has included part of her introduction in English translation. She introduces herself with photos that can be interpreted as traditional dance. Those images convey elegance and grace without depicting intense ritual sequences that might be repulsive to some viewers, such as animal sacrifice or lewd humour. In other words, the website does not expose visitors to visuals that might cause uneasiness (especially people who have not been to such rituals), by limiting its scope to activities that do not contradict perspectives of modernity and progress. This is an intentional choice of the manshin in hope to diversify the clientele.

Manshin Lee Hae-gyŏng, the main protagonist of the documentary film *Between*, was interviewed in many newspapers, and has maintained a personal blog, www.manshin.co.kr since 2006.[18] Such success in the media has often been criticized by colleagues and scholars as a sign for negligence of real healing in order to become a 'superstar shaman'.[19] However, as expected from a sincere spiritual healer, the daily practice of Manshin Lee consists mainly of treating the problems of her clients through supernatural communication.

Most manshin homepeiji are written solely in Korean. However, several manshin have extended their practice globally. Manshin Shin Myŏng-gi had a full version of her website, www.chuonbokhwa.com, in Japanese for several years as she used to also conduct services in Japan. Manshin Hi-ha Park, a UCLA graduate who has been initiated as a manshin in Korea, has been living in Germany for many years. Her website, www.hiahpark.com, which she calls Global Shamanic Healing, is in English and in German because she caters mostly to European clientele. On her website, Manshin Park advertises various workshops and performances that are far from being copies of ancient kut. Her terminology includes new age ideas that are absent from the Korean discourse of musok, such as unity of body and soul.[20] Her musok practice marks a new intercultural communication through rituals that used to be more locally oriented.

Documentation and evaluation of a kut ritual

In the spring of 2007, Manshin Kim Nam-sun was getting ready to commence a kut in a rented shrine near Seoul's downtown. The ritual was documented by Dr Yang. His positive impression of that performance contributed to Kim's nomination as Regional Intangible Cultural Asset Holder. Manshin Kim was excited about obtaining the title and therefore initiated a special ritual for this occasion. She proposed to her acquaintances to sponsor a kut for a minimal fee in order to allow Dr Yang to film and interrupt it freely for better documentation.

Before the ritual began, Manshin Kim attached a portable wireless microphone to her chest and handed a printed booklet to Dr Yang, telling him that it is a transcription by Professor Kim Tae-gon of the same ritual performed a few decades earlier by her *shinomoni* (spirit-mother). In Korean society, a neo-Confucian tradition of not doubting superiors results in a tendency to consider findings of previous scholars as objective truths. Well aware of this approach, Manshin Kim obtained and learned the booklet that she handed to Dr Yang. The performer and the evaluator followed the rules of the designation game. She performed a close version of the old transcription, and he in return could convincingly confirm that it is true to the 'original form'. No mention of the technological aspects of the performance appeared in the recommendation letter.

In the rented shrine, Manshin Kim began to sing and turn around repeatedly when the photographer noticed that the wireless microphone faltered. Dr Yang strode to the centre of the room and touched her wrist to suggest that she stops. A bit surprised, she stood still and allowed the two men to arrange the microphone again and test it before resuming her possession-trance dance. In an ordinary kut, a performer would not pause while becoming entranced, but in this new context, she was attentive to the scholars' needs. Furthermore, her ability to control herself during possession signified high level of professional skills and strengthened her plea to be nominated Ritual Holder. The assistants were clearly annoyed at the interference, but nobody protested. They all understood the implications of the event on their professional futures and accepted the need of technology-aided documentation. In stepping into the ritual arena, Dr Yang became an integral part of the performance. The evaluator who used electronic recording intervened in the ritual process and determined its pace.

Musok as an emblem of the 'Korean Spirit'

The need to choose preservation nominees among more than a hundred thousand practising manshin produced a complex designation process. A number of Korean folklore scholars, such as Dr Yang, are hired to evaluate various kut, and their conclusions are handed to a special committee to decide which rituals are the most valuable.[21] When people become clients of manshin, they search for ritual efficacy, its power to heal them or solve their personal problems. When folklore scholars look for kut to designate, they search for well-established practitioners whose work has already been appreciated by many clients. Within the relevant candidates, scholars then evaluate rituals by measuring their affinity with what is deemed to be the ritual's original form.

In the late 1800s and early 1900s, musok was documented mainly by Japanese ethnographers and by Christian missionaries.[22] The Japanese used musok to prove that Koreans and Japanese shared the same ancient culture, and through this *common origins theory*, they justified taking over Korea. Christian missionaries utilized their knowledge of folk religion to conceptualize Christianity in an appealing manner.[23] Pre-modern Korean scholars did not describe musok because it was deemed a lowly tradition. However, when the Japanese used Korea's vernacular culture for promoting their imperial goals, Korean scholars began to show interest in these folk beliefs. Local folklorists such as Ch'oe Nam-sŏn and Yim Suk-Jay discussed and documented kut in the early twentieth century and their valuable work became the oldest database for comparing contemporary rituals.[24]

Evaluating contemporary rituals through comparison with historic kut is problematic for various reasons. A lack of filming devices in the past produced mainly transcriptions of ritual songs with little attention to other performative aspects. The transmission of tradition is perceived in this comparison as an intergenerational imitation with no notice of manshin's agency and creativity in adapting text to context and altering ritual form and meaning according to their personal preferences. Events that precede and follow the actual ritual, such as altar construction, have not been studied. Cultural performances are sponsored through the Cultural Heritage Protection Act only if they are proven to be 'carrying great historic, artistic or academic values'.[25] This statement demonstrates how the evaluation criteria are based on analytic categories formulated by scholars, and not by performers and patrons who would emphasize the efficacy which is based on religious belief.

Designating kut as Important Intangible Cultural Heritage encapsulates a paradox because the wish to petrify rituals in order to connect the present with pre-modern Korean culture requires detaching the performance from its religious intention. Tradition is ever-changing, as shown in various case studies.[26] The Korean culture preservation policy seeks to establish a coherent corpus of officially recognized performances as a canonical representation of 'The Korean Spirit'. Most preserved kut are a living tradition in the performers' repertoire. However, contemporary kut are not always comparable to the ones archived by a previous scholar. Officially scripted rituals often prevent manshin from adapting the performance to specific needs of clients and are therefore performed for a general cause such as 'blessing the audience' or 'the wellbeing of the nation'. These kut are not perceived as fake or secular re-performances because blessing the audience and the nation is regarded a worthy purpose. As they follow the ritual's script, manshin feel comfortable to use various technologies such as sound amplification, lighting and impressive, commercially manufactured offerings to ensure the ritual's success that is measured in this case not by its efficacy but by achieving audience solidarity and enjoyment.

This examination of affinity with an 'original form' resembles discourses of *authenticity*. A survey of authenticity-related debates conducted by Regina Bendix demonstrated that it has been embedded in most academic cultural analysis from the initiation of folklore studies about 200 years ago.[27] While terminology such as *authentic shamanic rituals* has been utilized by many scholars of musok, it must be treated with prudence.[28] Performance authenticity is judged by different criteria depending on context and participants, thus producing contradictory meanings and usage.[29] Paradoxes and conflicts arise when some members of a community look for performers' sincerity and ritual efficacy while others are concerned with 'historic accuracy'.[30] Rituals and performances that have no antecedents in history have often been called *invented tradition, folklorism* or *fakelore*.[31] These labels suggest that some traditions are genuine and properly performed, while others are fake or contemporary inventions that have little value. Many of the examples set in Hobsbawm and Ranger's book *The Invention of Tradition* analyse technological innovation as contradictory to performance authenticity. However, *invented tradition* as a means for value judgement has been challenged by many.[32] Contemporary musok events in Korea might be labelled by some critics with the above quoted derogative terms, given all the technological innovations. Even musok practices that could be labelled genuine 'old ways' (following a continuous line of transmission), according to Hobsbawm's terminology, have often been restructured to fit new contexts and interests. An undisrupted line of transmission does not necessarily mean that contemporary performers are mere bearers of ancient traditions. Similar to Sponsler's observation regarding European rituals, kut are produced in our times after 'creative shaping to meet new ends'.[33]

The 'original forms' sought by Korean scholars are established on a shaky basis even in their own terms because the presumed originality of the earlier event to which they compare contemporary kut cannot be determined using the same standards. The documented performance eventually lacks a comparable antecedent. The scholars are left with the undisputable judgement of an earlier scholar as the sole originality determinant. The documentation process of an earlier scholar can be imagined as a quite arduous task as he writes down full transcription of ritual texts and a bit about the ritual's sequence and segments. The scholar becomes a mediator between the past performance and contemporary audiences that might include manshin and other scholars. Richard Bauman theorizes that mediation is an indexical relationship between a sequence of dialogues. In our case, the source dialogue is transcription of a historic kut, and the target dialogue is contemporary ritual. The source dialogue, which is an artefact of scholarship, reaches ahead to and has formative effect on the target dialogue, which is a shamanic performance.[34] The target dialogue reaches back and has a formative effect on the source dialogue because 'the source utterance anticipates repetition' and therefore 'the shaping of the source utterance prepares it for this decontextualization and recontextualization'.[35] Having a future repetition of the ritual in mind probably resulted in the scholar's inserting some intentional and unintentional deviations from the actual occurrence.

Let us imagine that several manshin participating in kut began arguing about the proper dance sequence. The early scholar would have probably excluded this dispute from the transcription and taken side with the prevailing party by recording only their version. Richard Schechner showed how in the documentary film *Altar of Fire* in 1976, disagreements between different ritual organizers were perceived by scholars and film-makers as irrelevant to the documentary because they disrupted the expected flow of the performance.[36] Dynamic attitudes to cultural research view such discrepancies and disagreements as opportunities to expose unspoken hierarchies and debates. However, the general tendency in early-modern Korea was to produce clear and consistent culture descriptions that seemed objective. Early scholars ignored not only moments of fuzziness within the research community, but also their own role in the event, as did the filming crew of *Altar of Fire*. Consequently, valuable descriptions of historic kut are lacking in context. Such stripped documentation processes used to be perceived as prerequisite for texts to outlive their time. Without filtering the complex and somewhat chaotic kut atmosphere, it would have been impossible to prepare a coherent ritual transcription that could serve future re-enactments.

Contemporary Korean scholars are expected to use these stripped descriptions when writing recommendations for designating rituals as National Assets. They are forced to speculate on aspects that are lacking in the historic document, such as altar settings and dance movements. As explained above, it is impossible to grasp a full effect of performance including its non-verbal aspects when it is transferred into an archived textual representation.[37] In order to enrich the documentation, designated rituals are photographed and filmed, acknowledging more performative aspects, but few of the contextual elements. Such documentation is prepared mainly in order 'to ensure that if a current heritage holder dies without leaving a successor . . . people will be able to revive their heritage by using these resources as points of reference'.[38] In spite of existing video documentation, the official demand of designated manshin remains to re-perform the ritual, following closely the texts and sequences that have been described in words by the evaluator, while very little attention is dedicated to the mise-en-scène.

Conclusion

In contemporary South Korea, musok has been appreciated and preserved as an ancient indigenous tradition. The South Korean government understands the importance of indigenous culture to the nation-building process and funds selected manshin. Korean scholars participate in this enterprise by evaluating kut rituals for the government. During the process of nomination as National Cultural Assets, manshin attest that they are mediating a genuine tradition by striving to follow texts that transcribe historic kut rituals, rather than emphasizing their religious sincerity.

As members of a highly commercialized consumer society, contemporary manshin in South Korea enjoy the technological enrichment of their tradition. They buy factory-made props and offerings, including some made of durable synthetic materials. Rituals' filming and recording are used for self-promotion, are sold in musok goods stores as ritual learning aids, and are broadcast on television and through the internet. Such innovations in musok are not perceived by Korean manshin and scholars as a signifier of tradition alteration because the evaluation of kut is based on assessing 'original form' by verbal measures. Material, performative and communicative aspects of kut beyond the ritual itself are absent from the evaluation criteria. The examples set in this essay demonstrate how technology is an integral part of culture and how Korean scholars and government agencies ignore the effect of technology on musok in order to maintain their stance of preserving 'original rituals' while at the same time using technology for the dissemination of ritual documentation in their effort to promote a unique national image.

Performing Jewish Prayer on Stage:
From Rituality to Theatricality and Back

Sarit Cofman-Simhon

The use of Jewish rituals in theatre, dance and music by religiously observant artists is a relatively new phenomenon in Israel. These shows present hermeneutic strategies of exploring the prayers from diverse perspectives. It is an intriguing endeavour, for through it these artists have an opportunity to experience and assess their religious practice in a non-religious setting, to mirror it to themselves by means of theatricalization and public presentation.

In this essay, I shall focus on a theatre performance, a dance performance and a vocal performance, all making use of Jewish prayers onstage. My inquiry started by asking the artists how they reconcile the supposed convergence between ritual and performance, and how they handle the possible collision along the continuum between their own daily practice and their staged presentations. Very rapidly my question was relegated to a non-question and elegantly set aside. Their statements were concise, even when not explicitly expressed: for them, the stage is merely a continuation of worship – by other means.

The performances I analyse here are associated with the modern orthodox Israeli community. The actors and the dancers in the first two pieces are young religious men, though not ultra-orthodox, whereas the vocal artist is a woman who represents a special case that I will problematize as opposed to – and complementing the others.

The phenomenon of artists who practise an orthodox lifestyle, and theatricalize their religious practice in order to deepen it, is not self-explanatory: it has to do with characteristics of Jewish prayer. For religiously observant Jews, the time of prayer is meant to be a time of self-judgement and self-evaluation, and it constitutes a part of their everyday life. Observant Jews pray three times a day every weekday and additional times on Shabbat and holy days. Moreover, prayer in Judaism is not meant to influence God as a defendant influences a human judge who has emotions and is susceptible to change – rather it is the worshipper who is changed.[1]

In this view, prayer is not a conversation; it is intended to inculcate certain attitudes in the one who prays, making his prayer into a challenging *agon*. Prayer turns inwards towards the realm of individual commitment. It is an intimate act. This is both the point of departure and the complexity of theatricalizing Jewish prayer.

For orthodox worshippers, ritual practices reinforce stability through the codification of repetitive modes of behaviour and fixed texts. In religious ritual, the performance is (more or less) the same every time the ritual is performed. Roy Rappaport qualifies ritual as 'more or less invariant', not absolutely so.[2] Although over time rituals clearly change within orthodox culture, they nevertheless tend to maintain as many of their details unchanged as possible. Speaking of those details, Rappaport explains that formality is simply acting in accordance with an extant form. Yet most importantly, this form is 'not encoded by the performers'.[3] This is to say the formal actions specified for performance in a given ritual are not decided by the performers of that ritual. They constitute a sacred 'restored behavior' (as Richard Schechner termed it, meaning: 'habits, rituals, and routines of life'),[4] which for the believer acquire a formative, epistemological quality.

To bring all these points together, the artists who pray daily are in fact instilling spirituality into a fixed prayer, by carrying out actions adhering to certain forms and according to specifications set by somebody else, with more or less no change from one instance to the next. The potential range of personal input into the form of the ritual is almost non-existent. They have no possibility of altering the prayer in order to benefit from more flexibility, unless they choose to practise 'lighter' orthodox Judaism (or modern conservative Judaism, or reform Judaism). As long as they consider themselves orthodox Jews, their prayers are fixed, and all that is left for them is to invest the prayer with personal meaning, thrice daily on ordinary days and additional times on holy days. Certainly, many orthodox Jews practise the prayer routinely, without achieving (or only partly attaining) the internalization and spiritualization of their religious acts. However, these artists who have chosen to explore their worship by means of theatricalization do seek a state of elevated existence. For them, the stage functions as an arena for bodily reinterpretation of their daily endeavour, a site of questioning themselves and their prayer in a manner impossible during worship itself.

Performing prayer: *Maʾamarot*

Maʾamarot[5] was a production based on the Jewish Morning Service, performed in Jerusalem at Ha-Zira Performance Art Arena by a group of seven orthodox male actors, and had a long run, between 2000 and 2004. The production made use of the Morning Service (*Shaharit*), the most elaborate of the three prescribed daily prayers. Subtitled: 'A voice and movement performance', *Maʾamarot* explored the practice of praying, which for these actors is a fixed and obligatory part of their daily routine.

The actors and the director Avi Assaraf first met in 1996 at the Maʾaleh School of Television, Film and the Arts, in Jerusalem. At the time, it was the only place in Israel where religiously observant students could study acting in an exclusively male environment. Assaraf taught movement lessons. He had returned from Italy, after a 3-year period of training with Jerzy Grotowski at his Workcenter in Pontedera. On graduating, seven of his students at Maʾaleh decided to continue to work together.

Maʾamarot is based on a fascinating and daring idea: onstage an imagined Morning Service is taking place, while the actors make visible and audible the introverted conflict the worshipper undergoes in the course of the prayer: his intimate struggle. For the devoted worshipper, praying is a complex process because a myriad of thoughts, worries and doubts can distract him from the prayer.[6] The stage presents one man who prays, split by the performance into seven characters. Such a choice makes possible a physical and vocal expression of the various states of the worshipper's soul while praying. As the programme states: 'Within the inner world of the worshipper, polar forces confront each other, although still side by side: doubt and certainty, proximity and alienation, suffering and joy, spiritual crisis and spiritual resolve.'[7]

The actor who opens the performance symbolizes the condition prior to the existence of prayer (*Shaharit* is traditionally attributed to the patriarch Abraham): the actor represents 'primordial man', the one who arouses all being (according to the Zohar),[8] the inventor and keeper of time. The second actor engages with the spiritual crisis of a man who cannot regain his former attachment to prayer. His situation reflects a state of difficulty, despite the will to pray. In the course of the performance, this actor assumes the task of expressing the philosophical facet of prayer. He is the 'philosopher'. The third actor represents 'foreign thought', the thought that interferes, questions the prayer and infiltrates the worshipper's mind with mundane questions. During the performance, he is seated on the podium, wearing a pink silken veil – quasi-prayer shawl, quasi-serpent – wrapped around his neck, teasing the other characters who try hard to pray. Two others explore the polarity of material versus spiritual facets of the prayer. To depict the material facet, the fourth actor performs a scene dealing with the Temple service: the business having to be transacted pertaining to the offerings, the materiality of the ancient service. Conversely, the fifth actor, who symbolizes the spirit of the worshipper – the quintessence of undisturbed, total prayer – the 'spiritual man' – stands on tiptoes, detached from materiality, as if seeking with his prayer to ascend to the heights. The sixth actor deals with severe divine judgement and enfolds his body in red fabric. He struggles with the restrictive side of the worshipper's personality, the harsh self-judgement that limits him, demands perfection and forbids any human error, any falling or stumbling. The seventh actor probes on stage the awareness of prayer and the theoretical attachment to it, examining letters, sounds and meanings, weighing up the text's poetic value. He is the 'literary man'. All seven performers act simultaneously onstage for the entire length of the performance, rendering present the internal physiognomy of the worshipper. The plot of the interaction onstage unfolds according to the chronology of *Shaharit*: starting with waking up and the Morning Blessings, each phase shows how the worshipper undergoes the process of pulling himself together, distancing foreign thoughts and harsh self-judgement, listening to the text, chanting it. He desires a state of absolute spirituality. The goal is reached when all seven characters cooperate and become synchronized in the effort of praying, in their movement and chanting.

The piece was presented to mixed audiences of secular and religious Jews. They praised the piece in post-performance discussions, although both religiously observant and secular spectators had a hard time understanding the 'plot', as one woman candidly put it: 'Why is it so difficult for you to pray?'[9] Yet the actors did not rise to the challenge of explaining, they merely smiled enigmatically.

The group then added a detailed explanation in the programme. The artists' explanations remained purposely vague. For example, the programme stated that 'we are aware of the fact there is something very intimate here among us; it is utterly ours, not something we present to others. We only allow a narrow opening to afford a glimpse of our world.'[10] Such declarations shed light on the extent to which the work was for the actors an emotional exposure, thus relegating the audience to the role of voyeur (reminiscent, not surprisingly, of some of Grotowski's productions). The difficulty of deciphering the performance stemmed from the fact that it operated as an idiosyncratic text containing primarily signifiers of inner experience. The signified were not any ritualistic forms, but the worshippers' thoughts and feelings during prayer, to which the audience had only indirect access. The question of representation became precarious, because the stage operated as an interface between the theatrical medium and the emotional realm.

As both performers and people at prayer, the actors of *Ma'amarot* worked to achieve moments of pure presence of authentic self, before the audience, as before God. As a result, some moments of the production were puzzling to the degree that one could question whether the actors were 'acting praying', or really praying. These were fascinating, even disturbing, instances. The production's ability to achieve ecstatic expression simultaneously with the actors' individual explorations of the experience of prayer in a non-religious setting generated a unique phenomenon: the audience was permitted to witness the intimacy between worshippers and their God. In particular, the actor playing 'the spiritual man' looked almost in trance, panting, moaning and heavily breathing, with his eyes shut. It is worth mentioning that in the performance, the morning prayer is performed in the evening – an anachronism which seems significant when the men look as not 'acting praying' but actually praying.

Theatre critics praised the piece for its authenticity and originality yet considered it non-communicative, cryptic and only remotely intended for public exposure – more for the sake of the actors' personal quests. Albert Souissa wrote: 'A unique work of art . . . an exceptional cultural revelation, beyond artistic judgment. . . . It breaks conventions of body art and performance. . . . The audience underwent an archetypal catharsis.'[11] Hayoota Deuthsch was excited as well: 'On the stage I have seen a struggle, I have heard voices of love and of protest . . . harsh gestures of birth, of death, of fear, of longing.'[12] Shai Bar-Yaacov was more explicit: 'Even those who do not practice praying can perceive something of the complex inner world of the prayer, by means of this performance, even if it is difficult to translate it into words.'[13] Finally, Hanoch Daum, an orthodox journalist, was happy with the fresh look at the prayer: 'This authentic encounter between voice and movement sheds a sort of vitality over our clumsy prayer. . . . The actors deserve a hug for daring to deal with such a painful subject. They do it in a fashion that fluctuates between abstract and avant-garde . . . even though such a performance requires virtuosity that they still lack.'[14]

In post-performance discussions some spectators raised the issue of possible profanation of the prayer, even of sacrilege. Such issues were to be expected; the actors themselves had raised them during their work process, and on the contrary, they considered the performance as a way of deepening their religious practice, not as profanation. Young and inexperienced at the time, they felt their work was intended to refine, clarify and intensify their daily ritual. In other words, for these actors, the stage functioned as a site for reassessing and renewing the tradition. What was unexpected was the 'danger' built into the encounter between ritual and theatre, for religiously observant actors. A new susceptibility came to the fore: some of the actors became aware of the fact that the experience of 'praying' onstage in front of a human audience could be more powerful for them than praying in synagogue before the divine spectator. They were worried by the narcissistic dimension of acting onstage, as if they had 'betrayed' both the prayer – and themselves.[15] Not all of them felt that way, and not always. However, these questions surfaced during the run of *Ma'amarot* and haunted the project. The crossing of borders between performing ritual in life and performing it onstage was perceived as dangerous.

Dancing prayer: *Highway No. 1*

All the members of *Kol Atzmotai Tomarna* ('all my bones shall say') are male, and the majority of them religiously observant Jews. The name is taken from Psalms 35:10, 'All my bones shall say: Lord, who is like unto Thee.' The group's website reads:

> Kol Atzmotai Tomarna is an educational and research-oriented framework based in the Ephron Dance Centre in Jerusalem. The programme's contents are drawn from the fields of dance and movement. The learning process is accompanied by thorough attentiveness to the spirit of Judaism. It is a new and experimental form of research, aimed at opening doors to the secrets of the body's wisdom and the world of dance, while exploring the meeting-point between body and spirit, according to the world of Jewish spirituality.[16]

Established in 2007 and headed by the non-religiously observant dancer and choreographer Ronen Izhaki, graduates of the dancing programme later founded the ensemble *Ka'et* (now). The ensemble numbers seven dancers and creates performances based on gestures from daily prayer, movements along with chants and synagogue attire, reframing them as contemporary dance. 'We are using the stage to awaken a new discussion between our lives and our bodies,' says Amitai Stern, a member of the group.[17] Typically, the audience is drawn from the orthodox community, but many spectators are secular, as the ensemble is a fringe, yet unique, group.

Highway No. 1 is widely considered their most engaging piece, certainly the most successful. The name refers to the highway connecting Jerusalem and Tel-Aviv. It symbolizes the two opposing ways of Jewish life in Israel: Tel-Aviv is a secular city, while Jerusalem accommodates a large orthodox population. The artists explain in post-performance discussions: 'Highway No. 1 connects east and west, hills and sea, Jerusalem and Tel-Aviv. Where does the line pass between the religious and the secular, between party-goers at a rave and worshippers at a synagogue? How will ritual prayer look in 2046?'[18]

This statement constitutes, in fact, the very core of the half-hour long piece that deals with the possible infiltration of secular rituals, such as rock music and dance, into the canonized prayer. This intrusion both alters the tradition and renews it. The performance starts with the group standing in one corner, barefoot, wearing black trousers and bluish-grey shirts. They move as if praying in synagogue, with the canonical motions and gestures associated with Jewish prayer, although not overtly bowing and swaying. On the opposite side, one single dancer moves differently, with a more unrestrained and wild motion. He then approaches the group, joins them and disturbs their praying with his wild movements. They resist the disturbance, yet one by one start to imitate him, and eventually all of them, including the intruder, segue into a sort of trance party. The music changes accordingly. Eventually, their movements are tamed and the group finds a new tempo for getting back to praying.

Figure 17 *Highway No. 1* – Prayer turns into trance party. Choreography: Ronen Izhaki. Dancers: Ehud Yehuda Segev, Hananya Schwartz, Ohad Stein, Amitay Stern, Alon Reich. Photo: Nir Shaanani.

As in *Ma'amarot*, we encounter concern for the men's prayer – not any particular prayer, but the idea of praying. The piece makes an abstraction of diverse prayers, and focuses on the issue of remaining faithful to tradition, when everything around is changing so fast and infiltrates the worshipper's life.

Reactions to the troupe have been split. Some dance writers and bloggers were commenting on the dancers' lack of technique, while sold-out house cheered. Hananya Schwartz, a young rabbi and a performer in Ka'et, was anxious about his own rabbi seeing him dance onstage. His anxiety wasn't entirely misplaced: after the performance, his rabbi quoted a passage from the Talmud that Schwartz said could be summed up as 'interesting but you are wasting your time'.[19]

Several of the dancers noted that in the performance they do actually find themselves praying – so intently that if the director stops them in rehearsals with a correction, they are annoyed at the interruption. Izhaki sees a connection and says admiringly: 'They brought to their bodies the focus they use in studying a Talmud page'.[20] Moreover, Izhaki, influenced by his work with the dancers, has started attending synagogue himself and participates in services.

The American chorographer Donald Byrd, during a trip to Jerusalem, praised the integrity of the group's work:

> There was one performance I attended that was truly surprising and definitely not disappointing, Ka'et Ensemble. . . . They brought a level of honesty and earnestness to their performance that I rarely see on the professional dance stage. There was neither a hint of the professional dance post-modern irony, nor twenty-first century apocalyptic jitters, nor amateurish smiley cutesiness. It was spirited, spiritual and full of a radiant joy, as only true believers (religious and artistic) seem to possess. And their joy was contagious. I caught a glimpse of a few of the "dancers," their faces washed in the afterglow of their performance, speaking with friends and relatives after the performance, and their joy was projected onto and reflected back on the faces of those who had experienced the performance and to whom they were now speaking. Their joy was not a "look I'm dancing" joy or the community centre's dance troupe's proudness (maybe a tad) but something much deeper and profound. It was transcendent with a touch of the holy, the spirit elevated. It was beautiful![21]

Byrd expresses admiration for the dancers, despite being unsure if he has understood their work:

> This is a kind of religious dance, I think (but it is also serious and rigorous choreography that any contemporary dance company could conceivably perform). It seems to me that what Ronen Izhaki (choreographer), his music/sound

collaborator Emmanuel Witzthum along with these men has done is to create a form of "charismatic" modern orthodox body-based prayer, especially with the piece *Highway No. 1*.[22]

I asked the dancers whether they do not sense that the presence of spectators is an intrusion into what is such a personal, intimate experience. On the contrary, they said, we need to communicate with other people, to establish a dialogue on our religious concerns.

Victoria Hanna: 'Secular' prayer?

The Israeli vocal performer Victoria Hanna constitutes a case *sui generis*: although she comes from an ultra-orthodox family, she no longer self-defines as such, and not even as modern orthodox. I chose Hanna's work as an exception corroborating the phenomenon of praying onstage: she has inverted the use of theatricality based on rituality. After abandoning orthodox practice, she is reconfiguring prayer, paradoxically declaring: 'The stage offers me an opportunity to pray.'[23] Thus, her 'secular' prayer and performance concerns are utterly religious. Hanna enacts a unique presentation of sacred Hebrew texts and prayers in a contemporary context, which amounts to 'a strong sense of ritual and a connection with something deep and ancient. Her voice undulates over a pulsing, vibrating drone, it has the feel of a prayer or incantation.'[24]

Hanna juxtaposes sacred texts with digital sounds, ring tones and rock music accompaniment. She is also the composer of her songs, and has performed all over the world. Vivek Ahuja, an Indian critic, following her performance in New Delhi in 2006, says: 'The fresh interpretations of original and ancient Jewish songs and texts provided an intimate evening, which was emotionally fiery, subtle and lyrical.' At the 2006 Singapore Arts Festival, Hanna's performance triggered an unexpected reaction from the Malaysian critic C. H. Loh, who reviewed her in both artistic and political terms, as representing 'a deeply spiritual people [who] also long for . . . love and connection with G-d – told through the bizarre vocal antics of . . . Victoria Hanna'.[25] These two reviews exemplify the impression of religious sense and the impact of Hanna's work, even in a distant cultural context.

Hanna's 2005 show, *Signals*, directed by Ruth Kanner, combines spoken language, theatre, electronic music and video art, with ancient prayers and

Hebrew texts. I would like to address three scenes, from teaching the alphabet of the holy language (Hebrew) to the *Song of Songs,* and to thanking God in blessings for our bodily functions.

> In the opening scene of *Signals*, Hanna . . . stands behind a podium in the centre of an empty and dark stage. Didactically, she pronounces each letter of the Hebrew alphabet, re-enacting a tutoring practice of the biblical language that originated in the Orthodox Jewish communities in the Diaspora. Hanna performs this traditional teaching method, through which she also re-embodies the voice of her father, a rabbi.[26]

Another scene presents the beginning of the love scene from the *Song of Songs*: Hanna lies down covered by large sheets of paper on which Hebrew letters are projected, and sings: 'I sleep, but my heart waketh; Hark! My beloved knocketh: Open to me, my sister, my love, my dove, my undefiled; for my head is filled with dew, my locks with the drops of the night.' She presents this imagined dialogue while switching her own voice to the male voice of the lover, and simulating his knocking, 'emphasizing the consonants in the dialogue with her voice, tongue and lips'.[27] This scene was particularly praised by the Indian critic Vivek Ahuja:

> She went on to sing "My Dove," and ancient Jewish prayers for the Holy Day of Atonement and the New Year. Victoria compellingly fused sacred and contemporary heritage into a total theatre experience, and brought to the audience music of the spiritual and eternal city of Jerusalem. She sang with confidence, with only an accompanying keyboard, and no drum for beat. Her notes came from her heart as she sang, giving a memorable evening to all in the auditorium.[28]

The third scene I would like to discuss takes us in a totally different direction: Hanna makes use of a blessing ritually used for thanking God for our basic corporeal functions: *Asher Yatzar* (traditionally a prayer said after one has used the toilet): 'Blessed are you God, who formed me with wisdom, hollows and openings. If one of them were ruptured or blocked, I could not stand before You even for one moment. Blessed are you who heals all flesh and performs wonders.'[29] She sings the text while stressing each syllable, and enumerating the words on her fingers as if counting all the wonders of God.

These scenes exemplify the dual uniqueness of Hanna's performance in terms of religious liturgy: first, a woman is appropriating and interfering with prayers that have traditionally been performed by males. And second: Hanna literally embodies the texts in a subversive manner, thus offering them a new, daring reading. It seems that her work oscillates between longing for her past experience of praying, and critically reinterpreting it. Hanna deliberately makes use of men's prayers, although there are (almost) parallel women's prayers. And yet she maintains that by performing prayers onstage she is addressing the Almighty:

> On stage I research in real time the other Stage, far above me and above my audience. I am sending my voice much higher. My belief is so strong, that I need to research it. On the stage I can see very clearly the limits of what humans can do, and I try to reach far away, to break through, to a higher Stage.[30]

If so, Hanna's rebellious attitude goes hand-in-hand with nostalgia for her ultra-orthodox past. On the one hand, she is not practicing orthodox Judaism. On the other hand, she is examining it, while still observing Shabbat. In terms of gender, her defiance of the patriarchal religious limitations imposed on women offers new perspectives on understanding and executing the ancient texts. Carol Martin describes this daring choice as a special contribution to reinscribing liturgy, rather than confronting it:

> These texts are part of a tradition of liturgy that is spoken, sung, and written in prescribed ways. Hanna's contribution to documenting this liturgy is to underscore its corporeality. To the degree that she incorporates a tradition, Hanna is part of the repertoire.[31]

Hanna's body and voice thus become a site containing both the traditional male liturgy and her personal rhetorical relationship with it. She distinguishes between performances of vocalists versus actors: 'In music there is something more direct and clean,' she says; 'the sounds pass through you', meaning that singing comes closer to praying, closer than when enacting prayers.[32] Still, hers is, after all, a public performance, and Hanna stresses the intimacy of praying in front of an audience:

> There is a contrast between the stage and religious worship. Ultimately, on the stage you express yourself and are concerned with the outcome, with the audience, even if you see yourself as a vessel for the sacred. It's not like when I pray alone, then I am as if in another sphere, *li'shma* (for its own sake), according to the *peshat* (simply put).[33]

Indeed, Victoria Hanna negates certain types of ritual performance onstage, particularly those that she is observing:

> Lighting Shabbat candles or making a blessing over them, I would say, that is different. The limit is the exploitation of the ritual, making use of it.

This is not absolute, it depends on who is the person. The limit is not to exploit something very intimate. The stage might abuse, violate intimacy, and become embarrassing.[34]

Hanna is using the rituals 'as a vocal artist, by taking the texts to an artistic field',[35] and thus, making them her own.

Conclusion: Back to rituality[36]

For centuries, orthodox Jews have developed a hermeneutic relationship with sacred texts and rituals, even when the intention was primarily to keep the practice as is. What we see here is yet another mode of doing just that: the artists enrich liturgy not by changing it, but by executing it with renewed intentions and intensity.

Avi Assaraf, the director of *Maʾamarot*, emphasizes that acting should be first of all a personal internal journey. Otherwise, he says, prayers onstage become merely 'acting oneself, distancing from the self'.[37] What he is interested in is 'personal experience in the world of prayer'.[38] To a certain extent, what he is describing here is the subsidiary role of the performances discussed: they operate as a continuation of worship by other means. This may be very well the reason that all three performances seek 'alternative' forms of theatricality, rather than 'mimetic' representation.

Yair Lipshitz mentions 'the ability of the theatre as a medium to create its own specific *Midrash*,[39] as well as the profit that the Jewish hermeneutic heritage may reap from theatrical interpretations'.[40] Lipshitz emphasizes that rethinking Jewish heritage 'in conflictual, dialogic and polyphonic terms'[41] is a significant and fruitful addition to the traditional Jewish hermeneutic activity.

To conclude, in the evening, the artists of *Maʾamarot* and *Highway No. 1* perform prayers onstage, interrogating and treating Jewish liturgy with emotions running the entire gamut from wild irreverence to extreme awe. At the end of the evening, they receive applause and go home, only to wake up next morning to the daily routine, to labour for God, to execute the same canonized, fixed, and obligatory acts and prayers that were subject to theatricalization the previous night.

This journey from rituality to theatricality and back sustains their religious practice, imbues their prayers with additional meaning and helps in their struggle to conquer the prayer every day anew. The experience onstage assists them in the extreme effort and tension of daily prayer. The shows thus constitute an attempt to elucidate the observance of prayer, beyond the fixation which is susceptible to rendering religious ritual sterile.

Victoria Hanna, by contrast, dissociates herself from the necessity to reinterpret prayers in order to substantiate them. Apparently, she has opted for a fair dichotomy: rituals she observes do not reach the stage, while other rituals and sacred texts are subject to subversive handling of a most artistic sort. Does the difference between Victoria and the other two groups mean that in order to bring Jewish rituals to the stage, the artist has first to stop religiously observing them? This might very well be the reason for her openness to discussing her work, whereas the artists of the other two groups are rather reluctant to clarify their special relationship with their performances.

Applied Performance Studies: Therapy, Activism and Education

Audacity and Insane Courage:
Dream Doctors' Secret Remedies

Atay Citron

"I am not funny. . . . What I am is brave."
> – Lucille Ball to *Rolling Stone*, 23 June 1983[1]

The stories I am going to relate here – stories of heroism and folly – are stories I heard from Dream Doctors. These are professional medical clowns who have been working in Israeli hospitals since 2002.[2] I have observed many Dream Doctors at work, with both paediatric and adult patients since 2006, when I created the first academic training programme for medical clowns at the University of Haifa's Theatre Department. I recorded interactions of Dream Doctors with patients, patients' families and hospital staff, and interviewed the medical clowns in order to understand the nature of their work, the methods they employ and their evaluation of the contribution they make to the healing process and well-being of hospitalized patients. In those interviews, I occasionally heard astounding stories about medical clowns behaving outrageously in order to manipulate unresponsive or uncooperative patients. Since in the early phase of my work I was interested in a general understanding of medical clowning, I tended to classify these unusual stories as marginal and did not probe into them. Later, however, I began to realize that their ostensible marginality masks a function and a meaning that are very central to the development of the Dream Doctors' organization. These stories, which I label 'stories of audacity and insane courage', have been told by their generators not only to me, but to peers (orally, and in writing, in the Dream Doctors' closed internet forum), to other researchers and to therapists who facilitate the organization's guidance and support groups, which in their regular gatherings allow participants to vent their emotional stress and discuss ethical issues of the profession. The repetitive articulation of these stories on different occasions and in different forums has shaped them as the building blocks of a Dream Doctors' mythology.

Any living organization that functions and develops produces a mythology, in the light of which norms are prescribed and preserved, novices are educated and initiated and deviations are addressed and treated. An investigation of the narratives that make such a mythology may reveal the organization's ethos and values. The Dream Doctors' mythology, which has been in formation for a little over a decade, is a fresh one to be sure, and it will probably continue to develop and change. At present, its heroes are characterized by independent spirit, audacious self-confidence and brash sense of humour. Its ethos seems to be that of bold innovation, similar to (and perhaps inspired by) that of historical avant-garde performance, adventurousness, individual courage, risk-taking and creativity. This is not to say that all ninety Dream Doctors that work in twenty six of Israel's hospitals are of the same mould. Nor is it true that there is an explicit orientation towards bold and risky behaviour, or that every individual Dream Doctor aspires to reach a high level of audacity. On the contrary, the professional training of the organization emphasizes careful, sensitive listening and attentiveness as well as compliance with hospital rules and cooperation with the staff. In the organization's lore, however, the most highly esteemed clowns are the jesters that play central roles in the audacity and insane courage narratives below.

There are hundreds of clown doctors' organizations in the world today, and although the services they offer are of similar nature and their fundamental values may be the same, they differ in approach, clowning techniques and other aspects of the work, including its ethos. I have had the opportunity to observe medical clowns at work in Canada, the United States, New Zealand and Australia, and on several occasions, I interviewed Dutch, German, Russian and Brazilian clown doctors. In the data that I collected, there are no stories that resemble the audacity and insane courage narratives of the Israeli Dream Doctors. A discussion of the possible reasons for that will be offered elsewhere, since here I have to focus on the stories' contents and on what we may learn from them. Before I delve into that, however, here is a brief introduction to medical clowning.

A brief history of medical clowning[3]

Most people who have heard about clowning in hospitals would identify it with the name Patch Adams that became known due to the international success of the 1998 Hollywood film bearing this name, with Robin Williams in the title role. Adams was indeed among the pioneers that used humour therapy in hospitals in the 1970s, when it was considered provocative and unacceptable. Although he personally continues to clown to this day, his focus has shifted to broader health policy issues, which he addresses as head of the *Gezundheit Institute*. Medical clowning as a profession has been in existence since 1986, when the New York-based Big Apple Circus launched its clown care unit under the leadership of Michael Christensen.[4] Expansion to other countries was relatively rapid, and professional development and growing cooperation with hospital staff brought about appreciation of the contribution of medical clowns to patients' general well-being and healing process. Since the 1990s, medical clowns in Europe, North and South America, Australia and a few countries in Asia are no longer altruistic volunteers, but trained professionals who get paid for their work by charitable organizations or by the hospitals that employ them. Most medical clowns, or clown doctors, as they are often called, work in children's hospitals or paediatric wards, but in recent years, significant expansion has begun, to include adult cancer and dialysis patients, geriatric patients and demented residents of old-age homes.

As clowns have become more present and more involved in hospital life, evidence of their intrinsic input to patients' recovery process was required. The abundance of anecdotal material provided by doctors, nurses, patients and their families was impressive, but evidence-based medicine progresses on the basis of published scientific studies. Consequently, medical clowns' work has been the subject of various published studies. These studies have demonstrated that medical clowns can be instrumental in stress and anxiety reduction in paediatric patients, particularly in pre-operative patients.[5] They have a positive effect on people suffering from dementia.[6] In Israel, medical clowns facilitate the procedure of injecting corticosteroids into the joints of patients suffering from idiopathic juvenile arthritis.[7] They assist in the performance of forensic examinations in adolescent victims of sexual abuse.[8] They substitute for sedative agents in paediatric patients undergoing radionuclide scanning.[9] They conduct the initial emergency-room encounters with shell-shock patients.[10] They have even proven effective in enhancing positive outcome of in vitro fertilization.[11] Clearly, clown doctors today are more than mere entertainers who put smiles on the faces of ailing patients. They are professionally trained to employ a variety of therapeutic methods, and they are being integrated into the medical teams in many hospitals around the globe.

While there are still many clowns who volunteer in hospitals, often with little or no professional training, a growing number of organizations recruit members only after auditions, trial periods, professional workshops and supervised practicum.[12] The University of Haifa launched the first full-time undergraduate programme, which combines training in clowning with studies in nursing, social and medical sciences. Some organizations in other countries are interested in developing similar programmes. After they start working, professional medical clowns continue their training on a regular basis, with international exchanges, professional workshops and seminars, and in most cases, 'mental hygiene' or support groups for the clowns, led by therapists. Some organizations run workshops for hospital staff as well, in order to improve communication with the clowns and to polish interpersonal skills through humour. There are also specialty areas, such as clowning with mental patients, or intellectually challenged children, rehabilitation hospital clowning and clowning in disaster zones.

The occupational hazards of clowning

Whereas most medical clowns stay in the safe zone of offering patients amusing diversion and playful interaction, there are a few Dream Doctors that on occasion take unusual measures and, within their role as clowns, behave outrageously. The risk of such conduct is failure, first and foremost. Not every person appreciates radical humour. A patient may find it offensive and withdraw as a result, or act defensively. A complaint may be filed, and the clown may be reprimanded or even fired. None of the above has happened so far, to the best of my knowledge. In my attempt to understand the tolerance of ailing patients to the clowns' audacity, I explored historic and ethnographic work that documents clowns' extreme behaviour. It appears that the few Dream Doctors that engage in such conduct, the ones that take risk of defying decorum, belong to a long line of ritual clowns and fools. These ancestors, if you will, while being blasphemous, are considered sacred, and while enjoying the protection of the establishment, are in permanent peril.

It may seem strange to tie together clowning and risk. After all, in the circus, it is trapeze artists and sword swallowers who seem to be risking their health and lives, not the clowns who fall on their padded bottoms or get hit on the head by a giant rubber hammer. But danger comes in many guises, as history and ethnography teach us. In the fourth chapter of her book, *Fools Are*

Everywhere: The Court Jester Around The World, Beatrice K. Otto writes about beatings, banishment and beheadings of court jesters who had gone too far with their audacious social critique.[13] For the fool, she tells us, 'overstepping the limits of his license was an occupational hazard'.[14] Instead of using caution to avoid this hazard, however, fools have consciously flirted with it. The risk was titillating apparently, and its significance to the clown's creativity and ability to function was crucial. Otto quotes the editor of a Hungarian humour magazine, saying that under Communism humour flourished because 'telling a joke is more interesting when you can be put in jail for it'.[15] This brings to mind satirists like Frank Wedekind, who was indeed jailed for publishing a poem spoofing Kaiser Wilhelm II,[16] or Lenny Bruce and his frequent arrests on charges of obscenity.[17] In these cases, as in many others, the charges filed against the audacious jesters turned them into instant folk heroes and intensified public expectations for more fearless, provocative satire.

Otto collected reports from various countries and eras in which jesters were reprimanded by their patrons for their insolence, and at times, also physically punished. China's Emperors Wenzong and Lizong, England's Henry VIII and France's Henry III and Louis XIII all at one time banished their fools from their courts, and some Chinese court fools were beheaded or otherwise executed for their scandalous humour.[18] In Otto's detailed record of those cases, one aspect seems particularly relevant to our discussion. It is embodied in a quote from *Gopal The Jester*, in which the Bengali king, as he banishes the fool from his court says, 'if you were not a clown, I would have had you hanged'.[19] Apparently, even when punished by authority, the clown may enjoy certain absolution. His status is unique because he is expected to constantly test the boundaries of decorum, even to overstep his license. This is the core of his being, his *raison d'être*. He operates under immunity from the authority so that he can criticize that very same authority in ways that no other subordinate is allowed. Both clown and ruler know that this immunity can be abruptly withdrawn, leaving the former at the mercy of the latter. When will it be withdrawn? The rules are intentionally vague, as this is the nature of the game, its source of suspense. With the blade hanging over his head, the clown must be witty and boldly truthful. If he doesn't come close to overstepping his license, he risks becoming conventional and boring. If he crosses the line, woe to him . . .

Why is the clown allowed to be provocatively critical and uninhibitedly truthful in the first place? William Guinee, writing about the Koyemshi – members of the ritual clown order of the Zuni in New Mexico – observes that a meta-statement of impotence and deformed idiocy is fundamental to their performance and protects them.[20] Like the 'natural fools' of medieval Europe – midgets, hunchbacks and other freaks of nature – they are perceived as polluted, lacking social status, and at the same time, possessing mysterious powers. The Koyemshi mud head masks have no noses, and large bulges of clay-smeared cotton cloth protrude over their ears, eyes and mouths. Their clay-smeared bodies are barely covered by rags, and according to Bunzel, they tie cotton cloth around their penises, 'which makes erection impossible and represents their innocent impotence'.[21] In Zuni mythology, as narrated by Cushing, the Koyemshi are exceptionally ugly, childish and impotent because they are the offspring of an incestuous relationship between siblings – the son and daughter of a primordial priest. Madly lusting for his sister, the son was scratching his face with his fingernails as he was chasing her. Rolling in the mud in despair, clumps of bloodied soil were stuck to his facial wounds, until his sister took pity on him. They lived together in a cave. Their nine sons looked like their father (hence the masks) and were impotent simpletons, whose ridiculous commentary on the sacred Kachina dance and on Zuni life in general was a delightful mixture of wisdom and stupidity.[22]

Manifest impotence (as that of eunuchs), sexual ambivalence and transvestitism, which are common in clown types around the world, neutralize the potential threat to a ruler posed by true males. As much as a sovereign is suspicious of the flattery of his courtiers, who may at any moment plot to dethrone him, he can trust a person who openly presents himself as impotent and proposes truth instead of flattery. The court fool's cap, like the Koyemshi wrapped penis, denotes impotence with its flaccid peaks from which bells are hung. It is the reverse image and parody of the king's crown that boasts erect peaks with precious stones. Its meta-message is 'I am impotent and therefore no threat to power'. This is where the clown's immunity originates.

Paradoxically, this submissive meta-message allows clowns to publicly display unusual abilities and powers. Clowns of the Né-we-kwe ('Gluttons') secret society of the Zuni, for example, are known for their gift to consume endless quantities of vegetables and fruit, along with pebbles, refuse, live and dead animals. 'They favor feces or urine', the astonished Cushing reported in 1896, 'but will eat almost anything'. This ability makes them 'medicine men *par excellence*', specializing in curing 'all diseases of the stomach – the elimination of poisons from the systems of the victims of sorcery and imprudence'.[23] The Zuni worship their Né-we-kwe and delight in their pranks. These sacred clowns, who undergo long and arduous training and initiation, are known as champions of reversal: they say the opposite of what they mean, they choose names for themselves that convey the opposite of their manifest characters, they walk and talk (and dance) backwards. In short, they embody society upside-down.[24]

Pueblo clowns are also known to perform dangerous and funny stunts, such as climbing down ladders from rooftops with their heads first, as they tell sexual and scatological jokes. Similarly, in American rodeo, this 'ritual drama of cattle culture', as Beverly Stoeltje describes it, the clown puts himself in dangerous situations in order to allow the bucked-off rider escape from the raging bull.

> He must attract the bull's attention to himself and away from the cowboy when the cowboy is bucked off, but he must challenge the bull and place himself in danger from the bull, acting like a crazy fool when he does so. Acting simultaneously as fool and hero, the clown's role is of major importance to the cowboy . . .[25]

During the cowboy's bull ride, the clown's buffoonery is thus a true life-saving act. The crazier, riskier and more idiotic his comic bullfighting pranks are, the louder the audience expression of admiration will be. The clown is also 'a verbal artist of bull', adds Stoeltje. Between rides, he mimes scatological jokes, which the rodeo announcer verbally interprets. As in all ritual clowning, the jokes assault decorum in regard to 'bodily functions, sexuality [and] social relations'. Hence 'bull' is physical danger from rampant virility, and at the same time, it is dung-stinking verbal caricature of social values.[26]

Defying authority

It took time for the hierarchically organized hospitals to get used to the Dream Doctors' unruly conduct. Miki, a seasoned medical clown, who works in several hospitals, told me one story that exemplifies the clown's natural resistance to authority and how it was effectively used to achieve therapeutic goals.[27] He was working in one room when he heard a child's cries of protest from another room. When he entered that room, he realized that the physical therapist was trying to force a boy out of his bed to exercise. The boy, having iron braces on his legs, was fearful of the pain the exercise might cause him and threw a tantrum. Miki instantly sided with him. 'Nobody likes to be controlled,' he says, 'and when the staff uses physical force to make a kid perform some task, the result is poor.' Miki told the boy not to listen to the physical therapist. 'No one can tell you what to do here, and you'll do exactly what you want,' he said. He then demonstrated how he, the clown, did only what he wanted. His silly demonstration made the boy smile and state that what he wanted was to play soccer. Miki brought a ball and a balloon, and within minutes, the boy was out of bed, playing with Miki and ready for physical therapy. The clown showed him a way out of the crisis by giving him control over his situation, or, as Miki puts it, 'by turning the hierarchical pyramid upside down and putting him on its top'.

Another Dream Doctor who defied authority is Amnon, who worked in Ashkelon, at Barzilai Hospital, which serves the Israeli population living near the border with the Palestinian Gaza strip.[28] In 2007, during one of numerous Israeli-Palestinian hostilities, a Hammas rocket had exploded next to a bus driving elementary school children to their homes in the town of Sderot. No one was physically hurt, but the traumatized children were sent to Barzilai, where they were met by paediatricians, nurses, psychologists, psychiatrists and social workers. Only the clown had not been summoned. Upon hearing the news, Amnon hurried to the hospital dining room, where the children were gathered. He saw the chief psychiatrist sitting with the children in a circle. The physician made a hand signal for Amnon to leave, but Amnon chose to ignore the signal and walked straight to the circle, to sit himself down among the children. In the process, his bag fell open on the floor, with his clown props scattered all over the place. The session was abruptly stopped, as giggling children left their seats to help the clown collect his props. One can imagine the radical change of mood, as clown and kids were trying out tricks, and funny whistles and squeaks were heard. When I asked Amnon about the psychiatrist's reaction to the unexpected mini-carnival of shell-shocked children, he said he had no idea. He was totally absorbed in his interaction with the children and never had another look at the psychiatrist. That silly kind of mood prevailed through lunch, when Amnon started a French fries battle with the staff and the children. Following that, the children were released to their homes.

Amnon says that he did not hesitate for a second about his move. 'There was no dilemma,' he recalls, 'only a strong drive to bring about a radical change of mood.' A witness to that scene was the hospital's deputy general manager. A week after the incident, he invited Amnon to his office, not for reproof, but to tell him how impressed he was by what he had seen. Consequently, the hospital protocol was changed, and when a missile fell on a shopping mall in Ashkelon, the medical clowns were the first to encounter the shell-shocked patients in the emergency room. Amnon was fortunate to have such an understanding and appreciative representative of medical authority witness his audacious action.

Provocative therapy

Since 2003, Yaron Sancho Goshen, aka Professor Sancho de la Sponga, has been a Dream Doctor at Ha'Emek Medical center in Afula. In those years, he effectively demonstrated his skills and won the trust, appreciation and cooperation of the hospital staff. Of the many stories he recounted from his experience, the report on his continuous work with Lisa, written in 2007, is among the best known in the Dream Doctors' community, and a telling example of the subject under discussion here.[29]

Lisa was an amyotrophic lateral sclerosis patient, an adolescent girl from a Palestinian town in the centre of Israel. Completely paralysed, she could only roll her eyes and move her tongue, thumbs, one elbow and one knee. One day, Sancho walked into her room, where Arabic music was playing, and without hesitation, invited her to dance. When I questioned the tact of that move (in a conversation we held 5 years later), Sancho admitted that as a person, he would have never dared to make such an audacious invitation, 'but it was the clown that did this crazy thing, inviting her to dance', he explained, 'because the clown is blind to her condition and lacks any pity or compassion. The clown is there to play with the healthy side of the patient, whereas the medical staff works with the ailing side'.

Figure 18 Professor Sancho de la Sponga in the operating room (the words 'operating room' are printed in Hebrew on the back of the shirt of the man in the background). Sancho is seen here with full theatrical makeup, which he wears for the special occasion of the Jewish holiday of Purim. Normally, he wears only a red nose because elaborate makeup is thought to be potentially scary to children. Photo courtesy of Y. Goshen.

Before we go on, two issues must be discussed: first, the issue of compassion, mentioned by Sancho, and second, the distinction he made between his person, and his clown persona, Professor Sancho de la Sponga.

Miki, who sometimes acts as Sancho's partner, contends that whereas compassion may be a prerequisite for a person choosing medical clowning as a profession, for the working clown it is a hindrance because it reaffirms the passivity and the acceptance of the patient's suffering. To illustrate this, he relates the story of a paediatric oncology patient, a weak, miserable-looking boy who under the influence of pain killers, was uncooperative and lacking any joy.' We decided to force him into life', Miki recalls:

> We started an agitated argument. That quickly led to an angry [toy] sword fight next to his bed, during which we occasionally slapped him. The kid began to get involved in our fighting, and soon, he was transformed into a heroic knight, brandishing his sword in all directions, slaughtering the pathetic clowns. Afterward, the nurse said that we acted as antidotes to the drug he had been given.

When he was asked once by a social worker why he was not kind to a patient and had not asked him how he was feeling that day, Miki replied that his job was to take the patient's mind away from how he felt. 'If I take the job of a nurse and show empathy,' he explains, 'I shall not be doing my own job.' Amnon takes a different stand. He believes that empathy is essential to the building of trust and rapport with the patient, and even if not verbally articulated, it is transmitted through non-verbal channels.

American psychotherapist Frank Farrelly addressed the same issue in his 1974 book, *Provocative Therapy,* and in numerous other writings and lectures.[30] Farrelly believes that contrary to the preconceived notion of empathy as fundamental to therapy, a therapist's scornful provocation can often be effective in transforming a client/patient from a self-pitying, helpless and passive person into an active adversary, willing to defend him/herself against the therapist's derision. Farrelly describes cases in which conventional therapy brought no progress, whereas one session of provocative therapy resulted in significant change. Farrelly himself is not a professional clown, but his sense of humour, together with his warm and authoritative personality, play an important part in the therapeutic encounters. A key chapter in his book is dedicated to humour in provocative therapy. Farrelly believes that provocative therapy should always be humorous, or else it may be offensive and inefficient.[31]

When Sancho distinguishes between his own persona and that of the clown, he practises a typical dissociation, says Rachel Lev, head of the Graduate

School of Creative Arts Therapy at the University of Haifa.[32] She explains that dissociation is a defence mechanism that enables an individual to handle dire situations by separating his/herself from his/her body or actions. Lev explains that dissociation protects the ego when a person is confronted with a trauma it cannot contain. Permanent dissociation is considered pathology, but when the clown performs and functions well on other levels, dissociation can help maintain his sanity. Medical clowns, she notes, spend days in wards with very sick children, and in order to function, they must dissociate themselves. It is interesting to note that Guinee, writing about the Koyemshi ritual clowns, also observes that 'the clown impersonator himself disassociates from the clown', as [his] mental state is that of 'precarious balance'.[33]

Let us go back to Lisa, lying motionless on her back in her hospital bed. She declined the invitation to dance, and Sancho invested endless efforts to persuade her. He filled her room with flowers and potted plants – all 'borrowed' from other rooms in the ward. He asked her to tell him if there was anything in his appearance that could be improved so that she would change her mind. He expressed his suspicion that she might have a gentleman with whom she was dancing. In the following sessions and throughout a year, he deliberately constructed a romantic role for Lisa, inflating her image as a desirable young woman. He crowned her 'Miss Umm el Fahem (the name of her town)'. He confessed his love to her mother, and asked other colleague clowns to make guest appearances in the grand soap opera that he and Lisa were creating. In retrospect, he said that his initial invitation to dance – crazy as it was – had given Lisa the option of refusal, which she had never had before. Instead of being unable to move, Lisa was suddenly choosing (for her own reasons) not to move.

Shlomit Bresler, a therapist who was facilitating two Dream Doctors' support groups, is familiar with Lisa's story as told to the group by Sancho.[34] She believes that the core of that interaction was the image of the body. In this disease, she explains, body image is very problematic. In the new dramaturgy proposed to Lisa by Sancho, her paralysed body was suddenly put in (imaginary) motion. She refused to dance, not because she was unable to do so, but because she was not sufficiently pleased with the man who had asked her to dance. This girl was being courted by a man, albeit a clown, and in that novel position she was establishing a new body image for herself. As Sancho was trying to win Lisa's heart, and as she persisted in her refusal to dance with him, her role of the desirable, unattained woman was gaining volume, and she was empowered. Laughing her way through that silly game, she could not but imagine a different body for herself, a woman's body that could, at any moment, start dancing with a man. That process was launched by Sancho's intuitive urge to do something crazy and audacious with Lisa.

Death

Death is a constant presence in the life of medical clowns, and it is often in its shadow that they need to be most creative, particularly because denial is prevalent even in the last moments. It is with chronic patients that the clowns have the most meaningful and long-lasting interactions. They know the patients' family members, who often take part in their silly shenanigans. They visit those patients regularly over months and sometimes even years. They are briefed by the staff about those patients' medical condition, and when death appears at the door, they feel they must do something special.

A few weeks after I had interviewed Amnon for this piece, he sent me the following death-bed dialogue he had with David, an adult cancer patient. The long-term clown-patient rapport seems to have allowed this bold farewell dialogue, in which the patient is no lesser clown than the Dream Doctor.

A: Buongiorno, David, how are you?
D: Soon I am going to stop farting.
A: It's time. Everybody has been suffering.
D: Yes, but my kids have gotten used to the smell.
A: They, too, suffer.
D: Well, at least I am leaving some money. Money doesn't smell.
A: Listen to a joke about farting . . . [he tells the joke]
D: They said I was terminal and suggested I move to the hospice.
A: Wow, it's a real suite down there, it's good.
D: Yes, I heard they have a garden too.
A: I'm not letting you move out until you give me all this medically-prescribed grass you promised me.
D: Forget it. I'll need every ounce of it.
A: Oy, David, we had some good time. . . . Remember we were in a movie together [a hospital publicity film]?
D: . . . we were fantasizing about Hollywood . . . O.K. Sing for me, but not a lullaby.
A: Are you crazy? I don't need you to fall asleep. I am going to be charged with Euthanasia.
D: Perhaps this Louis Armstrong song, "What a Wonderful World!"

A: I want to compose a song for you [beginning to play and sing] David, you are a very special and wonderful man, a gifted farter, I love you.

D: I love you too. We clicked immediately.

A: So you won't get to 120.

D: I won't get to 120, but I am at peace with myself, and this is worth something too.

A: This is worth a lot. Goodbye, David.

I shall conclude with the story that triggered the writing of this essay. It exemplifies my understanding of the notion of 'audacity and insane courage' and addresses the subjects of risk and taboo violation that were discussed above. I heard that story from Sancho, who also posted it in the Dream Doctors' closed internet forum, where it provoked an intensive debate on moral and ethical issues.

It is the story of an adolescent girl in intensive care. Sancho walked to her bed and asked her why she was there. He recalls that she smiled sweetly and said, 'I swallowed twenty-five pills.' Sancho's jaw dropped in amazement when he said, 'Co-o-o-l! But wait a minute, you are not dead, how come? What pills did you take?' The girl reported that it was Sedural – a prescription drug for urinary tract infection. She then described in detail how she tried to commit suicide after her boyfriend had left her. Sancho listened and was miming the plot with occasional exaggeration. At every stage, he interrupted the narration in order to find out if she was dead, and to express disappointment upon hearing a negative answer. When a doctor walked in, Sancho asked him, 'Tell me, doc, please, if one wishes to die, Sedural would not work, right?' When the doctor confirmed that Sedural was a poor choice for that purpose, Sancho continued to investigate: 'so what would you recommend?' The shocked doctor began to stutter, as Sancho continued: 'Would twenty-five pills of Valium kill her?' The doctor giggled and nodded as Sancho mentioned a few more lethal drugs. The doctor left the room. The girl was laughing.

When the girls' parents entered, Sancho recounted the entire interaction to them. The mother's weary smile made him ponder for a minute, after which he ceremoniously announced: 'Lady, I have something to tell you . . . your daughter is going to die'. He met the mother's eyes, paused, and then continued, 'and you are going to die as well'. The father, quick to grasp the gist, added, 'and I, too, am going to die', to which Sancho triumphantly replied, 'exactly, and me too. Beautiful!' After another brief pause, he said: 'but not now. She still has a lot to do. She needs to find love'.

Following a conversation about death and love with the parents, Sancho performed what I would call 'a closing ritual'. He pulled out a roll of pink heart stickers from his pouch and placed one on the girl's pajamas, saying, 'Mother loves you.' Another sticker – 'and father loves you.' Towards another heart sticker, positioned on the wall and representing the boyfriend who had left, Sancho and the girl contorted their faces, making vulgar sounds and gestures of disgust. Additional love stickers representing siblings' and other family members' love were placed on and around the girl, as Sancho was leaving, playing the tune from the film *Life is Beautiful*.

Sancho believes that the girl was receptive to his clowning because unlike everybody else, he responded to her story with childish enthusiasm that surprised her. He says that during the interaction, the girl's affirmative signals gave him license to proceed. One Dream Doctor who read the story pointed out that using irony and absurd, Sancho offered the girl a new, external perspective on her suicide attempt, and that by inviting the doctor and the parents to participate, Sancho made it possible for them to openly relate to aspects of the crisis which had previously been suppressed. Sancho remarked that he would probably not play that game with any doctor but that particular one, who knew him well and trusted his judgement.

While expressing admiration of Sancho's performance, one Dream Doctor wondered if by mentioning the names of specific drugs, Sancho was not helping

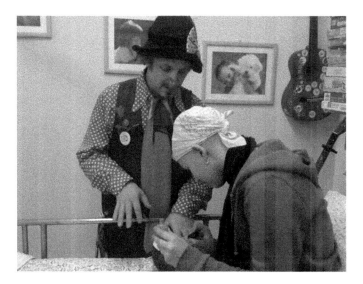

Figure 19 A girl applying polish on Sancho's nails in order to initiate him into the position of her 'best girlfriend'. Photo courtesy of Y. Goshen.

the girl with her next suicide attempt. Another clown wrote that Sancho's tightrope act was impressive but dangerous – he could fall and hurt himself and others. Sancho replied that if the girl was determined to put an end to her life, she would eventually find a way to do it. Her safety was the responsibility of her parents and the medical team. Medical clowning, he added, does not replace therapy. The clown is never aware of the complexity of a situation. He is oblivious to danger. His role is to expose hidden truths. If he is afraid of overstepping the limits of his license – to use Otto's term – he will never be able to walk the tightrope, to do his job. 'I am a great believer in the god of the clowns,' Sancho wrote in the internet forum, 'it is he who directs me to the place where I need to be and where I need to give a gift'.

Performing the World: The Performance Turn in Social Activism

Dan Friedman and Lois Holzman

The performance turn is widely acknowledged. The premise that all (or much) of human practices are performed, that humans, through performance, function as the active social constructors of their world is not only embodied in the discipline of performance studies, but has become part of the dialogue in anthropology, linguistics, ethnography, folklore, psychology, sociology and history.[1] What is generally less recognized, both by many scholars and by political activists themselves, is the performance turn in social activism.

The collapse of the Communist revolutions of the twentieth century have called into question the value of ideology (in particular) and cognition and knowledge (in general) to provide a way out of the developmental dead ends – pervasive poverty, constant warfare and violence, the rapidly expanding gaps in wealth and opportunity – that appear to have trapped humanity.[2] Acknowledging this, a growing number of political and social activists, community and youth organizers, progressive and critical educators and therapists, and others have been turning to performance as a way of engaging social problems, activating communities and experimenting with new social and political possibilities. This shift is allowing social change activists in both modern and traditional cultures to organize, through performance, something new with what exists. The performance turn has the potential to be socially and culturally transformative/ revolutionary because, in our view, performance is a creative social activity that allows human beings to break out of old roles and old rules.[3]

This chapter will focus on several aspects of the performance turn in social activism that have been made manifest at and through Performing the World (PTW), seven conferences that have taken place since 2001. PTW is a cross-disciplinary gathering of performance practitioners and scholars from every continent, many of them grassroots community organizers. It not only provides the opportunity for participants to learn from and inspire each other, but also to create informal international networks and collaborations.

In unpacking the origins and development of PTW and in analysing the larger performance turn, the authors draw upon their insider position. Both are leaders of the performance community that initiated and organizes PTW and both have been engaged in performance activism for three decades. Holzman, a developmental psychologist, along with the late Fred Newman, is the founder and remains the key organizer of PTW. Friedman is the artistic director of the Castillo Theatre in New York City, and as such he has interfaced with the theatre world relative to performance activism.

Performance activism has a number of distinct, albeit related, origins. Political, experimental and educational theatre is one vital source. Another is the performance turn in psychology and the social sciences, part of the larger embrace of performance associated with some versions of postmodernism. A third is to be found in the grassroots community and political organizing led by Fred Newman and his colleagues in New York City beginning in the early 1970s.

Political, experimental and educational theatre

We begin with political theatre, in particular with agit-prop, the amateur theatre activity of urban workers that emerged in the years following the Russian Revolution in both Germany and the Soviet Union and spread across the globe with the encouragement of the communist movement.[4] The 1960s saw the re-emergence of amateur political theatre, most immediately relevant, 'guerrilla theatre', the legacy of which continues in groups like the Guerrilla Girls, Improv Everywhere and the Yes Men, as well as in the contemporary phenomena of flash mobs.[5] Additionally, from the professional avant-garde came environmental theatre, which eliminated the clear distinction between the audience's and the actors' space, thus expanding the performance space beyond the stage.[6] The Living Theatre, during the same period, worked to transform the dynamic of the theatre from one in which actors perform a story for a passive audience, into one in which actors and audience both take part in a performed ritual.[7] These experiments helped to make clear (as agit-prop did a generation earlier) the possibility of performance by non-actors and to tie this conviction to a progressive politic.

Another theatrical stream flowing into the emerging river of performance activism has been educational theatre. Educational theatre has come to refer to the use of theatre as an educational tool in schools, as well as in settings outside formal educational institutions. In this latter sense, educational theatre has given birth to Theatre for Development, a term used primarily in Africa and Asia, to describe explicitly didactic theatre produced to educate communities on subjects ranging from HIV/AIDS to agricultural techniques, etc. Often this theatre work is funded by European-based NGOs or religious organizations that see theatre as a tool in the arsenal of helping the poor country to 'develop', hence the label.

Closely related to educational theatre is 'theatre for social change', a label more often used in the wealthy countries, particularly the United States, for theatre functioning at the grassroots level, often outside of formal theatre buildings, with the goal of fostering social change. In some ways it is the contemporary manifestation of the agit-prop and street theatre traditions of the twentieth century, although it is usually created by trained theatre artists who bring plays and/or the theatre-making process into communities from the outside. The most influential current within this stream is Theatre of the Oppressed in all its multiplying variations. While the Theatre of the Oppressed does not go as far as bringing performance *off* the stage into daily life, it does encourage the non-actor to take the stage.[8] Another current in the mix is Playback Theatre, which uses improvisation to bring people's lived experiences directly onto the stage, as actors 'playback' theatrically life stories told by audience members.[9]

In recent years these various tendencies within educational theatre and theatre for social change have embraced a common identity as 'Applied Theatre'. The label refers to the common approach of *applying* theatre as a tool to teach, engage communities, spark conversations, etc. about social, political, educational and cultural issues. Many practitioners who identify with this label, and for whom applied theatre and theatre activism are synonymous, have made PTW their home over the past decade.

Performative psychology

Another source of performance activism is the coming together of on-the-ground community organizing for progressive social change with the emergence of a performance turn within psychology and the other social sciences, of which Holzman and Newman are a part.

Among academics and practitioners critical of the social-scientific mainstream (on ethical, political and/or scientific grounds) who make a shift from a natural science-based and individualistic approach to understanding human life to a more cultural and relational approach, some have come to understand human life as primarily performatory. Contrary to mainstream psychology's premise that the essential feature of human beings is our cognitive ability (often accompanied by a subordination of our affective ability), performative psychology puts performance 'center stage'. To performative psychology theorists, researchers and practitioners, people's ability to perform – to pretend, to play, to improvise, to be who we are and 'other' than who we are – is simultaneously cognitive and emotive. It is seen as an essential human characteristic, essential to our emotional-social-cultural-intellectual lives – but dramatically overlooked by mainstream psychology.

This shift has breathed new life into qualitative research within the social sciences, spawning the methodology known as 'performative social science' or 'performative inquiry'. This approach involves breaking out of the typical academic performance of text, graphs, tables and Power Points and developing alternative modes of communicating psychological concepts, research and practices. Originating in the work of Ken and Mary Gergen[10] (and a few other qualitative researchers) in the 1990s,[11] performative social science is 'the deployment of different forms of artistic performance in the execution of a scientific project. Such forms may include art, theater, poetry, music, dance, photography, fiction writing and multimedia applications. Performance-oriented research may be presented in textual form, but also before live audiences, or in various media forms (film, photographs, websites)'.[12] Among the dozens of topics they cite are health and medical treatment for women with breast cancer, involving patients playing roles in a theatre production, and immigration, bringing audience members into interactive relations with artefacts and activities related to Mexican immigrants.[13]

Another direction performative inquiry has taken is studying performing by creating opportunities for people to perform in new ways. For example, there are practitioners who use theatrical performance techniques in non-theatrical settings to support the expression of people's creativity and sociality. Included here are various non-traditional therapies, including psychodrama, social constructionist, collaborative and narrative approaches.[14] There are also educators who have made this performance turn, becoming attentive to creativity as *socially performed* and learning itself as a creative activity. Some relate explicitly to teaching and learning as improvisational[15] and develop performatory practices of student-teacher engagement.[16]

This is the direction taken by the community we the authors are part of. We became convinced that performing in new ways is key to ongoing human development and that ongoing human development is a necessary bicondition of global cultural and political transformation.[17] Our brand of performance activism links performance inextricably to human and community growth and development. PTW was born as an organizing tactic of this community; we now offer a brief intellectual history of its activities.

We began by working in the poorest communities of New York City in the 1970s and have gone on to organize middle-class and wealthy people to work with us to support poor people to develop and provide leadership to the process of positive social change, free of government, corporate or university dependence. This organizing has led to, among many other things, the development of outside of school youth programmes, a theatre, a research and training centre, social therapy practices, independent electoral campaigns and self-governing organizations on a national and international stage.[18]

In the course of nearly four decades of this work, we have come to understand performance as a human capacity to be both who we are and who we are not at the same time (as actors on the stage are themselves and their characters). It is this ability, we believe, that allows human beings to develop beyond instinctual and socially patterned behaviour. This understanding of performance has, for us and increasing others, changed the very nature of social change activism.

In coming to this understanding/practice of performance, our organizing experience was enriched by Newman's training in analytical philosophy, the philosophy of science and the foundations of mathematics, and Holzman's training in developmental psychology, psycholinguistics and cultural-historical activity theory – and by the embrace by Newman, Holzman, et al. of the early methodological writings of Marx, the later writings of Austrian philosopher Ludwig Wittgenstein and the work of Soviet psychologist Lev Vygotsky.

From Marx we took his dialectical methodology and insistence that human beings are not isolated individuals: 'As society itself produces man as man, so it is produced by him. Activity and mind are social in their content as well as in their origin: they are social activity and social mind.'[19] For Marx, the transformation of the world and of ourselves as human beings is one and the same task: 'The coincidence of the changing of circumstances and of human activity or self-changing can be conceived and rationally understood only as revolutionary practice.[20] Revolutionary practice, we came to understand from Marx, is not so much the organizing towards a specific goal as it is a new conception of method, a conception of method that involves a unity of human beings and the world we've created/are re-creating.[21]

From Wittgenstein, we came to an understanding of the limitations of language (and, by extension, of ideology). His later writings present a way of doing philosophy without foundations, premises, generalizations or abstractions.[22] His method exposes 'the pathology' embedded in language and in conceptions of language, thoughts and emotions and introduces the concept of *language-games* Playing language-games 'bring[s] into prominence the fact that the *speaking* of language is part of an activity, or of a form of life'[23] (Wittgenstein 1953, *PI*, 23) and 'the mental mist which seems to enshroud our ordinary use of language disappears. We see activities, reactions, which are clear-cut and transparent' (Wittgenstein 1958, *BBB*, p. 17).[24] Extending Wittgenstein, we concluded that clearing the mental mist required performance.[25]

Vygotsky[26] brought Marx to bear on issues of human, particularly childhood, development and learning and formulated Marx's dialectical method in the following manner:

> The search for method becomes one of the most important problems of the entire enterprise of understanding the uniquely human forms of psychological activity. In this case, the method is simultaneously prerequisite and product, the tool and the result of the study.[27]

Continuing to build on Marx's dialectical method, Newman and Holzman expanded Vygotsky's statement of method and posited that human beings not only make and use tools but we also make new kinds of tools – *tool-and-result tools*. In fact, people develop through tool-and-result methodology. Vygotsky showed how little children become speakers of a language by playing language games with us, and in their pretend play. In both activities, the tool or process, and result or product, come into existence together.

Vygotsky said, 'In play it is as though a child is a head taller than he is. Play is a leading factor in development.'[28] He is telling us that in play, we are who we are *and* who we are becoming *at the same time*. He noted that children learn by playing with the adults and older children around them, creating performances of learning. Newman and Holzman,[29] building on this and looking at the organizing work being done by hundreds of their colleagues, came to realize that human development happens, not just with children, but with people of all ages, when we relate to them as 'a head taller', that is, as who they are becoming. Just as a baby and mother perform conversation before the baby speaks correctly, school age children can perform reading or math or science before they know how, and adults can learn how to run their world by performing power.

Relating to each other 'a head taller' is what the performance community that created PTW does with thousands of inner-city children and adolescents, with people in emotional distress, with adults who want to learn to be better parents – with each other, with everyone. We all have the capacity to play as children do, to do what we do not yet know how to do, to be who we are and other than who we are at the same time. This is performance. Performing is taking what exists and creating something new out of it. This is our performance activism.

Our performance activism on the ground

The theoretical work outlined above has been done under the aegis of the East Side Institute for Group and Short Term Psychotherapy (founded by Holzman and Newman)[30], which has functioned as the conduit/interface between the community organizing and the performance turn in psychology and other social sciences. An international non-profit education, research and training centre, the Institute has introduced and organized thousands of educators, mental health and medical workers, scholars and community organizers across the globe to the performance approach outlined here.

One key Institute activity is the ongoing research and extension of social therapy, which Newman began practicing and developing in the late 1970s as a group therapy in which building the ensemble, as distinct from analysing the individual, is considered the curative, development activity.[31] Out of the experience of social therapy (with its group-building activity based in conversation and improvisation) emerged social therapeutics as a method of organizing for social change and development in which human beings are related to as creators of their culture and ensemble performers of their lives. Increasingly, over the last two decades, social therapeutics has understood the core of its method to be performance and its core activity as that of bringing performance and play into daily life.

The All Stars Project (ASP)[32] has greatly expanded the reach of this approach. Founded in 1980 by Newman and developmental psychologist and community and political activist Lenora Fulani, the ASP is a non-profit almost totally funded by individual contributions. Under the leadership of Gabrielle L. Kurlander, an actress and director, who has been its president and CEO since 1990, the ASP has expanded from a local New York City talent show raising money on the streets to one of the leading youth development efforts in the United States. Kurlander has built a fund-raising operation, based on building strong relationships and the active participation of donors, that has raised some $80 million for its performance-based programmes, and interfaced with educators and policy-makers.

The oldest and largest of the ASP projects is the All Stars Talent Show Network (ASTSN), which is active in New York City, Newark, New Jersey, Chicago, Illinois and the San Francisco Bay Area in California. Starting as a modest event in church basement in the South Bronx in the early 1980s, today the ASTSN involves approximately 10,000 young people aged 5–25 each year who produce and perform in talent shows in high school auditoriums. The Development School for Youth is a year-long training and enrichment programme functioning in four US cities in partnership with corporate executives to provide 'cosmopolitanizing' business and cultural experiences, leadership training and paid internships to young people. The programme gives working-class youth the experience of trying out the performance of the business world, in the process discovering that they *can* create new performances, all kinds of new performances. Youth Onstage! (YO!) is the ASP's performance school and youth theatre. It provides young people with some of the tools of the theatre – most importantly, we think, improvisation and ensemble building – to make use of in their daily lives.

YO! also functions as the youth theatre of Castillo.[33] Founded in 1983, the Castillo Theatre brings professionals and community performers together on stage, produces many original plays derived from the issues and concerns of the communities from which it has emerged, and serves as a conduit for the influence of political and avant-garde theatre to New York's working-class and poor communities.

The most recent organizational project of the All Stars is UX, a free school for adults, where the most popular courses are Improv for Everyone, Acting for Everyone and Public Speaking. In its first 3 years, it has had over 3,500 students, 80 per cent of them adults, overwhelmingly Black and Latino.

Figure 20 *A Season in the Congo*, Photograph by Ronald L. Glassman/Courtesy of the Castillo Theatre © 2009.

What all of these programmes and activities have in common is encouraging participants to build social ensembles within which they can perform (as distinct from simply behave, that is, act our well-learned roles) in their daily lives; these projects embody and generate our version of performance activism.

A brief history of PTW

PTW was initially a coming together of the academic turn to performance in psychology and other social sciences, represented by the Gergens, and the on-the-ground work of helping people to create new performances off stage, represented by Newman and Holzman.

Their collaborations began in the 1990s with two conferences merging academic content and performance: the Institute-sponsored 1997 conference, 'Unscientific Psychology: Conversations with Other Voices', experimenting performatorily with the content and form of academic presentations, and a series of Performative Psychology symposia at American Psychological Association Conventions using plays, poetry, dance, comedy and other performance genre to present postmodern ideas to audiences of psychologists.

The success of these ventures, coupled with the desire to bring performance activists together with performance scholars, led to the first PTW in 2001, co-sponsored by Newman and Holzman's Institute and the Gergens' Taos Institute. 'Performing the World: Communication, Improvisation and Societal

Practice' was held in the seaside village of Montauk, New York, 1 month after 11 September. It included theatre artists, dancers, performance studies academics and young people from the All Stars youth programmes. Most of the 250 participants came from the United States, with about two dozen from other countries.

There has been both continuity and transformation over the seven PTW gatherings that have taken place between 2001 and 2012. The number of participants has doubled, and international presence has increased to more than 50 per cent, with 35–40 countries now represented. The 'performance politic' of the activists who launched PTW was there from the beginning, but was difficult to see until the conference became co-sponsored by the ASP and moved to its headquarters on 42nd Street in Manhattan's theatre district in 2008. The ASP's presence in working-class communities fused the PTW movement more deeply with the Black and Latino populations of New York. This created an overall environment in which the real host of these gatherings of 400–500 people from dozens of countries was not two organizations but the actual community created by the All Stars and the Institute. Nearly 200 volunteers – poor, working-class and middle-class young people and adults – staffed PTW; another 100 + across the five boroughs of New York City were housing hosts, providing attendees with a place to sleep (often a living room couch) and come home to each night. These experiences – for South African theatre professors, Brazilian teachers, youth workers from Peru, Park Avenue businessmen, unemployed mothers in Bed-Stuy, Brooklyn, non-profit managers in Manhattan's East Village, and high school students in Harlem – were not only once in a lifetime developmental moments for individuals, but embodied the methodology of the community.

One ongoing PTW theme has been the role of the performance approach to youth development, particularly poor youth and youth of colour. PTW 2008 featured a plenary, 'Performing Youth: A Conversation Across Borders', with Fulani and youth from New York, Johannesburg and Juarez, and an International Youth Talent Show. PTW 2010 explored 'The Performance of Blackness' through a mass theatrical performance, songs, raps and conversation involving scores of youth and adults. In 2012, PTW participants joined 200 young people at their All Stars Talent Show Workshop in Harlem and youth organizers from nine countries participated in a pre-conference training in how to bring the All Stars Talent Show to their communities.

The nature of social transformation and the means of achieving it has been another significant thread in the PTW tapestry. One especially provocative performance was that of critical psychologist Ian Parker and the Institute's Newman. In a PTW plenary session, 'What is Revolution?' they shared their very different views on Marx, political action and psychology. Parker argued that knowledge and ideological positions are essential to making revolutionary change, while for Newman, 'the critical revolutionary activity is the creating activity, not the knowing activity'[34]

The two major activities from which PTW participants have been drawn over the years – psychology and theatre – have been in dialogue throughout PTW's history. The plenary, 'Theory/Practice: Culture and Psychology, Therapy and Theatre', in 2010 featured – among others – Woodie King, Jr, founding producing director of the New Federal Theatre, Judith Malina, founder and artistic director of the Living Theatre and Patch Adams, a medical doctor and pioneer of performance as therapeutic for the sick. The 2012 plenary, 'The Therapeutic Power of Performance', featured seven leading play and performance activists and psychologists from Taiwan, France, Colombia and the United States who explored with each other and the audience the developmental potential of the therapeutic turn in performance and the performance turn in therapy.[35]

Perhaps, most relevant to this volume has been the ongoing conversation between the academic discipline of Performance Studies and the social change methodology of performance activism. Although this conversation remains in its early stages (this chapter is, in fact, a part of that conversation), as early as 2008 Richard Schechner led a PTW session entitled, 'The Performance of Studying Performance: Building Bridges Between the Academy and Performance Communities'. In 2012, Schechner and Friedman led a plenary on 'What is Performance and How Do We Know It?' In this session, Friedman unpacked the specifics of this community's approach to performance activism and Schechner called for a 'New Third World' of those neither allied with capitalism nor religious fundamentalism spearheaded 'by performance theorists and performance artists', persons who understand that 'playing deeply is a way of finding and embodying new knowledge, renewing energy and relating on a performatory rather than an ideological basis'.[36]

Performance activism around the world

There are many ways to perform activism and hundreds of them have been demonstrated and documented at PTWs over the years. Here we can offer only a tiny sample.

Alexandra Sutherland of South Africa's Rhodes University's drama department works with the theatre company Ubom![37] to challenge the fixed identity of the disenfranchised and poor. The 'Art of the Street Project' creates devised plays with township children who perform them in the National Arts Festival. This performance of who they are becoming (actors in an arts festival) transforms who they 'are' (poor children who beg on the streets). Similarly, Alex's theatre-making workshops with prisoners are more than 'rehabilitation' – they are, again, an identity-challenging, 'becoming' activity.

In Peru, Ursula Carrascal's VIDA involves children from very poor areas polluted by marine debris, lead and trash, in performance activism through 'Eco Dance', her environmental education dance programme. A regular PTW presenter, in 2012 Ursula led 'Dance to Survive', a performance created by children of the indigenous Cantagallo people who live on a garbage dump next to the Rimac River in Lima. Their dance gives them possession of their people's traditional culture and, at the same time, puts forward their demands for environmental clean-up and concerns about global climate change.

Sanjay Kumar leads the Pandies' Theatre for children, women, slum-dwellers and the homeless in New Delhi. Sanjay's recent PTW presentations have been plays devised from scenes created from the lives of boys who live on the train platforms – as part of an effort to bring about humane legislative policies towards the rape of boys in India. In Calcutta psychologist Ishita Sanyal teaches improvisation to the schizophrenic outpatients at Turning Point. Their performances in public squares are designed to develop both the patients and the community by changing the perception they both have of the mentally ill.

All of the PTWs have had titles. In 2010, we made its title the question that underlines performance activism – 'Can Performance Change the World?' Two years later, with the world situation appearing even bleaker, we asked, 'Can Performance ~~Change~~ Save the World?' Of course, the answers to these questions will not emerge intellectually or abstractly. They can only be performed.

Social Performance Studies: A New PS School with Chinese Characteristics

William H. Sun and Faye C. Fei

The advent of SPS

In his breakthrough *TDR* essay 'Performance Studies: The Broad Spectrum Approach' in 1988, Richard Schechner advocated that:

> Performing arts curricula need to be broadened to include courses in performance studies. What needs to be added is how performance is used in politics, medicine, religion, popular entertainments, and ordinary face-to-face interactions. . . . Courses in performance studies need to be made available not only within performing arts departments but to the university community at large. Performative thinking must be seen as a means of cultural analysis. Performance studies courses should be taught outside performing arts departments as part of core curricula.[1]

Eleven years later, a new brand of performance studies with Chinese characteristics, SPS, broke ground in a completely different setting. In 1999 we returned to China, after 15 years of studying and teaching in North America. Sun was a doctoral student of Schechner's at NYU and became a Contributing Editor of *TDR* in 1988. Fei, PhD in theatre from CUNY, edited and translated the first Western language book of Chinese theories of theatre and performance, prefaced by Schechner who uses the book in his courses on Asian Performance and theories.

Shanghai was completely different than 15 years earlier. While theatre productions became scarce, quasi-theatrical performances were rampant everywhere. Many makeshift stages were set up in shopping malls where salespeople and/or hired performers put on endless gigs to promote products, ranging from genuine brands to fake ones. Government officials began to address the press and the public, but these communications were characterized by scripted clichés and stiff manners.

Mass media played an extremely important role in the rise of various social performances. Television was full of various lively vaudeville-type entertainments, in which most performers appeared as themselves, not as characters. A popular news magazine, *New Weekly* (*Xin zhoukan*), carried a cover story series entitled 'I Show, Therefore I Am', including such articles as 'Demonizing Show Making', 'Costs of Show Making', 'Show Making from an Economist's Perspective', '33 Cases of Show Making', '12 Major Shows in Chinese Cities'.[2] All of them refer to social performances – as opposed to artistic performances in the legitimate theatre.

Responding to those overwhelming impressions, Sun published a paper, 'Performance Matters: An Introduction to Social Performance Studies', in the fall, 1999, issue of *Theatre Arts*, a leading theatre journal in China, and started teaching a course titled 'Social Performance Studies' at Shanghai Theatre Academy (STA).

STA had started a brand new 4-year programme in 'Television Anchoring', training hosts of TV entertainment shows. STA professors had been engaged in a debate with their counterparts at the Beijing Academy of Broadcasting, which had been training radio and television news announcers for decades. According to the doctrine of the Beijing school, evolved from the Communists' guerrilla war era radio broadcasting, no acting was allowed in broadcast anchoring. The new Shanghai school argued that television anchoring is acting as well as reporting. When some STA colleagues read or heard of Sun's introduction to performance studies, especially the brand new 'social performance studies', they were delighted to learn a new perspective according to which acting/performance, which can be translated into only one Chinese word, *biaoyan*, is not exclusive to the acting profession but is also applicable to many other professions.

Inundated with countless new performances and arguments about performance, we realized that performance studies could shed light on many of China's new developments: social, academic and professional. Yet it would need to be redefined to fit the reality of China. The new term social performance refers to actions performed outside of the theatre that have a definite impact on a particular audience.

Three major factors since 1992 contributed to the drastic development of various social performances in China. First, the Communist Party and central government's decision in 1992 to adopt the market economy greatly accelerated economic growth and made almost all products commercial commodities to be promoted performatively, from vegetables to electronics to human talents. Second, the rapid increase of television and cable TV, resulting in probably the largest number of channels an average TV set receives in the world, not only stimulated more TV entertainment, but could often turn common people's everyday activity into a TV show, be it a talk show, news or a commercial. More and more work units began to work on their PR teams and strategies, getting ready for TV cameras. Last but not least, the government realized it had to face the people more upfront in order to make them accept its policies. Officials had to be able to talk to the people persuasively and convincingly.

Yet talking well in front of the camera or live public was no easy task, because there had never been speech or theatre courses in China's general education system. The common criterion for good students is *tinghua*, meaning a good listener. Chinese schools had never been required to teach students to speak and perform well in public. The suddenly increasing need of social performance skills put most people in an awkward position. Many realized they could not even complete a Chinese sentence once a microphone was put in front of them. Others improvised using their instinctive skills, often fabricating and stumbling. There were no rules governing those performances. One often saw two extremes: inadequate poor performances on the one hand and free but fake performances on the other.

What was badly needed in China was SPS, a new research field focusing mainly on urban professional performances such as those of teachers, doctors, lawyers, salespersons and government officials. The goal of SPS was, and is, to analyse various kinds of social performances, in order to improve the inadequate ones and to falsify fake ones. In a sense, one of the missions of SPS is to study and develop appropriate standards and disciplines of performance in and across all professions.

Theories and examples

From the perspective of SPS, all human social actions, or behaviours, are negotiated between social disciplines and individual freedom. As a cross-disciplinary field, China's SPS is derived from the conjoining of Schechner's performance studies, Confucian tradition of rites based on social types, and Marxist theory of socially constructed human nature.

In a broad sense, SPS is a new branch of performance studies, as opposed to 'artistic performance studies' (which goes beyond the performance aspects of the theatre to include all genres of performing arts such as opera, dance, acrobatics, music, etc.). In a narrow sense, SPS differs from Schechner's performance studies in that Schechner's approach places, relatively, more emphasis on individual freedom, whereas SPS places more emphasis on social discipline and normative trainings. It is to explore the appropriate casting of long-term social roles, and to find ways to help performers adjust themselves and play these roles better. The Confucian concept *Li*, commonly translated as 'rites', meaning a system of rituals and related individuals' manners based on a strict hierarchy of social order, pigeonholed almost every person into a fixed social role and imposed on her with physical and mental rules. While this is definitely unacceptable in a modern society, the practice of putting people in class/groups for study and training is similar to that of Marxism, and Chinese opera training as well. Friedrich Engels theorizes about historical causes of men's actions:

> Men make their own history, whatever its outcome may be, in that each person follows his own consciously desired end, and it is precisely the resultant of these many wills operating in different directions and of their manifold effects upon the outer world that constitutes history. Thus it is also a question of what the many individuals desire. . . . On the one hand, we have seen that many individual wills active in the history for the most part produce results quite other than those intended – often quite the opposite; that their motives, therefore, in relation to the total result are likewise of only secondary importance. On the other hand, the further question arises: What driving forces in turn stand behind these motives? What are the historical causes which transform themselves into these motives in the brains of the actors?

Marxists believe that economic relations are the primary organizers and causes of society. How the economy is structured results in class divisions, as Engels argues in the same thesis:

> The possibility of purely human sentiments in our intercourse with other human beings has nowadays been sufficiently curtailed by the society in which we must live, which is based upon class antagonism and class rule.[3]

In fact 'class antagonism and class rule' are by no means the only important social confines within which people live. Karl Marx states that 'the human essence is no abstraction inherent in each single individual. In its reality it is the ensemble of the social relations. . . . The abstract individual . . . belongs in reality to a particular form of society'.[4] 'The ensemble of the social relations' includes many kinds. Gender and ethnicity/culture are also important 'particular forms of society', which can be seen as among the most determinant factors for all social performances.

Many social performances are derived from certain social disciplines, and often become demonstrative performances to prolong and perpetuate the social disciplines. Parents, teachers and models in commercials are routinely involved in carrying out those kinds of performances in front of novices. Take a simple example, eating. One can say eating is a universally innate human instinct. Yet eating of certain types of food, say, bread, rice or noodles, with certain utensils such as knife and fork, chopsticks or just fingers, is socially and culturally constructed. Chinese people usually eat with chopsticks. That is taught to children by parents or other guardians who demonstrate in performances showing the proper way of using chopsticks. Nowadays some Chinese children opt for Big Mac and/or KFC over rice. Such a choice is a result of the omnipresent brainwashing commercial performances on TV. Powerful TV advertisements can use all the resources to choreograph the most effective performance to convert potential young consumers, often defeating their elders' cultural traditions. On the other hand, in the past decades, Chinese restaurants have gone into many countries in the world. Many non-Chinese have learnt to use chopsticks. It takes quite some practice and closely following their teachers' demonstrations. Many Westerners who have learnt to handle chopsticks would not use them when they eat alone, but use them only when there is an audience, to show off their newly acquired skills – or to appear 'at one' with their Chinese hosts, friends and business associates.

Another related example may seem to be a biological, not a social, one – left-handed people. It seems there are many more lefties in the United States than in China. Several recent American presidents sign documents left-handedly. But rarely can one see a high ranking Chinese official sign with his left hand. It's not because American genes are so different from those of the Chinese. While left-handedness is inherent, whether to use left hand to eat or to write is socially determined. Chinese children are a lot more strictly ordered than today's Americans to conform to the social norm of eating and writing with the right hand, regardless of their inherent leaning. Their parents believe left-handedness is a social disability that can be corrected by more practice adhering to the norm. Most lefties in China are corrected when they are very young and just begin to learn to eat or write. By comparison, there are more people eating with left hand than those writing with left hand, because children learning to write have to go through both their parents' and teachers' disciplinary supervision, whereas when they learn to eat, usually only their parents supervise. When teachers teach their pupils to write, they not only make sure pupils use right hands, but also check specific postures of holding the writing instrument repeatedly against the ideal model, which is a recurrent item in the Chinese education system. The concept of ideal model representing the expected norm and standard is similar to Plato's theory of the primary form and idea, and also coinciding with Denis Diderot's ideal of acting as stated in his famous thesis *The Paradox of Acting*, 'constant imitation of some ideal type.'[5] On the other hand, the comparatively 'feel-good' American education in recent decades gives children a lot more freedom in deciding how to hold a pen and how to write.

The freedom enjoyed during childhood in choosing which hand to eat or write with, however, may not necessarily be enjoyed lifelong. Lefties who eat and

Figure 21 Chinese school children must learn the standard way to hold the brush before learning to write Photo by Peng Yongwen.

write with their left hands may encounter problems when they have to use tools designed for right-handed people. Studies suggest that lefties using 'regular' tools designed for the majority of right-handed people have higher accident rates. Yet manufacturers usually deem it economically unsound to design and make tools especially for lefties, therefore leaving the 'normal' tools a hidden danger for lefties. This danger is less prominent in China, because most lefties have been corrected, to some degree, by many years' repeated practice in eating and writing. For those whose lefty leaning is not too strong, it is possible that their acquired right-handedness could become their second nature, thus reducing the risk of operating 'regular' tools.

This acquired second nature through raining is similar to that of certain performers trained in extraordinary ways. For example, China's foremost Beijing Opera performer Mei Lanfang, after decades of practicing, had made appearing feminine his second nature, sometimes even in daily life. This second nature of his was analogous to a left-handed child 'tamed' to be right-handed. In short, even some biologically determined behaviour patterns can be reconstructed by social disciplines because humans are social animals after all. If a socially engineered ideal model is well chosen and well rehearsed, it may be well performed by people who have to overcome biological obstacles.

Needless to say, there must be a limit to using socially engineered ideal models to curtail biologically determined behaviour patterns. A notorious example in China is foot-binding. When young girls were forced to have their feet bound in old days, it was the patriarchy that set up its ideal model of feminine beauty and subjectivity. That model of tiny female feet catered to the rich and powerful men's perverse aesthetic taste, sacrificing women's well-being and freedom of mobility. Various cruel disciplinary measures imposed in European prison systems and hospitals, examined throughout Michel Foucault's *Discipline and Punishment*, are similar examples.

A far more common case of over-normalization is the criminalization and forced correction of homosexuals. Religious conservatives believe homosexuality is not inherent but acquired, and insist on 'correcting' it by enforcing discipline. This strict rule has made homosexuals disappear for centuries in many countries. But that was just the facade, under which many homosexuals learnt to disguise themselves, even by marrying the opposite sex and having children. Over-restrictive regulations often lead to rampant deceptive performances. The prohibition against alcohol in the United States is another case in point.

In Chinese history there have been numerous heavy-handed regulations like that. Between 1968 and 1976 during the Cultural Revolution, in the cities healthy secondary school graduates in the millions had to go and farm in the countryside. Sun was one of them. Many of those who didn't want to go pretended to be sick and got fake medical certification. When the Cultural Revolution was over and everybody was allowed to take the college entrance examination in 1977, almost all those supposedly sick city dwellers recovered overnight. Up until the late 1990s, college students in China were not allowed to have romantic relationships till after their graduation. They had to learn how to conceal their love relationships, especially in front of their professors and school administrators.

After decades of repression and forced 'correction' under an ideology ignoring individual freedom, the sudden adoption of the open door policy and then market economy set loose many Chinese people's innate urge to take free actions, often ignoring disciplines, or before proper disciplines were established when people rushed into new fields such as sales, advertising, law, public relations and so on. Having seen too many free-wheeling improvisations, including many groundless performances, more and more leaders groping in those new fields realized there should be more disciplines. Yet new disciplines often look like empty facade when people working in the fields have not been properly trained and therefore remained far away from the ideal models. For example, press conferences became a norm because the government needed to communicate with the people, yet most spokespersons could only read or recite pre-scripted words and often refused to answer questions except those pre-arranged, or gave clumsy answers that would often result in their quick dismissal. Some of the leaders in those fields are eager to look for effective ways to train themselves and their employees.

Some practical projects

At those people's request, Sun and his STA colleagues have done pilot projects in several professions, including state prosecutors, salespeople, and mayors and bureau heads at the Pudong Cadre Institute, China's new and highest level official civil-service training institution. Dr Ji Dongming, a surgeon turned general manager of Moller Villa Hotel, a state-owned luxury hotel, felt strongly that he needed a new way of thinking and training for his employees to meet his standard. And SPS he learnt about from reading Sun's published paper, titled 'Social Performance Studies and the Harmonious Society',[6] was exactly what he needed to turn his employees into professional service people schooled in proper etiquette. After being contacted by Ji, Sun took Peng Yongwen, who wrote his doctoral dissertation on social performance training, and some acting teachers to his establishment to start a series of training sessions. A speech and voice teacher taught receptionists how to improve their quality of voice and telephone manner. An acting teacher offered courses on general interpersonal reactions and postures under different circumstances. Augusto Boal's forum theatre technique was modified to help them experiment with various ways of dealing with difficult customers. For example, the managers told the teachers that a conventional first question after the hotel employee greeted a new customer, 'Do you have a reservation?', often upset the customer. They were puzzled about whether they should abandon that standard question or change it into a different one. The STA teachers began a series of simple forum theatre pieces with a professional actor playing various offended customers the hotel employees had to cope with. When one employee did not perform well enough to appease the customer, another would replace him and try a different way. After experimenting with many approaches in different forum theatre pieces involving all trainees, they gradually established a series of somewhat standard measures for the employees to take in meeting various customers.

Training programmes like this made us more acutely aware that basic social performance training should start in schools through educational theatre programmes. But so far little progress has been made in the national education system despite scholars' and practitioners' efforts to put theatre into school curricula for more than 10 years. Aside from the government inertia and lack of teachers, a major problem is the imported Western paradigm of creative drama based on individual creation, which in theory calls for everyone in the classroom to tell her story and create her drama. In the reality of highly structured school timeframe, it could only end up serving a few 'smartest and prettiest' students in after-school programmes and those of well-off parents in off-campus commercial acting programmes. In order to serve all school children, we need to create educational theatre in China with an alternative approach, based on a series of theatre etudes modelled after music education. The reason why music is fully implemented in all schools is that it's the most disciplined art form that can be taught efficiently through collective imitation of etudes, a series of short pieces measured to escalate in technical challenge and complexity step by step. To make theatre teaching viable in schools, teachers must learn from the music pedagogy and teach standard etudes first to all students, not just to the brightest and prettiest few. In other words, we have to give up certain degrees of spontaneity and creativity educational theatre could inspire in students, which is theatre's greatest potential benefits, so that we can give every student an opportunity to enjoy performing in the first place. Even imitative theatre-making can train children to speak well and give them hands-on experience in practical team projects. Once the foundation is laid for everybody, teachers can gradually move on to make more original theatre, for those students who seek freer creations at advanced stages.

Imitative theatre-making may sound odd to most Western theatre teachers, especially those for young students, because they are accustomed to playful, spontaneous exercises of improvisation. Yet in China the oldest and still most popular theatre model is Chinese opera whose training is very similar to music, focusing on repetitive practice of etudes. In early 2008, China's Ministry of Education took the first measure to implement theatre in school curriculum, asking schools to teach children 16 Beijing opera arias they selected. This measure, however, was a spectacular failure because many people questioned the Ministry's choice of the 16 arias, which were either too dated or politically problematic – chosen from the 'revolutionary model operas' during the Cultural Revolution. The failure of this attempt suggests that few existing Chinese opera pieces are suitable as etudes for today's school children. We must create new sets of etudes for them.

It is for this purpose that Sun and his colleagues and students at STA began working, in 2009, on a project of short plays based on etudes, generally entitled *Confucius Disciples*, for school students to perform. It is an open-ended series about China's greatest educator Confucius (551–479 BC) and his three fictional teenage disciples. Modelled after classic novel *Journey to the West* about Buddhist monk Xuan Zang (602–664) and his three disciples, including the famous Monkey King, this project is set during Confucius' historic travels to various states promoting his philosophy. While the plays are essentially allegories dealing with issues relevant to today's people, all characters are based on major role types of Chinese opera rendered in stylized performance patterns, similar to those of commedia dell'arte. The core characters are Confucius, old male type; Zilu, painted face, short-tempered warrior type; Zitu, clown type; and Qinran, martial female type who impersonates a man (like Mulan). Additional characters, also in types, are various local people they encounter en route. In one of the plays, *Rules of the Game*, a combat game takes place between Confucius' three disciples and a general's three fighters. The general cheats, by secretly changing his fighters' ranks, to win the rank-based game. Confucius and students argue whether they should've also cheated in order to win.

This ongoing series has been created with two rationales: for Chinese students, it is a medium of educational theatre; for non-Chinese, it is an introduction to Chinese culture, including Confucian ideas and Chinese opera. For both groups, etude is the key because a well-selected/created set of etudes makes up the base of training.

In his book *The Dictionary of Theatre Anthropology*, Eugenio Barba asserts that the most important feature of a universal 'secret of the performer' is the pre-expressive aspect of her acting, which is especially crucial in traditional Asian theatres. He is right if this pre-expressivity refers to physical and vocal drills in the training stage. Etudes are designed or selected to serve such a purpose. They can be repeated many times in groups till each individual finds a unique connection with the piece. The STA training programme begins with pre-expressive etude drills all students do together. In so doing, each of them gradually discover her individuality and fit in a certain role type. After finding a type, resulting from mutual consultation between the student and her teacher, each student begins working on more specific etudes associated with her type. In the second stage of the training, they can combine different pre-expressive etudes to render a short story, expressing something without having to rely on a written script. These etude combinations are usually improvised yet may also become composite etudes at a higher level. After this, students are given expressive characters in written scenes to enact. They usually start with imitating their teacher's ideal models repeatedly until they can fill into the characters with their own emotions and flavours, which means feeling free in enacting these actions, ultimately making super-expressive theatre.

These are the two main areas of application the Chinese SPS practitioners currently focus on – professional training and educational theatre. In both areas they start with some ideal models for student/trainees to emulate, before entering next phase of free improvisations and experimentations.

Negotiations between discipline and freedom

We believe that between social discipline and individual freedom, there is a great deal of negotiation in choosing the ideal model and right way to rehearse and adjust for any type of social performance. We choose to use the term 'discipline' and steer clear of 'conformity' or 'regulation' because the latter two seem to blatantly emphasize coercion over choice. The Chinese word *guifan* for discipline as opposed to *ziyou*, freedom, in fact contains two characters meaning 'rule' and 'model', respectively. Discipline seems to be closer to these two concepts. Currently in China, there are many problems on both ends of this negotiation. There are many disciplines that do not take reasonable human freedom into consideration, such as strictly fixed majors and course requirements for university students. One can then think that there is also too much freedom that ignores necessary *guifan* or disciplines, for instance, when people smoke in clearly marked non-smoking areas, litter in the streets and fib during job and press interviews. The ideal 'golden mean', which is a philosophical idea shared by Confucius and Aristotle, meaning the desirable middle between two extremes, is freedom within the socially accepted confines, much like Stanislavsky's succinct comment on Mei Lanfang's performance after he saw it in Moscow in 1935: 'regulated free actions'. For a performer to achieve that, it takes long and vigorous training till she feels freedom and unaware of regulations, which have in fact become her second nature. First of all, the performer has to choose, define and refine the right role within the artistic disciplines.

Theoretically, SPS follows dialectic materialism and proposes to analyse three basic dualisms underneath all social performances. The first pair, echoing Diderot's theory of acting, is the 'ideal model' of the role versus the performer's self, representing the social norm and the individual, respectively. There is certainly some distance between the two. SPS helps social performers to choose or design the former and then train the latter to shorten the distance in fitting into the former. This can be done from inside out, in the Stanislavskian way, or from outside in, in the Meyerholdian way. In some very special cases such as undercover investigation, Brechtian distancing techniques may also be used to make sure that the performer always keeps a clear mind, never getting lost in the ostensible role s/he is playing. The second pair, echoing Erving Goffman, is front stage of public performance versus backstage of the individual performer. SPS helps develop rules in separating the two in order to achieve better performance on the front stage, while checking the appropriate distance to protect the performer in relaxation and/or preparation phases. Oftentimes the line between the two is manipulated in such a way as the private life of public figures can be shown as front stage, or a choreographed performance is made to look like backstage because certain private secrets are intentionally disclosed. SPS analyses these kinds of frame manipulations. The third pair is prepared script versus live presentation with improvisations, each leaning towards the social norm and towards the performer's freedom, respectively. How scripted each social performance should be, which determines how much room there is for improvisation, depends on the overall given circumstances and careful character analysis, just like a participatory theatre performance.

One can find all these elements in any given social performance, though in many different forms. The SPS perspective gives scholars a great deal of freedom in choosing new research subjects in countless fields such as sociology, psychology, communication studies, management, political science, history and so on, just like Schechner's performance studies which opened a door to a borderless world more than three decades ago. Yet SPS proposes that all such researches pay attention to these three pairs of key elements, which reflect the academic discipline of the new field.

As Schechner would say, to study human beings cannot help being a performance. Any project of SPS is inevitably a regulated free performance.

Motion VIII

Performance Studies and Life Sciences

What Is Performance Anyway?
A Cognitive Approach

Tomasz Kubikowski[1]

I claim that performance in its most general sense is a natural occurrence: the operational mode of another natural phenomenon, consciousness. As it underlies consciousness and spans the Realised with the Not-Realised, itself it is hard to be realised; however, it is being indirectly singled out and thematized in cultural performances, which we should regard as 'twice-performed performances'.

Performance: English, idiomatic, indefinable?

Is 'performance' a notion, a homonym, a keyword? My title not only refers to Schechner's seminal text 'What Is Performance Studies Anyway?'.[2] It expresses the essential concern encountered by everyone, to whom the word 'performance' is not common, as it does not belong to his or her mother tongue.

Although it can be regarded, through its Latin roots, as part of the universal European heritage, in my native Polish this word has never existed. Depending on context, in the whole range of its meanings, it usually gets translated by no less than 24 different nouns.[3] Do we really need one word for all these meanings? Is not the whole issue based on mere equivocation? Or even worse: perhaps coining one single word for all these twenty plus senses is somehow culturally specific? Perhaps it expresses hidden presumptions, characteristic for the globalized US American culture? Then accepting it means yielding to this overwhelming, dominative culture and leads only to the impoverishment of the native language, thought and identity. Such accusations are quite common.

The native users of the word 'performance' do not help their foreign fellows, carefully guarding the word's unrestricted dynamics and thus restraining from any too precise definitional attempts. From various writings we can learn, that 'performance' is 'an essentially contested concept', 'a term hard to pin down', which 'problematizes its own categorisation'; 'indefinable' and yet there are so many definitions disparate in so many different books.

Bauman's definition and its merits

I choose one of all these numerous definitions to start with; it seems the most comprehensive and instructive. Given by Richard Bauman, it states that performance 'involves a consciousness of doubleness, through which the actual execution of an action is placed in mental comparison with a potential, an ideal or a remembered original model of that action'.[4] This definition suggests a certain morphology. It points at three elements, implicitly found also in other explanations of the term 'performance'. One of these three elements always comes as somehow established or settled outside the current moment: it is thus named *potential*, *idea* or a *model*. The second, opposite element is in turn momentous, current and actual: it is an *execution of an action*, perhaps an act of restoring a behaviour, an actual presentation of skills or carrying out a certain plan. There is however a third element, which is even more ephemeral than the second: some kind of meta-element, which links or separates these former elements, making them the two poles of the same structure, itself emerging from their polarity. It is the already-mentioned *comparison*, which may take form of the evaluation of an act, the intention of success or the will to display skills. In every case it constitutes the superior, crowning bond of the performance structure (Figure A).

According to performance theorists such as Jon McKenzie or Erika Fischer-Lichte, this superior bond has a dynamics of feedback.[5] Models and criteria shape current actions, efforts or attempts, and simultaneously get verified, modified or perfected through them.

These are all useful details, that tripartite structure. What seems the most exciting and important in Bauman's definition, however, is that it anchors the whole morphology, dynamics and very existence of performance in a field, which is unquestionably pre-cultural and thus can make a good ground for our effort at universalizing the notion of 'performance'. As Bauman claims, performance 'involves a *consciousness*'.

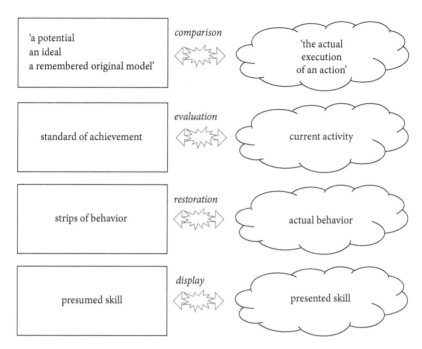

Figure A The 'Baumanian' tripartite morphology of performance.

Performance and consciousness studies

It is remarkable that the famous 'theory explosion' in performance studies in the early 1990s occurred simultaneously to a similar turn in the research on consciousness. This turn occurred after many years of a stall, during which consciousness had not been generally regarded as a serious, scientific topic, but rather as an epiphenomenon, and, in fact, a troublesome conceptual relic of the Descartes era. As John R. Searle noted in his 1990 paper: 'as recently as a few years ago, if one raised the subject of consciousness in cognitive science discussions, it was generally regarded as a form of bad taste, and graduate students, who are always attuned to the social mores of their disciplines, would roll their eyes at the ceiling and assume expressions of mild disgust'.[6] Daniel Dennett's famous *Consciousness Explained* (1991)[7] can be regarded the climax of this reductionist trend. However, over the next two decades and through the efforts of many diverse writers, foundations were set for the naturalist, non-reductionist and at the same time non-Cartesian notions of consciousness, creating a new, fascinating landscape of research, insights and findings.

I choose a few of these distinguished writers for a lodestar: Searle, one of the 1960s' frontrunners of the science of the performative, and the author of ground-breaking books: *The Rediscovery of the Mind* (1992)[8] and *The Construction of Social Reality* (1995).[9] The other is Gerald Edelman, a neurophysiologist, who in 1972 received the Nobel Prize for his research on the immune system, and who later published a trilogy devoted to our topic: *Neural Darwinism* (1987), *Topobiology* (1988) and *Remembered Present* (1990), summed up in *Bright Air, Brilliant Fire* (1992), with its ideas further developed in *A Universe of Consciousness: How Matter Becomes Imagination* (2000, with Giulio Tononi).[10] Findings of the philosopher and of the physiologist add up, based on which I construct three interconnected threads, woven around three fundamental oppositions: cognition/recognition, optimization/degeneracy and instruction/selection.

Recognition

As Edelman puts it, 'there is no explicit information transfer between the environment and organisms that causes the population to change and increase its fitness'.[11] Our environment does not contain any information to be extracted and utilized; the world never teaches us anything.

Therefore my mind does not *cognize* the world directly. The only thing I can do is to *recognize* my situation in the world, and to create, through this recognition, my own information, knowledge and wisdom. What does it mean? While dealing with the world, receiving its stimuli and the stimuli of my own

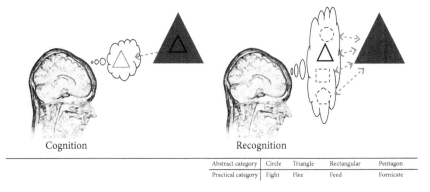

	Cognition		Recognition	
Abstract category	Circle	Triangle	Rectangular	Pentagon
Practical category	Fight	Flee	Feed	Fornicate

Figure B Cognition/Recognition.

organism, in my brain I create certain categories, patterns which I subsequently try to apply. These categories can be theoretical, but first of all shall be practical, like the famous ethological 'four F words' (fight, flee, feed, or . . . fornicate), which describe four basic modes of reaction to the presence of the alien organism: these practical categories serve as instructions for the behaviour in the animal life (Figure B).

Creating categories and trying to apply them strengthens those of them, which seem the most adequate, that is, which lead to the homeostasis of the organism. Obviously, in some next turn, I can create variants of the successful pattern and try them further, in order to select the fittest. Out of these patterns, their variants, and their relations I create my information, my knowledge: all by myself.

How is it all done, physically? The answer constitutes the core of the Edelman's 'theory of neural group selection' (TNGS), commonly known as the 'neural Darwinism'. To put it briefly: systems of synaptic connections, different 'neural maps' compete for the best available reaction to the stimuli. These numerous maps, with their diverse configurations, form the physiological basis for various patterns-categories figuratively pictured above. Those patterns/maps which best contribute to the organism's homeostasis qualify for further development: their neural connections toughen. The patterns/maps that do not prove useful weaken or even break.

Memory

The well-established patterns remain operational even after they have gone out of current use. They remain dormant, ready to be reactivated, sometimes by some unexpected factor, like the taste of a madeleine in Proust. These established neural patterns, once useful now out of use, serve namely as the base for memory. In this theory memory is not understood as any kind of an information storage: it is neither an archive, nor a biological RAM or ROM. For his part, Edelman defines memory as an 'ability to repeat performance': the performance of recognition, reaction and categorization.

Then essentially, there is no information in memory itself. We can regard memory as an information storage capacity only through a bold and radical abstraction, similar to this, which allows us to look at a brain as an information processing unit. Both of these are very artificial characteristics regardless their phenomena's nature: it is exactly as describing a mechanical typewriter as a 'text processing unit'. Memory is a neural performance ability. We can abstract its output as 'information' if we wish to.

We have learnt to depose all our self-made information in external repositories, in writing, picture and recording. Out of them we can retrieve knowledge and thus cognate the world through works of culture. Being secondary and mediated, this *cognition* inevitably differs from a direct, primary *recognition*. It is a book learning, different from any live knowledge.

The principle of the Nibelung

This state of things has its profound consequences. The most important is: I will learn nothing of the world, unless I actively try out suitable categories: unless I myself initiate the cognitive process with my own original proposal. To state it simply and metaphorically: the world does not give answer to any question I have not asked first. It is possible, however, that the world through its circumstances can suddenly demand such an answer from me.

No matter how great our knowledge, we can be surprised by any little something we have not managed to imagine, to foresee and to prepare for it. In time, in every moment I have a right to suspect that I do not know a response for some question, which in the next moment may become crucial. I never know whether I am aware of the most important.

Once I have called this existential condition 'the principle of the Nibelung', remembering the dwarf Mime from Wagner's *Siegfried*, who failed to ask the god about what was for him the most vital (viz. how to repair the sacred sword). He did not ask, he did not learn. All of the sudden, the god posed the same question to the dwarf, and as the poor dwarf did not know the answer, it cost him his life. Wagner apparently hated Mime, but gave him much of his own characteristics. We are all Mimes: Darwin guaranteed this.

In yet other words: in order to learn anything about the world, we must initiate a performance. The categorical model, according to which we act, serves as its scenario. This performance can succeed or fail, or succeed partially. We create our information, our knowledge and our wisdom out of the nuances of these successes and failures, out of the series of these nuances, of their outcomes and of the verifications and modifications done to the categorical models on the base of these outcomes.

The major differences between the two cognitive modes can be summed up as follows:

Cognition	Recognition
• Passive	• Active
• Information gained from outside	• Information produced/generated
• Memory is an information storage	• Memory is the ability to repeat performance
• Perceptive	• Performative

Degeneracy

The neural group selection is not too strict. All these groups which function, remain, not only those which function *best*. Our consciousness is never optimized. Just the opposite, according to Edelman and Tononi, it works on a basis of *degeneracy*. 'All selectional systems share a remarkable property that is as unique as it is essential to their functioning: in such systems, there are typically many different ways, *not necessarily structurally identical*, by which a particular output occurs. We call this property degeneracy. ... Put briefly, degeneracy is reflected in the capacity of structurally different components to yield similar outputs or results.'[12] We can perceive, feel, experience and comprehend the same thing in several ways at once: not only in the way which in this very moment appears as the most perfect. This degeneracy (which serves here as a technical term, but not apart from its common use) 'is not just a useful feature of selectional systems; it is also an unavoidable consequence of selectional mechanisms. ... The ability of natural selection to give rise to a large number of non-identical structures yielding similar functions increases both the robustness of biological networks and their adaptability to unforeseen environments.'[13]

There is a benefit in degeneracy. The system poorly adapted to the extant circumstances can unexpectedly become perfect after a rapid change in environment. The optimal system, the only legitimate one, can fail beyond the circumstances for which it was optimized. Optimization fails to the unpredictability of the world. 'Without [degeneracy], a selectional system, no matter how rich its diversity, would rapidly fail.'[14] We can survive in our diverse, changing environment, only because we are degenerate to a degree.

Selection and instruction

'A selectional system' mentioned in the last quotation hints at the core of our issue. Let us repeat the key phrase in Edelman, at this time up to its conclusion: 'There is no explicit information transfer between the environment and organisms that causes the population to change and increase its fitness. *Evolution works by selection, not by instruction.*'[15]

Willing or not, we live in the selectional system: this is the basic biological given. The world works like this. All living entities are being continuously selected and for this major selection, their single features are being selected too. In some circumstances, each of these features can decide about survival, prosperity and reproduction.

In this selection, no living creature is being conducted. There is no *spiritus rector*, no revealed guidelines; the will cannot affect evolution either. In organisms, however, various organs and processes have developed, which proved to enhance chances for withstanding selection; the most notable among them is the brain. This brain is a wonderfully complicated anticipational machine, and the consciousness, which arises in the brain as an emergent quality, and refers to the experiences of the whole organism, create our own instructions for survival in the ruthless world in which we live. Everything mentioned above: information, knowledge and wisdom; categories, patterns, models and conjectures are all instructions for certain actions, which purposely may enlarge our chances to survive. There is no instruction outside consciousness, but within consciousness, all serves instruction.

Selection and *instruction* are thus the two basic processes, to which all living beings endowed with consciousness are subject. Recognizing our situation in the world, we create an instruction of how to behave in this world. We try to improve this instruction through the subsequent performances of recognition. In the case of failure, we can dismiss the instruction and call up another from our degenerative storage, if we have one and if the situation allows for it. We die miserably in case of an extremely unhappy performance, and neither the most perfect instruction nor the most abundant degeneracy can ever fully prevent it. But what we usually can do is to let our instructions die for us in the front line.

In this way, instructions get selected. Subdued to the selection according to the never-fully known rules, just for enduring if only a moment longer, we create out of our deeds and ideas imperfect, degenerate instructions for survival.

The definition of performance

The life of every being endowed with consciousness runs then in a continuous clash of the two basic processes: the process of selection (to which every life is subdued) and the process of instruction (initiated by consciousness to withstand the former). This is our most basic mode of existence.

In other words: in the world of Darwinian selection, in some organisms there developed an ability of instruction to enhance chances of survival. We belong to those organisms.

Our brains create some arrangements, and these serve as a base for our behaviour. As a result of this behaviour, as a response to its consequences, these arrangements can be strengthened, modified or rejected. Arrangements, current behaviour and some meta-bond between them: the structure of the whole procedure retains the formerly abstracted 'baumanian' form of performance.

The biological role of consciousness is to create instruction and oppose it to the selection. The confrontation of instruction and selection displays the structure, which we have formerly singled out as characteristic of performance. In fact, I claim that the named confrontation is The Performance; the core performance, which forms the basic mode of existence for all conscious beings. All that we call 'performance' in our theories and in everyday life is grounded in this basic mode and should be regarded as its derivative.

This leads us to a new definition of performance. Namely, **performance happens when processes of selection meet processes of instruction.**

The levels of instruction/selection

There seem to be three levels of selection/instruction within a performance. First, actions are selected which best fulfil the instruction. Second, instructions are selected to use the most adequate and effective of them. Third, whole performances are selected (Figure C).

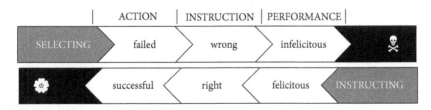

Figure C Levels of selection/instruction.

Obviously, as the diagram suggests, there exists also a fourth level: the continuous selection of the performing subjects.

Feedback and re-entry

The question remains about the exact character of the instruction/selection confrontation. As mentioned before, theorists tend to assign to it the feedback structure. However, another important lesson can be taken here from the research of Edelman, the theorist of the selectional systems. Both in his own books and in his writings together with Giulio Tononi, he discovers in those systems a different dynamics, which can serve as an alternative to feedback, and which Edelman calls *re-entry*.

'It is important to emphasise that re-entry is not a feedback', as 'feedback occurs along a *single* fixed loop made of reciprocal connections using previous *instructionally* derived information for control and correction, such as an error signal. In contrast, re-entry occurs in *selectional* systems across *multiple* parallel paths where information is not prespecified.'[16] It 'is a process of ongoing parallel and recursive signalling between separate brain maps',[17] and 'indeed, if we were asked to . . . name the *unique* feature of higher brains, we would say it is re-entry'.[18]

Edelman points out re-entry as a crucial point of his neural Darwinism theory.[19] At the same time, while feedback can be easily visualized as an elegant infinity loop, 'because of the dynamic and parallel nature of re-entry and because it is a process of higher-order selection, it is not easy to provide a metaphor that captures all the properties of re-entry'.[20] Edelman himself tried to visualize it on various occasions,[21] but indeed, his diagrams are not too communicative.

How to imagine re-entry, then? My own association is a host of little balls, flying blind between two areas – many of them miss, but those which hit, proliferate and spring back, and the dynamics of these all throwbacks, the cloud of balls being in the air at the same moment, create some ephemeral structure of higher degree. This picture differs much from the closed railway circuit of a feedback, where information trains run to and fro between the well-defined terminal stations, and the whole net of meta-informative telegraphs and semaphores has been constructed around to assure proper communication.

No matter how difficult it is for us to imagine re-entry, this difficulty rises now exponentially. If performance should be understood as a clash of selection and instruction, one can suspect that the dynamics of feedback coincides there with the dynamics of re-entry. How it happens exactly, our research has not yet revealed.

It is beyond the extent of this paper to analyse the topic more thoroughly. It is easy, however, to discover the re-entrant dynamics in the situations, which have so far been described by the performance scholars by the diagram of the feedback loop. In the basic theatrical event, of which Fischer-Lichte conducts her feedback model, in the confrontation of the actors and the audience, both sides are guided by certain instructions: the script, the mise-en-scène, the rules of behaviour, the social codes of communication. The actors operate according to their strict prescriptions; they are active. The audience remains more passive but at the same time they are more free in their expression: they can laugh, cry, applaud, boo and remain silent. There is much networking here: those who react in a certain way, inspire and provoke each other. These spontaneous networks, 'spectatorial maps', chart the audience reaction; their signals affect the actors, who react according to their condition, position, fantasy, discipline or composure. The audiences' favourites get their boost, other must overcome the viewers' indifference and thus their own disconcert. Some wish to show up. Some fight for better understanding. Various kinds of performers also form networks: all in all, between the stage and the auditorium, the complicated, multiple dynamics of a *selectional* character arises: the dynamics of re-entry. This fact has obviously been overlooked by the former researchers of performance, tending to describe such situations only from the instructional side, in its feedback aspect.

Two remarks

There are two more important remarks, which may help us avoid misunderstandings. Our statement, that performance is the basic mode of existence for all conscious beings (or rather: beings endowed with consciousness), does not mean that we must perform 'consciously' in the sense: intentionally, deliberately or knowingly. 'Consciousness' in its broadest sense is like a whole field or a pyramid, of which actual awareness, the focused consciousness forms only the narrow, pointed vertex. This focused consciousness is very limited (its capacity estimated for up to 16 bits per second) and, as Edelman and Tononi argue, 'the informativeness of consciousness should not be based on how many more or less independent "chunks" of information a single conscious state might contain. Instead, it should be based on how many different conscious states are ruled out by the occurrence of the particular state that we are experiencing at a given moment.'[22] The focused consciousness forms, as we might say, a special task force: its effectiveness consists not in its vast coverage, but in its precision and accuracy. However, the main effort in our battle with the world is made by the main forces, numerous activities which are not our current focus. Presently we are not aware of them, but we need consciousness to perform them and we have needed consciousness to learn them at all. I can drive my car while talking to the passengers; however, I needed all my consciousness when, years ago, I learned to drive.

It should be made clear: in the terminology used here, there is nothing like the 'subconscious' or the 'unconscious'. Searle devotes the whole chapter of *The Rediscovery of the Mind* to this issue and concludes, that 'the ontology of the unconscious is strictly the ontology of a neurophysiology capable of generating the conscious'.[23] My automatized behaviours are then not being performed 'unconsciously': they are performed by means of the processes 'capable of generating the conscious', so they belong to the domain of consciousness.[24] In Edelman's neurophysiological terms, the re-entrant neuronal mapping, which controls them, does not subside to the 'dynamic core' of consciousness.

The second important issue: it is not so that every single act done by the beings endowed with consciousness must be a performance. Certainly, not every organic act of restoring homeostasis reveals instruction and thus engages consciousness. I do not really think that I am performing my goosebumps when I feel cold: I simply break out in them.

At this moment, at the present level of knowledge, it is probably not possible to draw a complete, distinct and unquestionable border between the activities where consciousness intervenes and the activities happening without such intervention. However, this would be the border of the domain of performance.

A twice-performed performance

Perhaps the most important consequence of our notion of performance is that it essentially eludes comprehension and verbalization. The reason is simple: discourse belongs to the sphere of instruction. Performance spans instruction and what-is-beyond-it: the unspeakable rest, which always precedes and exceeds any instruction. Never explored, never discerned and always existent: Darwin vouches for it. This may be the reason, that performance is 'essentially contested', and 'problematizes its own categorisation'. 'Performance' is the word, which always leads to the unspoken, points at the unseen; it is the irrational number (or perhaps even the complex number) of our speech.

It is then really, as Schechner says, 'a term hard to pin down'. To accept performance as our basic existential condition is to appreciate this unspoken, unseen and unthought, which mounts a constant challenge for the mind, and which always remains beyond discourse.

How to achieve such appreciation? And is it at all possible to make a cultural expression of it? There is an obvious answer: perhaps it is achievable through 'performance', this time in its common meaning as a cultural practice. In my view, any cultural performance should be regarded as a performance of the second degree, a meta-performance, a 'performance squared', or referring to the Schechnerian formula of performance as a 'twice-behaved-behaviour': a twice-performed-performance. Safely framed within culture, it may be perceived and may sensitize us for what is ubiquitous outside these frames. It is just like we can only feel the air when it is pressurized within a balloon. When it is out of such frames, we remain immersed in it imperceptibly, never feeling it but living thanks to it.

Dramatic performance

As a special kind of twice-performed-performance, the familiar European tradition of drama theatre may be of special interest: it is the one that attempts to thematize common human performance. Although never directly, as by its very nature it cannot be, the performative clash of instruction and selection seems to be revealed in theatre, as a cursory inspection suggests, in at least two basic ways.

First, it gets revealed through the ways theatre functions as a social phenomenon or institution. Preparing and staging a theatre production is always agonistic, it is a fight for survival: success or flop. No matter how well prepared (instructed), it may lose in the selective confrontation with the audience; on the other way something very appearing only, as it seems, by degeneracy may raise acclaim, hit the point and blaze trails for the future; the history of theatre is full of examples.

So it lasts in the popular imagination. Lives and careers of the comedians have always served as an epitome of unpredictability with their sudden turns of success and failure, through their necessity of the continuous struggle for survival and of the constant confrontation with the ever-changing tastes of the public. From *Hamlet* through Proust, we have this struggle written in numerous works of culture and also well embedded in common conviction. Generally, almost since its institutional conception theatre has served as a constant referent of the great, all-embracing metaphor ('all the world's a stage), providing masses with elementary reflection on dreams and reality, twisting fates and *peripeteias*.

Second, the performative clash is being reflected in drama. We can find its presence in dramatic plots and several works of the European canon seem to point at it more clearly. It can be well traced in the tragedy of Oedipus, where all fortunate performances lead to the ultimate misfortune, darkly enlightening the whole final part of the cycle; with the hero who in Colonus delivers the powerful monologue about the limits of his consciousness. In many ways it can also be traced in *King Lear*, the tragedy bearing some distinct resemblances of *Oedipus in Colonus*. *King Lear* is sometimes being recognized as Shakespeare's most 'naturalistic' tragedy, the dispute about the 'nature' plays there an important part, and indeed, the play may be easily summed up in purely 'evolutionary' terms: a population dies out after the hereditary mechanisms went wrong, with the whole network of many characters' unfortunate instructions and performances, too intricate to analyse it here.

It may be supposed, in brief, that Edgar, the sole survivor of this tragedy, succeeds only because he was able to put all his former instructions at stake and succumb to total degeneracy, thus finding some new homeostasis by means of pure performance (which proves mortal for his fellows and which definitely drives the old king mad). In that, he differs from his mate in disinheritance, Cordelia. A faithful follower to her noble rules, she is unable either to play or to degenerate and so she perishes along with her father, her sisters, Gloucester, Edmund and the fool, no matter how adverse were their aims, views and attitudes. Indeed, in one of its numerous aspects, *King Lear* may be regarded as a great drama of the survival value of performance.[25]

The ways, in which the instruction/selection principle, the performative and never articulated work of consciousness reflect themselves in theatre and in culture, lead to the vast and so far unexplored field of research and analysis.

I have now mentioned the two above ways only to show that the much abstract deliberations of the previous paragraphs translate directly to the accessible cultural practices. As the principle governs all our life, its reflections and resonances can be found much more often; in other places I have also gone on these topics at more length.[26]

The Mirror Game: A Natural Science Study of Togetherness

Lior Noy

Prologue: A meeting point

I am interested in the liminal area between science and the arts. The separation of the two is evident in our culture[1]: science, objective and logical; art, subjective and intuitive. For me this separation was always a bit strange. I am a performer, an actor in Playback Theatre, an improvisation form based on real-life stories.[2] I am also a scientist, trained as a computational neuroscientist. In 2008, the last year of my PhD studies, I received an offer to bring together my two vocations. Prof Uri Alon, a renowned physicist and molecular biologist and a fellow Playback actor, invited me to explore with him the possibility to study performance from a scientific perspective.

This was the beginning of a journey that started, as it often does in research projects, with a long time of wandering in 'the cloud'[3] while searching for the right research question and methodology. We met one evening to try to break our impasse. Sitting at the bar of our favourite place in Tel-Aviv, we had a moment of grace. As Uri is trying to gauge what I am *really* interested in studying, I found myself talking about the mirror game, a basic theatre exercise in which two actors mirror each other, creating coherent motions together. I recalled an experience from a time I was teaching theatre at a youth ward in a psychiatric hospital. A young man, who did not participate in other activities in the ward, had come to my class and had joined the activity only when we played the mirror game, and only when his favourite guide could play with him. It seemed that the game offered this young man an opening which was not present elsewhere. Talking about this experience, we instantly realized that the mirror game could be a fascinating object for a scientific investigation. We felt that the game relates to the profound human experience of being in a state of *togetherness*, while being simple enough to be studied quantitatively. This insight led to the study I shall describe here, and later, to the establishment of a Theatre Lab at the Weizmann Institute of Science, a hub of research at the meeting point of science and performing arts.[4]

Applying a natural science approach to the study of performance

Several current research fronts study elements of performance using a natural science approach. I am referring here to the natural sciences in order to focus on studies applying rigorous measurements, controlled experiments and mathematical modelling to study performance. These studies belong mainly to the field of neuroscience, which in the last two decades has expanded into new territories in the behavioural and social sciences, including studies of elusive phenomena such as meditation[5] and the human moral sense.[6] A recently emerging subfield is *social neuroscience*, aiming to apply the tools of neuroscience to study social interactions[7] such as joint action[8] and storytelling.[9]

Much of the recent progress in neuroscience is the result of advances in brain imaging techniques, most notably the introduction of functional magnetic resonance imaging (fMRI). For studying performance, an fMRI experiment poses a serious challenge: participants are expected to lie still for an hour or so, situated within a claustrophobic metal tube. This experience is quite different from that of, say, a performing Jazz musician. Due to this challenge, most studies in the field focus on studying the experience of *perceivers* of a performance, most notably during the perception of music, with only a handful of studies applying brain imaging to study the production of performative acts in music[10] and in dance.[11]

Studying a full performance, Ivana Konvalinka has recently measured physiological arousal in a fire-walking ritual in rural Spain.[12] Measuring the heart rates of spectators and performers, she found a pattern of physiological synchronization: while the heart rate of the current fire-walker was in-sync with that of related spectators (close friends and family members), it was out-of-sync with that of unrelated spectators. This work echoes previous studies of the physiological basis of trance states in rituals[13] and suggests a link between behavioural and physiological synchronization, a hypothesis currently being explored in our lab.

A few recent studies examined the brain activity of *improvising* performers.[14] Charles J. Limb and Allen R. Braun found that during improvisation, Jazz musicians exhibit different patterns of brain activation, including a deactivation of extensive parts of the pre-frontal cortex, an area containing the *executive functions* of the brain, and regulating other brain areas. The inhibition of pre-frontal activity during improvisation might be related to the concept of an *inner critic*, defined by improvisation pioneer Keith Johnstone as the part of our mind that constantly monitors and censors our actions. Johnstone suggested that in order to promote the emergence of spontaneous improvisation, the inner critic needs to be inhibited, and suggested practical methods of achieving this such as trance masks work.[15] A speculative hypothesis can relate the deactivation in the pre-frontal cortex of improvising Jazz musicians with Johnstone's inner critic.

Son Preminger suggested that theatre improvisation could be used as a method for neurocognitive rehabilitation. She describes similarities between known theatre improvisation exercises and methods used to assess damage to pre-frontal brain area, claiming that both engage similar cognitive functions. In her work, improvisation exercises are integrated into a practical framework for neurocognitive rehabilitation, an example for the potential of new discoveries at the intersection of neuroscience and the performing arts.[16]

Whereas the aforementioned studies focus mainly on studying brain activation of viewers and performers, we have taken a different approach, rooted in physics. We wished to reduce a complex behaviour pattern during performance to a *model system*. A model system is a relatively simple system that can be studied rigorously, attaining insights that can be projected onto more complex systems. An example of a model system commonly studied in molecular biology is the *E. coli* bacterium, an organism with a relatively short genome that contain many of the genetic regulations mechanisms that appear also in the human genome. A good model system enables researchers to conduct controlled experiments, and to extract simple measurements that can be analysed mathematically, while keeping contact with the phenomenon of interest. We suggest that the mirror game exercise can be employed as a model system for studying togetherness in performance.

Togetherness and the mirror game

A group of people acting together can enter a unique state of spontaneous and highly synchronized action. Director Peter Brook describes such moments during rehearsals, in which group creativity is at its peak: 'For these moments, when feelings, words, and movements came together and fused into new life, depended on the "running of a current," an opening to which all present contribute.'[17] Avant-garde musician Holger Czukay recalls similar moments: 'I have good memories about nights or concerts where we didn't play the music rather . . . the music played us.'[18]

I refer to moments in which the 'music played us' as moments of togetherness. A related term is Victor Turner's *communitas*, the experience of a group going through a ritual transition, where gender and class boundaries are dissolved, and group members experience unmediated direct connections.[19] Amy E. Sheams, in her book on Chicago's 'Second City' improvisers, describes *being in the zone*: '. . . a state of unselfconscious awareness in which every individual action seems to be the right one and the group works with apparently perfect synchronicity.'[20] *Being in the zone* is also a familiar term in group sports.[21]

To study these moments, we used the mirror game, a common exercise from theatre and dance practice.[22] In the basic form of the exercise, two players stand in front of each other, making eye contact. The players are instructed to produce synchronized mirror-like motions. The game starts with periods in which the players explicitly alternate between leading and following. Following an external cue, the players enter a period of co-creation, producing the synchronized motion together without a designated leader. Usually the mirror game is used as a tool to achieve concentration, attention, listening, and is typically employed as a warm-up exercise. Richard Schechner emphasizes the centrality of mirroring in performance: 'The theatrical event is fundamentally a mirroring; an ensemble company is a group of mirrors reflecting each other.'[23] In his work, he extensively used different mirror games to promote togetherness. Describing a mirror game involving four actors, he writes: 'Ego boundaries between individuals are breaking down. The progression . . . is one of breakdown and reformation on the basis of mirroring until from four individuals one entity emerges.'[24]

We employed the mirror game in an experimental setting to study togetherness. The requirement to produce identical motions establishes a natural way to quantify the dyad's performance by recording the motions of the two player motions and measuring their similarity. Our working hypothesis was that it is possible to detect markers of the subjective feeling of togetherness in the dyadic motions in the game. Our aim was to define these markers and to suggest a possible mechanism for the emergence of togetherness.

The experimental setting

Measuring the motions in the mirror game exercise entails a non-trivial task: the recording and analysing of the entire body motion of two actors. To overcome this, we simplified the experimental system and studied a reduced version of the mirror game in which only linear motion of the hands are allowed. For this purpose we developed a custom device for measuring the linear motion of two players (Figure 22, top-left). The players face each other, holding handles that can move along parallel tracks half a metre long, and the motion of the handles is accurately recorded. The one-dimensional mirror game enables players to produce rhythmic motions at different amplitudes and frequencies. Interesting motion patterns can be discovered; for example, a continuous increase in motion frequency leading to a clear crescendo (Figure 22, top-right). With this device,

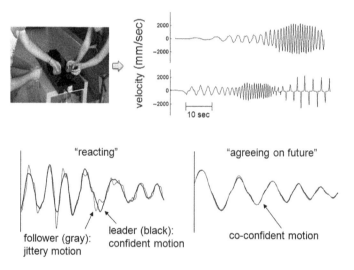

Figure 22 Top: the one-dimensional mirror game set-up. Two actors move handles along a line, mirroring one another with or without a designated leader. A custom-made device accurately measures the motion of the two handles. Two velocity traces, taken from rounds without a designated leader, show synchronized motions with complex patterns, for example, crescendos and diminuendos. The motion trace of one of the players was omitted here for clarity. **Bottom: a kinematic marker of togetherness.** A typical motion traces when one player is leading (black line) and the second player is reacting (grey line) are shown on the left. Notice the additional jittery motion on top of the leader's confident motion. In contrast, in joint-improvisation rounds, players can enter periods where they both produce synchronized and co-confident motion, without the typical jitter of followership. We suggest that in these periods the players do not react to each other, but instead agreeing on the current 'game', entering a momentary state of togetherness.

players were asked to play together and the goal of the game was defined as 'enjoy creating motion together that is synchronised and interesting'.

Moments of togetherness are rare in life, and it is difficult to capture them in the lab. To enhance our chances of detecting such moments, we focused on expert improvisers, operationally defined as actors or musicians with over 10 years of experience in joint improvisation. A similar approach was used in brain studies of meditation, where researchers investigated extremely experienced Tibetan monks in order to study meditation under laboratory conditions.[25] As a control group we also tested people without prior experience in improvisational arts.

We analysed the behaviour of pairs of expert improvisers in the simplified mirror game.[26] Players played a game composed of nine one-minute rounds, alternating between leader-follower rounds (with a designated leader) and joint-improvisation rounds (without a designated leader). Rounds were separated by ten-second breaks in which the players were allowed to remove their arms from the handles. The short rounds and the breaks were designed to assist players not to stay in a posture that might be uncomfortable for a long time. This was a limitation of the developed set-up, and we note that the duration of the rounds is shorter than what is commonly found in the mirror game exercise.

A game started with a short practice to allow players to get used to the possible motions. The progress of game rounds was conveyed to the players via a set of lights on the device, and a bell sound. Players were asked not to speak during the game. To allow for an intimate space, the experimenter left the room during the game.

The experimental results

Our findings show that expert improvisers create complex and highly synchronized motion together (Figure 22, top-right). To evaluate synchronicity in the motion, we segmented the velocity traces of the handles' motion into segments between stopping and found that the difference in segments stopping-times between the two players was often smaller than the minimal human reaction time (around 100 milliseconds). This suggests that players do not only react to the motion of each other but also use a prediction mechanism to anticipate the future motion.

Comparing the stopping time-differences in leader-follower and joint-improvisation rounds, we found that on the average, expert players were more synchronized in joint-improvisation rounds.[27] Moreover, when comparing both the speed of the motions and the produced errors, we found that in joint-improvisation rounds players were able to reach a region of performance that was not reached in leader-follower rounds.

We also analysed the behaviour of novices, people without improvisation experience, and showed that novices display the opposite pattern: they are less synchronized in joint-improvisation rounds, and show a smaller range of motions, showing that the joint-improvisation task is inherently challenging.

We then applied a detailed analysis of the motion traces to understand the source of the enhanced performance in the joint-improvisation rounds. We found in the motion traces of the follower a characteristically high-frequency motion that oscillates around the leader's confident motion, and we termed it *jitter* (Figure 22, bottom-left). This motion is typical of a scenario in which one agent (e.g. a hunting dog) chases another one (e.g. a rabbit). The dog is only reacting to the motions of the rabbit, without an ability to predict its future motions. As the rabbit changes its course, the dog zigzags across the rabbit's path, over- and under-shooting due to the inherent delay in reacting.

Previous studies of eye and arm movements describe similar jitter motion when tracking a target whose motion is not predictable.[28] This jitter motion was considered to be the result of an inner corrector, a reactive component in the brain that tries to correct the current error between the motion of the eye and the motion of the target. Similarly, we suggest that the jitter motion pattern found in the motion traces of the follower in the game is the result of an inner corrector, reacting to the perceived error between the motion of the leader and the follower. The detected jitter can thus be used as a *marker of followership* in the mirror game, characterizing periods when one player reacts to the motion of the other.

This aforementioned analysis allows us to show that during joint-improvisation rounds, expert improvisers not only switch (implicitly) between leader and follower roles, but also enter periods in which they create the motion together. We find that in about 15 per cent of the time in joint-improvisation rounds, expert improvisers produce smooth and synchronized motion, with neither of them displaying the characteristic jittery motion of a follower (Figure 22, bottom-right). Borrowing a term from drawing, we defined the smooth and synchronized motion of the two players as *co-confident* motion. These periods lasted usually for 5 to 20 seconds. The co-confident motion periods usually contained some development of the motion, for example, an increasing frequency up to some breakup point. We suggest co-confident motion periods as an operational description of moments of togetherness in the mirror game. As a control, we note that pairs without improvisation experience almost never exhibit this pattern of joint motion.

Finally, we developed a mathematical model for the behaviour of the players in the game. The motion of each player is the sum of two controllers: a *reactive* controller, which attempts to match the produced motion to the perceived motion of the other, and a *predictive* controller, which attempts to learn the motion of the other player and to predict it in advance. In simulations, this model produces motions that resemble the experimental results, including the emergence of co-confident motion when two such models are linked in mirror configuration. The model suggests that high synchronization in the mirror game is the result of a temporary cancellation of the reactive behaviour.

To summarize our results: we have shown an experimental paradigm to study joint-improvisation, presented an operational definition of moments of togetherness and suggested a mechanism for the emergence of these moments, based on reactive-predictive controllers. We are currently conducting several follow-up studies extending these results. We are particularly intrigued by a possible connection between the jitter in the mirror game, the mathematical reactive controller discussed above and the improvisation concept of an 'inner critic', and are exploring ways to bridge these concepts.

Regarding the reductionist nature of our approach

There is an inherent reduction in a scientific study of performance, where one attempts to reduce a nebulous concept to a well-defined experimental system. In this study the phenomenon of togetherness is reduced to a set of measurements of liner motions, a substantial move, from the transcendent to the very grounded. We aim to *distil* the phenomenon of togetherness, but in reducing it so much, do we manage to keep in touch with the original phenomenon?

I encourage the reader to come up with her or his own judgement for this question. Personally, I believe the answer is yes, that the moments of high synchrony in the mirror game reflect the subjective state of togetherness. In any case, there is a need for modesty: we did not *explain* the mystery of togetherness. We took, hopefully, a small step towards studying togetherness in a rigorous manner. We are currently taking further steps in this direction by performing further studies on the simplified mirror game, and by developing new paradigms to study more complex systems of joint-improvisation, such as the regular mirror game and joint drumming.

Another possible concern regarding our approach is that it will be so successful as to 'explain away' the phenomenon, reducing the magic of being in the zone to a set of mechanistic equations. I regard this concern in two manners: first, I do not think this scenario is very likely. As a performing improviser, I have a direct (subjective) access to the intensity and the complexity of joint-improvisation. I believe that the type of intuitive group decisions that we constantly make on stage is extremely difficult to analyse and model. But even if I am wrong, and one day someone will fully model a group going into the zone, this will not explain away the *experience* of these moments. The subjective experience in the moments when the 'music is playing us' is so vivid, and so unique, that any objective explanation will not replace it. An objective description can only co-exist alongside our subjective reality. Personally, I am slowly coming to grip with the notion of *multiple realities*, suggesting that we can simultaneously comprehend an objective description of a human experience *and* be fully in touch with its subjective reality. In the end, accepting the simultaneous existence of objective and subjective realities might be the final manifestation of togetherness.

Epilogue: A performance

Ruth Kanner is a renowned Israeli experimental theatre director, famous for her staging of non-dramatic texts. We recently started a dialogue that led her to suggest the following experiment: what would happen if we employ her group's skill to transform a *scientific* text to the stage? We decided to perform Kanner's experiment, and to have her actors improvise on the scientific paper describing the work presented here, to improvise on a text on joint-improvisation.[29] We planned a three-part performance: a flash presentation of the mirror game science project, a piece from a previous production of Kanner's group, which was influenced by scientific ideas about chaos and randomness, and then, a live experiment: four actors improvising on the text of the scientific mirror game paper, working their way from the most technical lines ('$p < 0.05$' – try to sing it!) towards the more comprehensible conclusions.

Something very intense was created as the performers explored their way through the text. At least for me, the performance had a transformative quality. Hearing the actors' voices, I felt that they manage to extract from the text the frustration and the joy of 3 years of hard work. They manage to unpack emotions that were condensed into the technical 2,500 words of the published paper. It was Playback Theatre at its best: my story coming to life on stage, illuminating words with hidden meaning. We wrote 'Togetherness' with an implicit agenda: 'it is so nice to be together!'. There is also a dark side to togetherness, which the actors managed to feel and to convey. Towards the end of the piece, the four actors started a wonderful joint singing of our key concept: 'To – ge – ther--rrr-ne—ssss'. In the midst of this collective work, one of them rebelled. Diverging away, she flew into her solo adventure, telling us that she prefers not to march in order, not to adhere to our definition of 'togetherness'. She prefers to play now, if we do not mind, and can we, please, not take ourselves so seriously.

Performing Science

Uri Alon

In 1999 I became a principal investigator, a scientist with my own lab, coming like a speeding train from my postdoc. I was ambitious and wanted desperately to succeed. My colleagues wanted me to succeed. My parents wanted me to succeed.

I walked into the whitewashed rooms of my new lab and felt like the walls and ceiling were collapsing on me. I panicked, because I realized that I didn't know what to do in my new job. How to find students, how to mentor them, how to resolve conflicts, how to choose good projects, how to build motivation, how to interview, how to write papers and grants.

I had studied thousands of hours of physics and biology, but not 1 hour on how to perform the day-to-day interpersonal tasks of doing science. No wonder that I made many basic mistakes. For example, when I interviewed potential students I talked a lot, trying desperately to convince them to join my lab. What I did not do was listen – so I had little idea of what the student was like. As a result I hired people who didn't fit with me or with each other. Soon, conflict arose between students, and I was torn in mediating between them, having no concepts about conflict resolution. Finally, I had to fire two students, after many sleepless nights of deliberation.

The lack of discussion or education on the subjective aspects of science contrasts with the detailed attention we give to objective aspects. When we buy a new microscope, we make sure to give it the best optical table and filters to work optimally. But when a new person joins our lab, what do we know about how to create an environment that will enable her to reach her full potential as a scientist working with a team of other scientists trying to build narratives about the natural world?

I started looking for knowledge about how to perform science, and found rich sources of information outside of science. One source came from doing improvisation theatre – I participated in an ensemble that does an improvisation form called playback theatre.[1] Improvisation theatre takes a group of actors into the unknown by listening and building on each other's ideas. It uses rituals to build trust and flow in the group. This was powerful experience for building a research group that goes into the unknown together. I also learned concepts from humanistic psychology from my partner Galia Moran, a clinical psychologist focusing on rehabilitation of people with mental illness. This helped me to perform what may be called interaction-centred science.

Bringing these notions and practices into my scientific mentoring made my group charged with intrinsic motivation, cooperation, playful and attentive amplification of each other's ideas and mutual support. This helped us pioneer a scientific field between physics and biology. Much of our success was due to the focus on the subjective and interpersonal performance of science by us, human beings.

Why don't we professionally discuss or teach the human aspects of doing science? The reason has to do with values. As pointed out by Evelyn Fox Keller, natural science has a cultural myth, in which the doing of science is purely objective and rational.[2] Just as the knowledge we seek is objective, so is the person doing the seeking. But when we label something as objective and rational, the other side – the subjective and emotional – is labelled as non-science or even threatening to science. Scientists sometimes write about their subjective journey – a classic example is James Watson's 'Double Helix' – but this remains extra-curricular reading, not part of the mainstream scientific education or discourse.

Natural science thus stigmatizes discussion – discussion within professional settings, that is – of the emotional and subjective aspects of doing science, our biases, our performances as interacting storytellers. We are assumed to be smart enough to figure out how to perform on our own or through observing our mentors. Subjective and emotional problems are pushed under the table. This leads to a form of self-oppression, in which scientists are increasingly unhappy with the 'system', and at the same time feel powerless to change it.[3]

Commiseration and complaint is a mainstay of private conversations when scientists meet – the academic reader may resonate with topics such as needless aggression from anonymous reviewers, systematic waste of talent of PhD students by certain mentors, promotion systems based on publication statistics rather than merit, grants that go to the least daring and creative proposals, and so on. On a deeper level, our lack of discussion of the emotional content of scientific communication and interaction limits our ability to do science, as I will argue below. But these recurring topics are rarely discussed in the public sphere in conferences, journals, classrooms, because they are considered subjective and therefore non-science or anti-science.

When viewed as a cultural phenomenon, one can gain hope for improving the culture of science. After all, culture can be changed and ways to change culture are well researched and understood. The key is what we discuss and don't discuss in professional settings. Public discourse shapes people's behaviours. For example, 100 years ago women could not vote. Public discussion relegated women to the home, so why should they vote on public matters. Most people agreed. Except for those who didn't, and after a few generations of struggle, won the vote for women. Today, people with chauvinistic opinions still exist, but they don't say 'take back the vote' – that is no longer a conceivable option. What we talk about and the way we talk about it makes such a statement unlikely.

Peer groups of scientists create a space for culture-changing discussion

Science is in a good position to widen its focus and improve its culture. After all, discourse can be changed by education, and science extensively deals with education. In recent years, I promoted an effective way to change the culture at an institution: starting a peer group of scientists. A group forms when 10–15 scientists at the same stage (PhD students, new faculty, etc.) get together and invite a workshop on communication skills for scientists that presents simple concepts on active listening, conflict resolution and leadership (I like the workshops given by the company HFP consulting). This nucleates a core for meeting regularly, say once every 2 weeks.

The peer group creates a space for discussing the subjective and emotional aspects of science, and build leadership to make changes as the group members increasingly get involved in running the institution. The inspiration is women's empowerment groups in the 1960–70s, with their motto 'the personal is political'. In the meetings, one person presents a conflict or issue they are facing now, the others share related stories. The facilitator notes the group state, and sees that people aren't getting into modes of giving advice, preaching, joking or any of the other barriers to effective communication. Scientist peer groups are running at Harvard, Yale, the Weizmann Institute and other universities.[4] Members report that the meetings provide mindfulness about how to perform science, how to carry out the different roles of being a scientist. Bonds of solidarity are formed between group members. Established groups have helped newcomers to start second-generation peer groups. Cultural change has heredity: once a peer group is founded, it becomes part of the normal offering to scientists.

To enhance discussion and education on the subjective and emotional aspects of our craft, we need a good curriculum. In the remainder of this essay, I lay out some suggestions for how performance studies – in the wide sense encompassing literature, anthropology and theatre – can help build such a curriculum and inspire deeper understanding of how to perform science.

The scientific conversation and improvisation theatre

Scientific conversations are where many ideas are generated, motivation is gained and insight achieved. They can also be meetings that suppress ideas and lead to de-motivation.

If we consider the scientific conversation as an attempt to journey into the unknown, we can analyse it using concepts from improvisation theatre in which two actors try to build an unscripted scene. The main principle in improvisation is saying *Yes And*, as described by Keith Johnstone. This skill includes making clear offers that the other can understand, accepting the other's offer and developing it clearly. The opposite of saying *Yes And* is called blocking. Blocking sounds like this:

> Here's a pool of water.
> No, that's just the stage.

> The scene ends, actors are frustrated.

> Saying *Yes And* sounds like this:

> Here's a pool of water
> Let's jump in!
> Ooh- there's a whale.
> Yeah, let's grab it by the tail.
> Wow, it's pulling us to the moon!

> --------------

Scientific conversations which block ideas prematurely tend to demoralize the participants and to prevent 'stupid' ideas from combining with other ideas to become breakthroughs.

Thus, good scientific conversations require mindfulness of blocking and saying *Yes And*. Skilled improvisers are able to recover from blocks and use them as material for new turns in the scene. This skill can be taught to science students, to help them co-lead discussions.

More fundamentally, performing a scientific conversation well allows us to tap into deep sources of intuition. For this, saying *Yes And* has a crucial importance: it is a way to bypass the inner critic. Improvisation theatre recognizes an inner critic that stops us from saying things, so we won't be considered crazy, obscene or unoriginal. In science nowadays, the inner critic is strong, and we don't say things so that people won't think we are not smart. Saying *Yes And* is one way to bypass the critic to allow access to material that is sometimes surprisingly salient and deep.

When I talk about this to scientists, they sometimes object that this picture excludes criticism of errors. In fact, current education in science places a premium on criticism – finding out where the other is wrong. This objection is valid, and a balanced scientific conversation can be thought of as a diamond shape pattern – first a phase of opening of ideas, even preposterous ideas, that are played with to generate the material for discussion, followed by a stage of critical examination. Too much *Yes And* may lead to an unproductive mess of mistakes, but also too much criticism can stifle creativity and prevent new ideas from originating. More likely, with skilled performers, both modes can go on at the same time, just as improvisation actors say *Yes And* while steering the scene to meaningful unexpected directions.

Improvisation actors also use their body to help bypass the inner critic. Before stepping into the scene, they go into an upright and relaxed body stance called 'Up and Happy'[5] and they make eye contact with their partners. They take a deep breath. All of this prepares the entry into the unknown together. Other body stances, such as eyes cast down and closed posture, seem to enhance a type of planning and thinking that interferes with spontaneous flow of the scene. I have become increasingly aware of my body stance during scientific conversations. Simple awareness of whether I'm attending to the other, for example, by turning my shoulders to face my discussion partner and attempting not to slouch, seems to improve my listening and sharpens the potential for playfulness in the discussion. Such body rituals may help scientists enter the scientific conversation better prepared for good interaction.

There is much to explore in scientific conversations: How can we enhance the chance of bypassing the inner critic, and gain access to inner voices that are not normally heard – voices that may carry insights that can take our understanding forward.

Scientific articles and The Art of Dramatic Writing

We are not taught to write compelling papers in science. No wonder that writing is a painful experience for many scientists. The fruit of our labours is, all too often, equally painful to read. In this section and the next, I address the issues of clarity and narrative structure in scientific writing. I have discussed the performance aspects of oral scientific communication elsewhere.[6]

The clarity of my writing was transformed by ideas from theatre, as described in Lajos Egri's book, *The Art of Dramatic Writing*.[7] Egri's message is that a play must have a premise: a central idea – a full sentence – that unifies all choices in the play. The play Macbeth has a premise: ruthless ambition leads to its own destruction. The premise is evident in every character, and in every detail. It gives the play artistic unity, the sense that all things hang together with nothing arbitrary.

The same applies to a good scientific article. Clear writing starts before a single word is written, by the effort to find a premise. The premise is a full sentence, conveying the main message. If one sets out without a premise, or with more than one premise, the result is difficult for readers to comprehend. A single premise can guide the writer and reader, and is the unifying principle for the paper. Include only material that relates to the premise. Drop the rest – even if it means dropping work that took much time.

Finding a premise takes effort. It is hard to boil down our work into a single sentence, and to commit to it. I start with a session of premise finding with my co-authors. A premise must be a full sentence. 'Complex networks of molecules in the cell' is not a premise; it is only a sentence fragment. 'We can understand complex networks by seeing that they are built of a small set of recurring patterns' is a premise.

My co-authors and I talk, give ourselves freedom to say stupid things, say *Yes And* and come up with several premises for our data. We then plot them out along two axes. The first axis is 'How interesting is this premise to us?' – interesting to us rather than what we imagine would be interesting to others. The second axis is: 'How well-supported is the premise by our data?' Readers tend to close up their attention if the premise is not matched by good support of the data.

Now our premises are plotted as points on a graph, defined by the two axes of interest and support. If one premise is better on both axes than the other premises, we choose it. Often, however, two premises show a trade-off – the duller premise is better supported than the intriguing one. In this case, if we have time constraints, we might choose the less interesting and better supported premise. If time and resources are available, we can see what research needs to be done to better support the more interesting premise. In this way, writing is part of research because it generates new experimental ideas.

With a premise in mind, we draw out the figures in a progression made to lead the reader step by step through our story. We try not to make big jumps, but to let each piece of description lead naturally into the next.

Science articles and the morphology of the Russian wonder tale

The scientific article, in the myth of rationality, is a technical exposition of data. The goal is to let the data speak for itself, a stream of encoded information injected into the reader's brain. To do so, we are taught the dry mechanics of writing the introduction, results and discussion sections. In reality, the quality of storytelling in an article is of central importance: papers that leave a lasting emotional impression, and tell an unexpected yet credible story (with a single well-supported and interesting premise), are the ones that make a difference.

To guide the transformation of data into a compelling story, I use an analogy to Vladimir Propp's classic structural analysis of the Russian wonder tale.[8] This is only one of many possible ways to form a narrative, suggesting a rich field for additional study.

In Propp's analysis, the Russian wonder tale is made of a series of plot modules, carried out by specific character types (hero, villain, magic donor, etc.). The modules appear in a universal order. I describe here a very simplified form of the original analysis. The Hero has a miraculous birth (born in a cabbage flower). Trouble descends on the land (sorcerer lays a curse), and the hero decides to do something about it and goes on a journey, meets a magical donor (fairy godmother) that tests him and provides a magical boon (magic sword), with which the hero combats and defeats the villain. Hero returns to the land but a false hero (the pretender) arises, and is unmasked. The hero attains the throne and marries the princess.

Here is how this maps to a scientific article. The introduction begins with the work of previous pioneers (miraculous birth), but there is a gap in our understanding (trouble), and we set out to address it (go on a journey). For that purpose we develop with some effort a technology (magical donor) and overcome technical difficulties (combat villain), to find new knowledge. We return to the land in the conclusions section and restate our main findings, but caveats and limitations are noted (false hero) and are addressed (unmasked). Marrying the princess means potential for royal offspring, and we conclude the article by suggesting the potential for new science and applications.

Hero miraculous birth	Pioneering origin of our field
Trouble descends upon land	But there is a gap in our knowledge
Hero decides to go on journey	Here, we address this
Meets magical donor	To do so, we developed a technology
That tests him and provides magical boon	And overcame technical challenges
Hero fights and defeats villain	To make new finding
Returns to land	Summary of new knowledge
False hero appears, is unmasked	Caveats and limitations are noted, and addressed
Hero marries princess, potential for royal offspring	Potential for more science, applications

As in the wonder tale, part of the appeal of an article is in the specific details (the glass slipper). Good articles provide idiosyncratic details, curiosities and specifics. But it is the overall plot modules that provide the sweep, context and timing for these details to enhance rather than obstruct the emotional experience – the narrative truth that, as Velleman[9] noted, guides the reader through a defined series of emotions. The wonder tale structure takes the reader, as in ritual structure described by van Gennep and Turner,[10] from the known, across the threshold into the unknown, and safely back transformed with new understanding. Not technical and dry, science writing can be like composing an adventure story.

Looking at an article this way opens the discussion of different ways for making narrative for conveying scientific findings. The wonder tale form, as any form, restricts us in important ways. For example, there is no scope for failure – indeed it is hard to publish negative results (lack of confirmation of hypotheses), dooming scientists to go down the blind alleys already visited by others. We also avoid non-linear and ramifying tales, without a beginning middle and end. Science can benefit from additional forms to guide readers through such non-linear accounts. In summary, widening the discussion of ways to tell scientific stories will provide better scope for scientists to communicate and enrich the kinds of stories we can tell about the natural world.

Dramatic metaphors, robust mathematical models and limitations on scientific understanding

Science is about making stories about nature. Here our subjectivity can collide with the objective goal of understanding nature. I'll use as an example the current struggle to understand the networks of molecular interactions within living cells.

How can we begin to understand how molecules interact if we never saw them with our eyes or felt them with our hands? Nanometre-sized molecules are alien to us. As noted by Fox Keller, Lakoff[11] and others, scientists wrap their ignorance by using metaphors as working tools. With metaphors we can entail properties of the known onto the unknown. Scientists use metaphors of space and visual metaphors to make abstractions. We have no choice but to use metaphors that are grounded in our bodies and our social mindset.

A class of metaphors that have long been used to understand molecules relates to drama – the way that two, three or more characters interact. Consider the words antagonist, hydrophobic, affinity. Molecule X binds molecule Y is talked about as if X loves Y (has high affinity for Y), molecule X may fear water (hydrophobic), X may be inhibited by its enemy (antagonist) and so on.

Things get more complicated when we try to understand the dynamics of circuits of molecules – how their story evolves with time. Here is an example of a story that is so enticing that it long dominated the way that biologists think of signalling in cells. It is the story of the bucket brigade. X hands a bucket to Y, which hands it to Z etc. If you know the initial conditions – X is given a bucket – you can predict the story at future times: the bucket will go step by step down the brigade. If you block the cascade – using a drug to inhibit Y, for example – you can predict exactly where the bucket will stop.

Such stories translate into mathematical models that are structurally robust: many details and parameters do not matter, and the equations give the same qualitative dynamics for many different parameters. In the model, changing the affinities of the molecules to each other may change timescales, but not the essential fact that we can feel in our bones: the bucket will reach the end of the cascade.

A bucket brigade model is an example of a story module. Other story modules are also intuitively understandable to our dramatic mindset. Three-character stories like 'the enemy of my enemy is my friend', and 'two friends agreeing about a third character', are well-known elements of social networks.[12]

But not all stories are as understandable to our minds as bucket brigades and love triangles. As all playwrights know, we can't truly understand stories with many more than three characters (unless they are arranged in a bucket brigade, in teams or other simple forms); a story with ten equally important interacting characters is beyond us, unless separated into simpler stories. The principles of Egri and Propp also relate to such limitations. In fact, we can't keep in mind more than a limited number of chunks of information and a limited number of simultaneous 'theories of mind'. This is crucially important because in order to understand an entire cell, we need to understand the story of thousands of interacting molecular characters – a feat comparable to understanding an entire village.

Thus, our limited ability to fathom drama may restrict the kinds of stories we can tell about nature. Unless biology is built of modules simple enough to understand, we won't be able to make sense of it – not in the intuitive grounded sense that I mean here. We may be able to follow through complex stories by means of computer simulations, but simulations don't lead to intuitive understanding if they can't be decomposed into parts[13] and mapped to simple metaphorical situations. It is thus conceivable that biology could be too tough for us to ever understand. Biology evolved to survive, not for scientists to understand.

Now comes a wondrous turn, or the hope of one. In 2001, we found to our surprise that complex networks of interacting molecules in the cell are much simpler than they could have been – they are made up of a small set of recurring patterns.[14] We called these recurring patterns network motifs. Each network motif is a small circuit, in which molecules interact in specific ways. Each network motif appears again and again in the network, each time with different molecules. Experiments suggest that each network motif carries out a specific dynamical function in the cell.

The network motifs found so far are built in ways that are understandable. The mathematical models that describe them have structural robustness: you don't need to know the precise parameter values in order to grasp the kind of dynamics they can display. For example, the incoherent feedforward loop is a network motif in which X does two opposite things, it activates Z directly, but also activates Y which is an inhibitor of Z. This circuit can cause a pulse of Z:X first activates Z. Then, at a delay, it activates the antagonist Y that causes Z activity to go down. If you understand this pulse, you understand what I mean by intuitive understanding. More subtle functions of this circuit can be revealed by mathematical analysis.

The same network motifs have since been discovered in every organism analysed. This raises the hope that biology may be universally built of modules simple enough to understand using stories of two and three characters, with robust math. It may be that evolution selected and kept these few circuit types because they are the simplest circuits (most economical in terms of number of components) that carry out needed functions in a way that is robust enough to work in the noisy environment of the cell. Once you understand the network motifs, you can in principle comprehend the dynamics of the entire networks out of the dynamics of each of its simple building blocks. A similar situation exists in engineering: complex electronic devices are built of a small set of recurring circuit elements, each simple enough to be understandable and to work robustly.

The understandability of biology, like that of engineering, is probably not a coincidence. It stems from three facts: (1) Systems that function in the real world apparently must be made of small, robust units, otherwise they cannot evolve to meet changing needs. (2) Thus, complex biology evolved to be built of small, robust modules. (3) These modules can be mapped to stories that our mind can understand, because we evolved the capacity to intuitively grasp stories that lead to reliable (structurally robust) predictions about the social world.

Biology may thus turn out to be more satisfying than physics, at least to scientists interested in intuitive understanding. Physics deals with non-evolved matter, which is mostly un-understandable. We can understand the harmonic oscillator, but not a meshwork of thousands, or even three, non-linearly interacting objects. Biology, on the other hand, may offer us centuries of research on systems we can deeply understand.

This optimistic conclusion for biology may of course turn out to be false. It is possible that parts of biology are built differently, more like villages not decomposable into simpler parts. Perhaps the neocortex or the immune systems are examples. In my bones, I feel these will also turn out to be understandable in terms of simple building block circuits – here is an exciting avenue for scientific research.

Conclusions

The myth of a lone scientist, purely objective and rational, suppresses discussion within the scientific professions of the subjective and emotional aspects of doing science. As a result scientists are increasingly isolated from each other, and are left without important concepts on how to do science. Our profession currently focuses on the results, not the process of science. It is rife with self-oppression and ignorance of basic communication skills, leading to loss of talent and potential.

A better metaphor for science is perhaps a group of explorers and storytellers, each resonating with some aspects of nature, trying to build increasingly rich and coherent stories. To improve science, we need to open discussions of the subjective and emotional aspects of our craft, so that both individual uniqueness and social communication can be enhanced. Through discussion, our limitations can be better addressed. The more we take into account our biases as human beings, the more objective the outcome of our science is likely to become.

In a practical way, this essay tries to touch upon topics for a future discussion of the subjective and emotional sides of science – a discussion not by outside observers of science, but rather by working scientists within the public sphere of science. Theatre can offer ways of practising and understanding scientific conversations, metaphors and scientific communication. Many more topics remain to be explored. My hope is that this grows into a living cultural change in science, rather than ending up an artificial set of self-help maxims. The thriving of peer groups that can create new culture locally, and the enthusiasm that scientists, especially of the current generation, express for these topics, gives hope.

Notes

Chapter 1

1 Richard Macksey and Eugenio Donato (eds), *The Structuralist Controversy. The Language of Criticism and the Sciences of Man*. Baltimore: The John Hopkins University Press, 2009, p. 152.

2 As detailed by François Cusset in *French Theory: How Foucault, Derrida, Deleuze, & Co. Transformed the Intellectual Life of the United States*, trans. Jeff Fort. University of Minnesota Press, 2008.

3 Richard Schechner, *Performance Studies: An Introduction*, Second edition. Routledge, 2006, p. 1.

4 John L. Austin, *How to do Things with Words*, Second edition. Cambridge, MA: Harvard University Press, 1975, pp. 21–2.

5 As writes Paul Eluard in his poetry 'The earth is blue' (1929).

6 Another way in the sense that we can see confronted here: the deconstructionist performativity of writing; performativity as an anthropological and esthetical reflexivity on theatrical performance; and the analytical performativity coming from the philosophy of ordinary language. In addition to the original exclusion of theatrical performance from the analysis of the performative by Austin, another antinomy arises between the use of the performative by Derrida and its elaboration by the tradition of analytical philosophy, by John Searle for instance.

7 *The Structuralist Controversy*, p. 13.

8 Plato, 'Io', *Early Socratic Dialogues*. London: Penguin Classics, 2005.

9 Aby Warburg didn't neglect in his iconological project the role of Dionysian impulses in the survival of forms. See Philippe-Alain Michaud, *Aby Warburg and the Image in Motion*. New York: Zone Books, 2004.

10 Antonin Artaud, *The Theatre and its Double*, trans. Mary C. Richard. New York: Grove Press, 1994, p. 5.

11 Ibid., p. 7.

12 Thierry de Duve, 'Performance here and now: Minimal Art, a Plea for a new Genre of Theatre', in *Open Letter*, 1983, n. 5–6.

13 Robert P. Crease, *The Play of Nature. Experimentation as Performance*. Bloomington and Indianapolis: Indiana University Press, 1993, p. 178.

14 Friedrich Nietzsche, *The Birth of Tragedy*, trans. Clifton P. Fadiman. New York: Dover Publications, 1995.

15 See Sigmund Freud, *The Origin and Development of Psychoanalysis*, Second lecture.

16 Jacques Derrida, 'Structure, Sign and play in the discourse of the human sciences', *Writing and Difference*, trans. Alan Bass. London: Routledge, 2001, p. 365.

17 Ibid., p. 367.

18 Ibid., p. 369.

19 Jacques Derrida, 'Force and signification', *Writing and Difference*, trans. Alan Bass. London: Routledge, 2001, p. 3.

20 Ibid., p. 21.

21 Ibid., p. 4.

22 Ibid., p. 24.

23 Ibid., p. 24.

24 Ibid., p. 31.

25 Ibid., p. 34.

26 Ibid., p. 31.

27 To a certain extent, these notions could be linked to some alternatives in biological theories: *preformism* terms for instance an approach of epigenesis (the idea that the living organisms are formed before their development) which will be criticized by the *transformism* of Lamarck and by the evolutionism of Darwin. A biological *performism* would mean that life forces are in excess over life forms, this excess leading to relative unpredictable plays and transformations.

28 'Force and signification', p. 34.

29 Ibid., p. 22.

30 Richard Schechner, 'Six Axioms for Environmental Theater', *Environmental Theater*. New York: Hawthorn, 1973.

31 Lucien Goldmann represented a Marxist fringe of structuralist literary criticism, opposed to a large extent to Derrida's deconstruction of structuralism.

32 Richard Macksey and Eugenio Donato (eds), *The Structuralist Controversy. Op. cit.*, p. 115.

33 Ibid., p. 153.

34 Ibid., p. 154.

35 Ibid., p. 155.

36 Jacques Derrida, 'The Theater of Cruelty and the Closure of Representation', *Writing and Difference*, trans. Alan Bass. London: Routledge, 2001, p. 293.

37 Ibid., p. 302.

38 Ibid., p. 310.

39 *Dionysus in 69* (by Richard Schechner and the Performance Group), directed by Brian de Palma, film B&W, 85'. 1970. Edited in DVD by Carlotta Films, 2003.

40 Jacques Rancière, *The Emancipated Spectator*, trans. Gregory Elliott. London and New York: Verso, 2009.

41 Richard Schechner describes how a transformation of consciousness needs an in between and not a simple exchange of positions in, for instance: 'Points of

contact between anthropological and theatrical thought', *Between Theater and Anthropology*. Philadelphia: University of Pennsylvania Press, 1985, p. 10.

42 Richard Schechner, 'The Crash of performative circumstances. A modernist discourse on postmodernism', *The End of Humanism*. New York: Performing Arts Journal Press, 1982.

43 Philip Auslander, 'Just be yourself', in Philip Zarrilli (ed.), *Acting (Re)Considered: Theories and Practices*. London: Routledge, 1995.

44 Shoshana Felman, *The Scandal of the Speaking Body: Don Juan with J.L. Austin, or Seduction in Two Languages*. Stanford: Stanford University Press, 2003.

45 Judith Butler, *Bodies that Matter: On the Discursive Limits of 'Sex'*. London: Routledge, 1993.

46 In his analysis of motion Aristotle distinguishes activity (*energeia*) from potentiality (*dynamis*). *Energeia* then designates the action of 'being-at-work'. This force in act is what best resembles our modern notion of performance, because it can be seized in its very process and not through an actualized end (which would be the *entelechia* in Aristotle's term). Aristotle, *Physics*, III, I.

Chapter 2

1 Jon McKenzie, *Perform or Else: From Discipline to Performance*. London: Routledge, 2001, p. 50.

2 See Henry Bial, 'Today I Am a Field: Performance Studies Comes of Age', in James Harding and Cindy Rosenthal (eds), *The Rise of Performance Studies: Rethinking Richard Schechner's Broad Spectrum*. New York: Palgrave Macmillan, 2011, pp. 85–96.

3 Richard Schechner, *Performance Theory*, Revised and Expanded edition. London: Routledge, 1988, p. 6.

4 Victor Turner, 'Foreword', in Richard Schechner (ed.), *Between Theatre and Anthropology*. Philadelphia: University of Pennsylvania Press, 1983, p. xii.

5 Victor Turner as quoted in Richard Schechner and Willa Appel (eds), *By Means of Performance*. Cambridge: Cambridge University Press, 1990, p. 1.

6 For more on the speech communications strain of performance studies, see Shannon Jackson, *Professing Performance: Theatre in the Academy from Philology to Performativity*. Cambridge: Cambridge University Press, 2004; and Sheron Dailey (ed.), *The Future of Performance Studies: Visions and Revisions*. Annandale, VA: National Communication Association, 1998.

7 Judith Butler, 'Performative Acts and Gender Constitution: An Essay in Phenomenology and Feminist Theory', in Henry Bial (ed.), *The Performance Studies Reader*. London: Routledge, 2004, p. 158.

8 Peggy Phelan, 'Introduction', in Peggy Phelan and Jill Lane (eds), *The Ends of Performance*. New York: NYU Press, 1998, p. 3.

9   Joseph Roach, *Cities of the Dead: Circum-Atlantic Performance*. New York: Columbia University Press, 1996, p. 4.

10 Diana Taylor, *The Archive and the Repertoire: Performing Cultural Memory in the Americas*. Durham: Duke University Press, 2003, p. 16.

11 Cf. Richard Schechner, *Between Theater and Anthropology*. Philadelphia: University of Pennsylvania Press, 1985, p. 113: 'A performance "takes place" in the "not me . . . not not me" between performers; between performers and texts; between performers, texts, and environment; between performers, texts, environment, and audience'.

12 David Zerbib, responding to a draft of this chapter, suggests that this kind of complex relationship created on the network between collective and individual, live and archive, presence and absence, deconstructs the opposition between PS 1.0 and PS 2.0 and thus 'PS 3.0 is the proof that PS 1.0 and 2.0 are part of the same OS'.

13 Richard Schechner, *Performance Studies: An Introduction*. London: Routledge, 2002, p. 21.

14 Henry Bial, 'Introduction', in Henry Bial (ed.), *The Performance Studies Reader*. London: Routledge, 2004, p. 1.

Chapter 3

1   Steven Pinker, *The Better Angels of Our Nature*. New York: Viking, p. 672.

2   Jawaharlal Nehru, 'Speech to Bandung Conference Political Committee, 1955'. http://www.fordham.edu/halsall/mod/1955nehru-bandung2.html.

3   Pinker, pp. 404, 413–14.

4   James Thompson and Richard Schechner, 'Why "Social Theatre"?' *TDR The Drama Review: The Journal of Performance Studies*, Vol. 48, No. 3 (2004), pp. 11–16.

5   Guglielmo Schinina, 'Here We Are: Social Theatre and Some Open Questions about Its Developments', *TDR*, Vol. 48, No. 3 (2004), pp. 17–31. See also '"Far Away, So Close": Psychosocial and Theatre Activities with Serbian Refugees', *TDR*, Vol. 48, No. 3 (2004), pp. 32–49.

6   Carol Martin, 'Introduction to "The Pixelated Revolution" by Rabih Mroué'. *TDR*, Vol. 56, No. 3 (2012), pp. 22, 24.

7   Erik H. Erikson, *Identity and the Life Cycle. Psychological Issues*. Vol. 1, No. 1 (1959), pp. 18–171.

Chapter 4

1   *The Agony and the Ecstasy of Steve Jobs* sparked a controversy over the proper domains of theatre and journalism. Daisey was accused of, and admitted to, some fabrication of sources and dramatization of events that made his work less than

factual according to accepted journalistic ethical standards. Much was written about this controversy, which was widely reported in a number of places; these materials are readily available on the internet. Partly for this reason, and partly because it lies outside the specific focus of my essay, I shall not discuss that interesting controversy here.

2 I saw *The Agony and the Ecstasy of Steve Jobs* at The Public Theatre in New York in the fall of 2011 and *33 rpm and then some* at the Malta Festival in Poznan, Poland in the summer of 2012.

3 Alison Forsyth and Chris Megson, *Get Real: Documentary Theatre Past and Present.* Performance Interventions. London: Palgrave Macmillan, 2009, p. 6.

4 Carol Martin (ed.), *Dramaturgy of the Real on the World Stage.* Studies in International Performance. London: Palgrave Macmillan, 2006, p. 195.

5 James K. Rilling, 'Neuroscientific Approaches and Applications within Anthropology'. *Yearbook of Physical Anthropology, Am. J. Phys. Anthropol. Suppl.*, Vol. 47 (2008), pp. 2–32.

6 Mike Daisey, *The Agony and the Ecstasy of Steve Jobs*, 2011. http://mikedaisey.blogspot.com/p/monologues.html, p. 10.

7 Ibid., p. 10.

8 Ibid., p. 19.

9 Ibid., p. 24.

10 Ibid., p. 43.

11 Rabih Mroué and Lina Saneh, *33 Rounds per Minute and then Some.* Unpublished manuscript, unpaginated, 2012.

12 Ibid.

13 Ibid.

14 See 'Uploaded and Unsanctioned: Introduction to *The Pixelated Revolution* by Rabih Mroué'. *TDR*, Vol. 56, No. 3 (T215, 2012), pp. 19–25.

15 Daisey, p. 45.

Chapter 5

1 Théâtre du Soleil, *1789* and *1793*. Paris: Théâtre du Soleil, 1989.

2 Margaret Croydon recounts Ronconi's interest in Schechner's theorizing in Chapter 9 of her *Lunatics, Lovers and Poets: The Contemporary Experimental Theatre*. New York: Delta, 1974, pp. 193–227.

3 Croydon, *op. cit.*

4 Christian Biet and Christophe Triau, *Qu'est-ce que le theater*. Paris: Gallimard, 2006; and David Wiles, *A Short History of Performance Space*. London: Cambridge, 2003.

5   Joan MacIntosh, Interview by Cindy Rosenthal in James Harding and Cindy Rosenthal (eds), *The Rise of Performance Studies: Rethinking Richard Schechner's Broad Spectrum*. Basingstroke, Hampshire: Palgrave Macmillan, 2011, pp. 196–212.

6   See Richard Schechner's comments on the intensity of performance in Chapter 1 in Richard Schechner, *Between Theatre and Anthropology*. Philadelphia: University of Pennsylvania Press, 1985, pp. 3–33.

7   For a history of this evolution, see 'Introduction' to Harding and Rosenthal (eds), *op. cit.*, 1–10.

8   Part of this essay has appeared in Judith Miller, 'Ariane Mnouchkine's *Dashed Hopes*', *Theater*, Vol. 41, No. 2 (Summer 2011), pp. 120–33. The analysis of the productions of *1789* and *1793* is based on five viewings by the author between 1970 and 1973. The analysis of *Les Naufragés du fol espoir*, including quotations/ translations from the unpublished play-script, is based on two viewings: 14 February 2010 and 19 June 2010.

9   See Freddie Rokem's analysis of *1789* for a broader conceptualization of what performing history implies: *Performing History: Theatrical Representation of the Past in Contemporary Theatre*. Iowa City: University of Iowa Press, 2007.

10 Richard Schechner, *Environmental Theatre*. New York: Applause, 1994 [1973].

11 Théâtre du Soleil, *l'Age d'or*. Paris: Stock, 1975.

12 Ariane Mnouchkine, *Méphisto, le roman d'une carrier*. Paris: Solin/Théâtre du Soleil, 1979.

13 Le Centre de Recherche et de Documentation Pédagogique (CRDP) has produced an excellent dossier with documentation and photographs of the creation and production of *Les Naufragés du Fol Espoir*. See http://crdp.ac-paris.fr/piece-demontee/piece/index.php?id+les-naufrages-du-fol-espoir.

14 To begin to create the text for this play, Cixous used parts of Jules Verne's *En Magellanie*, an unpublished manuscript finally published in 1987 by La Société Jules Verne (Paris) and his son's, Michel Verne's, adaptation of it, *Les Naufragés du Jonathan*. Paris: Pierre-Jules Hetzel, 1909.

15 Théâtre du Soleil, *Molière*. DVD Bel-Air Classiques, 1978.

16 Hélène Cixous, *Le Rire de la Méduse et autres ironies*. Paris: Galilée, 2010 [1975]. For a discussion of the ways in which Cixous's notion of *écriture féminine* can be found in Mnouchkine's staging, see Judith Miller, 'Medusa and the Mother/Bear: The performance text of *l'Indiade*', in David Williams (ed.), *Collaborative Theatre: The Théâtre du Soleil Sourcebook*. London: Routledge, 1999, pp. 131–7.

17 Théâtre du Soleil, *Le Dernier Caravansérail (Odysées)*. DVD Bel Air Média, Arte France, 2006.

18 Edouard Glissant, *Introduction à une poétique du divers*. Paris: Gallimard, 1996.

19 See Claire Bishop's account of how ethics can define spectatorship in *Artificial Hells: Participatory art and the Politics of Spectatorship*. London: Verso, 2012.

Chapter 6

* This research was supported by The Israeli Science Foundation (grant No. 435/10). Unless otherwise indicated, all the translations from German are mine. G. K.

1 Hans-Thies Lehmann, 'Wie politisch ist Postdramatisches Theater?', in Jan Deck and Angelika Sieburg (eds), *Politisch Theater Machen. Neue Artikulationen des Politischen in den darstellenden Künsten.* Bielefeld: Transcript, 2011, p. 34.

2 Hans-Thies Lehmann, *Postdramatisches Theater.* Frankfurt am Main: Verlag der Autoren, 1999. References are from the English translation by Karen-Jürs-Munby (*Postdramatic Theatre.* New York: Routledge, 2006).

3 Patrick Primavesi, 'Theater/ Politik – Kontexte und Beziehungen', in Deck and Sieburg, p. 49.

4 Michael Merschmeier, 'Die Stunden der Wahrheit', *Theater heute*, Vol. 38, No. 2 (February 1997), p. 8.

5 Gad Kaynar, 'German Theatre, Summer 2003: Journey Impressions', *Teatron*, No. 12 (February 2004), p. 31. (Hebrew).

6 Jean-Luc Nancy, *Singulär plural sein.* Berlin: Diaphanes, 2005, p. 20.

7 Anja Quickert, 'Temponauten mit Geschichte', *Theater heute*, Vol. 51, No. 6 (June 2010), p. 13.

8 Jacques Rancière, *Das Unbehagen in der Ästhetik.* Wien: Passagen, 2007, p. 32. See also: Florian Malzacher, 'The Scripted Realities of Rimini Protokoll', in Carol Martin (ed.), *Dramaturgy of the Real on the World Stage.* London: Palgrave Macmillan, 2010, pp. 80–7.

9 See, e.g.: Marvin Carlson, *Theatre is More Beautiful than War: German Stage Directing in the Late Twentieth Century.* Iowa City: University of Iowa Press, 2009, pp. 143–4.

10 Lehmann, 'Wie politisch ist Postdramatisches Theater?', p. 31.

11 Cathy Turner and S. K. Behrndt, *Dramaturgy and Performance.* Houndmills: Palgrave, 2008.

12 See Gad Kaynar, 'Pragmatic Dramaturgy: The Text as Context as Text', *Theatre Research International*, Vol. 31, No. 3 (2006), p. 252.

13 'The implied spectator' is the addressed and referred to dramatis persona of the intended spectator as s/he emerges from the rhetorical system of the performative event. See: Gad Kaynar, 'Audience and Response-Programming Research and the Methodology of the Implied Spectator', in Günther Berghaus (ed.), *New Approaches to Theatre Studies and Performance Analysis.* Tübingen: Max Niemeyer, 2001, pp. 159–73.

14 Bettina Milz, 'Conglomerates: Dramaturgy for Dance and Dramaturgy of the Body', *Teatron*, No. 28 (summer 2010), pp. 82–3. (Hebrew).

15 Patrice Pavis, 'Introduction: Towards a Theory of Interculturalism in Theatre?', in Patrice Pavis (ed.), *The Intercultural Performance Reader*. London: Routledge, 1996, p. 7.

16 Pavis, Ibid., p. 9.

17 Richard Schechner, *Performance Theory*. New York: Routledge, 1988, p. 177.

18 Jean-Pierre Sarrazac, *L'Avenir du Drame*. Belfort: Circé, 1998, p. 191.

19 Augusto Boal, *Games for Actors and Non-Actors*. London: Routledge, 1992, p. xxx.

20 Primavesi, 'Theater/ Politik – Kontexte und Beziehungen', p. 63.

21 These interviews have been made in the context of an Israel Science Foundation research, and were analysed in my seminars at Tel Aviv University's Department of Theatre Arts. This essay, partly is a radically revised version of my article: 'Dramaturgical translation in the post-dramatic era: Between fidelity to the source text and the target "dramaturg-as-text"', *Journal of Adaptation in Film & Performance*, Vol. 4, No. 3 (2011), pp. 225–40.

22 Gad Kaynar, 'A Prophet, and Not in His Town: With and About Jossi Wieler', *Teatron*, Vol. 8 (May 2002), p. 35. (Hebrew). For further reading on the contemporary German theatre, refer to: Carlson, *Theatre is More Beautiful than War*, and to the article of Matthias Naumann, 'Trials and Errors: On the German-Speaking Theatre Today', *Teatron*, Vol. 32 (2011), pp. 56–8. (Hebrew).

23 Primavesi, 'Theater/ Politik – Kontexte und Beziehungen', pp. 41–2.

24 *Theater heute* No. 8/9 (August–September 2009), p. 18.

25 Ibid.

26 Naumann, 'Trials and Errors: On the German-Speaking Theatre Today', p. 59.

27 Oren Laor and Niv Schoenfeld, 'Mud and Memory', *Teatron*, No. 32 (2011), pp. 87–90. (Hebrew).

28 As typical examples for these traditional notions see for example: Eivor Martinus, 'Translating Scandinavian Drama', in David Johnston (ed.), *Stages of Translation*. Bath: Absolute Classics, 1996, p. 110; Egil Törnqvist, *Transposing Drama: Studies in Representation*. Houndmills: Macmillan, 1991, pp. 7–8.

29 Gad Kaynar, 'Pragmatic Dramaturgy: Text as Context as Text', *Theatre Research International*, Vol. 31, No. 3 (2006), pp. 245–59.

30 Richard Schechner, *Performance Theory*, p. 77.

31 Hermann Beil, interview with Gad Kaynar, Berlin, 10 February 2005.

32 'When I consider a play for production – be it a Shakespeare, an Ibsen, a Goethe or the like – I might find the structure that the author devised in order to be adhered to interesting. . . . But if I fail to find any kind of actual meaning in the play, then I would not produce the play'. Hans-Joachim, interview with Gad Kaynar, Munich, 4 July 2003.

33 Turner and Behrndt, *Dramaturgy and Performance,* p. 175.

34 Stefanie Carp, interview with Gad Kaynar, Zurich, 22 June 2003.

35 Carlson, *Theatre Is More Beautiful Than War*, pp. 117–18.

36   Ibid., p. 127.

37   Stefanie Carp, interview with Gad Kaynar, Zurich, 22 June 2003.

38   Irina Szodruch, interview with Gad Kaynar, Tel Aviv, 6 August 2009.

39   Bettina Milz, 'Conglomerates: Dramaturgy for Dance and Dramaturgy of the Body', p. 84.

40   André Lepecki, cited in Turner and Behrndt, *Dramaturgy and Performance*, p. 178.

41   What seems to be a radically novel practice might be seen as echoing practices of ancient ritual theatre through which the 'memory of the production' is conveyed by the counterparts of Western dramaturgs as in the Ramlila of Ramnagar in which, as Schechner reports: 'The directors of the spectacle, the *vyases*, stand behind the performers, open regiebuchs in hand, correcting word and actions: making certain that everything happens according to the book.' Richard Schechner, *Over Under and Around: Essays in Performance and Culture*. Calcutta, New Delhi: Seagull Books, 2004, p. 189.

42   Tilman Raabke, interview with Gad Kaynar, Munich, 6 June 2003.

43   Leslie Hill and Hellen Paris (eds), *Performance and Place*. Houndmills: Palgrave, 2006, p. 3.

44   Carl Hegemann, interview with Gad Kaynar, Tel Aviv, 26 May 2008.

45   Richard Schechner, *Performance Studies: An Introduction*. New York: Routledge, 2002, p. 28.

46   Victor Turner, *Drama, Fields, and Metaphors*. Ithaca: Cornell University Press, 1974, pp. 37–41.

47   Richard Schechner, 'Who Is Rama?', in Lance Gharavi (ed.), *Religion, Theatre, and Performance: Acts of Faith*. New York: Routledge, 2012, p. 190.

48   Carl Hegemann, interview with Gad Kaynar, Tel Aviv, 26 May 2008.

49   Heiner Müller, *Material: Texte und Kommentare (Material: Texts and Commentaries)*. Leipzig: Reclam, 1990, p. 19.

50   Gad Kaynar, 'German Theatre, Summer 2003: Journey Impressions', p. 30.

51   Stefanie Carp, interview with Gad Kaynar, Zurich, 22 June 2003.

52   Primavesi, 'Theater/ Politik – Kontexte und Beziehungen', p. 47.

53   Heiner Müller, 'Gespräch mit Ruth Berghaus und Sigrid Neef (1987)'. In *Gesammelte Irrtümer* 2. Frankfurt/Main, 1990, p. 73.

Chapter 7

1   For analyses of the relations between theatre, architecture, and space, see for example: Marvin Carlson, *Places of Performance: The Semiotics of Theatre Architecture*. Ithaca: Cornell University Press, 1993; Gay McAuley, *Space in Performance: Making Meaning in the Theatre*. Ann Arbor: University of

Michigan Press, 2000; Mike Pearson, *Site Specific Performance*. New York: Palgrave Macmillan, 2010; and Erika Fischer-Lichte and Benjamin Wihstutz (eds), *Performance and the Politics of Space: Theatre and Topology*. New York: Routledge, 2012.

2 Nicolas Bourriaud, *Relational Aesthetics*. Dijon: Les Presses du Réel, 1998, p. 14.

3 David Seamon, 'Merleau-Ponty, Perception, and Environmental Embodiment: Implications for Architectural and Environmental Studies', a chapter prepared for: Rachel McCann and Patricia M. Locke (eds), *Carnal Echoes: Merleau-Ponty and the Flesh of Architecture*, forthcoming 2014; available at http://www.academia.edu/948750/Merleau-Ponty_Perception_and_Environmental_Embodiment_Implications_for_Architectural_and_Environmental_Studies (accessed 15 April 2013).

4 Henri Lefebvre, *The Production of Space*, trans. Donald Nicholson Smith. Oxford: Blackwell, 1991, p. 101.

5 For discussions of socially engaged art and performance in relation to social space, see for example Shannon Jackson, *Social Works: Performing Art, Supporting Publics*. New York: Routledge, 2011; Claire Bishop, *Artificial Hells: Participatory Art and the Politics of Spectatorship*. London: Verso, 2012; Martha Rosler, 'Place, Position, Power, Politics', in Carol Becker (ed.), *The Subversive Imagination: Artists, Society, and Social Responsibility*. New York: Routledge, 1994, pp. 55–76. See also Eva Brenner's essay in this volume.

6 The term 'meitzag' in Hebrew conjoins two words, installation art 'meitzav' and theatre performance 'hatzaga', and means 'performance art'. It was coined by art critic Gideon Ofrat.

7 See: http://www.miklat209.org.il/. See also: *(?) Ensemble 209: Contemporary Theater; Artistic Director Tamar Raban*, Catalogue Marking 25 Years to Shelter 209, ed. Yaron David. Tel Aviv: Performance Art Platform, 2012. About Raban see Roselee Goldberg, *Performance: Live Art since the 60s*. New York: Thames and Hudson, 2004, p. 59.

8 See more on this in M. Ben-Peshat and S. Sitton, 'Visual Literacy for Deciphering Cultural Identity: The New Central Bus Station in Tel Aviv', in Phil Fitzsimmons and Barbara McKenzie (eds), *Refocusing the Vision, the Viewer and Viewing Through an Interdisciplinary Lens*. Oxford: Inter-Disciplinary Press, 2010, pp. 69–78; and M. Ben-Pashat and S. Sitton, 'Glocalized New Age Spirituality: A Mental Map of the New Central Bus Station in Tel-Aviv, Deciphered through its Visual Codes and based on Ethno-Visual Research', *Journal of Visual Literacy*, Vol. 30, No. 2 (2011), pp. 65–91.

9 Sharon Rotbard, *White City, Black City*. Tel Aviv: Babel, 2005, p. 275. (Hebrew).

10 Kulanu omrim: toda, bevakasha, slicha; Am yafé am echad.

11 *Ensemble 209 The Second Law of Thermodynamics*, Program, p. 16.

12 Ibid., p. 5.

13 For an English version of the performance text, see: Tamar Raban and Guy Gutman, *Old Wives' Tales: Rise Woman and Make Us a Cake*, in Sharon Aronson-Lehavi (ed.), *Wanderers and Other Israeli Plays*. New York: Seagull Books, 2009, pp. 337–62; For a discussion of the performance from a feminist perspective, see Sharon Aronson-Lehavi, *Gender and Feminism in Modern Theatre*. Raanana: Open University Press, 2013, pp. 169–78; (Hebrew).

14 Michel Foucault, *Of Other Spaces*, trans. Jay Miskowiec, *Diacritics* (Spring 1986), p. 24.

Chapter 8

1 See PM web-sites: http://publicmovementenglish.blogspot.co.il/ & www.publicmovement.org.

2 See Claire Bishop, *Artificial Hells: Participatory Art and the Politics of Spectatorship*. London: Verso, 2012, pp. 1–40.

3 Ibid., p. 3.

4 Ibid., pp. 49–66.

5 Ibid., pp. 11, 77–104.

6 See: http://www.rebrandingeuropeanmuslims.org/; http://www.afterall.org/online/artists-at-work-public-movement.

7 In this regard, PM contrasts with other notable collective Israeli performance groups, such as the Zik Group and Where Is Dana. Zik Group was founded in 1985 and is still active. Its extensive work is documented and discussed in Daphna Ben-Shaul, *Zik Group, Twenty Years of Work*. Jerusalem: Keter, 2005 (Hebrew). Where Is Dana, a collective of artists, started to co-create in 2004. See Dror Harari, 'Performing Homage: Towards a New Order of Parody'. *Assaph: Studies in the Theatre*, Vol. 24 (2010), pp. 17–34.

8 My special gratitude to Richard Schechner for his comments on an early draft, mainly regarding the ceremonial performances, first presented under the title 'Public Movement and the Ceremonial Crisis' at the RS & PS conference at Haifa University, 2010.

9 I am deeply grateful to Saar Székely, a member of PM since its inception, for an ongoing dialogue about the group's work and for providing additional information about the group's performances.

10 In 2009–12, *Also Thus!* was performed at Lodz, Hamburg, Berlin and Santarcangelo, Italy, in addition to Israeli venues. In 2012 the performance took place at the square in front of the Tel Aviv Museum of Art as part of PM's fifth anniversary.

11 The Acco Festival was then artistically directed by Daniella Michaeli. For an overview of this festival, mainly under the directorship of Atay Citron, 2001–04, see Dorit Yerushalmi, 'From a Transient to a Resident: The Acco Festival of Alternative Theatre, 2001-2004'. *TDR*, Vol. 51, No. 4 (T 196, Winter 2007), pp. 47–67.

12 A precedent to this act was PM's first action *Accident* (2006) performed as a street intervention (without uniforms). It was followed by *Ceremony* (2007) which was elaborated into *Also Thus!*. In Germany, as part of a series of actions titled *Performing Politics for Germany* (2009), under the auspices of Hebbel-Am-Ufer (HAU) Theater, Berlin, the *Accident* ended in a police arrest.

13 See for example: Bishop 2012, pp. 18–26; 275–83.

14 The most familiar reference to this issue is Walter Benjamin's discussion of the relationship between the political and the aesthetic, particularly in his epilogue to *The Work of Art in the Age of Technological Reproduction* (1936), where he distinguishes between Communist politicization of art and Fascist aestheticization of political life.

15 Eyal Naveh and Esther Yogev, *Histories: Towards a Dialogue with the Israeli Past*. Tel Aviv: Babel (Hebrew), 2002, p. 36.

16 In Mircea Eliade's terms, *illo tempore* is the sacred realm of the first days or the beginning of things, when a ritual was first performed by a god, an ancient father or a hero. See Mircea Eliade, *The Myth of Eternal Return: Or, Cosmos and History*. Princeton: Princeton University Press, [1949] 1991, pp. 1–48.

17 PM does not declare itself a micronation, a term denoting a group that bases its activity on national characteristics but is not a legitimate nation under international law. In 2010 PM collaborated with the Slovenian artistic collective Irwin of NSK (Neue Slowenische Kunst), a self-defined micronation whose delegates meet representatives of the State and the military in the countries they visit. In Israel, sponsored by the Israeli Center for Digital Art in Holon, PM was invited as a self-declared representative of the State, and created an official welcoming ceremony.

18 See Michel Foucault, 'The Birth of Biopolitics', in Paul Rabinow (ed.), *The Essential Works of Michel Foucault, 1954-1984: Ethics, Subjectivity and Truth*. Vol. 1, trans. Robert Hurley et al. New York: The New Press, [1979] 1997, pp. 73–9.

19 See for example, Sylvère Lotringer and Paul Virilio, *The Accident of Art*, trans. Michael Taormina. New York: Semiotext(e), 2005; Paul Virilio, *The Original Accident*, trans. Julie Rose. Cambridge: Polity Press, 2007. See also Rokem's view of the notion of 'accident', bringing together the philosophical and performative spheres and focusing on Benjamin and Brecht in Freddie Rokem, *Philosophers & Thespians: Thinking Performance*. Stanford: Stanford University press, 2010, pp. 141–76.

20 Some verbal acts: the performers' bodies form the word 'NO' on the ground. They light up the fire inscription 'Now'. In Hebrew, the title of the performance, *Also Thus!* (*Gam Kach*) echoes the slogan 'Rak Kach', that is, 'Only Thus', of the Etzel – a paramilitary nationalist underground organization founded in Palestine in 1931 by Ze'ev Jabotinsky and his followers. The slogan has since accumulated additional meaning, for it was also used by Meir Kahane's Kach movement, outlawed in 1988 due to its fanatic right-wing politics. Ironically, the syllables 'Rak Kach' are also present in the name of the radical left-wing party Rakach. PM's title is therefore multivalent and doubt-instilling.

21 Translated from the Hebrew performance.

22 Eventually, the festival took place on a small scale several months later.

23 Zaka (Hebrew abbreviation for Disaster Victim Identification) is a voluntary organization activated since 1994 by Jewish Orthodox who assist the police and rescue forces.

24 Referring to emergency arenas and to the 9/11 Jihad and terrorism as performances, Schechner stresses an element of intentional specularity shared by terrorists and media alike: 'Things happen – but reporting and displaying the events and their aftermaths feed back into the events themselves' (Richard Schechner, *Performance Studies: An Introduction*. New York and London: Routledge, 2002, p. 274).

25 See Boris Groys, 'The Fate of Art in the Age of Terror', in Bruno Latour and Peter Weibel (eds.), *Making Things Public: Atmospheres of Democracy*. Cambridge, MA: MIT Press, 2005, pp. 970–7.

26 See Jacques Rancière, 'The Emancipated Spectator'. *The Emancipated Spectator*, trans. Gregory Elliot. London and New York: Verso, [2008] 2009, pp. 1–23.

27 In 2008 PM performed *The Lodz Actions* at the Festival of Dialogue of Four Cultures. In the same year, they created an action called *The 86th Anniversary of the Assassination of President Gabriel Narutowicz by the Painter Eligiusz Niewiadomski* (2008) at the Zacheta National Gallery in Warsaw.

28 The work was commissioned by Nowy Teatr in Warsaw in cooperation with the Zamek Ujazdowski contemporary art center.

29 See Jürgen Habermas, *The Structural Transformation of the Public Sphere: An Inquiry into a Category of Bourgeois Society*, trans. Thomas Burger. Cambridge, MA: MIT Press, [1962] 1989, pp. 1–26.

30 In keeping with Fraser's critique, public sphere can also include discrimination of counter-publics that are not associated with the bourgeois system. See Nancy Fraser, 'Rethinking the Public Sphere: A Contribution to the Critique of Actually Existing Democracy', in Craig Calhaun (ed.), *Habermas and the Public Sphere*. Cambridge, MA: MIT Press, 1992, pp. 90–142.

31 The police refused to participate in *University Exercise* on the Tel Aviv campus.

32 When performed in New York 2011, at Washington Square Park and Union Square, co-presented by the New Museum and Artis cooperation, Dana Yahalomi gave *Positions* a political context by cooperating with Occupy Wall Street movement.

Chapter 9

1 For a brief summary of Weinberg's work, see the Guardian obituary of 4 January 2000, http://www.guardian.co.uk/news/2000/jan/04/guardianobituaries.

Chapter 10

1   Jo Tollebeek, 'Historical Representation and the Nation-State in Romantic Belgium (1830-1850)', *Journal of the History of Ideas*, Vol. 59, No. 2 (4/1998), pp. 329–53.

2   Henri Pirenne, 'The Formation and Constitution of the Burgundian State (Fifteenth and Sixteenth Centuries)', *The American Historical Review*, Vol. 14, No. 3 (4/1909), pp. 477–502. Henri Pirenne is sometimes more a historical 'mythographer' than a scientific historian. He devoted most of his professional life to the genealogy of a Belgian nation after the Treaty of Verdun (843), in seven volumes of *Histoire de la Belgique*, written between 1900 and 1932.

3   Benedict Anderson, *Imagined Communities*. London: Verso, 1991, pp. 67–82.

4   A comprehensive account of this historical process is given in Els Witte, Jan Craeybeckx and Alain Meynen, *Political History of Belgium from 1830 onwards*. Antwerp: ASP, 2009.

5   Elodie Fabre, *Belgian Federalism in a Comparative Perspective*. Leuven: VIVES, 2009, accessed 6 February 2013, http://www.econ.kuleuven.be/VIVES/publicaties/discussionpapers/DP/DP2009/vivesdiscussionpaper5.pdf. Régis Dandoy, Geoffroy Matagne and Caroline Van Wynsberghe, 'The Future of Belgian Federalism through the Eyes of the Political Actors', paper presented at the ECPR Potsdam General Conference, 10–12 September2009.

6   Joseph Roach, *Cities of the Dead. Circum-Atlantic Performance*. New York: Columbia University Press, 1996, pp. 2–3.

7   Marc Reynebeau, *Onze kant van het bed. Mythes van de Belgische politieke crisis* [Our side of the bed. Myths about the Belgian political crisis]. Leuven: Van Halewyck, 2009, pp. 133–80.

8   Georges Duby, *The Age of the Cathedrals. Art and Society 980-1420*. Chicago: University of Chicago Press, 1983.

9   Jean Duvignaud, *Sociologie du théâtre. Sociologie des ombres collectives* [Sociology of the theatre. Sociology of collective shadows']. Paris: PUF, 1965, pp. 85–100.

10 Jean-Marie Apostolidès, *Le roi-machine. Spectacle et politique au temps de Louis XIV* [The King-Machine. Spectacle and politics in the age of Louis XIV]. Paris: Éditions de Minuit, 1981, pp. 133–59.

11 Steven N. Zwicker, *Lines of Authority. Politics and English Literary Culture 1649-1689*. Ithaca: Cornell University Press, 1993, pp. 91–3; and Klaas Tindemans, 'Nature, Desire and the Law. On Libertinism and Early Modern Legal Theory', *Journal for Early Modern Cultural Studies*, Vol. 12, No. 2 (Spring 2012), pp. 132–45.

12 Jay Fliegelman, *Declaring Independence. Jefferson, Natural Language & the Culture of Performance*. Stanford: Stanford University Press, 1993, pp. 89–94.

13 Klaas Tindemans, 'Représentation théâtrale et représentation démocratique. Notes sur la Révolution française, la théâtralité et la souveraineté populaire' [Theatrical representation and democratic representation. Notes on the French Revolution, theatricality and popular sovereignty] in Francine Maier-Schaeffer, Christiane Page and Cécile Vaissié (eds), *La Révolution mise en scène*. Rennes: Presses Universitaires de Rennes, 2012, pp. 109–18.

14 Walter Benjamin, *The Work of Art in the Age of Technical Reproducibility*. Cambridge, MA: Harvard University Press, 2008, pp. 19–55.

15 Timothy Raphael, *The President Electric. Ronald Reagan and the Politics of Performance*. Ann Arbor: University of Michigan Press, 2009, pp. 1–3.

16 Marc Swyngedouw, Koen Abts and Jaak Billiet, De verschuivingen in het stemgedrag 2007–2010 voor de Kamer in Vlaanderen. Analyse op basis van het postelectorale verkiezingsonderzoek 2010 [Shifts in electoral behaviour 2007–2010 for the Chamber in Flanders. Analysis based upon post-electoral research 2010]. Leuven: ISPO, 2012.

17 Bruno De Wever, *Greep naar de macht. Vlaams-nationalisme en Nieuwe Orde: het VNV 1933-1945* [To Seize Power. Flemish Nationalism and the New Order: the VNV 1933-1945]. Tielt: Lannoo, 1995.

18 Aline Sax, *Voor Vlaanderen, Volk en Führer. De motivatie en het wereldbeeld van Vlaamse collaborateurs tijdens de Tweede Wereldoorlog 1940-1945* [For Flanders, the People and the Führer. Motivation and Worldview of Flemish Collaborators during World War II 1940-1945]. Antwerp: Manteau, 2012.

19 Thomas Crombez, 'De arrière-garde in Vlaanderen: het katholieke massaspel tijdens het interbellum' [The *arrière-garde* in Flanders: the Catholic Mass Pageant between the Wars], *Etcetera*, Vol. 28, No. 120 (2010), pp. 6–10.

20 Bart De Wever 'Hedendaagse kunst' [Contemporary Art] in *De Standaard*, 8 November 2011. He writes: 'Today art is hardly able to touch the community, no matter how stubbornly some artists try with shock-effects. . . . A lot of contemporary art has withdrawn into a closed reservation, where art holds together a restricted circle, separate and distinguished from society.'

21 Bart De Wever, 'Wat Lisa Simpson ons over onszelf leert' [What Lisa Simpson teaches us about ourselves], *De Standaard*, 24 March 2012. In this essay, he defends historical myths as useful tools to affirm collective (political) identities, just as Lisa Simpson ultimately kept silent after discovering the local hero of Springfield was a fake.

22 Judith Butler extends the sociological denotation of the concept of *habitus* – coined by Pierre Bourdieu – in a bodily and thus performative direction: '. . . this bodily *habitus* is generated by the tacit normativity that governs the social game in which the embodied subject acts. In this sense, the body appropriates the rule-like character of the habitus through playing by those rules in the context of a given

social field'. See Judith Butler, *Excitable Speech. A Politics of the Performative*. New York: Routledge, 1997, p. 154. As if to prove that his *habitus* is not only the site of his sharp and witty speech, Bart De Wever lost more than 90 pounds of weight in four months, pursuing a heavily mediatized diet.

23 Maarten Hajer and Justus Uitermark, 'Performing Authority: Discursive Politics after the Assassination of Theo van Gogh', *Public Administration*, Vol. 86, No. 1 (2008), pp. 1–15.

24 On 9 July 2012, 2 days before Flanders' semi-official national holiday, De Wever held a speech at De Warande, a prestigious club of Flemish industrialists, in the heart of the Brussels governmental quarter. He combined an updated rhetoric of *kaakslagflamingantisme* ('slap-in-the-face-nationalism': every compromise is a defeat) with a message for deregulation and minimal governance. So he managed, by using the right speech and the right themes in the right place, to get more media space than the official speech of the Minister-President of Flanders, Kris Peeters. See Wim Winckelmans, 'Vlamingen vieren verdeeld' [Divided Flemish celebrations], *De Standaard*, 10 July 2012 and Bart De Wever, 'Alleen het gesproken woord telt/ De staat van Vlaanderen' [Only Speech Counts/The State of Flanders]. Brussel: N-VA, 2012, accessed 6 February 2012, http://www.n-va. be/files/default/generated/toespraak/11julitoespraak_de_warande_-_bart_de_ wever.pdf.

25 De Wever even sued this newspaper for libel when a guest-writer called him a 'negationist' – meaning the negation of the Judeocide, which is punishable under Belgian law – and his party sued the paper for hate speech. For a comment on these qualifications and De Wever's position, see Luckas Vander Taelen, 'De schizofrenie van *Le Soir*. Franstaligen kijken niet graag naar hun eigen gebreken' [The Schizophrenia of *Le Soir*. French Speakers Don't Like Looking at Their Own Faults], *De Standaard*, 25 March 2010.

26 Raymond Williams, 'Drama in a Dramatized Society', in Lizbeth Goodman and Jane de Gay (eds), *The Routledge Reader in Politics and Performance*. New York: Routledge, 2000, pp. 55–9. This is the transcript text of Williams' inaugural speech as Professor of Drama at Cambridge University in 1974.

27 Steven Samyn and Tine Peeters (eds), *De gevangenen van de Wetstraat* [The prisoners of the *Wetstraat*]. Ghent: Borgerhoff & Lamberigts, 2011, pp. 67–87.

28 Jörgen Oosterwaal, *Johan Vande Lanotte, dagboek van een politieke crisis* [Johan Vande Lanotte, Diary of a Political Crisis]. Antwerp: De Bezige Bij, 2012. Oosterwaal edited the revealing diary of Johan Vande Lanotte, now deputy Prime Minister, about this period. Bart De Wever wrote a foreword.

29 Victor Turner, *From Ritual to Theatre. The Human Seriousness of Play*. New York: PAJ Publications, 1982, pp. 70–1.

30 Hans Kelsen, *Vom Wesen und Wert der Demokratie* [About Essence and Value of Democracy]. Aalen: Scientia Verlag, 1929/1981, pp. 14–16. Kelsen demonstrates

how a representative democracy can only function properly if the unity of the nation is conceived as a mere 'normative postulate', not as a sociological fact or political objective. He wrote of course at a time when nationalist irredentism, in Germany and Austria in the 1920s, sought to revenge the humiliation of Versailles.

31 Marc Hooghe, 'Slechte Vlamingen bestaan niet' [Bad Flemings Do Not Exist], *De Standaard*, 14 October 2010.

32 B. Guy Peters, *Institutional Theory in Political Science: The 'New Institutionalism'*. New York: Continuum, 2005, pp. 123–38; and Guido Dierickx, *De logica van de politiek* [The Logic of Politics]. Antwerp: Garant, 2005, pp. 46–7.

33 Chantal Mouffe, *On the Political*. London: Routledge, 2005, pp. 19–21.

34 Alastair Campbell and Bill Hagerty, *The Alastair Campbell Diaries. Volume Two: Power and the People 1997-1999*. London: Hutchinson, 2011, pp. 309–58. Alastair Campbell was the (in)famous communications director of former British Prime Minister Tony Blair.

35 Hans Lindahl, 'Sovereignty and Symbolization', *Rechtstheorie*, Vol. 28 (1997), pp. 347–71. Lindahl focuses on the notion of 'symbolization', as it is reflected upon by Ernst Cassirer.

Chapter 11

1 Such is the main thesis of my book, published in April 2010, just before the crash: *Teatra polskie. Historie* (Theatres of Poland. The Histories). Warsaw: PWN, 2010.

2 See: Dariusz Kosiński, *Teatra polskie. Rok katastrofy* ('Theatres of Poland. The year of the catastrophy'), Instytut Teatralny im. Z. Raszewskiego, Warszawa 2013.

3 See for example the interview with Bronisław Komorowski for Radio Zet on 23 June 2010, online: http://wiadomosci.onet.pl/raporty/wybory-prezydenckie-2010/ komorowski-kaczynski-przebiera-sie-to-teatr-polity,1,3548039,wiadomosc.html.

4 In Polish, the Word 'peace' sounds the same as 'PiS' – the abbreviation of the name of the party 'Prawo i Sprawiedliwość' (Law and Justice).

5 Such commentaries were of course formulated mainly by Kaczyński's opponents. For example, in a radio interview given on 23 June 2010, Bronisław Komorowski stated that Kaczyński was disguising himself and playing 'political theatre' (see on-line: http://wiadomosci.onet.pl/raporty/wybory-prezydenckie-2010/ komorowski-kaczynski-przebiera-sie-to-teatr-polity,1,3548039,wiadomosc.html).

6 The Polish word for duck is 'kaczka', which echoes the beginning of the president's surname. This is the reason for the brothers' collective nickname, 'Kaczory' – the ducks.

7 Joseph Roach, *The Cities of the Dead. The Circum-Atlantic Performances*. New York: Columbia University Press, 1996, p. 3.

8   Bronisław Wildstein, 'Polska kultura jest katolicka' (Polish Culture is Catholic),
    an interview by Adam Puchejda, *Znak*, Vol. 267 (April 2011), p. 9.

9   Ibid., p. 10.

10 See: Benedict Anderson, *Imagined Communities: Reflections on the Origin and
    Spread of Nationalism*. London: Verso, 1983 (revised edition). On the role of the
    performances in inventing the nation and the national tradition, see: *The Invention
    of Tradition*, ed. Eric Hobsbawm and Terence Ranger. Cambridge University Press,
    1983.

11 Jon McKenzie, *Perform or Else: From Discipline to Performance*. London and
    New York: Routledge, 2001, p. 18.

Chapter 12

1   See: 'Manifest for a Theatre of Empowerment' (2006–09).

2   Joseph Beuys. In: Clara Bodemann-Ritter (Hg.), *Joseph Beuys, Jeder Mensch ein
    Künstler [Every Man an Artist]*. Ullstein: Press, 1997, p. 59.

3   Richard Schechner, 'Towards a Poetics of Performance', in *Performance Theory*,
    revised an expanded edition. New York: Routledge, 2003, pp. 153–86/170.

4   Victor Turner, *Dramas, Fields, and Metaphors*. Ithaca: Cornell University Press,
    1975; Richard Schechner, *From Ritual to Theatre*. New York: Performing Arts
    Journal Press, 1982.

5   Richard Schechner, 'From Ritual to Theatre and Back', in *Essays on Performance
    Theory 1970-1976*. New York: Drama Book Specialists, 1977, pp. 63–98/89 (First
    published 1974).

6   Schechner, *op. cit.*, p. 170. Claude Lévi-Strauss, *The Raw and the Cooked*.
    New York: Harper & Row, 1969.

7   See Schechner 1977, Ibid., p. 170.

8   See discussion on post-dramatics below.

9   See 'Transformance'-concept for political theatre (2014–17) in 'Red Vienna'
    social housing projects; see also Claudia von Werlhof, *Der unerkannte Kern der
    Krise*. Die Moderne als Er-Schöpfung der Welt: Arun Verlag, 2012, pp. 9–16.
    www.experimentaltheatre.com.

10 See discussion of the 'Theatre Reform' below.

11 See Maria Mies, Krieg ohne Grenzen 2005, p. 234. See Claudia von Werlhof,
    *Alternativen zur neoliberalen Globalisierung oder Die Globalisierung des
    Neoliberalismus und seine Folgen*. Wien: Picus Verlag, 2007, pp. 67–8. Jean Ziegler,
    Die Neuen Herrscher der Welt. München: Bertelsmann, 2002.

12 See Maria Mies, *Krieg ohne Grenzen*. Köln: PapyRossa, 2005, p. 234.

13 See Note 1.

14 Augusto Boal, *Theatre of the Oppressed*. London: Pluto Press, 1979, p. 17.

15 See Leitbild zur Wiener Theatrereform, 2002; Freies Theatre in Wien, Reformvorschläge zur Förderung Freier Gruppen im Bereich Darstellende Kunst, Wien 2003. See www.wien.gv.at/kultur/abteilung/pdf/leitbild-theatrereform.pdf, www.wien.gv.at/kultur/abteilung/pdf/konzeptfoerderung.pdf.

16 See reform-commentaries of Armin Anders, 2003–04, to appear in the new book 'Alternative Theatre 2000: Between adjustment and resistance' (2013).

17 Eva Brenner, 'Wie frei ist freies Theatre?', will appear in *Alternatives Theatre 2000*, ed. Eva Brenner. Vienna, 2013.

18 See Robert Sommer, 'Für immer auf Achse?', in Augustin, Nr. 305, 2011, p. 25.

19 See Eva Brenner, 'Manifest for a Theatre of Empowerment' (2006–09), www.experimentaltheatre.com; see gift, Zeitschrift für Freies Theatre 03, 2011. P. 14.20.

20 See Eva Brenner, 'Manifest for a Theatre of Empowerment' (2006–09), www.experimentaltheatre.com; see gift, Zeitschrift für Freies Theatre 03, 2011. P. 14.20.

21 Projects are funded by the city of Vienna, the Ministry of Culture, the district, and private sponsors. With a yearly budget of about €80–100,000, the company attracts over 2,000 spectators each year, with an additional 100,000 *via* community TV.

22 National government intercultural exchange and educational programme, focused on Eastern and Southern Europe.

23 See concept for Asylcafé 2008, submitted to *KulturKontakt* Austria, www.experimentaltheatre.com.

24 See Note 1.

25 See Eva Brenner, '*Ausbruch aus dem Off*, in Economy, Nr. 73, 2009, [Kommentar der Anderen], p. 33.

26 Press releases of Auf Achse', www.experimentaltheatre.com.

27 See programmes of On Axis 2011 and 2012, Ibid.

28 See 'Auszeichnng für Fleischerei', Wiener Bezirkszeitung, Nr. 44, 2010, n.p.

29 See Robert Sommer, 'Eine Fleischerei auf Achse', Eva Brenner will zum 'Aufschwung des politischen Theaters' beitragen', Augustin, 28 July 2010, pp. 26–8.

30 See Note 1. Most successful was the discussion-series 'KunstimDialog' (ArtinDialogue), a regular cultural-political programme on local television in cooperation with artists, civil society and community groups, political scientists, and media experts curated by Eva Brenner and socio-economist, Peter Kreisky (2004–10).

31 Peter Brook (1968), *The Empty Space*. New York: Penguin, 2008, p. 93.

32 Hans-Thies Lehmann, *Postdramatisches Theatre* [post-dramatic Theatre]. Frankfurt/Main: Verlag der Autoren, 1999; see Hans-Thies Lehmann, *Postdramatic Theatre*, trans. and with an introduction by Karen Jürs-Munby. London and New York: Routledge, 2006.

33 Post-structuralism was formulated as label by American academics to denote the heterogeneous works of a prominent French and some American intellectuals in the 1960s and '70s (Roland Barthes, Jacques Derrida, Jean Baudrillard, Michel Foucault, Gilles Deleuze, Judith Butler, and Julia Kristeva) closely related to postmodernism. See Jacques Derrida, *Grammatologie*, 1983, *Dissemination*, 1995; Jean Baudrillard, *Simulacres et Simulation*, 1981; see also: Francis Fukuyama, *The End of History?*, see Richard Schechner, *The End of Humanism*, 1982.

34 Hans-Thies Lehmann 1999, Ibid., pp. 30–1.

35 Ibid., p. 31.

36 Ibid., pp. 466–9.

37 Das politische Schreiben. Essays zu Theatretexten. (2002), Hans-Thies Lehmann, see Hans-Thies Lehmann, *Das Politische Schreiben* [Writing the Political]. Theatre der Zeit, Recherchen 12, Berlin 2002, p. 12.

38 Guy Debord, Kommentare, II, *Die Gesellschaft des Spektakels*. Berlin 1986 [La Société du Spectacle].

39 Ibid., pp. 14–15.

40 Ibid., p. 19.

41 Ibid., pp. 16–17.

42 (35) Ibid., p. 15, quote by György Lukács (1885–1971).

43 Jan Deck, in 'Politisch Theatre machen', in *Politisch Theatre machen*, Hrsg. Jan Deck und Angelika Sieburg, transcript Verlag, 2011; S. 11–28, S. 11/14. See Nikolaus Müller-Schöll, André Schallenberg, and Mayte Zimmermann, *Performing Politics*, Politisch Kunst machen nach dem 20. Jahrhundert, transcript Verlag, Bielefeld, 2012, pp. 7 and 136, pp. 136–48.

44 Jan Deck, in 'Politisch Theatre machen', Eine Einleitung, II. Künstlerische Strategien, in: *Politisch Theatre machen*, Hrsg. Jan Deck und Angelika Sieburg, transcript Verlag, 2011; S. 11–28, S. 14.

45 Ibid., p. 26.

46 See Ernst Bloch *Das Prinzip Hoffnung* (3 vols.: 1938–47), *The Principle of Hope*, MIT Press, 1986.

47 See Lehmann 1999, p. 459; see also Lehmann 2002, p. 13.

48 See *Performing Politics*, 2012, Ibid.; see Hans-Thies Lehmann, *Das Politische Schreiben*, Ibid., p. 13.

Chapter 13

1 As recounted by Simon Critchley, 'The Stone', *New York Times*, 2 January 2011, http:is/opinionator.blogs.nytimes.com/2011/01/02/stoned/.

2 The two archival photographs are from the WWI collection of the Photothèque of the BDIC-Musée d'histoire contemporaine. Musée des Invalides, Paris, France.

3 Susan Sontag, *Regarding the Pain of Others*. New York: Farrar, Straus and Giroux, 2003.

4 René Girard, *Violence and the Sacred*. Baltimore: The Johns Hopkins University Press, 1977, p. 36.

5 Smadar Lavie, Kirin Narayan and Renato Rosaldo (eds), 'Ritual, Violence, and Creativity', *Creativity/Anthropology*. Ithaca: Cornell University Press, 1993, p. 303.

6 Richard Schechner, *The future of ritual: Writings on Culture and Performance*. London and New York: Routledge, 1993, p. 256.

7 Samuel Hynes, *The Soldier's Tale, Bearing Witness to Modern War*. New York: Viking, 1997.

8 Ian Maxwell, 'The Ritualization of Performance (Studies)', in Graham St John (ed.), *Victor Turner and Contemporary Cultural Performance*. New York and Oxford: Berghahn Books, 2008, pp. 59–60.

9 Maxwell, Ibid., 60.

10 This exhilarating word is British author Salman Rushdie's, as he describes his own response to the Iranian *fatwa* declared on his life. 'I decided', he coolly remarked to a packed New York audience overseen by scores of police, 'to treat it with an ignoral'.

11 Johannes Fabian, *Anthropology With an Attitude: Critical Essays*. Stanford: Stanford University Press, 2001, p. 4.

12 Clifford Geertz, *Works and Lives: The Anthropologist as Author*. Stanford: Stanford University Press, 1988, p. 113.

13 Don Handleman, 'Why ritual in its own right? How so?' *Social Analysis*, Vol. 48, No. 2 (Summer 2004), pp. 1–32.

14 Handleman, Ibid., 16–17.

15 Elias Canetti, *Crowds and Power*, trans. Carol Stewart. London: Phoenix Press, 2000 [1960].

16 Richard Schechner, 'Living a Double Consciousness', in Catherine Bell (ed.), *Teaching Ritual*. Oxford: Oxford University Press, 2007, p. 25.

17 John Keegan, *A History of Warfare*. New York: Alfred A. Knopf, 1993, p. xvi.

Chapter 14

1 Combatants for Peace website: http://cfpeace.org/?page_id=2

2 Augusto Boal, *Games for Actors and Non-Actors*, trans. A. Jackson. London: Routledge, 1992, pp. 1–5.

3   Augusto Boal, *The Rainbow of Desire*, trans. A. Jackson. London: Routledge, 1995, pp. 72–3.

4   Ronald B. Adler and Neil Towne, *Looking Out/Looking In: Interpersonal Communication.* San Diego: Harcourt Brace College Publishers, 1999.

5   Rev. Martin Luther King Jr., *Strength to Love.* New York: Harper & Row, 1963.

6   Jan Cohen-Cruz, *Radical Street Performance: An International Anthology.* London: Routledge, 1998; Toby Emert and Ellie Friedland (eds), *Come Closer: Critical Perspectives on Theatre of the Oppressed.* New York: Peter Lang, 2011.

7   Gene Sharp, *The Politics of Non-Violence.* Boston: Porter Sargent Publisher, Boston, 1973, pp. 148–52.

8   Ramzi Suleiman, 'The Planned Encounter as a Microcosm: Psychosocial Perspectives', in R. Halabi (ed.), *Israeli and Palestinian Identities in Dialogue: The School for Peace Approach.* New Jersey: Rutgers University Press, 2000, pp. 31–47.

9   Richard Schechner, 'The Street is the Stage', *The Future of Ritual: Writing on Culture and Performance.* New York: Routledge, 1993, p. 86.

10 Sanjoy Ganguly, *Jana Sanskriti: Forum Theatre and Democracy in India.* New York: Routledge, 2010, pp. 88–9.

11 The term *spectator-actor* was coined by Boal in his first book *Theatre of the Oppressed* in which he discusses for the first time the concept of 'Forum Theatre', pp. 139–42. In Boal's second book, *Games for Actors and Non-Actors*, Adrian Jackson writes in the translator's introduction that 'spect-actor' is a Boal coinage to describe a member of the audience who takes part in the action in any way; the spect-actor is an active spectator, p. xxvi.

12 Augusto Boal, *Theatre of the Oppressed*, trans. Charles A. McBride and Maria Odilia Leal McBride. New York: Theatre Communications Group, 1979, pp. 143–7.

13 Augusto Boal, *Games for Actors and Non-Actors*, trans. A. Jackson. London: Routledge, 1992, pp. 277–88.

14 Ibid., p. 241.

15 The spaces that Boal notes as suitable for invisible theatre are streets, railway stations, ferries, restaurants, etc. Ibid., p. 277.

16 Ibid., p. 286.

17 Jill Dolan, *Utopia in Performance: Finding Hope at the Theatre.* Ann Aarbor: University of Michigan Press, 2005; Baz Kershaw, *The Radical in Performance: From Brecht to Baudrillard.* London: Routledge, 1999; Jan Cohen-Cruz, *Radical Street Performance: An International Anthology.* London: Routledge, 1998.

18 Fiona Wilkie, 'Mapping the Terrain: A Survey of Site-Specific Performance in Britain', *New Theatre Quarterly*, Vol. 18, No. 70 (2002), pp. 140–60.

19 Jill Dolan, *Utopia in Performance: Finding Hope at the Theatre.* Ann Arbor: University of Michigan Press, 2005.

20 Ibid.

21 Augusto Boal, 'Preface: The Unruly Protagonist', in *Theater of the Oppressed*, New Edition. London: Pluto Press, 2000, p. xxii.

22 In accordance with the Oslo Agreement, Area A is under Palestinian civil and security control, Area B is under Palestinian civil control and Israeli security control and Area C is under Israeli civil and security control. See: Yaacov Bar-Siman-Tov (ed.), *The Israeli-Palestinian Conflict: From a Peace Process to a Violent Confrontation: 2000–2005*. Jerusalem: Institute for Israel Studies, 2005. [Hebrew].

23 Giorgio Agamben, *State of Exception*, trans. Kevin Attell. Chicago: University of Chicago Press, 2005.

24 Sonja Kuftinec and Chen Alon, 'Prose and Cons: Theatrical Encounters with Students and Prisoners in Ma'asiyahu, Israel', *Research in Drama Education*, Vol. 12, No. 3 (2007), pp. 275–91.

25 Gene Sharp, *Non-Violent Resistance*, trans. Y. Amit. Jerusalem: Mifras Publishing House, 1984; p. 145. [Hebrew]

26 Augusto Boal, *Theatre of the Oppressed*, trans. Charles A. McBride and Maria Odilia Leal McBride. New York: Theatre Communications Group, 1979.

27 Augusto Boal, *Games for Actors and Non-Actors*, trans. A. Jackson. London: Routledge, 1992, p. 277.

28 Augusto Boal, *Theatre of the Oppressed*, trans. Charles A. McBride and Maria Odilia Leal McBride. New York: Theatre Communications Group, 1979, p. 147.

29 Frances Babbage, *Augusto Boal*. New-York: Routledge, 2004, p. 21.

30 Suzanne Lacy, 'Activism in Feminist Performance Art', in Jan Cohen-Cruz and Mady Schutzman (eds), *A Boal Companion: Dialogue on Theatre and Cultural Politics*. London and New York: Routledge, 2006, p. 93.

31 C. B. Driskell, 'An Interview with Augusto Boal', *Latin American Theatre Review*, Vol. 9, No. 1 (1975), p. 75.

32 Augusto Boal, *Theatre of the Oppressed*, trans. Charles A. McBride and Maria Odilia Leal McBride. New York: Theatre Communications Group, 1979, p. 147.

33 Suzanne Lacy, 'Debated Territory: Toward a Critical Language of Public Art', in Suzanne Lacy (ed.), *Mapping the Terrain: New Genre Public Art*. Seattle: Bay Press, 1995, p. 174.

34 Ibid.

35 Victor Turner, *From Ritual to Theatre; The Human Seriousness of Play*. New York: Performing Arts Journal Publications, 1982.

36 Clifford Geertz, *The Interpretation of Cultures*, trans. Y. Meisler. Tel Aviv: Keter Publishing House, 1990 [1973]. [Hebrew]

37 Richard Schechner, *Performance Studies; An Introduction*. New York: Routledge, 2002, p. 26.

38 Ibid.

Chapter 15

1 Umubyeyi, Jaqueline. 10 May 2011. Web.http://www.rcinet.ca/francais/emission/
   tam-tam-canada/archives/episode/10-40_2011-05-11-tam-tam-canada-10-05-
   2011/ (accessed 15 November 2012).

2 The National Unity and Reconciliation Commission of Rwanda. http://www.nurc.
   gov.rw. Web. (accessed 15 November 2012).

3 Richard Schechner, *The Future of Ritual*. New York: Routledge, 1995, p. 1.

4 Véronique Tadjo, *L'ombre d'Imana: Voyages jusqu'au Bout du Rwanda*. Paris: Actes
   Sud. 2000, p. 13.

5 Maurice Blanchot, *The Writing of the Disaster*. Lincoln: University of Nebraska
   Press, 1986, p. 7.

6 Chantal Kalisa, 'Theatre and the Rwandan Genocide', *Peace Review: A Journal of
   Social Justice*, Vol. 18, No. 4 (2006), p. 515.

7 Portions of the section on 'The Monument' have been reprinted from Jennifer
   H. Capraru and Kim Solga, 'Performing Survival in the Global City: Theatre
   ISÔKO's The Monument', in *Performance and the Global City*, ed. D. J. Hopkins
   and Kim Solga. New York: Palgrave, 2013, unpublished manuscript.

8 Solange Liza Umuhire, 'World Stage Behind the Scenes: Chat with "The
   Monument" Cast'. Youtube. Harbourfront Centre, 27 April 2011 (accessed
   3 September 2012). Web.

9 Colleen Wagner, 'The Monument'. Toronto: Playwrights Canada Press, 1996, p. 78.

10 Jennifer Herszman Capraru, 'Memory, Memorial, and The Monument'.
   Alt. theatre: Cultural Diversity and the Stage, Vol. 6, No. 3 (2009), pp. 14–23.

11 Wagner, Colleen, Ibid., p. 80.

12 Peggy Phelan, *Unmarked: The Politics of Performance*. London: Routledge, 1993,
   p. 146.

13 Farber Foundry Website. http://www.farberfoundry.com/molora-info.html
   (accessed 20 August 2012) Web.

14 Anne Carson, *Grief Lessons: Four Plays by Euripides*. New York: Review Books,
   2006, p. xi.

15 Wajdi Mouawad, *Littoral*, trans. S. Teperman. Toronto: Playwrights Canada Press,
   2011, p. 49. French text, Leméac Éditeur Inc., Montreal, 2009.

16 Walter Benjamin, 'On Some Motifs in Baudelaire', in *Illuminations*. New York:
   Schocken Books, 1969, p. 158.

17 Jean-Pierre Karegeye, 'International Seminar on Ethics and Childcare, UNESCO',
   2007, p. 4. Web. https://docs.google.com/viewer?a=v&q=cache:UL60hnRFaPE
   J:enfance-et-partage.org/pdf/colloque/FR/19-Fournier-Karegeye.pdf (accessed
   31 August 2012).

Chapter 16

1 Gayatri Chakravorty Spivak, *The Post-Colonial Critic: Interviews, Strategies, Dialogues*. New York and London: Routledge, 1990.

2 Homi Bhabha, *The Location of Culture*. New York and London: Routledge, 1994.

3 Edward Said, *Orientalism*. London, New York and other sites: Penguin Books, 2003.

4 Victor Turner and Richard Schechner, *The Anthropology of Performance*. New York: PAJ Publications, 1987.

5 Dwight Conquergood, 'Performance Studies: Interventions and Radical Research', *TDR, The Drama Review*, Vol. 46, No. 2 (2002), pp. 145–56; and Dwight Conquergood, 'Performing as a Moral Act: Ethical Dimensions of the Ethnography of Performance', in Petra Kuppers and Gwen Robertson (eds), *The Community Performance Reader*. London and New York: Routledge, 2007, pp. 57–70.

6 Jon McKenzie, Heike Roms and C. J. W. -L. Wee (eds), *Contesting Performance: Global Sites of Research*. London: Palgrave Macmillan, 2010.

7 McKenzie, Roms and Wee (eds), *Contesting Performance*, p. 12.

8 Alain Badiou, *Handbook of Inaesthetics*, trans. Alberto Toscano. Stanford: Stanford University Press, 2005.

9 Jazmin Badong Llana, 'Pilgrimage as Utopian Performative for a Post-Colonial Counterpublic', *Performance Research*, Vol. 16, No. 2 (2011), pp. 91–6. The core ideas and empirical material presented in this current paper originally saw print in the journal essay.

10 Fenella Cannell, *Power and Intimacy in the Christian Philippines*. New York: Cambridge University Press, 1999, p. 15.

11 Vicente L. Rafael, *Contracting Colonialism: Translation and Conversion in Tagalog Society under Early Spanish Rule*. Durham and London: Duke University Press, 1993.

12 Reynaldo C. Ileto, *Pasyon and Revolution: Popular Movements in the Philippines, 1840-1910*. Quezon City: Ateneo de Manila University Press, 1979.

13 Peter Hallward, *Absolutely Postcolonial: Writing between the Singular and the Specific*. Manchester and New York: Manchester University Press, 2001, p. 47.

14 The performers refer to themselves in the dotoc text as *peregrinos* – pilgrims.

15 A surviving copy of the 1895 text *Dotoc sa Mahal na Santa Cruz* used in the Baao dotoc is attributed to a priest. For the Canaman texts and those of Nabua and the komedya of Legazpi, the authors are not identified on

the extant copies. In conversations with practitioners, I learnt that certain performers like Pinay Esplana (of Baao, c. 1938–46) 'improved the music and changed the "wording" (phrasing)' of the dotoc for aesthetic purposes (Llana, Jazmin, 'The Bicol Dotoc: Performance, Postcoloniality, and Pilgrimage'. PhD thesis, Aberystwyth University, 2009, p. 166. I infer from this that most of the texts used in the dotoc held outside the church were already crafted by lay people.

16 'Heraclio' is Heraclius, Byzantine emperor of 610–41 A.D. and 'Cosrohas' is the Persian king Chosroes. See Jacobus De Voragine, *The Golden Legend*, trans. William Granger Ryan, Vol. I & II. New Jersey: Princeton University Press, 1993, p. 170. New material on Heraclius gives further details on the conflict between Heraclius and Khusro II (Chosroes) and the recovery of the True Cross that the Persian commander Shahrvaraz took during the violent sacking of Jerusalem in 614. See Geoffrey Regan, *First Crusader: Byzantium's Holy Wars*. New York and Hampshire, England: Palgrave Macmillan, 2003. For further details see Llana 2009 and Jazmin Llana, 'The Komedya in the Bikol Dotoc: Prelude or Main Event', *Philippine Humanities Review*, Vol. 11–12 (2010), pp. 121–48.

17 See Nicanor G. Tiongson, *Komedya, Philippine Theater: A History and Anthology*, Vol. 2. Quezon City: University of the Philippines Press, 1999, p. 1.

18 Almost always female, the director is a senior dotoc practitioner who volunteers her services, often also as her sacred vow to the Holy Cross. She is called 'autora' [author] in Nabua, 'maestra' [teacher] in Legazpi, 'parabalo' [trainer] in Baao, and 'notador' [prompter] in Canaman. Her dictation of every line uttered by the 'actors' establishes a distinct rhythm in the recitation of the komedya and the singing of the dotoc. However, this practice has disappeared in the cobacho dotoc of Baao and Legazpi and in the lagaylay of Canaman.

19 There are exceptions: in Canaman, the practice is supervised by the parish priest, managed by persons designated by the pastoral council, and held within the church yard/patio. I did not observe this set-up in Legazpi and Nabua, while in Baao the barrio representatives in the pastoral council also actively supervise the nine-day prayers and dotoc.

20 Llana, *Pilgrimage as Utopian Performative*, p. 94.

21 Webb Keane, 'Epilogue: Anxious Transcendence', in Fenella Cannell (ed.), *The Anthropology of Christianity*. Durham and London: Duke University Press, 2006, p. 316.

22 Alain Badiou, *Saint Paul: The Foundation of Universalism*, trans. R. Brassier. Stanford: Stanford University Press, 2003, p. 88, emphasis in original.

23 Feodor Jagor, *Travels in the Philippines*. Manila: Filipiniana Book Guild, 1965 [1875], p. 79.

24 Resil Mojares, 'Notes for the Production of a Brechtian Komedya', *Philippine Humanities Review*, Vol. 11–12 (2010), p. 57.

25 Vicente L. Rafael, *The Promise of the Foreign: Nationalism and the Technics of Translation in the Spanish Philippines*. Pasig City: Anvil Publishing, Inc. [Duke University Press, 2005] 2006, p. 117.

26 Vicente L. Rafael, 'Palabas: Essays on Philippine Theater History [Review]', *The Journal of Asian Studies*, Vol. 58, No. 4 (1999), p. 1195.

27 Rafael, *The Promise of the Foreign*, p. 115. Rafael uses the Spanish word *comedia*, whereas this essay retains *komedya* with a 'k' in deference to the idea that it was appropriated and came to be a distinct form. On this idea, see Doreen G. Fernandez, *Palabas: Essays on Philippine Theater History*. Quezon City: Ateneo de Manila University Press, 1996. Rafael's quotes from Guerra are from the latter's *Viajes por Filipinas de Manila a Tayabas* (1879) and *Viajes por Filipinas de Manila a Albay* (1887) cited in Nicanor Tiongson, *Kasaysayan ng Komedya sa Pilipinas, 1766-1862*. Manila: De La Salle University Press, 1982.

28 Rafael, *The Promise of the Foreign*, 121.

29 Ibid.

30 Ibid., 125.

31 Ibid., 116–17.

32 Cannell, *Power and Intimacy*, 248.

33 Ibid., 1.

34 Alain Badiou, *Metapolitics*, trans. Jason Barker. London: Verso, 2005, pp. 7–8.

35 Alan Morinis, *Sacred Journeys: The Anthropology of Pilgrimage*. Westport, CT and London: Greenwood Press, 1992.

36 Llana, *Pilgrimage as Utopian Performative*, p. 93.

37 Jill Dolan, *Utopia in Performance: Finding Hope at the Theatre*. Ann Arbor: The University of Michigan Press, 2005.

38 Llana, *Pilgrimage as Utopian Performative*, p. 93.

39 Dolan, *Utopia*, p. 8.

40 Richard Schechner, *Performance Studies: An Introduction*. London and New York: Routledge, 2002, p. 28.

41 Michael Pinches, 'The Working-Class Experience of Shame, Inequality and People Power in Tatalon, Manila', in B. J. Kerkvliet and Resil B. Mojares (eds), *From Marcos to Aquino: Local Perspectives in Political Transition in the Philippines*. Quezon City: Ateneo de Manila University Press, 1991, p. 177.

42 Peter Hallward, *Think Again: Alain Badiou and the Future of Philosophy*. New York and London: Continuum, 2004, p. 8.

43 Cf. Anthony Kubiak, *Stages of Terror: Terrorism, Ideology, and Coercion as Theatre History*. Bloomington and Indianapolis: Indiana University Press, 1991, p. 51.

44 Badiou, *Inaesthetics*, p. 55.

45 Alain Badiou, *Saint Paul: The Foundation of Universalism*, trans. Ray Brassier. Stanford: Stanford University Press, 2003, p. 93.

46 Adrian Kear, 'Thinking out of Time: Theatre and the Ethic of Interruption', *Performance Research*, Vol. 9, No. 4 (2004), p. 103.

47 Peter Hallward, 'Being and Event: On Badiou's Logics of Worlds', *New Left Review*, Vol. 53 (September–October 2008), p. 106.

Chapter 17

1 The Republic of Korea is referred to as South Korea or Korea. Romanization is according to the McCune–Reischauer system except for the use of shi instead of si to ease proper pronunciation.

2 Liora Sarfati, *Objects of Worship: Material Culture in the Production of Shamanic Rituals in South Korea*. PhD dissertation, Folklore department, Indiana University, Bloomington, 2010.

3 Laurel Kendall, *Shamans, Housewives, and other Restless Spirits: Women in Korean Ritual Life*. Honolulu: University of Hawaii Press, 1985, pp. 52–5, 72–9.

4 Tourist promotion bulletin of Danoje Festival, http://english.visitkorea.or.kr/enu/SI/SI_EN_3_6.jsp?cid=1066639 (accessed 25 February 2013).

5 http://jikimi.cha.go.kr/english/about_new/greeting.jsp?mc=EN_02_01_01 (accessed 29 October 2012). Emphasis added.

6 Jaihyon Lee, *A Handbook of Korea*. Seoul: Office of Public Information, 1955.

7 Sarfati 2010, p. 75.

8 Youngsook Kim Harvey, *Six Korean Women: The Socialization of Shamans*. St. Paul: West Publishers, 1979, pp. 125, 155, 168; Chongho Kim, *Korean Shamanism: The Cultural Paradox*. Aldershot: Ashgate, 2003, pp. 15, 65, 202, and Kendall 1985, pp. 23–35.

9 Keith Howard, 'Preserving the Spirits? Ritual, State Sponsorship, and Performance', in *Korean Shamanism Revivals, Survivals, and Change*. Seoul: Seoul Press, 1998, pp. 187–217.

10 Jongsung Yang, 'Investigative Research towards the Designation of Shamanic Village Rituals as Intangible Cultural Properties of the Seoul Metropolitan Government', *International Journal of Intangible Heritage*, No. 4 (2009), pp. 94–110, and *Folklore and Cultural Politics in Korea: Intangible Cultural Properties and Living National Treasures*. PhD dissertation, Folklore Department, Indiana University, Bloomington, 1994.

11 Claire Lee, 'Lotus Lantern Festival Designated as Intangible Cultural Heritage', *The Korea Herald*, 10 April 2012.

12 Yang 1994.

13 Sarfati Liora, interview with Prof Yim Dawn-hee, 10 November 2007.

14 Sarfati Liora, interview with Lee Yŏng-nam, a musok-goods store owner in Seoul, 15 October 2007.

15 Ibid.

16 Sarfati Liora, interview with Kim Nam-sun, Seoul, 20 April 2007.

17 Websites quoted in the text were accessed on 12 December 2012.

18 Between (*sai-eso*), 2006, directed by Lee Ch'ang-jae.

19 Chungmoo Choi, 'Nami, Ch'ae, and Oksun: Superstar Shamans in Korea', in Ruth-Inge Heinze (ed.), *Shamans of the Twentieth Century*. New York: Irvington, 1991, pp. 51–61.

20 Mariana Ruah-Midbar, *The New Age Culture in Israel: A Methodological Introduction and the 'Conceptual Network'*. PhD dissertation, Bar Ilan University, Israel, 2006.

21 Yang 2009.

22 Akamatsu Chijo and Akiba Takashi, *Chōsen fuzuko no kenkyū* (Study of Korean Shamanism). Tokyo: Osakayago Shōten, 1938. William Elliot Griffis, *Corea the Hermit Nation*. New York: C. Scribner, 1885 [1882].

23 Sarfati 2010, pp. 78–9.

24 Ch'oe Nam-sŏn, 'Sarman'gyo ch'aki' (Records on shamanism). *Kyemyŏng sibo*, Vol. 19 (1927), pp. 3–51, and Yim Suk-Jay (Im Sŏk-jae), *Mu-ga: The Ritual Songs of Korean Mudangs*, trans. Alan C. Heyman. Fremont, CA: Asian Humanities Press, 2005.

25 http://jikimi.cha.go.kr/english/search_plaza_new/state.jsp?mc=EN_03_01 (accessed 29 October 2012).

26 Ann Marie Shea and Atay Citron, 'The Powwow of the Thunderbird American Indian Dancers'. *The Drama Review*, Vol. 26, No. 2 (1982), pp. 73–88, and Henry Glassie, 'Tradition', *Journal of American Folklore*, Vol. 108, No. 430 (1995), pp. 395–412.

27 Regina Bendix, *In Search of Authenticity: The Formation of Folklore Studies*. Madison: University of Wisconsin Press, 1997.

28 Authenticity in kut is discussed in Laurel Kendall, *Shamans, Nostalgias, and the IMF: South Korean Popular Religion in Motion*. Honolulu: University of Hawaii Press, 2009; Dong-kyu Kim, *Looping Effects between Images and Realities: Understanding the Popularity of Korean Shamanism*. PhD Dissertation, University of British Columbia, 2012; and Kyo-im Yun, *Performing the Sacred: Political Economy and Shamanic Ritual on Cheju Island, South Korea*. PhD dissertation, Folklore Department, Indiana University, Bloomington, 2007.

29 Michelle Anderson, 'Authentic Voodoo is Synthetic'. *The Drama Review*, Vol. 26, No. 2 (1982), pp. 89–110.

30 Shea and Citron 1982.

31 Eric Hobsbawm and Terence Ranger (eds), *The Invention of Tradition*. Cambridge: Cambridge University Press, 1983; Šmidchens, Guntis, 'Folklorism

Revisited'. *Journal of Folklore Research*, Vol. 36, No. 1 (1999), pp. 51–70; and Richard M. Dorson, 'Is Folklore a Discipline?' *Folklore,* Vol. 84, No. 3 (1973), pp. 199–200.

32   Stephen Vlastos (ed.), *Mirror of Modernity: Invented Traditions in Modern Japan.* Berkeley: University of California, 1998; and Richard Handler and Jocelyn Linnekin, 'Tradition, Genuine or Spurious', *Journal of American Folklore*, Vol. 97, No. 385 (1984), pp. 273–90; and Glassie 1995.

33   Claire Sponsler, *Ritual Imports: Performing Medieval Drama in America.* Ithaca: Cornell University Press, 2004, p. 98.

34   Richard Bauman, 'Mediational Performance, Traditionalization, and Authorization of Discourse', in Helga Kotthoff and Hubert Knoblauch (eds), *Verbal Art Across Cultures: The Aesthetics and Proto-Aesthetics of Communication.* Tubingen: Guntar Narr Verlag, 2001, p. 93.

35   Ibid., p. 107.

36   Richard Schechner, 'Restoration of Behaviour'. *Studies in Visual Communication,* Vol. 7, No. 3 (1981), p. 11.

37   Diana Taylor, *The Archive and the Repertoire: Performing Cultural Memory in the Americas.* Duke University Press, 2003, pp. 20–6.

38   Yang 2009, p. 108.

Chapter 18

1   On these issues, see *Kavvana: Directing the Heart in Jewish Prayer,* https://sites. google.com/site/kadish67/kavvana-en.

2   Roy Rappaport, *Ritual and Religion in the Making of Humanity.* New York, Cambridge: Cambridge University Press, 1999, p. 24.

3   Ibid.

4   Richard Schechner, *Performance Studies: An Introduction.* New York: Routledge, 2002, p. 28.

5   The word *ma'amarot* ('sayings') designates the tenfold utterance with which, according to Judaism, the world was created. Parts of my discussion of *Ma'amarot* have been published in Sarit Cofman-Simhon, '*Ma'amarot*: Staging the *Agon* of the Jewish Morning Service', *Ecumenica Journal of Theatre and Performance*, Vol. 3, No. 1 (2006), pp. 41–56.

6   *Ma'amarot* is an all-male performance making this gender-specific phrasing appropriate.

7   Programme note, *Ma'amarot: A Voice and Movement Performance,* 2001.

8   The most important book of Kabbalah.

9   *Ma'amarot*, Post-performance discussion, Jerusalem 15 March 2002.

10 Programme note, *Ma'amarot: A Voice and Movement Performance*, 2001.

11 Albert Souissa, Rev. of *Ma'amarot. Achbar Col Ha'Yir* 2005: 36 in *Tair Theatre* file, Israel Goor Theatre Archives and Museum (IGTAM), Jerusalem.

12 Hayoota Deutsch, Rev. of *Ma'marot. Nekuda* 2005: 90 in *Tair Theatre* file, Israel Goor Theatre Archives and Museum (IGTAM), Jerusalem.

13 Shai Bar-Yaacov, Rev. of *Ma'marot. Yediot Aharonot - 24 Hours* 2005: 24 in *Tair Theatre* file, Israel Goor Theatre Archives and Museum (IGTAM), Jerusalem.

14 Hanoch Daum, Rev. of *Ma'marot. Tarbut Maariv* 2005: 15 in *Tair Theatre* file, Israel Goor Theatre Archives and Museum (IGTAM), Jerusalem.

15 Avi Assaraf (director in *Ma'amarot*), in discussion with the author, Jerusalem, 22 August 2012. All interviews were conducted in Hebrew and the translations are the author's.

16 Home page, 'Kol Atzmotai Tomarna', Website of dance theatre school Kol Atzmotai, http://www.othermove.com/site/index.asp?depart_id=46124&lat=en (accessed 5 March 2013).

17 Amitai Stern (dancer in Ka'et ensemble), '"Highway No.1" by Tammy and Ronen Izhaki', Website of dance theatre school Kol Atzmotai Tomarna, http://www.othermove.com/46124/Highway-no-1-1 (accessed 5 March 2013).

18 '"Highway No.1"', http://www.othermove.com/46124/Highway-no-1-1 (accessed 5 March 2013).

19 The Talmud is a central text of rabbinic Judaism. Hananya Schwartz (dancer in Ka'et ensemble), '"Highway No.1"', http://www.othermove.com/46124/Highway-no-1-1 (accessed 5 March 2013).

20 Izhaki (choreographer of Ka'et ensemble), in discussion with the author, Bat Ayin, 12 December 2012.

21 Donald Byrd, 'Jerusalem Journal, 11/12-11/17/2011', *Donald Byrd Blog*, 2 December 2011, http://spectrumdance.org/2011/12/jerusalem-journal-nov11-17-2011/.

22 Ibid.

23 Victoria Hanna (vocal performer), in discussion with the author, Jerusalem, 23 August 2012.

24 From *The Age* magazine quoted in Olamale Website, accessed 5 March 2013, http://www.olamale.com/htmls/victoria.htm.

25 Carol Martin, 'Living Simulations: The Use of Media in Documentary in the UK, Lebanon and Israel', in Alison Forsyth and Chris Megson (eds), *Get Real: Documentary Theatre Past and Present*. Basingstoke: Palgrave Macmillan, 2009, p. 86.

26 Ruthie Abeliovich, 'Envoicing the Future: Victoria Hanna's Exterior Voice', *Theatre Research International*, Vol. 34, No. 2, p. 60.

27 Ibid., p. 162.

28 'The voice to enthral', *The Hindu*, online edition, 29 September 2006, accessed 5 March 2013, http://www.hindu.com/fr/2006/09/29/stories/2006092902100200.htm.

29 Babylonian Talmud, Berachot 60b.

30 Victoria Hanna (vocal performer), in discussion with the author, Jerusalem, 24 February 2013.

31 Martin, 'Living Simulations', p. 84.

32 Victoria Hanna, in discussion with the author, Jerusalem, 23 August 2012.

33 Ibid.

34 Ibid.

35 Ibid.

36 The title pays homage to Richard Schechner's essay 'From ritual to theatre and back: the efficacy-entertainment braid' in his *Performance Theory*. New York and London: Routledge, 1988.

37 Avi Assaraf (director in *Ma'amarot*), in discussion with the author, Jerusalem, 22 August 2012.

38 Ibid.

39 *Midrash* ('investigation') means interpreting Jewish texts and praxis.

40 Yair Lipshitz, 'The Stage as a Space for *Midrash*: Theatre and the Jewish Hermeneutic Project', in Ahuva Belkin (ed.), *Jewish Theatre: Tradition in Transition and Intercultural Vistas*. Tel Aviv: Assaph Book Series, The Yolanda and David Katz Faculty of the Arts, Tel Aviv University, 2008, p. 11.

41 Ibid., 20.

Chapter 19

1 My thanks to Julie Pasqual – a wonderful clown doctor of New York City's Big Apple Circus Clown Care Unit – who had Ball's insightful comment on a sticker decorating her locker at Harlem Hospital.

2 Dream Doctors Project website: http://www.dreamdoctors.org.il/eng/

3 For a broader introduction to medical clowning, see Atay Citron, 'Medical Clowning and Performance Theory', in James Harding and Cindy Rosenthal (eds), *The Rise of Performance Studies: Rethinking Richard Schechner's Broad Spectrum*. London & New York: Palgrave Macmillan, 2011, pp. 248–63.

4 Big apple Circus Clown Care website: http://bigapplecircus.org/clown-care.

5 A. J. Smerling, E. Scolnick et al., 'Preoperative Clown Therapy For Pediatric Patients'. *Anesthesia & Analgesia*, Vol. 88 (1999), p. 306S. L. Vagnoli et al., 'Clown Doctors as Treatment for Preoperative Anxiety In Children: A Randomized, Prospective Study'. *Pediatrics*, Vol. 116, No. 4 (2005), p. 1013. Y. Gozal, 'Preoperative Anxiety in Children:

Medical Clowns vs Oral Midazolam'. Lecture at the *Medicine and Medical Clowning: The Dream Doctors International Conference*, 2011. http://www.youtube.com/watch?v=nn2688hprIw&list=SP7B130D71E6ACB427&index=7.

6 B. Warren and P. Spitzer, 'Laughing to Longevity – The Work of Elder Clowns'. *The Lancet*, Vol. 378, No. 9791 (2011), pp. 562–3. P. Spitzer, 'How to Raise a SMILE: The Sydney Multi-Site Intervention of Laughterbosses and Elder Clowns'. *Australian Journal of Dementia Care*, Vol. 1, No. 1 (2012), pp. 22–6.

7 A. Oren Ziv et al., 'Dream Doctors as Important Team Members in the Treatment of Young Children with Juvenile Idiopathic Arthritis'. *Harefuah* (in Hebrew), Vol. 151, No. 6 (June 2012), pp. 332–4.

8 D. Tener, R. Lev-Weisel et al., 'Laughing through this Pain: Medical Clowning During Examination of Sexually Abused Children: An Innovative Approach'. *Journal of Child Sexual Abuse*, Vol. 19, No. 2 (2010), pp. 128–40.

9 A. Koren, 'Dream Doctors instead Sedation in Radionuclide Scanning among young children'. Lecture at the *Medicine and Medical Clowning: The Dream Doctors International Conference*, 2011. http://www.youtube.com/watch?v=5IObmxZFzJU&list=SP7B130D71E6ACB427&index=12.

10 A. Raviv, 'Medical clowning with PTSD/ASD: My Work as a Clown Doctor, with Patients who Suffer From PTSD/ASD'. Lecture at the *Medicine and Medical Clowning: The Dream Doctors International Conference*, 2011. http://www.youtube.com/watch?v=e8LNsOanvxk&list=SP7B130D71E6ACB427&index=19.

11 S. Friedler et al., 'The Effect of Medical Clowning on Pregnancy Rates After in vitro Fertilization and Embryo Transfer'. *Fertility & Sterility*, Vol. 95, No. 6 (2011), pp. 2127–30.

12 As medical clowning becomes a paramedical profession, the issue of professional training divides hospital clowns, organizations and therapists in many countries and international forums. I obviously support systematic professional and academic training for medical clowns, and I have reason to believe that in Israel, such training will be eventually required as part of legislation regulating the field of creative arts therapies.

13 Beatrice K. Otto, *Fools Are Everywhere: The Court Jester Around The World*. Chicago & London: The University of Chicago Press, 2001, pp. 133–54.

14 Ibid., p. 134.

15 Ibid., p. 136.

16 Lisa Appignanesi, *The Cabaret*. New York: Universe Books, 1976, p. 44.

17 Ronald Collins and David Skover, *The Trials of Lenny Bruce: The Fall & Rise of an American Icon*. New York: Sourcebooks, 2002.

18 Otto, pp. 137–9.

19 Ibid., p. 142.

20 William Guinee, 'Confrontation and the Creation of Balance: Ritual Clowning Among the Zuni'. *Folklore Forum*, Vol. 18, No. 1–2 (1985), pp. 113–35.

21 Bunzel (1929) quoted by Guinee, p. 118.

22 Cushing (1896) quoted by Guinee, pp. 118–19.

23 Jesse Green (ed.), *Zuni*: Selected Writings of Frank Hamilton Cushing. Lincoln & London: University of Nebraska Press, 1979, pp. 323–4, 363.

24 Ibid.

25 Beverly J. Stoeltje, 'The Rodeo Clown and the Semiotics of Metaphor'. *Journal of Folklore Research,* Vol. 22, No. 2/3 (1985), pp. 171–2.

26 Ibid.

27 Interview with Miki Bash, conducted on 1 March 2012.

28 Interview with Amnon Raviv, conducted on 9 May 2012.

29 Interview with Yaron Sancho Goshen, conducted on 14 December 2011.

30 Frank Farrelly and Jeffrey Brandsma, *Provocative Therapy*. Cupertino, CA: Meta Publishing, 1974. I am indebted to Peter Spitzer, for referring me to Farrelly's writings and videotaped lectures.

31 Farrelly, pp. 95–118.

32 Interview with Prof Rachel Lev-Wesiel, conducted on 12 March 2012.

33 Guinee, p. 124.

34 Interview with Dr Shlomit Bresler, conducted on 29 May 2012.

Chapter 20

1 Marvin Carlson, *Performance: A Critical Introduction*. New York: Taylor and Francis Group, 1996; Richard Schechner, *Performance Studies: An Introduction*. London and New York: Routledge, 2002.

2 Fred Newman and Lois Holzman, *The End of Knowing: A New Developmental Way of Learning*. London and New York: Routledge, 1997.

3 Dan Friedman, 'Good-bye Ideology, Hello Performance', *Topoi: An International Review of Philosophy*, Vol. 30, No. 2 (2011), pp. 125–35.

4 Martha Bradshaw (ed.), *Soviet Theater, 1917-1941*. Ann Arbor: Edwards Bros., Inc., 1954; Ludwig Hoffman and Daniel Hoffman-Ostwald (eds), *Deutsches Arbeiter-theater, 1918-1933*. München: Rogner und Bernhard.

5 Guerrilla Girls, *Confessions of the Guerrilla Girls*. Perennial, 1995; Charlie Todd and Alex Scordelis, *Causing a Scene: Extraordinary Pranks in Ordinary Places with Improv for Everywhere*. New York: William Morrow, 2009; The Yes Men, *The Yes Men Fix the World*. DVD, 2009; Georgiana Gore, 'Flash Mob Dance and the Territorialisation of Urban Movement', *Anthropological Notebooks*, Vol. 16, No. 3 (2010), pp. 125–31.

6 Richard Schechner, *Environmental Theatre*. New York: Hawthorn Books, Inc., 1973.

7 Judith Malina and Julian Beck, *Paradise Now: Collective Creation of the Living Theatre*. Vintage Books, 1971.

8 Augusto Boal, *Theatre of the Oppressed*. Pluto Press, 2000.

9 Henrich Dauber and Jonathan Fox (eds), *Gathering Voices: Essays on Playback Theatre*. New Paltz, NY: Tusitala Publishers, 1999; Jo Salas, *Improvising Real Life: Personal Story in Playback Theatre*. New Paltz, NY: Tusitala, 1999.

10 Kenneth J. Gergen, *The Saturated Self: Dilemmas of Identity in Contemporary Life*. New York: Basic Books, 1991; Mary M. Gergen, *Feminist Reconstructions in Psychology, Narrative, Gender & Performance*. Thousand Oaks, CA: Sage, 2001.

11 Norman K. Denzin, 'The Reflexive Interview and a Performative Social Science', *Qualitative Research,* Vol. 1, No. 1 (2001); Kip Jones, 'Connecting Research with Communities through Performative Social Science', *The Qualitative Report,* Vol. 17, Review/Essay 18, (2012), pp. 1–8, http://www.nova.edu/ssss/QR/QR17/jones.pdf (accessed 21 November 2012).

12 Kenneth J. Gergen and Mary M. Gergen, 'Performative Social Science and Psychology', *FQS: Forum: Qualitative Social Research*, Vol. 12, No. 1 (2011), http://www.qualitative-research.net/index.php/fqs/article/view/1595 (accessed 21 November 2012).

13 Ibid.

14 Sheila McNamee and Kenneth J. Gergen (eds), *Therapy as Social Construction*. London: Sage, 1992; J. L. Moreno and J. Fox, *The Essential Moreno: Writings in Psychodrama, Group Method, and Spontaneity*. New York: Springer, 1987; R. A. Neimeyer and J. D. Raskin, 'Varieties of Constructivism in Psychotherapy', in K. Dobson (ed.), *Handbook of Cognitive Behavioral Therapies (2nd Edition)*. New York: Guilford, 2000, pp. 393–430; Tom Strong and David Pare, *Furthering Talk: Advances in the Discursive Therapies*. New York: Kluwer Academic, 2004.

15 Carrie Lobman, 'Improvising with(in) the System: Creating New Teacher Performances in Inner City Schools', in Keith Sawyer (ed.), *The Teaching Paradox: Creativity in the Classroom*. Cambridge: Cambridge University Press, in press; Keith Sawyer, *The Teaching Paradox: Creativity in the Classroom*. Cambridge: Cambridge University Press, in press.

16 Lois Holzman, *Schools for Growth: Radical Alternatives to Current Educational Models*. Mahwah, NJ: Lawrence Erlbaum Associates, 1997; Carrie Lobman and Barbara E O'Neill (eds), *Play and Performance,* Vol. 11, *Play & Culture Studies*. New York: University Press of America, 2011; Jaime E. Martinez, *A Performatory Approach to Teaching, Learning and Technology*. Rotterdam, The Netherlands: Sense Publishers, 2011.

17 Fred Newman and Lois Holzman, *Unscientific Psychology: A Cultural-Performatory Approach to Understanding Human Life*. Lincoln, NE: iUniverse Inc. (originally published Westport, CT: Praeger), 2006/1996; Fred Newman and Lois Holzman, *The End of Knowing: A New Developmental Way of Learning*. London; New York: Routledge, 1997.

18 Dan Friedman, 'Castillo: The Making of a Postmodern Political Theatre', in John W. Frick (ed.), *Theatre at the Margins: the Political, the Popular, the Personal, the Profane*. Tuscaloosa, AL: University of Alabama Press, 2000; Lois Holzman, *Vygotsky at Work and Play*. New York: Routledge, 2009.

19 Karl Marx, 'Economic and Philosophical Manuscripts', in E. Fromm (ed.), *Marx's Concept of Man*. New York: Frederick Ungar, 1967.

20 Karl Marx and F. Engels, 'Theses on Feuerbach', in *The German Ideology*. New York: International Publishers, 1974.

21 Fred Newman and Lois Holzman, 'All Power to the Developing', *Annual Review of Critical Psychology*, Vol. 3 (2003), pp. 8–23; Fred Newman and Lois Holzman, *Lev Vygotsky: Revolutionary Scientist*. London: Routledge, 1993.

22 Ludwig Wittgenstein, *Philosophical Investigations*. Oxford: Blackwell, 1953; Ludwig Wittgenstein, *The Blue and Brown Books*. New York: Harper, 1958.

23 Ludwig Wittgenstein, *Philosophical Investigations*. Oxford: Blackwell, 1953, p. 23.

24 Ludwig Wittgenstein, *The Blue and Brown Books*. New York: Harper, 1958, p. 17.

25 Fred Newman and Lois Holzman, *Unscientific Psychology: A Cultural-Performatory Approach to Understanding Human Life*. Lincoln, NE: iUniverse Inc. (originally published Westport, CT: Praeger), 2006/1996.

26 Lev S. Vygotsky, *Mind in Society*. Cambridge, MA: Harvard University Press, 1978; Lev S. Vygotsky, *The Collected Works of L.S. Vygotsky, Volumn 1, Problems of General Psychology*. New York: Plenum, 1987; R. W. Rieber, David Keith Robinson and Jerome S. Bruner (eds), *The Essential Vygotsky*. New York: Kluwer Academic/Plenum Publishers, 2004.

27 Lev S. Vygotsky, *Mind in Society*. Cambridge, MA: Harvard University Press, 1978, p. 65.

28 Ibid., p. 102.

29 Fred Newman and Lois Holzman, *Lev Vygotsky: Revolutionary Scientist*. London: Routledge, 1993.

30 http://www.eastsideinstitute.org

31 Fred Newman, 'A Therapeutic Deconstruction of the Illusion of Self', in Lois Holzman (ed.), *Performing Psychology: A Postmodern Culture of the Mind*. New York; Routledge, 1999, pp. 111–32; Lois Holzman and Rafael Mendez, *Psychological Investigations: A Clinician's Guide to Social Therapy*. New York: Brunner-Routledge, 2003.

32 http://www.allstars.org

33 http://castillo.org

34 http://vimeo.com/19625879

35 Video available at http://www.performingtheworld.org
36 Dan Friedman and Richard Schechner, 'Performance Studies/Performance Activism' Plenary presented at PTW 2012, 4–7 October 2012, New York City. https://vimeo.com/54674363.
37 http://www.ubom.co.za/index.php?p=130

Chapter 21

1 Richard Schechner, 'Performance Studies: The Broad Spectrum Approach'. *TDR*, Vol. 32, No. 3 (Autumn 1988), p. 6.
2 *New Weekly* (Xin Zhoukan, Guangzhou). 15 October 2000, pp. 12–37.
3 Friedrich Engels, 'Ludwig Feuerbach and the End of Classical German Philosophy', Marx and Engels. *Basic Writings on Politics & Philosophy*, ed. Lewis S. Feuer. New York: Anchor Books, 1959, pp. 218, 231.
4 Karl Marx, 'Theses on Feuerbach', Marx & Engles. *Basic Writings on Politics & Philosophy*, ed. Lewis S. Feuer. New York: Anchor Books, 1959, p. 244.
5 Denis Diderot describes his ideal actor as such: '. . . the actor who plays from thought, from study of human nature, from constant imitation of some *ideal type . . .* will be one and the same at all performances, will be always at his best mark'. (Italics by the citers) *Actors on Acting*, ed. Toby Cole and Helen K. Chinoy. New York: Crown Publishers, 1970, p. 162.
6 'Social Performance Studies and the Harmonious Society'. *Jiefang Daily* (Shanghai), 2 April 2006.

Chapter 22

1 I am much obliged to Joe Essid for correcting my English style.
2 Richard Shechner, 'What Is Performance Studies Anyway?', Peggy Phelan and Jill Lane (eds), *The Ends of Performance*. New York and London: New York University Press, 1998, pp. 357–62.
3 For not to sound hollow: przedstawienie, wypełnienie, wydajność, występ, dokonanie, odprawienie, spełnienie, dotrzymanie, mozół, wykonanie, słuchowisko, wyczyn, osiągnięcie, zachowanie, uczynek, osiąg, wystawienie, performancja, widowisko, spektakl, dopełnienie, popis, wykon, przeprowadzenie. Most of these are verbal nouns.
4 In: Marvin Carlson, *Performance: A Critical Introduction*, 2nd edn. New York and London: Routledge, 2004, p. 5.
5 'Feedback, then, offers us a metamodel applicable to the invention of a general theory of performance'. Jon McKenzie, *Perform or Else. From Discipline to Performance*. London: Routledge, 2001, p. 92. 'Performances are generated

and determined by a self-referential and ever-changing feedback loop'.
Erika Fischer-Lichte, *The Transformative Power of Performance: A New Aesthetics*, trans. Saskya Iris Jain. London: Routledge, 2009, Kindle Edition loc. 1011.

6 John R. Searle, 'Consciousness, explanatory inversion, and cognitive science', *Behavioural and Brain Sciences*, Vol. 13 (1990), pp. 585–96.

7 Daniel Dennett, *Consciousness Explained*. Boston: Little, Brown and Company, 1991.

8 John R. Searle, *The Rediscovery of the Mind*. Cambridge, MA and London: MIT Press, A Bradford Book, 1992.

9 John R. Searle, *The Construction of Social Reality*. New York: The Free Press, 1995. See also: John R. Searle, *Making the Social World. The Structure of Human Civilization*. New York: Oxford University Press, 2010.

10 Gerald M. Edelman, *Neural Darwinism*. New York: Basic Books, 1987. Gerald M. Edelman, *Topobiology*. New York: Basic Books, 1988. Gerald M. Edelman, *The Remembered Present*. New York: Basic Books, 1990. Gerald M. Edelman, *Bright Air, Brilliant Fire*. New York: Basic Books, 1992. Gerald M. Edelman and Giulio Tononi, *A Universe of Consciousness. How Matter Becomes Imagination*. New York: Basic Books, 2000.

11 Edelman 1992, p. 74.

12 Edelman and Tononi, pp. 86–7.

13 Ibid., p. 87.

14 Ibid., p. 86.

15 Italicized by T. K.

16 Edelman and Tononi, p. 85.

17 Ibid., pp. 105–6.

18 Ibid., p. 49.

19 'Indeed, re-entry . . . is the main basis for a bridge between physiology and psychology'. Edelman 1992, p. 85.

20 Edelman and Tononi, p. 49.

21 See figures in: Edelman 1990, Chapter 4, pp. 64–90; also figure 9–4 in: Edelman 1992, p. 90.

22 Ibid., p. 150.

23 John R. Searle, 1992, kindle edition loc. 2049.

24 Searle returns to this topic in Chapter 9 of his later book: *Mind: A Brief Introduction*. As he concludes: 'To say of an agent that he has such-and-such an unconscious intentional state, and that that state is functioning actively in causing his behavior, is to say that he has a brain state that is capable of causing that state in a conscious form, even though in a particular instance it may be incapable of causing it in a conscious form because of brain damage, repression, etc. I am not entirely satisfied with this conclusion, but I cannot think of an alternative

conclusion that is superior to it.' John R. Searle, *Mind: A Brief Introduction*. New York: Oxford University Press, 2004, Kindle Edition loc. 3230.

25 It may be worth here to compare *King Lear* to the play sometimes regarded its 'stillborn twin': *Timon of Athens*. Timon's famous paradox of the scene IV, 3: 'Promise me friendship, but perform none: if thou wilt not promise, the gods plague thee, for thou art man! if thou dost perform, confound thee, for thou art a man!' summarizes the fate of Cordelia: she did not promise, she performed, and she suffered twice.

26 Tomasz Kubikowski, *Reguła Nibelunga. Teatr w świetle nowych badań świadomości*. Warszawa: Akademia Teatralna, 2004.

Chapter 23

1 Charles P. Snow, *The Two Cultures*. Cambridge, UK: Cambridge University Press, 1993.

2 Jo Salas, *Improvising Real Life*. New Paltz, NY: Tusitala Publishing, 1993. See also: Jonathan Fox, *Acts of Service*. New Paltz, NY: Tusitala Publishing, 1994.

3 Uri Alon 'How To Choose A Good Scientific Problem'. *Molecular Cell*, Vol. 35, No. 6 (2009), p. 728.

4 The Theatre Lab was established in the end of 2011, and is supported by the Braginsky Center for the Interface between the Science and Humanities. It is composed of two interlaced groups, a scientific group and a performing group. The scientific group includes seven scientists, with a background in physics, molecular biology, computer-science and neuroscience, applying a natural science approach to study elements of performance. The performing group is the Kartoshkes Playback Theare ensemble. The ensemble spends one day each week at the Weizmann institute campus, practising Playback and providing inspiration and support to the scientific group, by taking part in discussions and designated workshops and participating in controlled experiments as expert 'guinea pigs'.

5 Antoine Lutz, Lawrence L. Greischar, Nancy B. Rawlings, Matthieu Ricard and Richard J. Davidson, 'Long-Term Meditators Self-Induce High-Amplitude Gamma Synchrony During Mental Practice'. *Proceedings of the National Academy of Sciences*, Vol. 101, No. 46 (2004), pp. 163–9.

6 Marc D. Hauser, *Moral Minds: The Nature of Right and Wrong*. New-York: Harper Perennial, 2007.

7 Riitta Hari and Miiamaaria V. Kujala, 'Brain Basis Of Human Social Interaction: From Concepts To Brain Imaging'. *Physiological Reviews*, Vol. 89, No. 2 (2009), pp. 453–79.

8 Natalie Sebanz, Harold Bekkering and Günther Knoblich, 'Joint Action: Bodies And Minds Moving Together'. *Trends in Cognitive Sciences*, Vol. 10, No. 2 (2006), pp. 70–6.

9   Greg J. Stephens, Lauren Silbert and Uri Hasson, 'Speaker-Listener Neural
    Coupling Underlies Successful Communication'. *Proceedings of the National
    Academy of Sciences*, Vol. 107, No. 32 (2010), pp. 14425–30.

10 Lawrence M. Parsons, 'Exploring The Functional Neuroanatomy of Music
    Performance, Perception, and Comprehension'. *Annals of the New York Academy of
    Sciences*, Vol. 930, No. 1 (2001), pp. 211–31.

11 Steven Brown, Michael J. Martinez and Lawrence M. Parsons, 'The Neural Basis
    Of Human Dance'. *Cerebral Cortex*, Vol. 16, No. 8 (2006), pp. 1157–67.

12 Ivana Konvalinkaa, Dimitris Xygalatasa, Joseph Bulbuliac, Uffe Schjødta,
    Else-Marie Jegindøa, Sebastian Wallotd, Guy Van Ordend and Andreas
    Roepstorffa, 'Synchronized Arousal Between Performers and Related Spectators
    in a Fire-Walking Ritual'. *Proceedings of the National Academy of Sciences*, Vol. 108,
    No. 20 (2011), pp. 8514–19.

13 Barbara Lex, 'The Neurobiology of Ritual Trance', in Eugene G D'Aquili et al. (eds),
    The Spectrum Of Ritual: A Biogenetic Structural Analysis. New York: Columbia
    University Press, 1979, pp. 117–51.

14 Sara Bengtsson, Mihály Cśikszentmihályi and Fredrik Ullén, 'Cortical Regions
    Involved in the Generation of Musical Structures during Improvisation in Pianists'.
    Journal of Cognitive Neuroscience, Vol. 19, No. 5 (2007), pp. 830–42. See also:
    Charles J. Limb and Allen R. Braun, 'Neural Substrates of Spontaneous Musical
    Performance: An fMRI Study of Jazz Improvisation'. *PloS One*, Vol. 3, No. 2 (2008),
    p. e1679.

15 Keith Johnstone, *Impro: Improvisation and the Theatre*. New-York: Routledge,
    1987.

16 Son Preminger, 'Improvisation for Prefrontal Neuro-Rehabilitation', in Idan Segev
    et al. (eds), *Augmenting Cognition*. Lausanne, Switzerland: EPFL Press, 2011,
    pp. 41–67; Son Preminger, 'Transformative Art: Art as Means for Long-Term
    Neurocognitive Change'. *Frontiers in Human Neuroscience*, Vol. 6, No. 96 (2012),
    pp. 1–7.

17 Richard Schechner, *Performance Studies*. New York: Routledge, 2006, p. 237.

18 'Interview with Holger Czukay – CAN', October 2005, http://www.czukay.de/
    history/interview/muzicisiface.php.

19 Victor W. Turner, *The Ritual Process: Structure and Anti-Structure*. New Jersey:
    Aldine Transaction, 1969, p. 96.

20 Amy E. Seham, *Whose Improv Is It Anyway?: Beyond Second City*. Jackson, MS:
    University Press of Mississippi, 2001, p. 64.

21 Kathleen M. Dillon and Jennifer L. Tait, 'Spirituality and Being in the Zone in
    Team Sports: A Relationship?' *Journal of Sport Behaviour*, Vol. 23, No. 2 (2000),
    p. 92.

22 Viola Spolin, *Improvisation for the Theater 3E: A Handbook of Teaching and
    Directing Techniques*. Evanston, IL: Northwestern University Press, 1999, pp. 61–2.

See also: Augusto Boal, *Theater of the Oppressed*. London: Pluto Press, 2000, pp. 129–35.

23   Richard Schechner, *Environmental Theater*. New York: Applause Books, 1994, p. 118.

24   Richard Schechner, *Environmental Theater*, p. 119.

25   Antoine Lutz, Lawrence L. Greischar, Nancy B. Rawlings, Matthieu Ricard and Richard J. Davidson, 'Long-Term Meditators Self-Induce High-Amplitude Gamma Synchrony during Mental Practice'. *Proceedings of the National Academy of Sciences*, Vol. 101, No. 46 (2004), p. 16369.

26   Lior Noy, Erez Dekel and Uri Alon, 'The Mirror Game as a Paradigm for Studying the Dynamics of Two People Improvising Motion Together'. *Proceedings of the National Academy of Sciences*, Vol. 108 (2011), pp. 20947–52.

27   The level of synchronization was defined by the error in segments' stopping time, discussed above, and by the error in the speed of the two motions, defined as the average of the absolute difference between the speeds of the two handles over one motion segment, normalized by the total speed in this motion segment.

28   Chris R. Miall, David J. Weir and John F. Stein, 'Intermittency in Human Manual Tracking Tasks'. *Journal of Motor Behavior*, Vol. 25, No. 1 (1993), pp. 53–63.

29   This performance was initiated and produced by Mr Guy Biran, the artistic director of 'The Arena', an alternative performance venue in Jerusalem.

Chapter 24

1   Jonathan Fox, *Acts of Service: Spontaneity, Commitment, Tradition in the Nonscripted Theatre*. New Paltz, NY: Tusitala, 1994; Salas, Joe, Improvising Real Life: Personal Story in Playback Theatre. New Paltz, NY: Tusitala, 1999.

2   Evelyn Fox Keller, *Reflections on Gender and Science*. New Haven: Yale University Press, 1985.

3   Carl M. Cohen and S. L. Cohen, *Lab Dynamics: Management Skills for Scientists*. New York: CSHL Press, 2006; Boice Robert, *Advice for New Faculty Members: nihil nimus*. Needham Heights, MA: Allyn and Bacon, 2000.

4   R. Milo and M. Schuldiner, 'Weizmann Young PI forum: The Power of Peer Support'. *Mol Cell*, Vol. 36 (2009), pp. 913–15.

5   Keith Johnstone, *Impro: Improvisation and the Theatre*. New York: Routledge, 1987.

6   Uri Alon, 'How to Give a Good Talk ', *Mol Cell*, Vol. 36 (2009), pp. 165–7; Uri Alon, 'How to Build a Motivated Research Group ', *Mol Cell*, Vol. 37 (2010), pp. 151–2.

7   Egri Lajos, *The Art of Dramatic Writing*. Merricat Publications, 2009.

8   V. J. Propp, *Morphology of the Folktale*. Austin: University of Texas Press, 1968.

9   J. D. Velleman, 'Narrative Explanation ', *Philosophical Review*, Vol. 112 (2002), pp. 1–25.

10 John G. Scott and Peter J. Carrington, *The SAGE Handbook of Social Network Analysis*. SAGE Publications, 2011.

11 George Lakoff and Mark Johnson, *Metaphors We Live By*. Chicago: University of Chicago Press, 2003; Evelyn Fox Keller, *Making Sense of Life: Explaining Biological Development with Models, Metaphors, and Machines*. Cambridge, MA: Harvard University Press, 2003.

12 P. W. Holland and S. Leinhardt, 'Local Structure in Social Networks', *Sociological Methodology*, Vol. 7 (1976), pp. 1–45.

13 Herbert A. Simon, *The Sciences of the Artificial*, 3rd edn. Cambridge, MA: MIT Press, 1999.

14 R. Milo et al., 'Network Motifs: Simple Building Blocks of Complex Networks', *Science*, Vol. 298 (2002), pp. 824–7; Uri Alon, 'Network Motifs: Theory and Experimental Approaches', *Nat Rev Genet*, Vol. 8 (2007), pp. 450–61.

About the Contributors

Chen Alon (PhD), is a theatre activist. His PhD dissertation from Tel Aviv University is about the polarized model of the 'Theatre of the Oppressed', regarding Israelis and Palestinians. As a Major (res.) he co-founded 'Courage to Refuse', a movement of officers and combatant soldiers who refuse to serve in the occupied Palestinian territories, an action for which he was sentenced to prison. Alon is also a co-founder of 'Combatants for Peace', a movement of Palestinian and Israeli combatants who have abandoned the way of violence, and struggle together non-violently against the occupation.

Prof Uri Alon is the Abisch professor of systems biology at the Weizmann Institute of Science. He studies how biological cells make decisions, using approaches from physics and molecular biology. He is also a playback theatre actor, with Kartoshkes ensemble, using improvisation to enact audience members stories on the spot with empathy. website: http://www.weizmann.ac.il/mcb/UriAlon/.

Sharon Aronson-Lehavi (PhD) is a tenured Senior Lecturer of theatre and performance studies at the Department of Comparative Literature, Bar-Ilan University. In 2012 she was appointed as a member of the Israel Young Academy, established by the Israel Academy of Sciences and Humanities. She is the author of *Gender and Feminism in Modern Theatre* (Open University Press, 2013, Hebrew), *Street Scenes: Late Medieval Acting and Performance* (Palgrave Macmillan, 2011), and editor of *Wanderers and Other Israeli Plays* (Seagull Books, In Performance Series, 2009). She holds a PhD in Theatre Studies from the Graduate Center, City University of New York (CUNY). Her awards include a Fulbright grant for doctoral studies, a Dan David postdoctoral research award, a membership in a German Israeli Foundation (GIF) research team, and the 2012 award for Excellence in Teaching, Bar-Ilan University. In 2013–14, she is a Lisa and Douglas Goldman Visiting Israeli Professor at the University of California, Berkeley.

Henry Bial is Associate Professor of Theatre and Chair of the Department of American Studies at the University of Kansas. He is the author of *Acting Jewish: Negotiating Ethnicity on the American Stage and Screen* (University of Michigan Press, 2005), the editor of *The Performance Studies Reader* (Routledge, 2004; Second Edition, 2007), and the co-editor of *Theater Historiography: Critical Interventions* (with Scott Magelssen, University of Michigan Press, 2010) and *Brecht Sourcebook* (with Carol Martin, Routledge, 2000). He has published essays in *TDR, Theatre Topics, The Journal of American Drama and Theatre*, and elsewhere, and currently serves as president of the Association for Theatre in Higher Education (ATHE). Bial holds a PhD in Performance Studies from New York University.

Dr Daphna Ben-Shaul is a senior lecturer at the Department of the Theatre Arts, Tel Aviv University. She is the head of the Actor-Creator-Researcher MFA Programme. Her publications are related to artistic reflexivity, voiding as a performative phenomenon, and performance analysis of contemporary Israeli performance. She is the editor and co-writer of an extensive book on the Israeli art and performance group Zik (Keter, 2005). She has published articles in numerous publications, including *Modern Drama, Theatre Research International, Gramma Journal of Theory and Criticism, Performance Research,* and *Assaph*. In 2005–10 she was a member of a research team, funded by GIF for Scientific Research and Development, with researches from Freie Universität, Berlin and Tel Aviv University. She is part of a unique programme that won the Humanities Fund for an innovative humanities teaching project – 'The Laboratory Program of Research and Practice in Theatre and Performance.'

Eva Brenner (PhD, MA, NYU, mag.art/Academy of Fine Arts, Vienna) is a theatre director, producer, author and film-maker. She has directed plays by Elfriede Jelinek, Marguerite Duras, Ingeborg Bachmann, Marlene Streeruwitz, Hanna Krall, Else Lasker-Schüler, Samuel Beckett and Heiner Müller (for Wiener Festwochen, dietheater Künstlerhaus, klagenfurter ensemble, Stadttheater Klagenfurt and her own company). In 1998, she opened Projekt Theater Studio in Vienna, an experimental laboratory for interdisciplinary performance work and in 2004 an intercultural theatre space, the FLEISCHEREI, dedicated to bringing together multicultural artists from Austria and abroad to create new working-formats. Brenner's recent international collaborations include the University of Valencia (Spain), the Castillo Theatre (New York) and the Arab-Hebrew Theatre of Jaffa (Israel), the University of Haifa (Israel), lectures, workshops and lecture-demonstrations in Spain, Israel, Poland and United States. Currently she is developing a new theatrical genre entitled 'social transformance' as a synthesis of her latest experiments and will publish a book on alternative theatre this fall. Her book on the development of 'Free Theater' in Vienna/Austria, *Surrender or Resistance: Independent theatre today. On the Loss of Diversity* (Promedia), is appearing in the fall of 2013.

Jennifer Herszman Capraru grew up in a haunted house in Montréal, and is artistic director of the award-winning Theatre Asylum (www.isoko-rwanda.org). In 2008 she founded Isôko Theatre Rwanda, and directed *Littoral* (touring to Congo in 2014) and *The Monument* in Rwanda, Toronto's World Stage, Montreal, Ottawa and Poland's Dialog Festival 2013. Directing includes *24 Exposures* for Canadian Stage Festival, *Lullaby* for Dark Horse (Dora Nomination) *Metamorphoses* (Phoenix Theatre), and *The Seventh Seal* (DB Clark). Her productions at Theatre Asylum, including *BéBé*, *The Trials* and *My Mother's Courage*, have toured Canada with The Theatre Centre, National Arts Centre, Intrepid Theatre, Harbourfront and Banff Centre. Jen has been a guest speaker and professor in Canada, United States, and Israel. She has been a nominee for the Hirsch and McGibbon awards, and a fellow at Schloss Solitude and the Lincoln Centre's Director's Lab, NYC. Jen holds an MA in Theatre Studies from York University and trained as a director in Germany at the Volksbühne and Landestheater Tübingen. www.theatreasylum.com.

Atay Citron is associate professor at the University of Haifa's Theatre Department and head of its Medical Clowning Academic Training Program, which he founded in 2006. He was department chair (2004–2009), artistic director of the Bat-Yam International Street Theatre Festival (2007–2010), the Acco Festival of Alternative Israeli Theatre (2001–2004), and the School of Visual Theatre, Jerusalem (1993–2000). His stage work was seen in the U.S., Canada, France and Israel. He is the recipient of several awards, among them the Rosenblum Award for Excellence in the Performing Arts and two Fulbright fellowships. He was the initiator and organizer of the 2010 international conference *RS & PS: Richard Schechner and Performance Studies* at the University of Haifa. He holds a Ph.D. from the Department of Performance Studies, Tisch School of the Arts, New York University, and his main academic interests are avant-garde performance, ritual, especially healing rites and shamanism, ritual clowning and medical clowning.

Dr Sarit Cofman-Simhon teaches in the School for Performing Arts at Kibbutzim College in Tel Aviv and at the Theatre Department at Emunah College in Jerusalem. She holds a PhD in Theatre Arts from the University of Minnesota, Minneapolis. Her main field of research is theatre and Judaism, and recent chapters she published include 'From Alexandria to Berlin: The Hellenistic Play *Exagoge* Joins the Jewish Canon', (in *Jews and Theater in an Intercultural Context*), 'Goldfaden and Romanian Theater' (in *Representations of Jewish Life in Romanian Literature*), and 'African Tongues on an Israeli Stage: A Reversed Diaspora' in *TDR* (fall 2013). She is completing a book in Hebrew on Ethiopian theatre in Israel, and as a researcher at the Hebrew University Vidal Sassoon International Center, she is writing on the representation of Jews in European drama.

Dr Faye Chunfang Fei, an internationally produced playwright, is professor of English and Drama, and director of Center for American Studies at East China Normal University, Shanghai; currently director of Confucius Institute at China Institute, New York City. Fei had taught theatre in the United States for 9 years before taking the present position. Her numerous scholarly publications include *Chinese Theories of Theatre and Performance from Confucius to the Present* (University of Michigan Press, 1999; 2002). She has had fellowships from NEH (United States), British Academy and ALFP (Japan).

Dan Friedman is the artistic director of the Castillo Theatre in New York City, which he helped to found in 1984. He is also the associate dean of UX, a free community-based school of continuing development for people of all ages also in New York. Friedman holds a doctorate in theatre history from the University of Wisconsin, and has been active in political, experimental and community-based theatre since the late 1960s. He is editor of *The Cultural Politics of Heiner Müller; Müller in America, Still on the Corner and Other Post-Modern Political Play by Fred Newman;* and co-editor with Bruce McConachie of *Theatre for Working Class Audiences in the United States, 1830-1980.* He has written or co-written 15 plays and, in addition to his work at Castillo, he has directed at La Mama, the Nuyorican Poets Café and at various New York City colleges.

Lois Holzman (PhD), is co-founder and director of the East Side Institute for Group and Short Term Psychotherapy, an international educational, research and training center for new approaches to human development, learning, therapeutics and community building. With her mentor and intellectual partner the late public philosopher Fred Newman, she has advanced social therapeutics, a 'psychology of becoming' that incorporates play, performance and practical philosophy as a practical-critical, postmodern Marxist alternative to modernist psychology. Lois is a founder and lead organizer of the Performing the World conferences. Among her books are *Vygotsky at Work and Play*, *Schools for Growth: Radical Alternatives to Current Educational Models* and (with Newman), *The End of Knowing*.

Prof Gad Kaynar is the chair of the Theatre Arts Department, Tel Aviv University. His research fields include Israeli, German and Scandinavian theatre. Kaynar is also guest professor at the Hebrew University, Jerusalem, the Institut für Theaterwissenschaft, LMU University, Munich, and Venice International University. His recent publications include *Another View: Israeli Drama Revisited* (coedited with Zehava Caspi, 2013), *The Cameri Theatre of Tel-Aviv* (2008); *The Reality Convention in Hebrew Theatre* (forthcoming 2014); and *German Dramaturgy at the Turn of the Millennium* (forthcoming 2015). He is the recipient of 'Israel Science Foundation' grants for research on *Applied Dramaturgy* (2004–2009) and *Rethinking Political Theatre and the Politics of Israeli Public Mainstream Theatre* (2010; with Shulamith Lev-Aladgem). He is co-editor of the quarterly *Teatron*, a dramaturg of Israeli repertoire theatres and festivals, chairman of the Israeli Organization for Theatre Research, a poet, an actor, a director and a translator (from German, Norwegian and Swedish). For his Ibsen translations and research, he has been appointed (2008) 'Knight First Class of the Royal Norwegian Order of Merit' by King Harald V of Norway.

Barbara Kirshenblatt-Gimblett, professor of Performance Studies at New York University, is programme director of the Core Exhibition at the Museum of the History of Polish Jews, Warsaw. Her books include *Destination Culture: Tourism, Museums and Heritage, They Called Me Mayer July: Painted Memories of a Jewish Childhood in Poland Before the Holocaust*, co-authored with her father Mayer Kirshenblatt, *The Art of Being Jewish in Modern Times* (edited with Jonathan Karp), and *Anne Frank Unbound: Media, Imagination, Memory* (edited with Jeffrey Shandler). In 2008, she was honoured with a lifetime achievement award by the Foundation for Jewish Culture and the Mlotek Prize for Yiddish and Yiddish Culture. She currently serves on Advisory Boards for the YIVO Institute for Jewish Research, Vienna Jewish Museum and Jewish Museum and

Tolerance Center in Moscow, and on editorial boards for *TDR The Drama Review*, *International Journal of Heritage Studies*, *Museum Worlds* and *Museum & Society*, among others.

Dariusz Kosiński is professor of Performance Studies in the Faculty of Polish Studies at the Jagiellonian University in Kraków, Poland. His research focuses on the uniqueness of the Polish theatre and performance tradition. He is the author of *Polski teatr przemiany* (The Polish Theatre of Transformation; Wrocław 2007), *Grotowski. Przewodnik* (Grotowski. A Guide; Wrocław 2009), *Teatra polskie – historie* (Polish Theatres: Histories; Warszawa, 2010), a synthesis of the history of Polish performing arts (German translation published 2012), and *Teatra polskie. Rok katastrofy* (Polish Theatres. The Year of the Catastrophe), an analysis of the large-scale performances after the crash of the presidential plane in April 2010. Since 2010 he is the research director of the Grotowski Institute, Wrocław.

Tomasz Kubikowski is deputy artistic director and dramaturge of the National Theatre, Warsaw. He is a professor (and the former vice-rector) at the Aleksander Zelwerowicz Theatre Academy in Warsaw. He has also guest lectured at the Music Academy in Warsaw, University of Warsaw, Stefan Wyszynski University in Warsaw and University of Richmond, Virginia. At the Theatre Academy, he was one of the initial organizers of the International Festival of Theatre Schools (2002), and is presently an organizer and director of the National Theatres' Meeting (2009, 2011). Kubikowski is a qualifier or jury member at numerous other theatre festivals, Polish and international. He is the author of *Siedem bytów teatralnych* (The Seven Theatre Beings, 1994), *Reguła Nibelunga* (The Principle of the Nibelung, 2004), *Doświadczenie teatralne Wilhelma Meistra* (Wilhelm Meister's Theatrical Experience, 2013) and over 150 reviews, essays and reportages, published mostly in 'Odra', 'Dialog', 'Teatr', 'Didaskalia'. He is also author of a drama (*Nauka o barwach – The Science of Colors*, TV production directed by Jan Englert, 1998) and a translator.

Jazmin Badong Llana (PhD, Aberystwyth University, UK) is associate professor of drama, theatre and performance at De La Salle University in Manila, Philippines. Presently she is an Executive Council member of the Committee on Dramatic Arts, (Philippine) National Commission for Culture and the Arts. Notable awards received are the Helsinki Prize 2008 from IFTR-FIRT, the Dwight Conquergood Award 2010 from Performance Studies international

(PSi), and the Ford Foundation International Fellowship from 2006 to 2009. Active affiliations are with the Performance Studies international and the newly organized Performance Philosophy Association. She is also convening the ad hoc group Performance Studies Philippines. She has published in, among others, a peer-reviewed congress book of the International Drama/Theatre and Education Association (2009), the *Philippine Humanities Review* (2010) and *Performance Research* (2011).

Carol Martin is a professor of Drama at Tisch School of the Arts, New York University. Her recent books include *Theatre of the Real* (Palgrave/Macmillan 2013) and *Dramaturgy of the Real on the World Stage* (Palgrave/Macmillan paper 2012, cloth 2010). Martin is the general editor of 'In Performance', a book series devoted to performance texts and plays published by Seagull books and distributed by The University of Chicago Press. Her essays and interviews appear in anthologies, in academic journals in the United States and abroad and in the *New York Times* and have been translated into Turkish, French, Polish, Chinese, Romanian and Japanese.

Judith Graves Miller is currently dean of Arts and Humanities at New York University Abu Dhabi. A specialist in French and Francophone Drama, both text and production, she has written widely on the Théâtre du Soleil, including a monograph on Ariane Mnouchkine for the Routledge Key Practitioners series (2007). She has translated some 20 plays, including works by Hélène Cixous, Koffi Kwahulé, Olivier Kemeid, José Pliya and Werewere Liking. She expects to publish an annotated anthology of plays by Ivoirian Koffi Kwahulé, translated by Chantal Bilodeau, in the near future.

Dr Lior Noy is a researcher at the Weizmann Institute of Science, studying group improvisation and creativity. Trained as a computational neuroscientist, he received his PhD from the Weizmann Institute, where he studied human movement imitation. He is also a performer in Playback Theatre, an improvisation form based on real-life stories. He is currently a member of the Kartoshkes Playback Ensemble. Dr Noy is the founder of 'Weizmann Playback' – a group of faculty and students regularly practicing Playback Theatre, and a co-founder (with Allon Weiner) of 'Jamii', a group of experienced Playback participants focused on community work. Together with Uri Alon, he co-founded in 2012 the Theatre Lab at the Weizmann Institute, a hub of research at the meeting point of science and performing arts.

Liora Sarfati is an adjunct professor at the Departments of East Asian Studies of Tel Aviv University and The Hebrew University, Jerusalem. She holds a PhD from the Department of Folklore and the Department of East Asian Languages and Cultures at Indiana University, Bloomington. She is now working on a book manuscript about Korean shamanism in rituals, museums, films, television and the internet. In this monograph she analyses new forms of reproducing knowledge and practice in mediated manners that add new contexts to rituals that reach back to pre-modern Korea.

Richard Schechner is university professor and professor of Performance Studies, Tisch School of the Arts, NYU. Editor, *TDR: The Journal of Performance Studies*. BA, Cornell University 1956; University of Iowa 1958; Tulane University 1962. Major interests: performance theory, experimental performance, Asian performance, stage directing. Founder of The New Orleans Group (co-founder), The Performance Group, and East Coast Artists. Books include: *Public Domain, Environmental Theater, The End of Humanism, Performance Theory, Between Theatre and Anthropology, The Future of Ritual, Performance Studies—An Introduction*, and *Over, Under, and Around*. His books and essays have been translated into more than 20 languages. Schechner has directed and devised many performances in the United States, Europe, Asia and Africa; he has led performance workshops and lectured on all continents except Antarctica. Fellowships include: Guggenheim, NEH, ACLS, Princeton, Dartmouth, Yale, and Cornell Universities, Erasmus Mundus, and Leverhulme. Prizes and Awards from PSi, ATHE and IATC.

William Huizhu Sun is a playwright, a director and a professor at STA; he is a consortium editor, *TDR, The Drama Review*; he is a director, UNESCO ITI Asia Pacific Bureau of Theatre Schools. He taught at four universities in North America for 10 years before returning to Shanghai in 1999. His research interests are in SPS, intercultural theatre, theatre narratology, etc. His recent publications are *Theatre in Construction and Deconstruction, Conflicts on Stage and Clash of Civilizations, What to Imitate? What to Express? Social Performance Studies*, etc. Sun and Fei co-authored a bilingual anthology *Reinventing Western Classics as Chinese Operas*.

Klaas Tindemans is PhD in Law and he works as teacher/researcher at the Drama Department of the RITS School of Arts (audiovisual and performing arts), where he coordinates the research programme. He also teaches at the Vrije

Universiteit Brussel, and at the Antwerp Conservatory (drama department). In the past he was dramaturge with theatre director Ivo van Hove (the current manager of Toneelgroep Amsterdam), research assistant at the K. U. Leuven, teacher at Tilburg University and general manager of the Flemish Theatre Institute. He is also active as dramaturg with the Antwerp-based actors' collective 'de Roovers' with Bronks, the Brussels youth theatre and with director Lies Pauwels. He wrote and directed two plays: *Bulger* (2006) and *Sleutelveld* (2009). For *Bulger* he received the 'Förderpreis für neue Dramatik' (Theatertreffen Berlin, 2008). As an academic, he publishes about legal-philosophical issues, politics and theatricality, ancient tragedy, contemporary (documentary) theatre and cultural policy.

Annabelle Winograd is a theatre historian, writer and director, based both in Tel Aviv, Israel, and at Dartmouth College, NH, United States. Materials from her book-in-progress *Performing War: Theatricality at the Western front, 1914-1918,* have appeared in anthologies in French and English, and in professional journals such as *Theater* [Yale]. She has been invited to lecture on her WWI work at many universities, arts academies and research institutes in the United States, Europe and Israel, including the Humbolt and Freie Universities, Berlin, the Getty Research Institute, LA, and l'Historial de la Grande Guerre, Peronne. She has given the distinguished Calloway lecture at NYU's Tisch School of the Arts, and most recently presented at the University of Paris/BDIC, conference: 'les mises en scène de la guerre au XXe siècle: théâtre et cinema'. Her immersion in the WWI period began with her research into performance alongside early twentieth-century art movements, which resulted in her widely cited *Dada and Surrealist Performance,* accorded the Hazan prize for twentieth-century art literature.

David Zerbib teaches Philosophy of Art and Aesthetics at the Geneva University of Art and Design and at the University of Paris 1 Panthéon-Sorbonne. His research interests concern the theory of performance and performance art, and contemporary aesthetics. He develops his activity through different academic, artistic and cultural contexts. Among his recent publications: 'The Four Parameters of the Ontology of Performance (and their doubles)' in *La performance, vie de l'archive et actualité,* AICA/Presses du réel (2013); 'The myth of the active subject: An interview with Claire Bishop', in *The Work of Art as Dispositif: Setting the Stage for Audience Participation,* France: CNRS (forthcoming); 'Is performance performative?' *Art press 2,* n 18, August–October

2010; 'The *performantial* regime of the work of art', (*Art Press 2*, November 2007–January 2008). He curated *Ce qui perd forme*, an exhibition devoted to the history of performance art, in Toulouse, France (2010) and is the editor of *In Octavo. Des formats de l'art*, (France: Presses du réel, 2014). Having organized one of the first lectures of Richard Schechner in a French University, he also participates in the translation and introduction of his essays in French.

Index